Children and the Responsibility to Protect

Children and the Responsibility to Protect

Edited by

Bina D'Costa
Luke Glanville

BRILL
NIJHOFF

LEIDEN | BOSTON

Cover illustration: The photo of a small boy from a nomadic tribe was taken with his consent at Pahalgam, Jammu and Kashmir by photojournalist Faisal Khanand and is reprinted on the cover with his permission.

This collection of essays was first published in the journal *Global Responsibility to Protect* (vol.10/1-2, 2018) as a special issue.

Library of Congress Cataloging-in-Publication Data

Names: D'Costa, Bina, editor. | Glanville, Luke, editor.
Title: Children and the responsibility to protect / edited by Bina D'Costa, Luke Glanville.
Description: Leiden ; Boston : Brill Nijhoff, 2019. | "This collection of essays was first published in the journal Global Responsibility to Protect (vol.10/1-2, 2018) as a special issue." | Includes bibliographical references.
Identifiers: LCCN 2019010122 (print) | LCCN 2019010680 (ebook) | ISBN 9789004379534 (Ebook) | ISBN 9789004284197 (pbk. : alk. paper)
Subjects: LCSH: Responsibility to protect (International law) | Children (International law)
Classification: LCC KZ4082 (ebook) | LCC KZ4082 .C45 2019 (print) | DDC 341.6/7--DC23
LC record available at https://lccn.loc.gov/2019010122

Typeface for the Latin, Greek, and Cyrillic scripts: "Brill". See and download: brill.com/brill-typeface.

ISBN 978-90-04-28419-7 (paperback)
ISBN 978-90-04-37953-4 (e-book)

Contents

Case Studies

Conclusion

List of Contributors

J. Marshall Beier
is Professor in the Department of Political Science at McMaster University. His current research inquires into issues of children's rights, security, and political subjecthood. He is the author of *International Relations in Uncommon Places: Indigeneity, Cosmology, and the Limits of International Theory* (Palgrave Macmillan, 2005, 2009), editor of *Indigenous Diplomacies* (Palgrave Macmillan, 2009) and *The Militarization of Childhood: Thinking Beyond the Global South* (Palgrave Macmillan, 2011, 1013), and co-editor with Lana Wylie of *Canadian Foreign Policy in Critical Perspective* (Oxford University Press, 2010). He has authored numerous book chapters and his articles have appeared in *Contemporary Security Policy, Critical Studies on Security, Global Governance, International Political Sociology, International Politics, International Studies Review, Security Dialogue*, and *Third World Quarterly.*

Letícia Carvalho
is an Assistant Professor in the Department of International Relations at PUC Minas, Brazil.

Bina D'Costa
is leading the migration research program at the UNICEF Office of Research–Innocenti. Her research interests span migration, children and conflict, gender, war crimes and justice. She has undertaken studies on refugees, stateless communities and IDPs, and has provided input and technical advice to Human Rights bodies, UN agencies and NGOs. Her publications include (with John Braithwaite) *Cascades of Violence in South Asia* (forthcoming 2018); (editor) *Children and Violence: Politics of Conflict in South Asia* (Cambridge University Press, 2016); (with Kim Huynh and Katrina Lee-Koo) *Children and Global Conflict* (Cambridge University Press, 2015); *Nationbuilding, Gender and War Crimes in South Asia* (Routledge, 2011, 2013); *Marginalisation and Impunity: Violence against Women and Girls in the Chittagong Hill Tracts* (CHTC and IWGIA, 2014, 2016); and (co-edited with Katrina Lee-Koo) *Gender and Global Politics in the Asia-Pacific* (Palgrave, 2010) and journal articles.

Myriam Denov
is a Full Professor at McGill University and holds the Canada Research Chair in Youth, Gender and Armed Conflict. Her research interests lie in the areas of children and families affected by war, migration, and its intergenerational

impact. A specialist in participatory research, she has worked with war-affected children and families in Africa, Asia, and the Americas. Dr. Denov has presented expert evidence in court on child soldiers and has advised government and nongovernmental organizations on children in armed conflict and girls in armed groups. She has authored and co-authored several books on the impact of war on children including *Child Soldiers: Sierra Leone's Revolutionary United Front* (Cambridge University Press) and *Children Affected by Armed Conflict: Theory, Method & Practice* (Columbia University Press). Her current research is exploring the intergenerational effects of wartime sexual violence and children born of wartime rape in multiple countries around the world. Dr. Denov is a Trudeau Fellow and was recently was inducted into the College of the Royal Society of Canada. She holds a PhD from the University of Cambridge, where she was a commonwealth scholar.

Luke Glanville

is a Fellow in the Department of International Relations, Australian National University. He is the author of *Sovereignty and the Responsibility to Protect: A New History* (Chicago: University of Chicago Press, 2014), and has placed articles on the politics, ethics, law, and history of R2P-themes in journals such as *European Journal of International Relations*, *International Studies Quarterly*, and *European Journal of International Law*. Luke is a co-editor of the journal, *Global Responsibility to Protect*.

Erin Goheen Glanville

is a SSHRC Postdoctoral Fellow in the School of Communication at Simon Fraser University, Vancouver, Canada. Erin's current project is a digital storytelling collaboration around asylum discourse and digital storytelling. She runs community workshops shaped by her doctoral research on refugee fiction as pedagogy and has published on narrative representations of refugees, globalisation, and diaspora fiction.

Michelle Godwin

has broad experience in the humanitarian and development sector. She has worked with NGOs, research groups and United Nations agencies. Her work has focused mainly on child protection and public health programmes in post-conflict and 'transition' contexts. She is currently Programme Manager with UNICEF Office of Research-Innocenti's initiative on adolescence.

Cecilia Jacob

is a Senior Lecturer in the Department of International Relations, The Australian National University. Her research focuses on civilian protection, internal conflict and political violence in South and Southeast Asia, and international norms of sovereign responsibility and protection. She is the author of *Child Security in Asia: the Impact of Armed Conflict in Cambodia and Myanmar* (Routledge, 2014), co-editor of *Civilian Protection in the Twenty-First Century: Governance and Responsibility in a Fragmented World* (Oxford University Press, 2016).

Dustin Johnson
is a research officer at the Roméo Dallaire Child Soldiers Initiative. His research interests include the recruitment and use of child soldiers, the prevention of mass atrocities, and the role of children in peace processes.

Atim Angela Lakor
is the founder of Watye Ki Gen (We Have Hope), a Ugandan organisation whose members are formerly abducted women held in the bush, working for the rights and the welfare of children born in captivity. Atim Angela was abducted from Aboke St Mary's College with fellow pupils by the Lord Resistance Army when she was 14 years old. She is co-author of The Lord Resistance Army (LRA) Forced Wife System and is currently studying for a Bachelors degree in Development studies at Gulu University, Uganda. She spoke at the Preventing Sexual Violence Initiative meeting on tackling stigma at Wilton Park in November 2016.

Katrina Lee-Koo
is a Reader in International Relations and Deputy Director of the Monash Gender, Peace and Security research centre at Monash University, Melbourne Australia. Her research interests include critical security studies, feminist international relations, children and global conflict and the United Nations Security Council's Women, Peace and Security agenda. Recently, she is the co-author of *Children and Global Conflict* (with Kim Huynh and Bina D'Costa, Cambridge University Press, 2015) and *Ethics and Global Security* (with Anthony Burke and Matt McDonald, Routledge 2015).

Ryoko Nakano
is an Associate Professor in the School of International Studies at Kanazawa University, Japan. She was formerly Assistant Professor at the Department of Japanese Studies, Faculty of Arts and Social Sciences, National University of Singapore. She is the author of *Beyond the Western Liberal Order: Yanaihara Tadao and Empire as Society* (Palgrave Macmillan, 2013), and published articles on global norm diffusion, East Asian politics, and Japanese perspectives of international relations. She received her Doctor of Philosophy in International Relations from Oxford University in 2005.

Jochen Prantl
is Deputy Director (International Engagement) of the Coral Bell School of Asia-Pacific Affairs and Associate Professor of International Relations at The Australian National University. His research focuses on global governance, international security, and strategic diplomacy. He is currently completing a book, *The Crisis of Liberal Institutions*, under contract with Oxford University Press. Dr. Prantl holds degrees in Political Science (M.A.) from the University of Bonn and International Relations (M.A.; D.Phil.) from the University of Oxford.

Jeremy Shusterman
has worked as Emergency Specialist with UNICEF in humanitarian responses in conflict and disaster affected countries in Africa, Asia, the Middle East and Haiti. Between 2005 and 2008 Jeremy worked at the United Nations Secretariat in New York. He serves on a number of surge rosters of humanitarian response specialists.

Hannah Sparwasser Soroka
is a research assistant for the Roméo Dallaire Child Soldiers Initiative and an undergraduate student in Early Modern Studies and Philosophy at the University of King's College in Halifax, Canada.

Timea Spitka
is a lecturer in the Political Science and International Relations departments at Hebrew University, Israel. She has researched, lectured and written on issues related to R2P, international intervention in violent conflict, mediation, gender and conflict resolution. Dr. Spitka has also worked in conflict zones for international organizations including the UN and Oxfam. Her book *International Intervention, Identity and Conflict Transformation: Bridges and Walls between Groups* was published by Routledge in 2015.

Jana Tabak
is a post-doctoral research fellow in the Institute of International Relations at PUC-Rio, Brazil. Her doctoral research was on the participation of children in armed conflicts and the dissertation will be published as a book by the University of Georgia Press (*The Child and the World: Child-Soldiers and the Claim for Progress*, Atlanta: University of Georgia Press, Forthcoming).

Shelly Whitman
is the Executive Director of the Roméo Dallaire Child Soldiers Initiative, based out of Dalhousie University in Halifax, Canada. The Dallaire Initiative is a global organization dedicated to progressively ending the use of children as soldiers. In addition, she is an Adjunct Professor of Political Science and International Development Studies at Dalhousie University.

Children and the Responsibility to Protect: An Introduction

Luke Glanville
Australian National University
luke.glanville@anu.edu.au

Abstract

This introduction outlines in broad strokes some key aspects of the relationship between the Responsibility to Protect (R2P) and the practice and scholarship of child protection. It lays out the parallel development of the R2P and Children and Armed Conflict agendas over the last two decades and surveys how key R2P documents developed during this period have engaged with issues of child protection. It then outlines the chapters that follow.

Keywords

Children – Children and Armed Conflict – Responsibility to Protect

...

> *'A bullet hit my foot. I think they shot me by mistake. They meant to shoot big people.'*
>
> MUHAMMAD YUNUS, *Rohingya child, 2017.*[1]

In situations of mass violence, children are particularly vulnerable. Far too often, they are intentional targets of violence, victims of indiscriminate violence, and traumatised witnesses of violence against others. They are disproportionately affected by war, being at greater risk of malnutrition and disease and

1 Video made and tweeted by UNICEF, 21 October 2017, https://twitter.com/UNICEF/status/921662347252551682 (accessed 1 January 2018).

 | DOI:10.30965/9789004379534_002

highly vulnerable to abuse and exploitation. Children make up more than half the world's 25.4 million refugees.[2] And things are only getting worse. At the close of 2017, UNICEF warned that children in conflict zones around the world are 'under attack at a shocking scale' as parties to conflicts blatantly disregard international laws designed for their protection:[3]

> In conflicts around the world, children have become frontline targets, used as human shields, killed, maimed and recruited to fight. Rape, forced marriage, abduction and enslavement have become standard tactics in conflicts from Iraq, Syria and Yemen, to Nigeria, South Sudan and Myanmar … Millions more children are paying an indirect price for these conflicts, suffering from malnutrition, disease and trauma as basic services – including access to food, water, sanitation and health – are denied, damaged or destroyed in the fighting.[4]

In Yemen, UNICEF details, three years of fighting has left 5,000 children dead or injured, 385,000 children severely malnourished and at risk of death, and more than 11 million children in need of humanitarian assistance. In South Sudan, four years of civil war has seen 19,000 children recruited into armed groups and over 2,300 killed or injured. In Myanmar, Rohingya children have suffered and seen horrific violence and comprise more than half of the 650,000 forcibly displaced to Bangladesh since mid-2017. In the Democratic Republic of the Congo, 2017 saw 200 health centres and 400 schools attacked and 850,000 children driven from their homes by violence. And in northeast Nigeria and Cameroon in same period, Boko Haram forced at least 135 children to act as suicide bombers.[5]

The Responsibility to Protect (R2P) and Children and Armed Conflict (CAAC)

At the United Nations (UN) World Summit in 2005, states unanimously acknowledged their responsibility to protect populations from atrocity crimes.

2 UNICEF, 'Figures at a Glance', http://www.unhcr.org/en-au/figures-at-a-glance.html (accessed 1 August 2018).

3 UNICEF, 'Children under attack at shocking scale in conflicts around the world, says UNICEF', Press Release, 28 December 2017.

4 Ibid.

5 Ibid.

In a section of the World Summit Outcome Document titled 'Responsibility to protect populations from genocide, war crimes, ethnic cleansing and crimes against humanity', heads of state and government accepted a responsibility to protect their own populations from these crimes, to encourage and assist other states to do the same, and, where necessary, to take peaceful and even coercive measures in accordance with the UN Charter to ensure that populations are protected.[6]

It is often forgotten that this landmark section of the Outcome Document was immediately followed by a section titled 'Children's rights'. In this section, heads of state and government expressed their 'dismay at the increasing number of children involved in and affected by armed conflict, as well as all other forms of violence, including domestic violence, sexual abuse and exploitation and trafficking' and their support for 'cooperation policies aimed at strengthening national capacities to improve the situation of those children and to assist in their rehabilitation and reintegration into society'. They committed themselves to 'respecting and ensuring the rights of each child without discrimination of any kind', and called upon all states to become parties to the Convention on the Rights of the Child, which the UN General Assembly adopted in 1989.[7]

Six months after the Summit, the UN Security Council unanimously adopted Resolution 1674 on the theme of Protection of Civilians, which reaffirmed both the provisions of the 2005 Outcome Document regarding the Responsibility to Protect (R2P) and the various resolutions adopted by the council since 1999 on the theme of Children and Armed Conflict (CAAC) that formed the basis for the Outcome Document's provisions for children's rights.[8]

The R2P and CAAC agendas have obvious commonalities. They both emerged during the 1990s and early 2000s in response to debates and dilemmas about how to protect civilians in conflict situations. Both are a product of a desire to conceptualise and cultivate effective local and international action to ensure such protection. While the seeds of R2P were being sown in the mid-1990s by Francis Deng and Roberta Cohen at the UN and the Brookings Institute, developing a concept of 'sovereignty as responsibility' in response to a crisis of internal displacement, and by policy-makers and commentators, wrestling with the controversial concept of 'humanitarian intervention' in response to the repeated outbreak of mass atrocities around the world,[9] others were thinking

6 '2005 World Summit Outcome', A/RES/60/1, 24 October 2005, para. 138–39.

7 Ibid., para. 141–42.

8 UNSC Resolution 1674, 28 April 2006.

9 Luke Glanville, *Sovereignty and the Responsibility to Protect: A New History* (Chicago: University of Chicago Press, 2014), pp. 171–89.

through how to better promote and protect the rights of children caught up in such crises. Most crucial was a report written by Graça Machel titled 'Impact of Armed Conflict on Children', submitted to the General Assembly in 1996.[10] The report drew attention to the disproportionate impact of war on children and stressed local and international responsibilities to ensure their protection, using language that anticipated R2P. 'Preventing conflicts from escalating is a clear responsibility of national Governments and the international community' and the impact of armed conflict on children is 'an area in which everyone shares responsibility and a degree of blame', Machel claimed:[11]

> It is unconscionable that we so clearly and consistently see children's rights attacked and that we fail to defend them. It is unforgivable that children are assaulted, violated, murdered and yet our conscience is not revolted nor our sense of dignity challenged. This represents a fundamental crisis of our civilization. The impact of armed conflict on children must be everyone's concern and is everyone's responsibility; Governments, international organizations and every element of civil society. Each one of us, each individual, each institution, each country, must initiate and support global action to protect children. Local and national strategies must strengthen and be strengthened through international mobilization.[12]

The following year, the UN Secretary-General appointed the first Special Representative for Children and Armed Conflict. The year after that, the Security Council held its first open debate on the theme of CAAC and issued a Presidential Statement expressing 'its intention to pay serious attention to the situation of children and armed conflicts'.[13] In 1999, the council adopted its first resolution on the theme, strongly condemning 'killing and maiming, sexual violence, abduction and forced displacement, recruitment and use of children in armed conflict', as well as attacks on schools and hospitals, and committing itself 'to remain actively seized of the matter'.[14]

That same year, NATO waged a controversial military intervention for the purpose of protecting civilians in Kosovo. Moved by both the heated arguments over the intervention, as well as the distressing failure to prevent genocides in

10 'Impact of Armed Conflict on Children', A/51/306, 26 August 1996.

11 Ibid., para. 254, 33.

12 Ibid., para. 317.

13 S/PRST/1998/18, 29 June 1998.

14 UNSC Resolution 1261, 25 August 1999.

Rwanda (1994) and Srebrenica (1995), UN Secretary-General Kofi Annan challenged the international community to resolve the seemingly intractable debate about humanitarian intervention. In 2001, the International Commission on Intervention and State Sovereignty (ICISS) responded with a report titled 'Responsibility to Protect'. This formed the basis for the 2005 agreement on R2P.

The R2P and CAAC agendas thus emerged in parallel with each other and were driven by shared concerns. However, as Jeremy Shusterman and Michelle Godwin emphasise in their contribution to this book, the connections between the two have always been more coincidental than purposeful. Certainly, there are clear overlaps and complementarities. The protection of children is an implicit if not always explicit aspect of R2P and protection against atrocities crimes is a necessary part of the broader task of protecting children in situations of armed conflict. But advocates and practitioners have done little to pursue or take advantage of such connections. I will leave it to some of the contributors to this book to consider questions about whether and how the two agendas might be brought into conversation to fruitfully inform and strengthen each other. For now, I will briefly outline how some key R2P documents have touched on related issues of child protection.

Where are Children in R2P?

Some of R2P's key documents have engaged with the vulnerability and agency of children in thoughtful and informed ways. But this engagement has tended to be scattered and tacked-on rather than consistently and deeply embedded in R2P's conceptual development. The 2001 ICISS report made four references to children. These included two references to the issue of child soldiers and one each to the need to protect children from starvation and the problem of weapons such as land mines that don't distinguish between children and soldiers.[15] The 2005 World Summit provisions for R2P made no mention of children, although as noted earlier they were immediately followed by a commitment to protect children's rights.

Since 2009, the UN Secretary-General has issued annual thematic reports on R2P, each dealing with a different aspect of the principle. The 2009 report, 'Implementing the Responsibility to Protect', gave a reasonable degree of attention to questions of child protection. Among numerous passages, it considered issues of sexual exploitation of women and girls; it noted the rehabilitation

15 ICISS, *The Responsibility to Protect: Report of the International Commission on Intervention and State Sovereignty* (Ottawa: IDRC, 2001), pp. 4, 14, 17, 24.

and reintegration of children associated with armed groups in Sierra Leone; it recognised the work of UNICEF with a number of Governments, including Colombia, the Philippines and the Sudan, to address how their judicial systems deal with children formerly associated with armed groups and accused of serious war crimes; and it noted other positive developments within Colombia, Uganda, and Rwanda with respect to child demobilisation, the banning of sexual exploitation, and troop training on children's rights.[16] While Shusterman and Godwin in this book criticise the report for offering a 'puzzling range of deliverables' for children, the report does at least evince a serious effort to incorporate children's needs into the remit of R2P.

While the Secretary-General's R2P reports in 2010, 2011, and 2012 made little mention of children, the 2013 report, focused on atrocity prevention, had more to say. It discussed the resolutions on CAAC that the Security Council had adopted since 2005, noting that they outlined useful means for combating specific crimes against children and suggesting that such means should be incorporated into atrocity prevention strategies. It also noted not only that the recruitment or forcible transfer of children can constitute atrocity crimes, but also that such recruitment and forcible transfer can be indicators of future perpetration of atrocity crimes (Dustin Johnson, Shelly Whitman, Hannah Sparwasser Soroka pursue this important idea in their contribution).[17] The 2014 report, focused on international assistance, briefly mentioned the role of UNICEF and the Secretary-General's Special Representative for CAAC in encouraging states to implement guidelines for child protection and to assist in the development of national action plans.[18]

The 2015 report, taking stock of the decade since the World Summit, was significant in that it was the first to highlight the need to account for the agency and voice of children. While his treatment of the matter was brief, the Secretary-General called on peacekeeping missions 'to be guided by more strategic and forward-looking assessments of threats to populations that incorporate the perspective and the protection strategies of local actors, particularly women and children'. The report also emphasised that R2P should not be disconnected from related activities on the protection and empowerment of women

16 'Implementing the Responsibility to Protect', A/63/677, 12 January 2009, pp. 14, 16, 17.

17 'Responsibility to Protect: State Responsibility and Prevention', A/67/929-S/2013/399, 9 July 2013, pp. 6, 7–8.

18 'Fulfilling Our Collective Responsibility: International Assistance and the Responsibility to Protect', A/68/947-S/2014/449, 11 July 2014, p. 9.

and girls.[19] While the 2016 report made no mention of children, the 2017 report, focused on accountability for prevention, lamented that the number of child victims of atrocity crimes had 'increased significantly over the past few years' and highlighted the role of the Special Representative for CAAC 'to speak on behalf of the vulnerable and raise protection concerns'.[20]

In short, several of the key international statements on R2P give at least some attention to key questions of child protection and they increasingly demonstrate recognition of the need to conceive of children not merely as objects in need of protection, but as people with agency, whose voices need to be heard and perspectives understood (Jana Tabak, Leticia Carvalho, Erin Goheen Glanville, and J. Marshall Beier consider the importance of this in their contributions). The absence of the agency and voice of children in earlier R2P documents was arguably a feature of how R2P advocates and practitioners had long tended to think about the protection of *all* vulnerable people. It is only in recent years that R2P's supporters have begun to seriously engage with the agency, perspective, autonomy, and potential resilience of those at risk of atrocity crimes. Those thinking about how R2P might further account for and support the subjecthood of vulnerable people would do well to engage with the valuable insights of scholarship and policy on child protection, both at the domestic and international levels.[21]

Insofar as the R2P concept plays a useful role in encouraging and habitualising local and global efforts to protect populations from atrocities, it is hopefully able to make some contribution toward promoting and protecting the rights of children. But this is by no means easy. And, indeed, R2P itself is under grave threat today, beset by entrenched disunity within the Security Council and other UN organs, rising nationalism, xenophobia, and neglect or even outright rejection of global responsibilities by so many states, and increasingly routine disregard for international humanitarian law in so many conflicts. And as the statements and statistics at the beginning of this introduction attest, children are bearing a disproportionate burden of the resulting suffering. There is an

---

19 'A Vital and Enduring Commitment: Implementing the Responsibility to Protect', A/69/981-S/2015/500, 13 July 2015, pp. 11, 16–17.

20 'Implementing the Responsibility to Protect: Accountability for Prevention', A/71/1016-S/2017/556, 10 August 2017, pp. 3, 15–16.

21 This large body of scholarship is discussed in several of the contributions that follow. For a sample of recent work, see Kim Huynh, Bina D'Costa, Katrina Lee-Koo, *Children and Global Conflict* (Cambridge: Cambridge University Press, 2015); J. Marshall Beier (ed.), *Childhood and the Production of Security* (Abingdon: Routledge, 2016); Bina D'Costa (ed.), *Children and Violence: Politics of Conflict in South Asia* (Cambridge: Cambridge University Press, 2016).

urgent need, therefore, for sustained engagement with the topic of this book: Children and the Responsibility to Protect.

The Plan of the Book

The chapters this book were originally published as articles in a special double issue of the quarterly journal, *Global Responsibility to Protect*, at the beginning of 2018.[22] The contributions are grouped in three sections.

Two Agendas: R2P and CAAC

The four contributions that comprise the first section examine various aspects of the R2P and CAAC agendas. They consider the relationship between the two agendas and explore the possibilities and limits of their potential to advance the rights of children. Jeremy Shusterman and Michelle Godwin note that, while the R2P and CAAC agendas emerged and were embraced by the international community around the same time as each other, R2P has had little influence on either the shaping of or the advancement of CAAC. They provocatively observe that, while so much debate about R2P remains mired in theoretical questions about whether it is a useful concept or one whose effectiveness is impaired by political and other constraints, those working on CAAC have more quickly turned to questions about how to actually protect children given these constraints. They conclude that R2P nevertheless can be of use for CAAC practitioners. It can be effectively deployed to frame and drive their efforts to protect children, particularly in extreme situations in which standard systems-based approaches prove unable to prevent the perpetration of atrocities.

Katrina Lee-Koo, in contrast, critiques the Security Council for its singular and 'overbearing' focus on protection when contemplating and implementing the CAAC agenda. In conceptualising children primarily as victims and focusing solely on their protection, the Security Council fails to engage with the ways in which children can at times resist, adapt, and survive conflict, acting as agents of their own protection and of community resilience. While the agency of children does not negate their need for protection, Lee-Koo argues, it does complicate it, generating questions about how protection programs might be better designed and implemented.

22 Bina D'Costa and Luke Glanville (eds), "Special Issue: Children and R2P," *Global Responsibility to Protect*, 10/1–2 (2018).

Cecilia Jacob argues that, while the CAAC agenda usefully advances the protection of children in situations of armed conflict, there is a need for a 'child-centric approach' to the prevention of atrocities that is consistently implemented not only in time of conflict, but also in time of peace. Rather than broadening the CAAC agenda to cover peacetime, Jacob suggests that the best way forward is the development of a 'child-centric focus' within R2P's atrocity prevention framework. She notes that, while long-term structural prevention strategies ought to include the strengthening of children's resilience, participation, and ownership of bottom-up approaches, there may be a need to turn to top-down international protection measures as atrocities become imminent.

Jochen Prantl and Ryoko Nakano seek to explain why existing legal and normative frameworks have had such little success in protecting children in conditions of armed conflict. They highlight the need to understand norm diffusion in global, regional, and domestic contexts and suggest two fundamental challenges confronting the R2P and CAAC agendas: the constraints posed by power politics both within and beyond the Security Council and the differing engagement with the 'global' R2P norm at regional and domestic levels. They conclude that R2P needs to be 'glocalised', carefully and flexibly calibrated for different local audiences, if it is to successfully advance the protection of children.

Representing Children

The three contributions that comprise the second section examine how the agency and vulnerability of children is represented and how their voices are heard in discussions of child protection and R2P. Jana Tabak and Leticia Carvalho analyse UNICEF's *Unfairy Tales* project, a series of animated films about children who have fled conflict zones. The authors cast this project as an intervention by UNICEF in a discursive battle about how displaced children should be perceived, framing them as vulnerable, at risk, and in need of protection, with the implication that they might otherwise develop in deviant and uncivilised ways such that they pose a future risk to the global community. Tabak and Carvalho grapple with how this understanding of childhood, and its assumptions about normal and deviant development, risks authorising and informing problematic protection practices.

Erin Goheen Glanville uses the example of a 2015 novel by Stella Leventoyannis Harvey, *The Brink of Freedom*, to demonstrate the potential for literary novels to overcome the limitations of the simplistic cultural trope of the vulnerable refugee child. Whereas the simplistic trope of vulnerability may generate intense reactions with shallow roots, Goheen Glanville explains, a novel can embed notions of shared responsibilities for the protection of the vulnerable within the more complex and often contradictory material reality of a displaced child. Such a creative cultural intervention can feed alternative an social imaginary of children that generates deeper and more sustainable political will for implementing R2P.

J. Marshall Beier suggests that the concept of protection is beset by a paradox: it is an imperative produced by diminished subjecthood and yet it demeans that same subjecthood In the case of children, this paradox can turn into a pathology. By representing children as quintessential innocents in need of protection and ignoring their voices, he claims, humanitarian actors problematically objectify children as part of the 'scenery' of the politics of protection and obscure their subjecthood. While recognising the need in certain circumstances to focus on the urgent protection needs of vulnerable children, Beier emphasises that the impulse to protect them needs to always be held in tension with their subjecthood and that voice should be given to this tension. This requires the adult world 'to cultivate an ethic of responsibility *to* young people rather than *for* them'.

Case Studies

The three contributions that comprise the third and final section explore some of the possibilities and difficulties of child protection in three cases: Israel/Palestine, northern Uganda, and Syria. Timea Spitka examines the plight of children in the ongoing Israeli/Palestinian conflict, highlighting their vulnerability to violence, exploitation, recruitment, and detention. Noting the apparent incapacity or unwillingness of local or international actors to ensure adequate protection of children in this conflict, Spitka suggests that there is a need to analyse both the effectiveness and also the unintended harms caused by existing tools for human protection. She also suggests that the development of a shared focus on the welfare of children among warring parties could potentially serve as an entry point for negotiations to resolve broader disputes, as has happened in some other cases.

Myriam Denov and Atim Angela Lakor draw on interviews with children born in Lord's Resistance Army captivity to explore what R2P might contribute to the protection of children born of conflict-related sexual violence (CBC). While they number in the thousands in northern Uganda alone, the reality and plight of CBC around the world has received minimal attention from scholars and policy-makers. In northern Uganda, these secondary and intergenerational victims of war are subject to significant stigma, violence, and other hardships and stand in need of the kinds of protection offered by the R2P framework, the authors argue. Based on the suggestions of the interviewed children themselves, Denov and Lakor conclude that specific provisions to advance the protection, health, and well-being of CBC that might be fruitfully incorporated into the R2P framework include access to education and vocational training, access to land and livelihood, sensitisation programs and workshops aimed at fighting stigma, and the establishment of protection laws at the national level.

Dustin Johnson, Shelly Whitman, and Hannah Sparwasser Soroka argue that violations of children's rights, especially their recruitment and deployment as child soldiers, are reliable early warning indicators of mass atrocities, and they lament that the international community has too often failed to adequately respond to such violations. Using the horrific crisis in Syria as an example, they suggest that had meaningful preventive action been taken in response to violations of children's rights in the early days of the crisis in 2011, the international community not only could have saved the lives of some children, but it also would have stood a better chance of heading off the outbreak of mass atrocities.

Conclusion

My co-editor, Bina D'Costa, concludes the book with some reflections based on recent field experience providing research support as part of UNICEF's Rohingya emergency response in Cox's Bazar, Bangladesh. D'Costa notes that questions remain about the relative responsibilities of different actors in the international community, emphasizing the need to clarify the roles and requirements not only of the United Nations and individual states, but also civil society and business actors in ensuring that the rights of children are protected. She particularly highlights the need to better protect children that are forcibly displaced or that fall through the cracks and are left vulnerable to trafficking and subjection to sexual exploitation, forced labour, and recruitment in armed forces.

Two Agendas: R2P and Children and Armed Conflict

∴

'Children Heard, Half-Heard?': A Practitioner's Look for Children in the Responsibility to Protect and Normative Agendas on Protection in Armed Conflict

Jeremy Shusterman
Humanitarian Affairs Specialist, UNICEF, Office of Research - Innocenti, Italy
jeremy.shusterman@gmail.com

Michelle Godwin
Programme Manager - Adolescence, UNICEF Office of Research, Innocenti, Italy
michellekgodwin@gmail.com

Abstract

When the United Nations (UN) agreed on a definition of the Responsibility to Protect (R2P) at the 2005 World Summit, the two paragraphs it endorsed articulated what R2P stands for, giving the concept a focused but narrow remit around protecting populations specifically from genocide, war crimes, ethnic cleansing and crimes against humanity in armed conflict. In its next paragraph, the UN Membership reiterated concerns on the impact of armed conflict on children echoing the landmark 1612 Resolution by the Security Council on Children and Armed Conflict (CAAC) adopted a few weeks before. Though side-by-side in the text, CAAC and R2P were not linked. To

* Disclaimer: The findings, interpretations and conclusions expressed in this paper do not necessarily reflect the views or policies of UNICEF. The ideas are those of the authors alone, and do not represent the position of any organisation, government or agency.

 | DOI:10.1163/9789004379534_003

this day, for international practitioners in emergency responses, the interaction between both remains unclear. While this simultaneous peak moment for R2P and CAAC may have occurred by chance, this article describes how both concepts (as advocacy tools and instruments for practitioners to 'respond') emerged out of similar concern for protecting civilians – including children – in conflict. However, the link between both concepts should not be overstated. While R2P and CAAC fit together for the intentions they share, this happened more coincidentally than purposefully. This article argues, taking an international practitioner's perspective, that both concepts should not be understood as always operating at the same level. CAAC has grown from an advocacy platform to an umbrella of different programmes, responses, tools and frameworks, including the Monitoring and Reporting Mechanism (MRM) on Children and Armed Conflict. Even if applied with variable success, these tools and approaches under the CAAC agenda chart some ways practitioners can hope to do more towards protecting children in conflict. But for those same practitioners, delivering on a Responsibility to Protect is a different question – one where their 'responsibility' is at best secondary and implicit, because R2P sits squarely as a primary and explicit responsibility of states – who are also the ultimate duty bearers for children's rights. While the echoes of a child rights agenda can be heard in the conversation around R2P, and while R2P can help frame and drive efforts by child protection practitioners to respond to some of the worst situations children face, R2P is, for the protection agency field officer, an aspirational goal, necessarily out of reach.

Keywords

child protection – conflict – Responsibility to Protect (R2P) – Security Council – United Nations – MRM

•••

... the children in the apple-tree
Not known, because not looked for
But heard, half-heard, in the stillness
Between two waves of the sea.

T.S. ELIOT, *The Little Gidding*[1]

•••

1 T.S. Eliot, *Four Quartets* (New York: Houghton Mifflin Harcourt, 1943), p. 49.

The last days of New York's summer in 2005 saw the United Nations headquarters abuzz. The world body was on the edge of convening the largest gathering of Heads of States ever seen, for a meeting aptly billed as the 'World Summit'. The UN launched a campaign appealing to New Yorker's patience and better nature, anticipating the frustrations of every-day commuters witnessing a large segment of their city slow down so that 170 Heads of States could gather all in one place all at the same time. Advertisements plastered the city and subway cars with apologies for the traffic gridlock and a pledge that the unfolding World Summit would hopefully 'break through a little political gridlock'. And it did. One major step forward, with the adoption of the World Summit Outcome document, was resolving the debate about an emerging candidate international norm, articulated by the International Commission on Intervention and State Sovereignty (ICISS) as the Responsibility to Protect.[2] Subject of controversy and debate in the lead-up negotiations, and needing high level advocacy to make it into the final document, the Responsibility to Protect was finally given a definition endorsed by the full United Nations membership. This endorsement moved the concept from candidate to agreed international norm – referred to in shorthand by international relations theorists as 'R2P'.

A few months before, on 26 July 2005, at a meeting opened at 10:20 AM and wrapped up by 10:25 AM, the Security Council adopted its 1612th resolution.[3] In this resolution the Security Council acted upon the recommendations laid out by then Secretary-General Kofi Annan[4] to establish a Monitoring and Reporting Mechanism (MRM) on Children and Armed Conflict (CAAC), and established a Working Group of Security Council Member States to actively review progress in rolling it out. Though not the first of the Security Council's pronouncements on the subject of Children and Armed Conflict, this new resolution – referred to in shorthand by practitioners as '1612' – was soon heralded as a landmark moment in advancing the issue of children in war on the international community's agenda. It was equally fundamental for the day-to-day workings of child-protection-mandated agencies, with the CAAC agenda being at the intersection of advocacy and practical implementation for the United Nations, including notably its Department of Peacekeeping Operations

2 International Commission on Intervention and State Sovereignty, 'The Responsibility to Protect – Report of the International Commission on Intervention and State Sovereignty', (Ottawa: International Development Research Centre, 2001).

3 S/RES/1612, 26 July 2005.

4 Kofi Annan, 'Children and Armed Conflict - Report of the Secretary General', A/72/361–S/2017/821, 9 February 2005.

(DPKO) and its funds and programmes, chief among which the United Nations' Children's Fund (UNICEF).[5]

The adoption of Security Council Resolution 1612 on Children and Armed Conflict and the World Summit agreement on a definition for the Responsibility to Protect (R2P) were a little over fifty days apart. Such close synchronicity could appear coincidental, but there are potential parallels beyond the schedule and timing of these critical moments for the two concepts. Both concepts echo each other, and it is in these echoes that we ask if the cause of children can be heard.

This article attempts to articulate the interaction between both concepts. It looks at how children feature and how the advocacy work of protection-mandated agencies, on various scales, includes agendas from high-flying normative frameworks – such as the outcome document of a World Summit and a Security Council resolution – in programming and advocacy 'toolkits'. Exploring how to link the two concepts, whether they can be linked, and what may (or may not) be the added value for children, is attempted using two main axes of analysis. First: has the R2P been a contributing, accelerating or on the contrary unrelated factor in the advancement of the CAAC agenda? Or put simply: has R2P worked to advance the protection of children and prevention of violence against children? Second: what is the connection between the concept of R2P and the everyday work of child-protection mandated agencies, what they do on the ground, and what they do to advocate for children's rights in conflict? Put simply: is R2P a useful lens through which to view the efforts of these agencies, and, vice-versa, is R2P a helpful guiding principle for these agencies to structure and direct their efforts? In unpacking the relationship between both concepts, the attempt in this article is not to demonstrate – or to disprove – an inherent programmatic or advocacy purpose or benefit in linking the two (R2P and CAAC). This article is not intent on being prescriptive, rather, the objective is to explore, with some consideration to programming realities, whether linking both concepts can bring about child protection outcomes (by definite intent, or fortuitous coincidence) or whether the link between both concepts is more of an artificial construct and/or merely accidental.

5 UNICEF, 'Guidance Note: UNICEF Roles and Responsibilities in the Children and Armed Conflict Agenda of the Security Council', November 2015.

The Responsibility to Protect ... as a Rallying Call for Children?

Children Heard, Half Heard in the Trajectories Advancing R2P and CAAC

The trajectory of R2P and the CAAC agenda in the lead-up to the summer of 2005 appear largely uncorrelated at first glance. The initial momentum behind the Children and Armed Conflict Agenda was the foundational study by human rights advocate Graça Machel in 1996 on the impact of conflict on children.[6] This study was released long before the equally foundational 2001 report by the International Commission on Intervention and State Sovereignty (ICISS) on R2P. Yet already, in 1996, Machel's words echo with foresight the language that would develop around R2P. She argues that 'preventing conflicts from escalating is a clear responsibility of national Governments and the international community',[7] and that 'governments bear the primary responsibility for protecting children from the impact of armed conflict'.[8] For Machel, the impact of armed conflict on children must be 'everyone's concern and *is* everyone's responsibility; Governments, international organizations and every element of civil society'.[9]

Machel's study launched the CAAC agenda around the issue of child soldiers and child recruitment into armed forces and groups, and shed light on many more aspects and dimensions of how conflict affects children.[10] Analysis and follow-up points were presented for action not only by the Security Council, but also for the entire UN architecture. Recommendations included, for example, suggestions on which agency should coordinate responses for internally displaced children (para. 292), calling on the Security Council to assess the impacts of its sanctions regimes against the universal benchmark of the Convention on the Rights of the Child (para. 131) and demanding all to realise that while 'thousands of children are killed every year as a direct result of fighting, from knife wounds, bullets, bombs and landmines, [...] many more die from malnutrition and disease caused or increased by conflict' (para. 137).[11]

In the intervening years between the publication of the Machel study (1996) and Security Council Resolution 1612 (2005), the CAAC agenda grew

6 Graça Machel, *Impact of Armed Conflict on Children*, A/51/306, 26 August 1996.
7 Ibid., p. 71, para. 254.
8 Ibid., p. 75, para. 270.
9 Ibid., p. 90, para. 317, emphasis in the original text.
10 Ibid.
11 Ibid., p. 41.

significantly. The same year UNICEF[12] dedicated a chapter of its yearly *State of the World's Children* report to 'Children in War'. The following year, a position of Special Representative of the Secretary-General for Children and Armed Conflict (SRSG-CAAC) was established at the United Nations.[13] In 1998 the Security Council declared it would 'pay serious attention to the situation of Children and Armed Conflict',[14] and by 2000 the Optional Protocol to the Convention on the Rights of the Child on the Involvement of Children in Armed Conflict was adopted, receiving ten ratifications and entering into force by 2002.[15]

Further advances took place in consolidating the Children and Armed Conflict agenda as an established priority of the international community and of its foremost body, the Security Council. The Council, for example, began holding regular thematic debates on the issue starting in 1998 and was seized of the matter as a recurring topic to be discussed on a continuing basis in 1999.[16] Others, including the European Union started issuing their own guidelines on the matter.[17] With Resolution 1460 of 2003 the CAAC agenda entered an 'era of application'[18] with regular high level reporting on efforts to stop the use and recruitment of children and a request by the Council to the Secretary-General to develop specific proposals on how to monitor and report on the application of international norms related to CAAC. By 2005, the Security Council had held several thematic debates on the matter, considered numerous Secretary-General Reports and a 'name and shame' list of parties using and recruiting children. The first premises of a UN-led Monitoring and Reporting Mechanism (MRM) were underway and a first 'Plan of

12 UNICEF, 'State of the World's Children 1996', (New York: UNICEF, 1996). This document references an earlier premise of the children and conflict agenda in the 1980s with the concept of 'children as zones of peace' and 'days of tranquillity' during which hostilities would be suspended to run immunisation campaigns and other humanitarian actions focused on children or with children as an entry point.

13 'Children and Armed Conflict – Timeline', Office of the Special Representative of the Secretary-General for Children and Armed Conflict, https://childrenandarmedconflict.un.org/mandate/timeline/, accessed 30 November 2017.

14 SC/6537, 29 June 1998.

15 Radhika Coomaraswamy, 'The Optional Protocol to the Convention on the Rights of the Child on the Involvement of Children in Armed Conflict – Towards Universal Ratification', *The International Journal of Children's Rights*, 18/4: 535–549 (2010), p. 537.

16 S/RES/1261, 30 August 1999.

17 European Union, 'EU Guidelines on Children and Armed Conflict', 9 December 2003, 15634/03.

18 S/RES/1460, 30 January 2003.

Action' was signed in 2005 in Cote d'Ivoire with the Forces Armées des Forces Nouvelles to demobilise children involved in the conflict and halt any further recruitment.[19]

In comparison, the foundational report behind R2P was not formed until 2001. It however also found its roots in events from the mid and late 1990s, with the first premises of the concept coming from earlier still, through the plea to reconcile sovereignty with human rights made by then UN Secretary-General Javier Perez de Cuellar.[20] Intervening years, however, saw the conflicts in ex-Yugoslavia, Rwanda, Somalia, to name a few. Then, as the 2001 ICISS report itself explains, 'NATO's intervention in Kosovo in 1999 brought the controversy [around the right of humanitarian intervention] to a head'. Over those years the Security Council did not issue Presidential Statements, or set up regular thematic debates on the right to intervention – as it did for CAAC as early as 1999.[21] Pondering the question of intervention might have been a little too self-referential and existential a debate, and besides, the Council, particularly divided from the aftermath of the Kosovo intervention, was perhaps not the most conducive environment.[22] It was instead one Member State, Canada, which took the initiative to establish the ICISS, giving it a mandate to 'bring back a report that would help the Secretary-General [of the United Nations] and everyone else find some new common ground'.[23]

Six years after the foundational Machel report, the 2001 ICISS report had a similar galvanising effect around the idea of R2P, and is credited with creating the momentum for the concept to be adopted only four years later at

19 Anita Knudsen and Michelle Godwin, 'Pinning Down a Paper Tiger: Some Practice Observations on the Monitoring and Reporting Mechanism in Nepal and Asian Contexts' in Bina D'Costa (ed.), *Children and Violence: Politics of Conflict in South Asia* (Cambridge: Cambridge University Press, 2016).

20 Luke Glanville, *Sovereignty and the Responsibility to Protect: A New History* (Chicago and London: The University of Chicago Press, 2014), p. 173.

21 S/PV.4037, 25 August 1999.

22 While the subject might not have been taken up by the Security Council as such, much discussion took place around redefining the concept of sovereignty as a power not without associated responsibilities, including delivering on human rights. This was further to the work and sometimes provocative propositions by successive United Nations Secretary-Generals from Javier Perez de Cuellar through to Boutros-Boutros Ghali and Kofi Annan, among others (Luke Glanville, *Sovereignty and the Responsibility to Protect: A New History* (Chicago and London: The University of Chicago Press, 2014) pp. 173–176).

23 International Commission on Intervention and State Sovereignty (ICISS), *The Responsibility to Protect* (Ottawa: IDRC, 2001), p. vii.

the World Summit.[24] The children's experiences captured in Machel's[25] work can be heard throughout the work and output of ICISS.[26] In describing the complexity and brutality of modern warfare, the International Commission lamented, for example, how the proliferation of small arms and light weapons meant that all too often these weapons find their way into the hands of child soldiers. It also welcomed the 1998 Rome Statute of the International Criminal Court which prohibits the enlistment of children as soldiers – although the 2011 ICISS report did not mention the recently adopted Optional Protocol from 2000. Perhaps where ICISS comes closest to addressing child protection is when it argues that R2P 'implies an evaluation of the issues from the point of view of those seeking or needing support'. Its call here is to 'refocus the international searchlight where it should always be: on the duty to protect communities from mass killings, women from systematic rape, and children from starvation'.[27]

A second important moment in the trajectory of the responsibility to protect was in the Secretary-General's High Level Panel on Threats, Challenges and Change[28] report in 2004. A key contribution in the context of discussions around UN reform, this report *A More Secure World: Our Shared Responsibility* spoke of a:

> growing acceptance that while sovereign Governments have the primary responsibility to protect their own citizens from […] catastrophes, when they are unwilling or unable to do so, that responsibility should be taken up by the international community.[29]

The report is however light on the issue of children and armed conflict, and, perhaps because of its broad scope from collective security conflict through to poverty, disease and environmental degradation, it only mentions in passing the minimum standards from international humanitarian law as 'applicable

24 Peter Singer, *One World Now* (New Haven & London: Yale University Press, 2016), p. 145.

25 Machel, 'Impact of Armed Conflict on Children'.

26 International Commission on Intervention and State Sovereignty (ICISS), *The Responsibility to Protect* (Ottawa: IDRC, 2001), p. 4.

27 Ibid., p. 17, para. 2.29.

28 See: High Level Panel on Threats Challenges and Change, *A More Secure World: Our Shared Responsibility*, (New York: United Nations, 2004); Carsten Stahn, 'Responsibility to Protect: Political Rhetoric or Emerging Legal Norm?', *The American Journal of International Law*, 101/1: 99–120 (2007).

29 High Level Panel on Threats Challenges and Change, *A More Secure World: Our Shared Responsibility*, p. 56.

to the most vulnerable in situations of armed conflict, including women, children and refugees [which] must be respected'.[30]

This comparison in trajectories between the R2P and CAAC agendas brings some nuance to the impression that the synchronicity seen in 2005 was merely coincidental. Yet it hardly proves a close conceptual link, or close connection between the two norms, or that both agendas advanced each other's purpose in a deliberate way. Whilst the concepts took different paths, they did find their source in some of the most glaring failures the international community had its hands in during the 1990s. Moreover the appeals put forward by both concepts – when taken as platforms for international advocacy – echo each other to some extent. These echoes are faint, only half-heard, but nonetheless are perhaps sufficient to warrant digging deeper – and to test whether R2P worked as not only a rallying call in the face of grave human right violations, but also as a rallying call and advocacy framework that helped bring attention specifically to the grave violations children face in conflict.

Somewhere Between: 'Hot Air', Added Value and Unnecessary Hype?

Bellamy[31] provides a useful approach for testing whether or not R2P had a mobilising effect overall, and this approach can be applied to test if it contributed to advancing the agenda of protecting children in war. Asking frankly if R2P has added value or is simply 'hot air',[32] Bellamy explains that R2P was designed by the authors of the ICISS report as a rallying cry to replace the call for the 'right to intervene'. He sets out to test it through a thorough analysis of international pronouncements and statements leveraging R2P, in relation to a series of cases of mass atrocities over January 2006 to June 2011, and analysing what Security Council action was taken, if any, around these cases. He shows how R2P was not necessarily that effective in *directly* triggering international community action, but how as a concept it did become gradually internalised in the workings of the Security Council.[33] Based on analysis of when and how R2P was invoked by the Security Council, the UN and other actors, and around what crisis, Bellamy does find a connection 'between the use of R2P language by governments, UN officials or NGOs and the *likelihood* that the [Security] Council will pass a resolution' (emphasis added) on the issue at hand.[34]

---

30 Ibid., p. 62, para. 232.

31 Alex J. Bellamy, 'The Responsibility to Protect: Added Value or Hot Air?', *Cooperation and Conflict*, 48/3: 333–357 (2013).

32 Ibid.

33 Ibid.

34 Ibid., p. 340.

The gravity of the crisis, however Bellamy cautions – not the potency of the concept – may be what explains Security Council action. Use of the concept could be a derivative of such gravity, rather than the other way around: 'The worse the situation is, the more likely it is both that actors will use R2P language and that the Security Council will adopt resolutions'.[35] The analysis is further nuanced, looking at the scale of civilian deaths in each case, finding that 'there is no clear linkage between the gravity of the problem in terms of civilian lives lost, the invocation of R2P and the likelihood of Security Council resolutions'.[36] This makes it a matter of perceptions, with R2P used as a concept in order to elevate a situation above 'normal politics' – or a discursive act of 'securitising' the issue.[37]

Extending Bellamy's angle of analysis, it is worth exploring if R2P has (or has not) served as a rallying cry specifically for children. Echoes of language reminiscent of R2P can be found in the discourse on CAAC even before R2P's formal definition was adopted. During the Council's third thematic debate on Children and Armed Conflict in 2003, several veto-wielding Security Council Member States hinted in muted terms at the premises of the R2P concept.[38] The 2005 thematic debate that the Security Council held in February saw Special Representative of the Secretary-General Olara Otunnu more directly leverage the concept of R2P in his remarks, linking the R2P and the CAAC agenda more openly. Otunnu couched his reference in a state-centric framework – anticipating the future angle the definition of R2P would take. In 2005 he invoked R2P as a rallying call to Member State's responsibility for the cause of children in armed

35 Ibid., p. 340.

36 Ibid., p. 341

37 Ibid., p. 341.

38 For example, the United States spoke of the 'special responsibility to make extra efforts to protect children caught in the destructive cauldron of armed conflict', while China argued that 'as far as the [Security] Council is concerned, taking effective measures to prevent, curb and eliminate armed conflict is its major responsibility in the protection of children in armed conflict'. S/PV.4684, 14 January 2003 and S/PV.4684 (Resumption 1), 14 January 2003. Of course these are hardly ground-breaking pronouncements, and both earlier and later debates saw other delegations arguing squarely that the responsibility to protect children in conflict starts and finishes with the State: S/PV.4176, 26 July 2000; S/PV.4176 (Resumption 1), 26 July 2000 and S/PV.4176 (Resumption 1)/Corr.1, 26 July 2000. They nonetheless merit attention for the juxtaposition of the two concepts and for when these statements were made, that is, when the Children and Armed Conflict agenda was on the edge of entering the 'era of application' and as debates on R2P were particularly tense in the context of the Iraq invasion earlier in 2003.

conflict, and also as a blueprint for what practitioners may wish to aim for in their day-to-day work towards implementation:

> With regard to the role of Governments, let me state as clearly as I possibly can that the primary responsibility for protecting children lies with the national authorities, and that the role of United Nations agencies and other international actors should supplement those efforts, not supplant them. In situations where, because of the protracted experience of war, national institutions have been weakened, the rejuvenation of those institutions should be a priority for all international partners.[39]

The near synchronised peak moments of Resolution 1612 and the adoption of a definition for R2P in 2005 even appears to open a period in which – discursively at least – both concepts are closely linked together in the language of international actors operating at the intersection of these agendas. For example, at the July 2006 Security Council thematic debate on children and armed conflict, R2P was invoked specifically by UNICEF's Executive Director at the time, Ann Veneman, who argued that Resolution 1612 can provide a mechanism for accountability and compliance in the wider context in which Governments have a 'fundamental responsibility to protect their populations'.[40] As the Security Council made it routine to hold thematic debates on the issue of children and armed conflict – at times even twice per year – a rudimentary review of the different statements[41] by Member States between 2005 and 2016 suggests a similar process of internalisation, with R2P being leveraged for advocacy around Children and Armed Conflict. A year after 1612, the Security Council's 2006

39 S/PV.5129 (Resumption 1), 23 February 2005, p. 24.

40 S/PV.5494, 24 July 2006, p. 5.

41 S/PV.7753, 2 August 2016; S/PV.7466, 18 June 2015; S/PV.7129, 7 March 2014; S/PV. 7259, 8 September 2014; S/PV.6980, 17 June 2013; S/PV.6838, 19 September 2012; S/PV. 6838 (Resumption1), 19 September 2012; S/PV.6581, 12 July 2011; S/PV.6581 (Resumption 1), 12 July 2011; S/PV.6341, 16 June 2010; S/PV.6341 (Resumption 1), 16 June 2010; S/PV.6176, 4 August 2009; S/PV.6114, 29 April 2009; S/PV.6114 (Resumption 1), 29 April 2009; S/PV.5936, 17 July 2008; S/PV.5936 (Resumption 1), 17 July 2008; S/PV.5834, 12 February 2008; S/PV.5834 (Resumption 1), 12 February 2008; S/PV.5494, 24 July 2006; S/PV.5494 (Resumption 1), 24 July 2006; S/PV.5573, 28 November 2006; S/PV.5573 (Resumption 1), 28 November 2006; S/PV.5235, 26 July 2005; S/PV.5129, 23 February 2005; S/PV.5129 (Resumption 1), 23 February 2005; S/PV.4898+Corr.1, 20 January 2004; S/PV.4898 (Resumption 1), 20 January 2004; S/PV.4684, 14 January 2003; S/PV.4684 (Resumption 1), 14 January 2003; S/PV.4422, 20 November 2001; S/PV.4422 (Resumption 1), 20 November 2001; S/PV.4176, 26 July 2000; S/PV.4176 (Resumption 1)+Corr.1, 26 July 2000; S/PV.4037+Corr.1, 25 August 1999; S/PV.4037 (Resumption 1), 25 August 1999.

resolution on Protection of Civilians mentioned both R2P and CAAC[42] and ten years on reverberations of Otunnu's statement continue to be felt, including in the words of Secretary-General Ban Ki-moon, who reiterated in 2016 that:

> States have the primary responsibility to protect the fundamental rights of the world's children. I call on Member States, civil society, United Nations entities and everyone who can make a difference to rise to this test and give all children the childhood they deserve.[43]

It is, however, much more difficult to find a cause-to-(indirect)-effect link – even a tenuous one – between R2P being raised in relation to Children and Armed Conflict, and Security Council action specifically on grave violations of children's rights in conflict. In fact, the same rudimentary review of Member States' statements made at thematic debates on CAAC demonstrates that references are made mostly in passing, without much articulation conceptually, and mostly as lofty pronouncements. These references were not calls to action on specific situations. Therefore, when considering whether R2P added value, or was just 'hot air' in advancing the CAAC agenda, the answer, it would seem, is somewhere in between. R2P and the CAAC framework fit together for the intentions they share, and both became internalised in the work of the Security Council – but perhaps this occurred more coincidentally than purposefully. As a result, the added value of R2P to CAAC is neutral, rather than a rallying call to action for children.

An important challenge to the very idea of attempting to link the two concepts comes directly from arguments in defence of R2P's added value. Gareth Evans (2008), one of the two co-chairs of ICISS, indeed warns of the risk of a number of 'misunderstandings' around R2P, including that 'R2P covers all human protection issues'.[44] Evans makes a plea to preserve the focus and 'bite' of R2P, for practical purposes, noting that 'if R2P is to be about protecting everybody from everything, it will end up protecting nobody from anything'.[45] Considering *how* the CAAC agenda and R2P are mentioned side by side in

42 S/RES/1674, 28 April 2006.

43 Ban Ki-Moon, 'Foreword' in *20 Years to Better Protect Children Affected by Conflict*, Office to the Special Representative of the Secretary-General for Children and Armed Conflict, https://childrenandarmedconflict.un.org/wp-content/uploads/2017/01/Twenty-Years-of-Work-Booklet_web.pdf, accessed 30 November 2017, p. 5.

44 Gareth Evans, 'The Responsibility to Protect: An Idea Whose Time Has Come ... and Gone?', *International Relations*, 22/3: 283/298 (2008), p. 294.

45 Ibid., p. 294.

Security Council pronouncements, Evans's words of caution resonate and seriously nuance the depth of any conceptual link between the two agendas, lending much more weight to the idea that they combined by coincidence, not by intent. Here it is worth quoting Evans in full to see how their combination may be merely circumstantial, and perhaps just for the sake of grand-sounding, but ultimately innocuous, public policy discourse:

> Of course one can argue, linguistically and as a matter of good public policy, that the international community has the responsibility to protect people from the ravages of HIV/AIDS worldwide; the proliferation of nuclear weapons and other weapons of mass destruction; the ready availability of small arms, and the use of landmines and cluster bombs; the impact of dramatic climate change, particularly on specific groups like the Inuit of the Arctic circle; and much more besides. But if one is looking for umbrella language to bring these issues and themes together, it is much more appropriate to use a concept like 'human security' than to say these are proper applications of the new international norm of 'the responsibility to protect'.[46]

Evans does not mention the CAAC agenda in this laundry list of matters the international community has a 'responsibility to protect' people from, but he might as well. This critique of making the link for the sake of making the link could also be made in reverse. Because it can be leveraged to elevate an issue to the level of an 'existential threat'[47] and a matter of international peace and security (using UN charter language),[48] whether or not it is worthwhile or wise to use R2P when talking about children is a concern. While this question is beyond the immediate scope of this article, the opportunity versus risks in making the CAAC agenda a matter of international security or a 'threat to peace' is an important one to raise. Perhaps there is already enough in the universal value attached to the idea of the child and childhood and we may risk eroding this. Machel has previously noted how children 'present us with a uniquely compelling motivation for mobilisation'[49] which has proven a sufficient drive for momentum behind the protection of children in war and the CAAC agenda.

46 Ibid., p. 294.

47 Bellamy, 'The Responsibility to Protect: Added Value or Hot Air?'; Eli Stamnes, 'Speaking R2P and the Prevention of Mass Atrocities', *Global Responsibility to Protect*, 1: 70–89 (2009), p. 77.

48 United Nations, 'United Nations Charter'(1945), Chapter VII.

49 Machel, 'Impact of Armed Conflict on Children'.

In that regard, despite grave violations against children in armed conflict deserving the highest level of attention – which it has – R2P as an umbrella is arguably over-securitising/politicising an issue which may not (and perhaps should not) need the extra hype, and where the extra hype may in fact be counterproductive.

Child Protection in Emergencies: Practice Guidance and R2P

Responsibility Dilemmas Challenging Practitioners

The former SRSG-CAAC Olara Otunnu's appeal at the thematic debate on CAAC in 2005 delineated a breakdown of roles and responsibilities of how different actors should 'practice' R2P. The 'primary responsibility to protect' children in armed conflict lies with national authorities, he says, and what other actors can do is 'supplement' (not supplant) and 'rejuvenate' national institutions when those have been weakened by conflict – which Otunnu identifies as the priority for all international partners.[50] By implication, this delineation of roles and responsibilities conjures up the idea of some form of implicit 'secondary' responsibility of international actors, subordinate to the primary responsibility of the state, but a responsibility nonetheless. Identifying what actions and concrete measures will fulfil this secondary responsibility is the challenge and onus taken up by child-protection-mandated agencies. The challenge of what is done, what action can be done, what can stick, and what fails, is a further angle of questioning around the practical use and purpose in linking R2P with the CAAC agenda, or the even broader child protection in emergencies[51] strategies and responses.

Some of the basic tools and guides that ground child protection action in emergencies and in conflict contexts show the same linguistic coincidence between what R2P aims for, and the objectives, benchmarks and standards that humanitarian actors strive towards. Identifying children as a particularly vulnerable category in humanitarian action and response, the 2011 Sphere Standards[52] – a key field handbook for practitioners – underline that the 'government and other relevant authorities are responsible for ensuring that the

50 S/PV.5129, 23 February 2005; S/PV.5129 (Resumption 1), 23 February 2005.

51 See UNICEF definition of this sub-set of child protection work (5 April 2012) available here: https://www.unicef.org/protection/57929_62178.html, accessed 30 November 2017.

52 The Sphere Project, *Humanitarian Charter and Minimum Standards in Humanitarian Response* (Rugby: The Sphere Project – Practical Action Publishing, 2011), p. 41.

rights of the affected population are respected and fulfilled', suggesting that humanitarian agencies should consider supporting these populations in claiming their rights. In the international humanitarian response architecture, 'Child Protection' is defined as an 'Area of Responsibility' under the Global Protection Cluster;[53] and the *Minimum Standards for Child Protection in Humanitarian Action*[54] employ a similar language and approach. Principle 3, for example, to 'Protect people from physical and psychological harm arising from violence and coercion' is explained thus:

> Although the primary responsibility to protect children from harm rests with government, all child protection responses should seek to make children more secure, facilitate children's and families' own efforts to stay safe, and reduce children's exposure to risks.[55]

Among international practitioners there has been a growing effort to rethink child protection work as delivering on the commitment to support national institutions in establishing a protective environment for children. The shift in international child protection efforts from single-sector issue-based

53 Coincidentally, 2005 was also a culminating moment for another agenda around Humanitarian Reform, which saw the formal launch of sectoral coordination mechanisms – called 'Clusters' – with a number of different agencies mandated to lead specific Clusters. Much discussion went into how to rationalise the work of actors operating in the area of Protection, and what was established was a 'Global Protection Cluster' led by the Office of the United Nations High Commissioner for Refugees (UNHCR). Because of the multiplicity of protection issues different 'Areas of Responsibility' were established under the Global Protection Cluster, each with a specific agency lead. In the case of Child Protection, the lead was given to the United Nations Children's Fund (UNICEF), while other areas of responsibility include Gender-Based Violence (led by the United Nations Population Fund – UNFPA), Land Housing and Property (led by the Norwegian Refugee Council) and Mine Action (led by the United Nations Mine Action Service – UNMAS), 'Global Child Protection Cluster – Governance', Global Protection Cluster, http://www.globalprotectioncluster.org/en/about-us/governance.html, accessed 30 November 2017; 'Global Protection Cluster – Who We Are', Global Protection Cluster, http://www.globalprotectioncluster.org/en/about-us/who-we-are.html, accessed 30 November 2017.

54 Child Protection Working Group (CPWG), 'Minimum Standards for Child Protection in Humanitarian Action', September 2012, https://reliefweb.int/sites/reliefweb.int/files/resources/Minimum-standards-for-child-protection-in-humanitarian-action.pdf, accessed 11 December 2017.

55 Ibid., p. 29.

interventions to a systems approach[56] has seen a move away from fragmented programming on discrete individual child protection risks – child trafficking, children working or living in the streets, child labour – towards a systems-strengthening approach. This approach encompasses the myriad of simultaneous and structural variables and dynamics that affect protection in a child's environment, acknowledging that the action needed is holistic, multi-level, often across sectors and requiring engagement of all actors – again with the government identified as a key broker or 'duty bearer' for children.[57] UNICEF came out with a systems-focused child protection strategy[58] in 2008, while Save the Children in 2010 committed to building rights-based national child protection systems under its *Child Protection Initiative*.[59] Looking at the specific case of emergencies and conflict, UNICEF's framework calls for strengthening national and sub-national child protection systems in conflict and natural disasters. Save the Children also warns of the risk of losing sight of working at systems levels in emergencies, explaining that:

> in situations of armed conflict or natural disasters, one of the most important issues to address is the question of the balance between attention to the immediate needs of vulnerable groups on the one hand, and longer-term systems building on the other.[60]

In the extreme situations that theoretically evoke the concept of R2P, and where the Security Council is seized under the CAAC Agenda (because of the severity of the violations affecting children) a critical question is what exactly can child-protection-mandated agencies do to supplement or rejuvenate national institutions which have failed, are failing, or may even be

56 Michael G. Wessells, 'Children and Armed Conflict: Introduction and Overview', *Peace and Conflict: Journal of Peace Psychology*, 22/3 (2016); Mark Canavera, Kiryn Lanning, Katherine Polin and Lindsay Stark, '"And Then They Left": Challenges to Child Protection Systems Strengthening in South Sudan', *Children & Society*, 30/5: 356–368 (2016).

57 See discussion of child protection programming approach 'UNICEF's Child Protection Strategy'(New York: UNICEF, 2008) E/ICEF/2008/5/Rev in Knudsen and Godwin, 'Pinning down a Paper Tiger', p. 249.

58 UNICEF (2008) 'UNICEF Child Protection Strategy,' ed. UNICEF (New York: UNICEF, 2008), E/ICEF/2008/5/Rev.1.

59 Save the Children, 'Building Rights-Based National Child Protection Systems: A Concept Paper to Support Save the Children's Work', 2010, https://resourcecentre.savethechildren.net/sites/default/files/documents/3250.pdf, accessed 31 November 2017.

60 Ibid., p. 6.

contributing to harming children. Kingsbury[61] alludes to this dilemma noting that oftentimes 'protection' means 'different things to different agencies' and draws on perspectives from protection practitioners in Sri Lanka from across UNHCR, UNICEF, World Vision and *Médecins Sans Frontières* in interviews conducted by the Integrated Regional Information Networks-IRIN.[62] Responding to the question 'How do you define your organization's protection role and where its protection limits lie?' World Vision said as an organisation they 'do not promise that children in our target communities will be safe' as this was not deemed possible. In a similar vein UNICEF's response, worth quoting in full here – as Kingsbury does – highlights the complexities in day-to-day work:

> The way we define protection varies a lot. UNICEF's [2008] child protection strategy states [that it] is 'preventing and responding to violence, exploitation and abuse to ensure children's rights to survival, development and well-being', but UNICEF also signs up to a broader, rights-based inter-agency definition of protection through the protection cluster.
>
> Whenever you engage with governments or non-state actors on protection of civilians against harm or abuse, you always have to have in mind their accountability. You are there to assist them, to see how they will protect people from abuse. You can't … be the agency taking on those responsibilities. In Haiti, when there was no police force up-and-running, and displaced people were experiencing abuse, we could not just stand by and do nothing, but we tried to build the capacity of remaining police forces to address it.
>
> We helped them establish police brigades. It was then the police who started monitoring airports to make sure children had appropriate documentation so they weren't trafficked out of the country. In Sri Lanka we advocated for the release of children in the LTTE [Liberation Tigers of Tamil Eelam], but we wouldn't start sending supplies to strengthen police forces, or hand out money that could be used to fuel conflict. It's

61 Damien Kingsbury, *Sri Lanka and the Responsibility to Protect: Politics, Ethnicity and Genocide* (New York: Routledge, 2012), p. 14.

62 'The Dangers of Promising Too Much,' IRIN News, in Damien Kingsbury, *Sri Lanka and the Responsibility to Protect: Politics, Ethnicity and Genocide* (New York: Routledge, 2012), p. 15.

> a thin line we tread. It can be more difficult to get ... non-state actors to address violations ... for instance, the LTTE in Sri Lanka was an organized rebel group, [so] the government of Sri Lanka would not accept if outsiders try to build up the LTTE's capacity to protect.[63]

This example illustrates where lies the conundrum for field practitioners faced with extreme violations of child rights, or pervasive violations that start triggering talk of R2P. How can child-protection mandated agencies deliver on an implicit secondary and supplemental R2P in such heightened contexts, and even more so when the perpetrator is a state? It is pertinent that the example here is Sri Lanka, as the response in that country was found to be a 'systemic failure'[64] by the United Nations in the face of grave atrocities. Charles Petrie,[65] who led the Internal Review Panel tasked with analysing the UN's failures in Sri Lanka, found that protection monitoring processes there – both general and on children – 'had a number of limitations', and concluded that:

> the UN, in headquarters and in Sri Lanka, did not appear to fully recognize the scope of its responsibility to respond to Government violations and did not realize until very late that its protection actions were largely empty.[66]

Petrie's report also found that the UN-led Monitoring and Reporting Mechanism (MRM) on CAAC in Sri Lanka was essentially 'compromised'.[67] The MRM, discussed in more detail later, is essentially a dedicated circle of stakeholders working at various scales (principally the country-level, UN Headquarters-level and the Security Council-level) to provide verified information on grave rights violations committed against children in armed conflict and to seek accountability to stop these violations. In a departure from usual practice, the Government was sitting on the body coordinating this mechanism in Sri Lanka, the mechanism itself was under-resourced by UN bodies, and the Internal Review Panel also found evidence of serious underestimation of violations

63 Ibid.

64 Ban Ki-moon, 'Renewing Our Commitment to the Peoples and Purposes of the United Nations', 22 November 2013, https://www.un.org/sg/en/content/sg/speeches/2013-11-22/renewing-our-commitment-peoples-and-purposes-united-nations-scroll, accessed 30 November 2017.

65 Charles Petrie, 'Report of the Secretary-General's Internal Review Panel on United Nations Action in Sri Lanka' (New York: United Nations, 2012).

66 Ibid., p. 19.

67 Ibid., p. 23.

within the mechanism's reporting. Meanwhile in New York the Member State driven Security Council Working Group on Children and Armed Conflict was only monitoring the situation in Sri Lanka 'periodically',[68] as a 'slender aspect of the situation'[69] and at a slow pace which meant in the end 'no impact on the wider situation'.[70] The Panel's overall assessment of the UN's protection role in Sri Lanka is unforgiving, as it concludes that the rights violation investigations, information gathering and the protection work of these actors and coordination bodies 'neither served as an effective platform for advocacy and Security Council engagement, nor did it serve as a documentation mechanism for accountability'.[71]

The wider failures in Sri Lanka triggered an effort at aggiornamento across the United Nations system on how it could do better when confronted with serious human rights violations in conflict. The Human Rights Up Front[72] initiative was designed to ensure that the full breadth of the United Nations' mandates is leveraged to help protect people at risk or subject to serious violations of human rights and humanitarian law. Operational agencies of the United Nations working in emergencies and humanitarian response were part of this initiative, and the Inter-Agency Standing Committee (IASC) – a coordinating body of major humanitarian agencies, with membership at Principals-level – adopted a statement to commit to the 'Centrality of Protection in Humanitarian Action'.[73] The IASC statement reiterated that while 'the primary responsibility to protect people' lies with states, the United Nations has an imperative to engage to 'protect people, wherever they may be' and that the 'same imperative to protect people lies also at the heart of humanitarian action'.[74] The IASC statement emphasised that in practical terms 'this means identifying who is at risk, how and why at the very outset of a crisis'. At the

68 Ibid., p. 24.

69 Ibid., p. 24.

70 Ibid., p. 24.

71 Ibid., p. 114.

72 See: Jan Eliasson, 'The United Nations' Human Rights up Front Initiative', *Academic Council on the United Nations Systems Quarterly Newsletter*, 2015; United Nations, '"Human Rights up Front" Initiative', https://www.un.org/sg/en/content/ban-ki-moon/human-rights-front-initiative, accessed 2 January 2018; the initative is also outlined in Jan Eliasson and Helen Clark's letter to United Nations Resident Coordinators (24 Februrary 2014).

73 Inter-Agency Standing Committee, 'The Centrality of Protection in Humanitarian Action – Statement by the Inter-Agency Standing Committee (Iasc) Principals', 17 December 2013, https://interagencystandingcommittee.org/sites/default/files/centrality_of_protection_in_humanitarian_action_statement_by_iasc_princi.pdf, accessed 23 November 2017.

74 Ibid.

country /field level, the onus is put on Humanitarian Coordinators (senior UN staff with the responsibility to coordinate the UN's humanitarian response at the country and crisis level), Humanitarian Country Teams (a coordinating body of heads of key agencies, NGOs and at times donor representatives) and all Clusters (sectoral coordination groups) to deliver on a responsibility to 'place protection at the centre of international humanitarian action'.[75] So the onus is not on the field *alone* (where some of the tensions inherent to working with multiple entities in open conflict are hard to overcome) the IASC Principals affirm that they too are accountable to provide support, including backing up advocacy and lending their voices from afar when local advocacy is delicate.

While the Human Rights Up Front initiative highlights a commitment by protection and child-protection mandated agencies to act, the leap from commitment to operationalisation by practitioners is difficult to unpack. The link to be made between day-to-day on the ground activities to protect children in armed conflict and the framework of R2P also remains tenuous and perhaps only conceptual. An independent whole of system review[76] of protection efforts in the context of humanitarian action pointed at the fact that the standard child protection interventions available tended to be off the mark.[77] Although the review found that 'child protection' tended to have a more universal and clear definition (as opposed to 'protection'), nevertheless response actions in child protection tended to follow 'routine prioritisation of particular issues such as displacement or the need for child-friendly spaces,[78] whatever

75 Ibid.

76 This review was commissioned by the Norwegian Refugee Council on behalf of the IASC and the Global Protection Cluster.

77 Norah Niland, Riccardo Polastro, Antonio Donini and Amra Lee, 'Independent Whole of System Review of Protection in the Context of Humanitarian Action', (Norwegian Refugee Council, on behalf of the Inter-Agency Standing Committee and the Global Protection Cluster, 2015).

78 UNICEF defines child-friendly spaces (CFS) as 'places designed and operated in a participatory manner, where children affected by natural disasters or armed conflict can be provided with a safe environment, where integrated programming including play, recreation, education, health, and psychosocial support can be delivered and/or information about services/supports provided. Generally, CFS refer to a relatively short to medium term programme response, and are very often operated from tents and/or temporary structures (i.e. in schools, under a tree or a vacant building). They are usually operated by NGOs or governments. UNICEF is involved in establishment and coordination, in addition to setting minimum standards for them.'(UNICEF, 2009, 'A Practical Guide for Developing Child Friendly Spaces', p. 9). This type of response action is standard across nearly all child-protection-mandated agencies, with the language and jargon varying

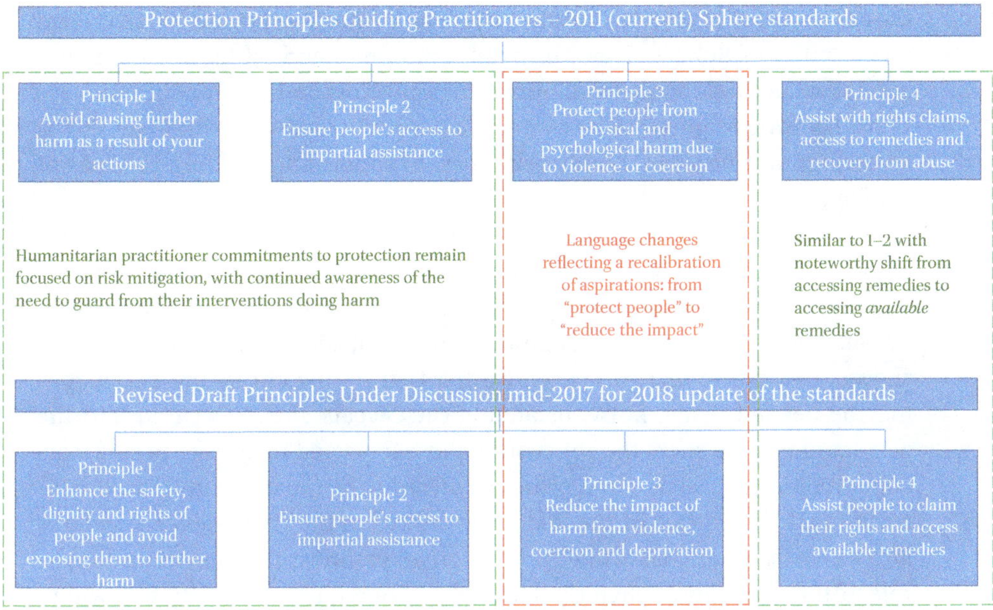

Adapted from The Sphere Project, Sphere (2011), and Changes in Protection Principles, Draft 1, Sphere (2017, unpublished)

FIGURE 1 *Changes under discussion to protection principles in the Sphere standards (2017).*

the nature of the crisis'.[79] It thus called for better and more joined up analysis, rather than predefined activities and rolling out child-friendly spaces as a default setting.

The inherent limitations child-protection-mandated agencies can face may emerge from being unable, as the IRIN interviews highlighted, to promise that the children they want to protect will be safe. It is therefore unsurprising, from this angle, that specialists and practitioners find it difficult to define protection activities within their response plans, and can struggle to identify transferable lessons. Examples can be drawn from the written guidance for field and UN practitioners. The practitioner's dilemma around protection and R2P, for example, is evident in current consultative efforts to revise the Sphere standards handbook on principles, minimum standards and quality of humanitarian action.[80] Figure 1: *Changes under discussion to protection principles in*

between Child Friendly Spaces, Safe Spaces (Save the Children), Safe Play Areas (ICRC) and so on.

79 Ibid., p. 28.

80 The Sphere Project, *Humanitarian Charter and Minimum Standards in Humanitarian Response* (Rugby: The Sphere Project – Practical Action Publishing, 2011).

the Sphere standards (2017) outlines the four 'protection principles' that form a core pillar of Sphere. These principles are not standard interventions but guiding values that apply to all humanitarian actors and all types of interventions. They are required to be taken into account whether the intervention is a vaccination campaign, building latrines, or supporting children in times of conflict.

SPHERE already recognised that the primary responsibility to protect rests with the state, but in the ongoing consultations and feedback to revise the protection principles, field practitioners cite that some principles may be too aspirational and are in need of recalibration to be realistic.[81] In particular, Figure 1 shows the move to recognise even further that setting out to 'protect people' may be beyond reach, notwithstanding the caveats already written into the 2011 standards. As such, the third principle is expected to change to softer accountabilities, focused on the principle of 'reducing the risk'. Similarly, the International Committee of the Red Cross (ICRC) in the *Professional Standards for Protection Work* insists that 'protection actors must not substitute for the role of the authorities when the latter have the requisite capacity and will to assume their responsibilities'.[82] Recognising such capacity might be lacking, the ICRC standards note that any direct substitution should only be last-resort, mostly one-off life-saving interventions ('the evacuation of wounded or sick from a battle zone',[83] or 'providing medical services following a violation'[84]). The discussion on revisions to core principles illustrates how, in addition to being short on capacity and mandate to protect people, protection activities (including, by extension, in the realm of child protection), principles, rules and professional standards developed from within the field have all directed practitioners against the temptation of aiming or wanting to be the primary provider of protection. One further example in this regard is the 2014 Aide Mémoire by the Office for the Coordination of Humanitarian Affairs (OCHA) on the Protection of Civilians. This specific guide for practitioners on what to do and what advocacy instruments, platforms and tools to rely on, underlines that the

81 Practitioners discussion hosted during the webinar 'Revising the SPHERE Handbook', 27 April 2017, International Association of Professionals in Humanitarian Assistance and Protection.

82 ICRC, 'Professional Standards for Protection Work Carried out by Humanitarian and Human Rights Actors in Armed Conflict and Other Situations of Violence', (Geneva: International Committee of the Red Cross, 2013) pp. 46–48.

83 Ibid., p. 47.

84 Ibid., p. 47.

primary responsibility to protect is always with the state, pointing out implicitly that practitioners' primary responsibility is to remind the state – or other parties in the conflict – of their responsibility, not to supplant them.[85] Furthermore, an earlier review[86] of Protection of Civilian mandates in peacekeeping operations noted that while there is a need to do more to better protect civilians, 'peacekeeping operations cannot "protect everyone from everything"', 'need to manage expectations' and 'do not and cannot "own" the concept of protection'.[87,88]

85 OCHA, 'Aide Memoire for the Consideration of Issues Pertaining to the Protection of Civilians in Armed Conflict', (New York: United Nations, 2014).

86 Victoria Holt, Glyn Taylor, and Max Kelly, *Protecting Civilians in the Context of UN Peacekeeping Operations: Successes, Setbacks and Remaining Challenges* (New York: United Nations, 2009), pp. 3, 12.

87 Ibid.

88 In addition to the above examples of practitioner guidance, and although a discussion of 'integrated missions' is beyond the scope of this particular article, one practical example can be found in 2013 when the UN peacekeeping operation in the Democratic Republic of Congo (DRC) was augmented with a 'special intervention brigade' under Security Council Resolution 2098. Among its roles was 'protection of civilians', and 'neutralizing' armed groups through 'targeted offensive operations'. Though it was to complement national capacity, the brigade was authorised to act 'unilaterally'. This offensive posture was bold ... but caused a stir inside aid agencies worried about humanitarian space. The most visible component of the international operation (humanitarian or otherwise), the peacekeeping mission, could now be seen to be (even more of) a *party* to the conflict, able to launch offensives, including for civilian protection. Humanitarian actors voicing concerns hinted at how they recognised that 'primary' provision of protection was not their mandate ... and was a risky concept when taken on by a (perceived) peer. Peacekeeping missions indeed tend to be lumped together in popular perception with humanitarian agencies, which was definitely the case in Congo. 'Perception-by-association' of having the same mandate was what humanitarian agencies wished to avoid, precisely because taking on a role that inches closer to a primary responsibility for protection means turning into quite a different actor, with quite a different mandate. Laid bare, the thorny question is what happens if the firewall is removed of the responsibility to protect staying with the state? How far does the mandate go to be the primary provider? One could be reminded of the example of 'shoot-to-feed', long ago advocated in the face of failure in Somalia ... warped into 'shoot-to-protect'. Even indirectly, the possibility of being perceived as having such a mandate had many uneasy on the ground at the time. Note: this example is based on the Author's field notes, Goma, DRC, July 2013. For further reference see respectively the Security Council resolution in question (S/RES/2098, 28 March 2013, pp. 6–7, paras. 12 (a), 12 (b)), as well as Aurelie Ponthieu, Christoph Vogel, and Katharine Derderian, 'Without Precedent or Prejudice? UNSC Resolution 2098 and Its Potential Implications for Humanitarian Space in Eastern Congo and Beyond', *Journal of Humanitarian Assistance*, 21

Finally, recent remarks from Secretary-General António Guterres, in the dialogue on the 2017 Secretary-General's report on R2P echoed this point in commentary on the role of protection agencies in advocating for vulnerable populations. Considering the increased attention to the capacities, rights and participation of affected populations in crisis situations – accountability to these groups has come into sharper focus[89] – the Secretary-General underlined the demand for global normative frameworks that link to advocacy efforts to represent the views and interests of vulnerable groups at the field level. He also noted the different roles by different actors – those who 'speak out' and those who need to 'listen' (and, presumably, act):

> In practice, it can sometimes be difficult to assure direct accountability to populations that are under stress owing to the risk of atrocity crimes. In such situations, those with mandates for protection must represent the views and interests of vulnerable populations. That includes, but is not limited to, the United Nations High Commissioners for Human Rights and for Refugees, the heads of United Nations field presences, my Special Representatives on Sexual Violence in Conflict and for Children and Armed Conflict and my Special Advisers on the Prevention of Genocide and on the Responsibility to Protect. *United Nations field presences have a responsibility to speak on behalf of the vulnerable and raise protection concerns, in public, if judged necessary, a responsibility reinforced by the Human Rights Up Front initiative. When they do so, they speak with my full support, but speaking out is only part of what is needed. Individual States and intergovernmental bodies must be prepared to listen.* It is imperative that the Security Council, the Human Rights Council and the General Assembly provide greater opportunities for those who speak on behalf of the vulnerable to relay their concerns, and those opportunities should be extended beyond the United Nations to others, such as humanitarian and civil society organizations that have field presences in affected regions.[90]

January 2014; and Leslie H. Gelb, 'Shoot to Feed Somalia', *New York Times*, 19 November 1992.

89 See for example 'IASC Task Team on Accountability to Affected Populations and Protection from Sexual Exploitation and Abuse (AAP/PSEA)', https://interagencystandingcommittee.org/accountability-affected-populations-including-protection-sexual-exploitation-and-abuse, accessed 30 November 2017.

90 Antonio Guterres, 'Implementing the responsibility to protect: accountability for prevention. Report of the Secretary-General', A/71/1016-S/2017/556, 10 August 2017, emphasis added; see also Antonio Guterres, 'Secretary-General's Remarks to General Assembly

Practice guidance exists and is continuing to develop to promote humanitarian actors' efforts to be more accountable to affected populations – including children.[91] The UN-led MRM, to which we now turn, can be one of these tools for advocacy to realise high level principles in practice, though it certainly faces challenges in linking up the various layers.

The Monitoring and Reporting Mechanism (MRM) on Grave Violations of Children's Rights as Sharpest Tool to Protect?

These latent challenges described above are evident when looking specifically at what international child protection practitioners can do to deliver on the CAAC agenda using a key operational implement in their toolkit. One of the most significant developments in the CAAC agenda since 2005, has been the Security Council resolutions that introduced the UN-led Monitoring and Reporting Mechanism (MRM) and its Action Plans as a way to document grave violations of children's rights, to inform advocacy efforts, to call to account groups that perpetrate violence against children and to stop the violations from occurring.[92] The UN-led MRM systematically monitors and reports on six grave violations committed against children: (i) killing and maiming

---

informal dialogue on the responsibility to protect', 6 September 2017, https://www.un.org/sg/en/content/sg/statement/2017-09-06/secretary-generals-remarks-general-assembly-informal-dialogue?platform, accessed 30 November 2017.

91 See for example, UNICEF's tools for accountably to children in emergencies: 'Accountability to Affected Populations (AAP) and Prevention of Sexual Abuse and Exploitation (PSEA)', http://www.unicefinemergencies.com/downloads/eresource/accountability_to_affected_populations.html, accessed 30 November 2017. Other monitoring frameworks that attempt to privilege children's own views in the measures of quality of services in child protection systems are also being applied in conflict settings such as the Promising Quality Framework. See for example 'IASC Task Team on Accountability to Affected Populations and Protection from Sexual Exploitation and Abuse (AAP/PSEA)', https://interagencystandingcommittee.org/accountability-affected-populations-including-protection-sexual-exploitation-and-abuse, accessed 30 November 2017. Within child protection programming at the national scale the Promising Quality (to children) Framework provides another example, now being piloted by UNICEF in Zimbabwe, South Sudan and parts of the Syria response. See E. Sammon, M. Godwin, L. Rumble, A. Nolan, A.B. Matsika and N. Mayanga, 'Make the promise true: A monitoring and evaluation framework for measuring quality in child protection service delivery in Zimbabwe', *Child Indicators Research*, 8(3): 623–640 (2015).

92 For a useful snapshot of key developments in the CAAC agenda from 1997–2014, see: Table 10.1 in Knudsen and Godwin, 'Pinning Down a Paper Tiger', pp. 246–248.

of children; (ii) recruitment or use of children by armed forces and groups;[93] (iii) rape and other forms of sexual violence against children; (iv) attacks against schools and hospitals; (v) abduction of children; (vi) denial of humanitarian access to reach children.[94] Of these 'six grave violations' the first five act as triggers for a perpetrator of violations to be added onto a public 'name and shame' list maintained by the Secretary-General.[95]

In 2005, the roles and responsibilities for operationalising the MRM were agreed between the Office of the Special Representative of the Secretary-General-CAAC assuming the mandate to 'conduct high-level political advocacy, raise awareness [… and] lead the drafting of the annual [CAAC-MRM] report of the Secretary-General'[96] and UNICEF which took on the core responsibility to set up taskforces in relevant countries hosting armed groups and forces committing violations against children. These taskforces are co-chaired by the UN Resident Coordinator (the organisation's most senior staff member in country) together with the head of UNICEF, and include a broad group of stakeholders including UN agencies, national government, international and local NGOs and affected communities. Programmatically, these taskforce members work together, strengthening capacity to monitor violations, verify reports of violations, collect, organise and store data about cases and produce high level reporting, ultimately feeding into the reports of the UN Secretary-General on Children and Armed Conflict.[97]

---

93 The linguistic distinction between armed 'forces' and 'groups' being intentional to allow focus on state armed forces and non-state actors and groups.

94 UNICEF, 'Guidance Note: UNICEF Roles and Responsibilities in the Children and Armed Conflict Agenda of the Security Council', November 2015, http://www.unicefinemergencies.com/downloads/eresource/docs/Global%20Norms%20and%20Standards/Guidance%20Note%20on%20UNICEF%20and%20CAAC%20Agenda.pdf, accessed 30 November 2017.

95 While the Special Representative of the Secretary General on CAAC makes a recommendation on what parties to list (drawing on field data and reports gathered through the MRM taskforce), ultimately the decision rests with the Secretary-General on which groups to include (and not to include) in the list. Also see: OSRSG-CAAC, UNICEF, and DPKO, 'Field Manual – the Monitoring and Reporting Mechanism (MRM) on Grave Violations against Children in Situations of Armed Conflict' (2014).

96 See: UNICEF, 'Guidance Note'; Letter from UNICEF Executive Director and the acting SRSG-CAAC to UNICEF Representatives, 14 October 2005, quoted in UNICEF's 'HA2 Position Paper: UNICEF's Roles and Responsibilities in the Children and Armed Conflict Agenda of the Security Council', August 2014.

97 UNICEF 'Guidance Note'.

In the course of this work, taskforce members (child protection practitioners) engage in active dialogue with parties to the conflict. Part of this engagement is to negotiate, co-develop and implement agreements with the armed group or force (Action Plans)[98] that have the goal to end and prevent violations against children and thus allow an offending party to improve their international reputation through removing them from the 'list of shame' in the high level CAAC report. The offending armed group or force, government and UNICEF can be signatories on these action plans.[99] Knudsen and Godwin note that in this way the MRM:

> not only puts in the spotlight the behaviour of the [offending] armed force or group, in regards to child right violations, but also highlights the responsibility of humanitarian child protection actors (UN and Government) in reducing threats to child safety. The MRM obligates the UN to squarely measure its own progress in the dialogue with armed forces or groups on this matter and in developing programmes to prevent and respond to the violations.[100]

In this way, by engaging with those responsible for the gravest violation of child rights in conflict, the MRM is a specific implement in the advocacy toolkit of child-protection-mandated agencies, as it seeks to act towards 'risk elimination' – and shared accountability to ending violations against children.[101]

Reichhold and Binder's[102] analysis of the spectrum of protection risk, places 'risk elimination' at one end and 'risk mitigation' on the other. Risk mitigation is the strategy logic behind emergency response interventions such as UNICEF'schild friendly spaces. The MRM acts more broadly, within its set of advocacy tools and activities it seeks to also eliminate risk by 'pressuring state and non-state authorities to change [...] behaviour that negatively affects civilian safety'.[103] Similarly, Slim and Bonwick's[104] practice handbook provides a framework of analysis using a risk-based model of protection, whereby

98 Ibid., p. 8.

99 Ibid., p. 8.

100 Knudsen and Godwin, 'Pinning Down a Paper Tiger', p. 249.

101 See Ibid.

102 Urban Reichhold and Andrea Binder, 'The Metrics and Ethics of Protecting Civilians', *Global Responsibility to Protect*, 6/2: (2014), p. 208.

103 Reichhold and Binder, 'The Metrics and Ethics of Protecting Civilians', p. 214.

104 Hugo Slim and Andrew Bonwick, *Protection – An ALNAP Guide for Humanitarian Agencies* (London: ALNAP/ODI, 2005).

humanitarian agencies act in order to influence the different variables within the 'protection equation' (reduce threats, reduce vulnerabilities and increase capacity). Knudsen and Godwin demonstrate that the MRM works on what Slim and Bonwick highlight should be the 'first programming priority' which is 'reducing threats' – achieved specifically by 'engaging responsibility':

> Reducing the level of threat is the first programming priority. This means trying to make states, armed groups and individuals meet their humanitarian responsibilities to protect people in war. This involves engaging those responsible – directly or indirectly – in an effort to prevent violations, end threats and respond to suffering.[105]

The MRM is perhaps the mechanism for international child-protection-mandated agencies to 'engage responsibility': UN-led MRM taskforces keep parties engaged, and monitor the level of implementation and compliance by armed forces and groups to the commitments and benchmarks set out in signed Action Plans. However, as practitioners have reflected, success is often highly contingent on a myriad of external security and political factors.[106]

Unique and useful though it can be in engaging different actors, the MRM is hardly a straightforward tool for delivering on an (implicit) responsibility to protect. It is also a mechanism whose protective results are hard to measure.[107] There are tremendous methodological challenges in reporting and measuring whether and when 'risk elimination' works. Without full post-conflict hindsight, measuring whether or not humanitarian protection actors are delivering on this implicit responsibility to protect involves unpacking highly complex and granular detail.[108] Indeed to categorise which actions undertaken

105 Slim and Bonwick, *Protection – An ALNAP Guide for Humanitarian Agencies*, p. 52.

106 Ibid.

107 Reichhold and Binder, 'The Metrics and Ethics of Protecting Civilians', 2014.

108 For example, an Action Plan may have worked nationally, but there may be pockets of remaining conflict at the community/village level, where protection issues have been left unaddressed – posing challenges to measure success in 'engaging responsibility' or in delivering – even directly by shoring up the state – on R2P. This is also illustrated in the difficulties encountered when trying to list the 'Mai Mai' militias in the Democratic Republic of Congo, which are highly localised non-state armed groups, sometimes at community or village level, or splinter groups of splinter groups, which the Annual Reports of the Secretary-General on CAAC has had to list under multiple variations, appending to each group the name of its field commanders – see 'Children and Armed Conflict, Report of the Secretary-General', S/2013/245, 15 May 2013, pp. 14–15 and list on p. 49.

for children under the MRM fall within the scope of R2P is an acrobatic and difficult task.

A considered read of the Secretary-General's regular reports on 'the responsibility to protect', for example, finds only vague and loosely connected mentions of children's issues in conflict. Most action described is about shoring up of the primary duty bearer's – the states' – responsibility, at, usually, a micro/meso-level. For example, the first in the series of Secretary-General reports on R2P – titled *Implementing the responsibility to protect* (2009)[109] – paints a puzzling montage of deliverables including: the publication of a child protection handbook for parliamentarians, 'an active publications programme across the human rights spectrum',[110] efforts for governments in Colombia, Philippines or the Sudan to reform their judicial systems to better handle former children associated with armed groups, or training for armed forces in the Economic Community of West African States (ECOWAS) region on children's rights before, during and after conflict. Laudable as these efforts are, it is hard not to think back to Evans' (2008) warning that over-broadening what falls under R2P risks rendering it meaningless. The third report of the Secretary-General (2011)[111] takes a less scattergun approach and better summarises what the UN can do, outlining capacity to help rebuild legal institutions and train police, prison and judicial officials in countries recovering from conflict. The link between R2P and the MRM/CAAC agenda is made off and on in R2P reports that followed – but rarely beyond acknowledgements, in-passing, that CAAC and 1612 are useful frameworks.

In addition, the ten-year review of what had been achieved for CAAC since the Machel study (2009) referred back to the World Summit's recognition of R2P, noting a concrete, practical and operational opportunity for peacekeeping operations to deploy 'where there is a need to protect populations, including children, from grave human rights' violations'.[112] Although the Machel Study 10-Year Strategic Review (2009) called for more robust mandates and more forceful means to protect children,[113] the question of mandates for

109 Ban Ki-moon, 'Implementing the Responsibility to Protect: Report of the Secretary General', A/63/677, 12 January 2009.

110 Ibid., p. 14.

111 Ban Ki-moon, 'The Role of Regional and Subregional Arrangements in Implementing the Responsibility to Protect: Report of the Secretary-General', A/65/877–S/2011/393, 27 June 2011.

112 UNICEF, *Machel Study 10-Year Strategic Review: Children and Conflict in a Changing World* (New York: Office of the Special Representative of the Secretary-General for Children and Armed Conflict, 2009), p. 50.

113 Ibid.

peacekeeping operations is a cyclical all-time favourite debate topic at and around the United Nations.[114] The latest contribution in that discussion to date, the 2015 Review report from High Level Independent Panel on Peace Operations, sadly returned a harsh diagnosis of untapped opportunity and unrealised potential in this regard. The text is worth quoting in full:

> 84. Over the past two decades, concerted efforts have been made to strengthen international protection frameworks. Those include the increasing prominence of human rights and protection-related mandates for United Nations peace operations, the responsibility to protect, as set out in General Assembly resolution 60/1 on the 2005 World Summit Outcome, and most recently the Human Rights Up Front initiative of the Secretary-General. In addition to the mandate of the United Nations High Commissioner for Human Rights, mechanisms of the Human Rights Council and the human rights treaty bodies, the Office of the Special Adviser on the Prevention of Genocide and the Office of the Special Adviser on the Responsibility to Protect, mandatory monitoring and reporting arrangements have been set out in General Assembly and Security Council resolutions on children in armed conflict and sexual violence in conflict. Policies, guidance and training have been developed on ways to implement human rights and protection-related mandates. Many United Nations peace operations now include protection of civilians advisers, child protection officers and women's protection advisers working alongside the mission's human rights component. *But that growth in concepts, standards, advocacy and specialised personnel has yet to transform reality on the ground, where it matters.*
>
> 85. The primary responsibility for the protection of civilians lies with their Governments. The Security Council and other international partners

114 The 2000 'Brahimi Report' for example warns that: 'There are hundreds of thousands of civilians in current United Nations mission areas who are exposed to potential risk of violence, and United Nations forces currently deployed could not protect more than a small fraction of them even if directed to do so. Promising to extend such protection establishes a very high threshold of expectation. The potentially large mismatch between the desired objective and the resources available to meet it raises the likelihood of continuing disappointment with United Nations follow-through in this area. If an operation is given a mandate to protect civilians, therefore, it also must be given the specific resources needed to carry out that mandate'. Lakhdar Brahimi, 'Report of the Panel on United Nations Peace Operations', A/55/305–S/2000/809, 21 August 2000.

> should seek to include that responsibility of the host Government clearly in a United Nations compact between the Secretariat and the host Government, proposed in paragraph 151, and hold host Governments to account for the protection of civilians. The presence of a United Nations mission or other protection actors does not diminish the obligation of host Governments to make every effort to protect their own civilians. But neither does that State responsibility dilute the obligation of United Nations missions to act within their capabilities when the host Government is not willing or able to protect its citizens.[115]

Though more is needed on the ground, peacekeepers and child-protection practitioners have made specific efforts at developing concrete guidelines around the MRM, beyond the dimension of 'engaging responsibility' to include service delivery for children affected by armed conflict.[116] The MRM not only reports on protection concerns, but engagement in the mechanism arguably strengthens the network of protection actors, improves coordination and deploys specific interventions for children, notably organising for the release and reintegration of children associated with armed forces and groups. Data collected for the purpose of tracking cases of child recruitment can also inform more effective case-management and service referral for child survivors, where they are available.[117] Responses also include repeat training with key state authorities (police, military, border forces) and non-state actors when possible on child rights, international human rights and international humanitarian law. Joint guidelines across the Office of the SRSG-CAAC, UNICEF and the Department of Peacekeeping Operations (DPKO) continue to explain that

115 High Level Independent Panel on Peace Operations, *Uniting Our Strengths for Peace: Politics, Partnership and People* (New York: United Nations, 2015), p. 37, emphasis added.

116 OSRSG-CAAC, UNICEF, and DPKO, 'Field Manual – the Monitoring and Reporting Mechanism (MRM) on Grave Violations against Children in Situations of Armed Conflict', June 2014, https://childrenandarmedconflict.un.org/wp-content/uploads/2016/04/MRM_Field_5_June_2014.pdf, accessed 11 December 2017; OSRSG-CAAC, UN-DPKO, and UNICEF, 'Global Good Practices Study – Monitoring and Reporting Mechanism on Grave Violations against Children in Situations of Armed Conflict', November 2013, http://www.mrmtools.org/mrm/files/MRM_Good_Practice_Study_-_27_Nov_2013.pdf, accessed 11 December 2017.

117 Ibid.; Child Protection Working Group (CPWG), 'Minimum Standards for Child Protection in Humanitarian Action'; Michael G. Wessells, 'Children and Armed Conflict: Interventions for Supporting War-Affected Children', *Peace and Conflict: Journal of Peace Psychology*, 23/1: 4–13 (2017).

'accountability is key to the MRM process and protection actors should be in a position to advise children and their families'.[118]

Yet the MRM faces serious obstacles in the face of large-scale violence with its limited ability to effect change in the behaviour of warring parties towards children – for example in Syria, Iraq or Yemen – and MRM partners can face backlash from Government when and if they engage with non-state actors. For practitioners working on the MRM in-country, the mix of public/private diplomacy and advocacy is often a particularly complex equation, where practitioners need to balance their relationship with Government, non-state actors, other United Nations agencies and peacekeeping forces, humanitarian NGOs, the best interests of individual children, and their organisation's internal geographical hierarchies (for example head office in the capital, regional and headquarter offices).[119] Others have pointed out how the continual bargaining with such risks is an everyday consideration for field officers, alongside dilemmas related to protection work in the height of conflict situations, as it relates to mandates, principles, access and operations (including staff safety).[120] Beyond these day-to-day frustrations for the field practitioner, the global MRM architecture can itself also be gripped by similar dilemmas on how to help deliver 'protection' and find itself caught in the middle of far greater external geopolitical considerations and influences. At the global scale, the controversial non-listing or de-listing of certain Member States and parties because of alleged pressure on the United Nations apparatus is one example.[121]

---

118 OSRSG-CAAC, UNICEF, and DPKO, 'Field Manual', p. 54.

119 By way of example, in July 2010, UNICEF's signature of an agreement with the Justice Equality Movement (JEM) in Darfur to demobilise children and prevent recruitment (facilitated by the Centre for Humanitarian Dialogue in Geneva) triggered some government backlash in Khartoum. See 'Sudan Summons Unicef Representative to Protest Jem Pact', *Sudan Tribune*, 25 July 2010; 'UNICEF Signs Child Protection Pact with Key Rebel Group in Darfur', UN News Centre, 21 July 2010, http://www.un.org/apps/news/story.asp?NewsID=35386#.WOe3FdJ96Hs, accessed 30 November 2017.

120 See for example Lang and Knudsen who explored what 'protection' work implied at the height of the conflict in Sri Lanka, with observations largely applicable to the protection of children in armed conflict, Hazel Lang and Anita Knudsen, '"Your Subject of Protection Is a Dangerous One": Protracted Internal Conflict and the Challenges for Humanitarian Agencies', *Norsk Geografisk Tidsskrift – Norwegian Journal of Geography*, 63/1: 35–45(2009).

121 In June-July 2015 there was much speculation among observers and child protection practitioners as to whether or not Israel and Hamas would end up on the annual 'list of shame' annexed to the Secretary-General's report on CAAC further to the 2014 conflict in Gaza, but neither was listed. A year later, the report by the Secretary-General for 2015 listed the Saudi-led coalition for actions in Yemen, but a few days later a statement was issued by the Secretary-General accepting a proposal by Saudi Arabia to review the cases

Institution-centricity of Normative Frameworks: Overlooking Community Based Protection?

There is a hint in the joint guidelines issued by UN-DPKO, OSRSG-CAAC and UNICEF towards the need for community-based responses by field practitioners in order to help better protect children and contribute to a protective environment. Shifting the spotlight to the local and community angle – as there are actors there – brings us to a critique that can and should be directed in equal measure both to R2P and the CAAC/MRM agenda/architecture. When speaking of R2P, or focusing on what child-protection actors do to create a protective environment for children (success in that being beyond their control), a lot of the tools, implements and practices are top-down and at best only nominally rooted in the communities those actors intend to help protect.[122] Furthermore,

---

and numbers cited in the report, with the statement saying that 'pending the conclusions of the joint review, the Secretary-General removes the listing of the Coalition in the report's annex'. The outcome of this proposed joint review appears to remain pending (two months later UN diplomatic sources expressed frustration that no information was being shared) but the Saudi-led coalition does still appear in the report. Another year later, in 2017, around the time the report on 2016 was expected (August/September) speculation reignited around the potential re-listing of the Saudi-led coalition. The decision to list or not to list was particularly anticipated as it was seen by many as a test for the new Secretary-General, António Gutteres. In October 2017 as the report came out the Saudi-led coalition was listed, although a new typology was created in the Secretary-General's list, differentiating between parties 'that have not put in place measures [...] to improve the protection of children' and parties that have, the Saudi-led coalition being listed among those that had put in place such measures. See: 'Statement Attributable to the Spokesman for the Secretary-General on the Annual Report of the Secretary-General on Children and Armed Conflict', 6 June 2016, https://www.un.org/sg/en/content/sg/statement/2016-06-06/statement-attributable-spokesman-secretary-general-annual-report, accessed 1 December 2017; Amnesty International, 'UN: Shameful Pandering to Saudi Arabia over Children Killed in Yemen Conflict', 7 June 2016, https://www.amnesty.org/en/latest/news/2016/06/un-shameful-pandering-to-saudi-arabia-over-children-killed-in-yemen-conflict/, accessed 1 December 2017; Human Rights Watch, 'Ensure Consistency in Children and Armed Conflict Report', 27 April 2015; Antonio Guterres, 'Children and Armed Conflict: Report of the Secretary-General'; Colum Lynch, 'Confidential UN Report Accuses Saudi Coalition of Killing Hundreds of Yemeni Kids', *Foreign Policy*, 16 August 2017, http://foreignpolicy.com/2017/08/16/confidential-u-n-report-accuses-saudi-coalition-of-killing-hundreds-of-children-in-yemen-conflict/, accessed 1 December 2017; Somini Sengupta, 'Saudi Arabia Resists Independent Inquiry on Yemen Atrocities', *New York Times*, 27 September 2017.

122 It is worth noting that language used across official reports and guidelines insists on inserting 'help' everywhere there is a reference to protection commitments – a further discursive acknowledgement that for child-protection-mandated actors from the

they can come across as missing the fact that communities, including children and adolescents – to use an old humanitarian adage – are oftentimes the first responders ... and can be the first protectors. There is an identified research gap in understanding how international actors interface with the local level and why some of their initiatives at building peace succeed and why others may fail in restoring a protective environment.[123] There is also a growing body of research pointing out the limited sustainability and insufficient local contextualisation of current approaches in child protection, with a call to stop thinking top down, and to rather adopt a combination of bottom-up, middle-out *and* top-down approaches.[124]

Considering South Sudan, Canavera *et al*[125] describe the work of international child protection actors, and find most efforts to be short-term, top-down and relying heavily on 'trainings'. Training sessions – on child rights, on international human rights and humanitarian law, on the responsibilities of different actors vis-à-vis children – were mainly issue-based, and revolved around imported concepts of child protection. Rarely was capacity building work consolidated, or the skills built transferable, and training frameworks on child protection were found to be misaligned with the overarching national systems. For CAAC programming, these trainings focus on police, gendarmes, military commanders and the rank and file, including from within the ranks of Blue Helmets deployed under the auspices of UN and regional peacekeeping operations.[126] Canavera *et al*'s key informants uniformly invoked the word 'unsustainable' to describe these and other 'capacity building' initiatives. However, together with child-friendly spaces, such training interventions are often the bread and butter of child protection in emergency response plans.

---

international community who are *not* the state, the concept of R2P applies only derivatively as a 'responsibility to *help* protect'.

123 Séverine Autesserre, 'International Peacebuilding and Local Success: Assumptions and Effectiveness', *International Studies Review*, Volume 19, Issue 1: 114–132 (2017).

124 Michael G. Wessells, 'Bottom-up Approaches to Strengthening Child Protection Systems: Placing Children, Families, and Communities at the Center', *Child Abuse & Neglect*, 43: 8–21 (2015).

125 Canavera et al., '"And Then They Left"'.

126 Recent cases in the Central African Republic of predatory behaviour with local children by peacekeepers is only one among many stark and sadly recurring reminders that the very forces deployed to protect civilians may come to be a threat themselves – and an issue the United Nations constantly seeks to address, with varied success. 'Report of an Independent Review on Sexual Exploitation and Abuse by International Peacekeeping Forces in the Central African Republic', A/71/99, 27 September 2016.

The diagnosis in South Sudan casts some doubt on the depth of the shift from a focus on specific child protection issues to child protection systems (at least in emergency responses). It also strengthens protection review findings that demonstrate that not only are activities and responses pre-packaged regardless of context, training contents also tend to be predefined,[127] insufficiently contextualised and rarely oriented to the communities' needs and own mechanisms to protect children. Another research gap[128] and important line of enquiry, is around child protection systems-building in developing countries and specifically investigating how the international community 'does' child protection system-strengthening in humanitarian contexts. As such, both R2P and CAAC are rooted in an approach that at times remains institution-centric, with efforts that sometimes prove 'unsustainable' because of the way they are conceptualised and delivered. What the two approaches may perhaps have in common is the failure to realise that strengthening institutions alone does not in itself provide protection for children – either in conflict or in the absence of conflict.

Practitioner Conclusions

The concept of R2P may not have had a central or critical role in advancing the profile of grave child protection issues. War crimes or crimes against humanity that specifically target or involve children are not explicit in the rhetoric and discourse around R2P. Strong and continuous momentum existed for a sharp international community focus on CAAC, independently and before the concept of R2P captured international attention.

Although the initial impetus of CAAC can be traced back several years before R2P was conceptualised, both concepts and agendas did come to a near-simultaneous peak moment in 2005. In that sense, while R2P may not have been central to advancing child protection and rights issues on the global agenda, it is probably fair to say that its conceptualisation was part of a wider fertile environment for the CAAC agenda. But given the pre-existing momentum around the issue of children in war and the protection discussions among humanitarian agencies during this period, it might be fair to say that the CAAC agenda had enough wind of its own in its sails. The CAAC agenda did not advance any faster due to the simultaneous rise of R2P. CAAC did not require the helping

127 Though in fairness, training on international humanitarian law and other key rights standards has some inherently uniform dimensions anywhere it happens.

128 Canavera et al., '"And Then They Left"'.

hand from R2P, and arguably R2P did not present much of an extra push in any case. Moreover, momentum and attention around the grave violations of child rights in conflict has arguably continued and expanded – including as an advocacy platform,[129] in the gradual – but often chaotic – mainstreaming of CAAC thinking in peacekeeping operation mandates, the new priorities of protection-mandated agencies and the operational guidelines for monitoring and reporting on the grave violations.

While these developments were underway, on the separate track of R2P, the concept became internalised and increasingly used in the work of the Security Council and the Human Rights Council,[130] though not without hitting obstacles both situational, political and definitional, and staying somewhat ensnared in debates about its intrinsic usefulness and added value. In fact, the debate around the 'responsibility to protect' appears, from this exercise of newcomer authors at least, to remain focused on whether it has intrinsic value,[131] and has been effective in moving protection forward or not. There is far less literature the authors could identify intent specifically on re-examining and challenging the idea that the CAAC agenda and its principles should benefit from international consensus and recognition. Of course, how much the CAAC agenda has done in terms of securing lasting change on the ground for children and eradicating the grave violations is still the subject of much discussion, and not considered in this piece. But failures in implementation and CAAC principles (not) becoming a reality on the ground is far less attributed to the value of the concepts themselves and much more argued to be a factor of local dynamics, translation of concepts and circumstances.[132] Failures of R2P are much more often invoked with a direct question levelled at the value of the concept itself, or with a jab about it ringing sorely hollow. In short, while scholars, diplomats and practitioners are still debating whether R2P is useful, they seem to have moved on for the norms around CAAC, the debate being on how to make it work, not whether it is a useful framework.[133]

---

129 In 2015 the Security Council passed S/RES/2225 which expanded the criteria for parties to be listed, asking the Secretary-General to also list parties that engage in abduction of children during armed conflict.

130 Maggie Powers, 'Responsibility to Protect: Dead, Dying, or Thriving?', *The International Journal of Human Rights*, 19/8: 1257–1278 (2015).

131 Bellamy, 'The Responsibility to Protect: Added Value or Hot Air?'; Powers, 'Responsibility to Protect: Dead, Dying, or Thriving?'.

132 Knudsen and Godwin, 'Pinning down a Paper Tiger'.

133 Beyond the question of R2P and children, other lines of enquiry have looked into additional linkages between R2P and other protection-oriented concepts, notably the International Refugee Protection Regime. Again, much of the point of debate is on the

Secondly, while at the global level the link between R2P and CAAC is somewhere between circumstantial and vaguely mutually reinforcing, there is a case to be made that in practice some of the day-to-day work of child protection actors has a connection with the grand R2P framework. However, these connections are loose and come with some serious caveats. Recognising the primary responsibility of the state to protect its citizens – and its children – child-protection mandated international agencies and actors in emergency and transition contexts do work at building the capacity of the state's apparatus and institutions to deliver on this mandate, and the tools and approaches they use support this goal. The question that remains has two closely related dimensions: one, whether the pinpointed, discrete actions at a near micro/meso-scale done by child-protection-mandated agencies (e.g. trainings, capacity building of state institutions) are worth actually framing in the much more macro-scale agenda that is R2P, and second, whether these highly specific actions – in time and place – have sustainable import and impact in achieving R2P by the state. What child-protection mandated agencies do on the ground for children, could be considered to be the small building blocks in a strategy to help states deliver on their responsibility to protect children, and, as the MRM does through monitoring and other child rights networks, strengthen the broader protection networks to which the state, NGOs and communities belong. However, in practice international emergency programming is limited in scope, tends to rely on default responses and not be rooted in local community mechanisms and systems. And the line is clear (but cause for much dilemma): this responsibility to protect is the state's, and child protection actors only bear at best a secondary – albeit frustrating – implicit responsibility to 'help' – with advice from within the profession not to go too far ... or indeed to promise too much.

The extent to which the R2P framework and the CAAC/MRM agenda provide tools to strengthen or influence the web of protection actors affecting children's lot in war and conflict requires more investigation. Nonetheless, R2P retains solid relevance as an advocacy implement, and it is still invoked by

---

added value of R2P. Looking into the European Union's refugee policy, some argue that R2P would 'add little' and be redundant. See for example Dan Bulley, 'Shame on EU? Europe, R2P, and the Politics of Refugee Protection', *Ethics & International Affairs*, 31/1: 51–70 (2017). Others meanwhile argue that a case can be made to link R2P and refugee responsibility sharing. See Alise Coen, 'Capable and Culpable? The United States, R2P, and Refugee Responsibility-Sharing' *Ethics & International Affairs*, 31/1: 71–92. This warrants further investigation but again underlines how debates on the concept of R2P, and on its linkages with other concepts, continue to revolve around whether the concept – and making the link with others – is or is not useful.

child-focused agencies in the face of some of the gravest violations children face in the world,[134] or in places less obvious but where states may need less of a rallying call and more of a 'wake-up call' with respect to their duties on child rights.[135] The connection between R2P and what practitioners do to help states deliver on their responsibilities for children does require and benefit from joining up the micro-level to a broader framework, and it expands the various layers in a practitioner's advocacy tool kit.

In many ways, echoes of a child rights agenda can be heard – half heard – in the ongoing conversation around R2P. Equally, R2P is a concept that can help frame – and drive – efforts by child protection practitioners in some of the worst situations children face and where systems-based child protection approaches prove difficult. R2P is an ambitious, necessary target that perhaps stays beyond the reach of field practitioner's direct action. It may simply be best left that way. The interplay between R2P and CAAC is a relationship of constant flux, perhaps best summarised, from a field practitioner's perspective, as seeing R2P as an admirable, though mostly unattainable, aspiration – but an aspiration always to look for.

---

134 Hanaa Singer, 'Statement by Hanaa Singer, UNICEF Representative for Syria on Attack on the Al Hayat Primary School in Eastern Damascus', 7 November 2014, https://www.unicef.org/media/media_76951.html, accessed 1 December 2017.

135 Dan Toole, 'Statement on the protection of the rights of children who may be transferred from Nauru to Cambodia', 17 April 2015, https://www.unicef.org/eapro/media_23969.html, accessed 1 December 2017.

'The Intolerable Impact of Armed Conflict on Children': The United Nations Security Council and the Protection of Children in Armed Conflict

Katrina Lee-Koo
Monash University, Australia
katrina.leekoo@monash.edu

Abstract

The United Nations Security Council's Children and Armed Conflict agenda is animated by a protection ethic. While the protection of children from violence in armed conflict is entirely appropriate, this article demonstrates that the Council's singular focus upon protection goes beyond merely appropriate, and borders upon overbearing. The article traces the ways that dominant conceptualisations of children as 'innocent victims' has animated an agenda that focuses primarily upon their victimisation that, in turn, reinforces the legitimacy of the protection ethic. It argues that this excludes a nuanced understanding of the lived experiences of children in conflict. In this sense, the agenda is closed to exploring the ways in which children resist, adapt, shape, and survive conflict in ways that position them as agents of their own protection and – in some circumstances – agents of community resilience amidst conflict. Ultimately, this article argues that re-visioning children's relationship to armed conflict provides a strategy to better ensure children's rights and reflects their relationship to peace.

Keywords

children – armed conflict – UN Security Council – protection – agency

Over the past two decades, the United Nations Security Council has established significant architecture to inform and support its Children and Armed Conflict (CaAC) thematic agenda.[1] Initiated in 1999 with the adoption of

1 The quote in the title is from United Nations Secretary-General, 'Secretary-General's message to Informal Meeting on 20th Anniversary of General Assembly Resolution 51/77 on Children and Armed Conflict', 8 February 2017, https://www.un.org/sg/en/content/sg/

 | DOI:10.1163/9789004379534_004

UNSCR 1261 – in a response to the 1996 UNICEF Report, *The Impact of Armed Conflict upon Children* by Graça Machel[2] – the agenda seeks to bring to the Council and UN Member States' attention the vulnerabilities and needs of children living in conflict-affected zones. At the time of writing, eleven resolutions informed the agenda, which has developed an impressive infrastructure with regards to specific issues, advocacy, implementation, and monitoring and evaluation. The relative strength and depth of the agenda speaks to the widespread support of this issue across the Security Council's membership[3] and demonstrates the overwhelming recognition by the UN and its member states that children – as a constituency – should be protected from conflict.

With this in mind, the Children and Armed Conflict agenda is built upon this single pillar: the protection of children. It is explicitly a protection agenda. This is reaffirmed in the preambulatory statements of several resolutions which reaffirm the commitment to create '*a comprehensive framework for addressing the protection of children affected by armed conflict*' (emphasis added). Protection is a familiar theme in the Security Council's interpretation of its responsibility to civilian populations affected by conflict as demonstrated in the Protection of Civilians (PoC), Women, Peace and Security (WPS), and the Responsibility to Protect (R2P) thematic agendas which all have substantial commitments to civilian protection.[4] This focus emerged from recognition, as outlined in the initial PoC resolution, that 'civilians account for the vast majority of casualties in armed conflicts and are increasingly targeted by combatants and armed elements' and an awareness of 'the consequent impact this will have on durable peace, reconciliation and development'.[5]

In establishing a link between protection of civilians and durable peace, the Council is connecting its primary mandate to maintain international peace and security with the protection of children. In acknowledging this Graça Machel argued in 1996 that the 'unregulated terror and violence' that

statement/2017-02-08/secretary-generals-message-informal-meeting-20th-anniversary-general, accessed 28 March 2017.

2 S/RES/1261, 25 August 1999; Graça Machel, *The Impact of Armed Conflict upon Children*, A/51/306/1996, 26 August 1996.

3 See Shamala Kandiah Thompson, 'Children and Armed Conflict,' in Jared Genser and Bruno Stagno Ugarte (eds.), *The United Nations Security Council in the Age of Human Rights* (Cambridge: Cambridge University Press, 2014), pp. 98–120.

4 See Gina Heathcote, 'Women and Children and Elephants as Justifications for the Use of Force', *Journal of the Use of Force and International Law*, 4/1: 66–85 (2017).

5 S/RES/1265, 17 September 1999, Preamble.

children suffer in conflict 'speak[s] of deliberate victimisation'.[6] By recognising that violence against children can constitute deliberate and intentional acts of conflict and disruptions to peace and security, the Council embraces as its own the responsibility for children's protection. This connection is acknowledged throughout the Council's work, recognising that the protection of children 'is an important aspect of any comprehensive strategy to resolve conflict'[7] and noting 'the harmful and widespread impact of armed conflict on children and the long-term consequences this has for durable peace, security and development'.[8] Drawing from this, the Security Council's approach to the protection of children in conflict is arguably a product of three imperatives: international legal responsibilities to uphold children's right to be free from violence, moral obligations to protect children from violence, and – importantly – instrumentalist claims that children's protection is a tool in the maintenance of peace and security.

Attacks upon civilian constituencies undeniably disrupt peace and security. However, the protection of civilian groups, while a priority, should not be the only attitude the Council develops towards the role of civilians in the maintenance of international peace and security. It should instead be reconceptualised as the first step in recognising the positive impact that civilians may have in societies experiencing conflict. UNSCR 1325, the landmark resolution of the Women, Peace and Security agenda recognises the impact that the targeting of 'civilians, particularly women and children' has on 'durable peace and reconciliation'.[9] Yet it also reaffirms 'the important role of women in the prevention and resolution of conflicts and in peace-building'.[10] This multi-pillar approach (inclusive of a gender perspective in Prevention, Participation, Protection, and Relief and Recovery) recognises the multiple subjectivities and roles of conflict-affected women. In short, it recognises that while women may be victims of conflict, this does not necessarily wholly define their experience. They may subsequently or simultaneously play other roles in conflict zones that support their communities. In this vein, this article reviews the focus upon protection of children in the UN Security Council's approach to children

6 Machel, *The Impact of Armed Conflict upon Children.*

7 Office of the Special Representative of the Secretary-General for Children and Armed Conflict, *The Six Grave Violations Against Children During Armed Conflict: The Legal Foundation,* November 2013, p. 9.

8 S/RES/1261, 25 August 1999.

9 S/RES/1325, 31 October 2000, Preamble.

10 Ibid.

in conflict-affected zones, and examines the spaces available to consider children's own agency as promoters of peace.

This article therefore argues that the Security Council's focus upon protection within the Children and Armed Conflict agenda is not simply overwhelming, but can be described as overbearing. It does not deny that violence against children is intolerable. Nor does it absolve the Council – or any adult constituency for that matter – of responsibility to ensure children's well-being amidst conflict. This article does, however, argue that the overbearing focus upon the protection agenda blindsides the Council to the breadth of experiences and multiple subjectivities of children in armed conflict. An analysis of these experiences can offer a more robust and nuanced understanding of how children survive in conflict and what aptitudes and competencies they demonstrate to support and rebuild their societies. Certainly they may be victims of unacceptable violence, yet they are also a unique and diverse group of civilians with intersecting identities (such as race, gender, ethnicity, familial status etc.) and evolving capacities and competencies (related to age, physical abilities, cognition, mental and emotional development, education, and health needs). For example, children – particularly older adolescent children – might be soldiers, carers, heads-of-households, workers, spouses, parents, or students while simultaneously being victims of conflict. This does not negate their need for protection (and younger children do require focused protection that is distinct from older children), but it does complicate it. It creates questions around the design and implementation of protection programs and the relationship between the protector and protected. The Council presupposes not simply that 'victim' is a child's primary identity, but in many cases that it is her/his only identity. In response, this article advocates for a nuanced approach to thinking about the fluidity of children's identities in relation to conflict.

Thus, this article takes childhood as a dynamic state, one that is unique and constantly changing. Children's agency may be typically diminished when compared to adults but might not always be absent. It is therefore argued that while the protection agenda should persist, it should be reconceptualised to accommodate a more complicated approach to children's identities. This should be done for two reasons: first, for the well-being of children, their development amidst difficult circumstances, and the protection of *the breadth of* their rights. Second, an approach that considers children's lived experiences promises an inter-generational commitment that recognises the role children do and will continue to play in post-conflict communities. It is therefore argued that the construction of the agenda upon a single pillar of protection promotes an unstable approach to building international peace and security. As the UN system re-evaluates its peacebuilding infrastructure in the light of failures to sustain peace across generations, it is an apt moment to also reconsider the role children might play in these processes.

With this in mind, this article begins with the case for children's agency in conflict. It then moves to an outline of the development of the CaAC agenda within the Security Council. It demonstrates that the focus on the protection agenda is more a reflection of the Council's conceptualisation of children and civilians rather than the lived experiences of children. It then moves to examine the exclusion of children's agency from the agenda. With the question of children's agency in mind, the article then looks outside the Security Council to see where nuanced approaches to children's experiences in crisis settings are promoted. Finally, it considers how this approach might shape the work of the Council itself.

Understanding Children's Agency in Conflict

Emerging research on the experiences of children in armed conflict present a nascent theoretical and empirical account of children's agency.[11] While agency is a contested concept,[12] for the purposes of this research it is understood simply as the capacity of individuals to make independent decisions about one's life, and to seek to enact those decisions in ways that shape that person's life trajectory and – in this way – also shape their environment. This understanding of agency is shaped by two literatures: first, the feminist conceptions of the term which seek to understand the operation of individual action – and limits upon that action – within hostile structures of power.[13] Second, it also draws from the notions of the everyday. According to de Certeau, agency can

---

11 See Michael G. Wessells, *Child Soldiers: From Violence to Protection* (Cambridge: Harvard University Press, 2006); Sverker Finnström, 'Wars of the Past and War in the Present: The Lord's Resistance Movement/Army in Uganda', *Africa: Journal of the International African Institute*, 76/2: 200–220 (2006); Carolyn Nordstrom, 'The Jagged Edge of Peace,' in Siobhan McEvoy-Levy (ed.), *Troublemakers or Peacemakers? Youth and Post-Accord Peace Building* (Notre Dame, IN: Notre Dame University Press, 2006); Lesley Pruitt, *Youth Peacebuilding: Music, Gender, Change* (New York: SUNY Press, 2013); Helen Berents, 'Children, violence, and social exclusion: negotiation of everyday insecurity in a Colombian barrio', *Critical Studies on Security*, 3/1: 90–104 (2015), among others.

12 See Gudrun Dahl, 'Sociology and Beyond: Agency, Victimisation and the Ethics of Writing', *Asian Journal of Social Sciences*, 37/3: 391–407 (2009).

13 Saba Mahmood, *Politics of piety: the Islamic revival and the feminist subject* (Princeton, NJ; Woodstock: Princeton University Press, 2012); Bina D'Costa, 'Marginalized identity: new frontiers of research for IR?' in Brooke A. Ackerly, Maria Stern and Jacqui True (eds.),

be practiced through the art of living as one's self within environments not of one's making.[14] For children, this might mean that everyday childish activities in conflict zones such as playing, going to school or disobedience can constitute resistance, tactical action, resolve and resilience.[15] In addition, it is important to recognise that children also undertake adult activities in lieu of absent parents/adults or in altered social structures. In this sense, it eschews the expectation that agency is constituted through lauded, loud or even visible impacts upon the structures or events of international relations. Rather everyday agency in this context might be simple negotiation of the conflict environment.[16] Such activities may demonstrate experience, skill, strength, cunning, political consciousness, capacity for judgement and ability to act, all of which – for the purposes of this research – qualify as a form of agency and all of which have the capacity to shape a child's immediate environment.

Significantly, grounded research has revealed numerous cases of children's agency enacted in both childish and adult ways. For example, Berent's fieldwork with conflict-affected children in the *barrio* communities of Bogotá analyses how children negotiate the insecurity of their everyday lives. She finds that children and young people 'are aware of the complexities of ... [the deeply embedded nature of insecurity, violence, and fear in many urban environments in Colombia] ... and can articulate the connections and dissonance of an absent or harmful state, violence of local gangs, and ongoing consequences of stereotyping'.[17] Yet, children not only understand their insecurity, they also engage in a range of activities to 'seek security within their everyday life'.[18] Berents finds that while children experience violence in armed conflict, they simultaneously demonstrate the capacity to act for their own and others' security. Similarly, Finnström finds that children operating in armed groups in Uganda self-identify as agents with the ability to make independent decisions and negotiate conflict environments.[19] Finally, in her account of Angolan

---

Feminist methodologies for International Relations (Cambridge; New York: Cambridge University Press, 2006).

14 Michel de Certeau, *The Practice of Everyday Life* (California: University of California Press, 1988).

15 Kim Huynh, 'Children and Agency: Caretakers, Free-rangers and Everyday Life.' In Kim Huynh, Bina D'Costa and Katrina Lee-Koo, *Children and Global Conflict* (Cambridge: Cambridge University Press, 2015), pp. 55–62.

16 Alison M.S. Watson, 'Resilience is its own resistance: the place of children in post-conflict settlement', *Critical Studies on Security*, 3/1: 47–61 (2015), p. 39.

17 Berents, 'Children, violence, and social exclusion', p. 91.

18 Ibid.

19 Finnström, 'Wars of the Past and War in the Present'.

children, Nordstrom demonstrates that despite the devastation wreaked on their lives by conflict, children nonetheless exhibited capacity for community-mindedness and resilience in processes that simulated, if not constituted, peacebuilding.[20] Thus while children's agency may be negative (as might be the case with child combatants) or positive (such as children involved in peacebuilding), there is growing evidence of both its existence and impact. The capacity of children to exercise agency through activities such as going to school, providing care for family or community members, running households, providing the family's income, volunteering to join armed forces, resisting political oppression, building networks with other children across conflict's fault-lines, and showing resilience in the face of unrelenting violence all constitute such agency.[21] It is important not to romanticise or overstate this. However a grounded approach to agency and a serious consideration of the lived experiences of children begins to reveal the multiple subjectivities of conflict-affected children and the links their activities may have to the broader politics and practices of peace and security.

This rethinking of children's agency challenges the dominant discursive construction of children as victims. Indeed, as outlined further below, there is a broad acceptance of 'childhood' as a discursive equivalent of 'victim'. Watson argues that this constructs children as passive in the face of conflict, as well as incapable of demonstrating agency. She argues that 'anyone classified as "victim" – by definition, often a condition of powerlessness and domination – finds it difficult to claim agency' because it is assumed that the state of victimhood renders their 'potential to act rationally and hence claim agency' suspect.[22] Victimhood, Watson argues, is therefore associated with passivity, stigma, and irrationality. It in fact constitutes a process of othering that conceives of children (and in many cases women) as damaged and outside of the realm of reason and action.[23] This is problematic for two reasons: first 'the portrayal of any marginalised group as "victim" has a direct impact on their ability to become political agents and thus claim their political rights' and second, it blinds us to the gambit of possibilities that children might be able to achieve, should we recognise their agency.[24] Acceptance of children's victim status transfers the

20 Nordstrom, 'The Jagged Edge of Peace'.

21 See Wessells, *Child Soldiers: From Violence to Protection*; Finnström, 'Wars of the Past and War in the Present'; Nordstrom, 'The Jagged Edge of Peace,'; Pruitt, *Youth Peacebuilding: Music, Gender, Change*; Berents, 'Children, violence, and social exclusion', among others.

22 Watson, 'Resilience is its own resistance', p. 47.

23 Ibid., pp. 47–49.

24 Ibid., pp. 47–48.

agency to address their needs into the hands of adults. Thus, the discursive framing of children as wholly victimised by conflict provides the foundational justification for an adult-enacted protection regime that marginalises children in its design and implementation.

This is further reinforced by representations of children as inherently apolitical and innocent beings, the very embodiment of "innocent civilian". Huynh notes that innocence operates in two ways with regards to children. In the first instance it is about freeing children of political responsibility: the 'appeal to innocence can mitigate responsibility for everything from social faux pas to crimes against humanity'. In the second instance the protection of childhood innocence performs a litmus test for society: 'innocence is not merely an excuse; it is also a quality that must be protected for the good of the child and the community'.[25] In this sense, innocence abrogates children's responsibility from the worst excesses of human behaviour but it simultaneously deprives children of recognition for their political activism. This is justified as a necessary condition for a healthy community. It is based upon an *a priori* acceptance of their naivety, bewilderment, and lack of experience in the public sphere. Like notions of victimhood, innocence imposes a passivity and meekness in the face of violent politics in a way that renders children irrational and denies capacity to respond to the politics around them. This idea is born of a particularly liberal imagining of childhood which sees children as blank slates or kinds of 'apprentice citizens' whose location in the private sphere acts to shield them from, but also deny them access to, political action.[26] This neat segregation further reinforces the appropriateness that adults should be the political caretakers of children affected by conflict and strengthens the moral justifications of the protection regime.[27]

Ideas that children are victims of conflict – innocent and apolitical – form the ontological foundations of the Security Council's protection regime. While it may be based upon idealised (and arguably reasonable) liberal claims that children should be separated from political violence, the lived reality is that that separation is never possible. Moreover, continuing to assert that children can be separated from the politics of conflict encourages analytical barriers to understanding the relationship between children's lived experiences and conflict. As this section has argued, at its most promising, children can become

25 Kim Huynh, 'Children and Agency: Caretakers, Free-rangers and Everyday Life', p. 39.

26 Michael Wyness, Lisa Harrison and Ian Buchanan, 'Childhood, Politics and Ambiguity: Towards an Agenda for Children's Political Inclusion', *Sociology*, 38/1: 81–99 (2004), pp. 82–84.

27 Huynh, 'Children and Agency: Caretakers, Free-rangers and Everyday Life', pp. 37–42.

agents in their own protection and the protection of their community. However, this is easily overlooked when 'the emphasis in the discourse on civilian protection … downplays human resilience and empowerment as vital strategies for promoting the human security of civilians'.[28] The extent to which this is evident in the UN Security Council's Children and Armed Conflict agenda is explored in the next section.

The Security Council and the Protection Agenda

Since its establishment in 1996, the UN Office of the Special Representative of the Secretary-General for Children and Armed Conflict has been 'the leading UN advocate for the protection and well-being of children affected by armed conflict'.[29] The Special Representative's mandate was established by the General Assembly in February 1997 and outlined as: assessing progress in strengthening children's protection in conflict, raising awareness and promoting the collection of data, and working collectively across the UN sector to ensure respect for children's rights.[30] The Special Representative reports annually to the General Assembly and the Human Rights Council and advocates on behalf of the agenda to the Security Council and other relevant actors. Moreover, it supports the gathering of data, and implementation and monitoring of the Council's CaAC agenda. While this has given the Office focus, it has also seen a narrowing of the work in this field in line with the Council's ontological framing of the issue. The dominance of the protection framework in the Council's work means the Office shies away from advocating a more robust implementation of the children's rights agenda to include, for example, children's active participation in peacebuilding or relief and recovery programs. The Council's protection agenda, as noted above, is alternatively animated by a view that children are innocent in the face of political violence, that they are defenceless against conflict, and they are not agents of their own security. Moreover, it scripts the Council into a paternal 'father-knows-best' role as protector of conflict-affected children.

---

28 Cecilia Jacob, '"Children and armed conflict" and the field of security studies', *Critical Studies on Security*, 3/1: 14–28 (2015), p. 18.

29 Office of the Special Representative of the Secretary-General for Children and Armed Conflict, 'Our Work', https://childrenandarmedconflict.un.org/mandate/our-work/, accessed 29 March 2017.

30 A/RES/51/77, 20 February 1997.

This protector role can be evidenced in a number of ways. First, the emphasis given to the six grave violations against children in armed conflict focuses entirely upon children's subjugation in conflict. These violations, which have been outlined in the resolutions and pursued by the Office of the Special Representative, are: the killing and maiming of children; recruitment or use of children as soldiers; sexual violence against children; attacks against schools or hospitals; denial of humanitarian access for children; and abduction of children. According to the Office of the Special Representative, these violations were chosen 'based on their suitability for monitoring and verification, their egregious nature and the severity of their consequences on the lives of children'.[31] These violations are undoubtedly egregious, as demonstrated in the annual reporting by the Secretary-General. The evidence which has been collected on these also reinforces their characterisation as grave violations and in turn justifies the resources dedicated to them in terms of advocacy, data collection and monitoring and evaluation. However, their positioning not just as the primary focus of the agenda but *the* agenda itself is problematic. It presents children as being wholly victimised by armed conflict in the worst possible ways. These issues and the reporting mechanisms that support them lack nuance or balance that speaks to how children might negotiate or deflect violence, build resilience to it, or indeed have other experiences or relationships with violence that are not covered here. Even though it appears to constitute the breadth of the agenda, it speaks only to some children's experiences some of the time.[32] However, it can be easily interpreted as representing all children's passivity in the face of inescapable violence and naturalises, even valorises, the Council's role as protector.

Second, the protection theme is demonstrated in the discursive representation of children's rights and the application of the 1989 United Nations Convention on the Rights of the Child (UNCRC). Children's rights are an important theme of the agenda. Indeed, the UNCRC is referenced in all eleven Security Council resolutions. However, there is a primary focus upon protection in the interpretation of these rights. All references to children's rights in armed conflict in the CaAC resolutions are made within a broader framing of the right to protection. In early resolutions 'the *protection*, well-being and *rights* of children' is noted (emphasis added), while from UNSCR1539 (2004) onwards the

31 Office of the Special Representative of the Secretary-General for Children and Armed Conflict, *The Six Grave Violations Against Children During Armed Conflict: The Legal Foundation,* November 2013, p. 9.

32 Katrina Lee-Koo, 'Children and Armed Conflict: Mapping the Terrain'. In Huynh, D'Costa and Lee-Koo, *Children and Global Conflict*, pp. 21–32.

language moves to 'the *protection and rights* of children', and from UNSCR1612 (2005) references to rights are dropped in favour of simply 'the protection of children'.[33]

This coupling of protection and rights corresponds with a marginalisation of elements of the Convention that deal with children's agency. Article 12 of the UNCRC notes that:

> State Parties shall assure the child who is capable of forming his or her own views the right to express those views freely in all matters affecting the child, the views of the child being given due weight in accordance with the age and maturity of the child.[34]

While all the CaAC resolutions call upon the UNCRC's enforcement, engaging the element of the UNCRC which calls for children's voices to be heard is not a priority of the Council. This attitude is not confined to the Council of course. Watson argues that the neglect of children's agency in favour of focusing upon children's roles as dominated subjects within the international system is common.[35] There is long-standing criticism of the widespread neglect of Article 12 in numerous sites around the world in favour of endorsing an adult advocate to speak for the child.[36] In this sense, the UNCRC overwhelmingly 'emphasis[es] children's welfare over their autonomy'[37] and this is reinforced by the Council's approach.

Third, there are very few references to children's participation in the agenda, and all localised in the earlier resolutions. Arguably, passive acknowledgement of children's agency is evident in references to the inclusion of children in disarmament, demobilisation and reintegration (DDR) processes[38] as well as in promoting 'the availability of alternatives for children to their participation in armed conflict'.[39] The use of the language of inclusion in DDR programs acknowledges both children's experiences of soldiering (which is a central theme of the CaAC agenda) as well as the need for them to be demilitarised. In

33 S/RES/1539, 22 April 2004; S/RES/1612, 26 July 2005.

34 A/RES/44/25, 20 November 1989, Article 12.

35 Alison M.S. Watson, 'Saving More than the Children: The Role of Child-Focused NGOs in the Creation of Southern Security Norms', *Third World Quarterly*, 27/2: 227–237 (2006), p. 231.

36 Alison M.S. Watson, 'Resilience is its own resistance', p. 52.

37 Huynh, 'Children and Agency: Caretakers, Free-rangers and Everyday Life', p. 42.

38 S/RES/1314, 11 August 2000, OP 11; S/RES/1460, 30 January 2003, OP 13; S/RES/1539, 22 April 2004, OP 8.

39 S/RES/1261, 25 August 1999, OP 13.

this way it could be argued that there is an unstated acknowledgement that as child soldiers children have participated in conflict, thus implying some form of active engagement in conflict. The reference to promoting alternatives for children recruited to conflict also passively implies that children may 'choose' to voluntarily recruit into armed forces due to a lack of options.

In a clearer and more active acknowledgement of children's agency, the language of children's empowerment and voice is used in relation to peace processes. In addition to the involvement of children in DDR, UNSCR 1314 (2000) also requests children's involvement in 'peace negotiations and peace agreements'[40] and further encourages support for 'the involvement of young persons in programmes for peace consolidation and peace-building'.[41] UNSCR 1379 (2001) calls upon all parties to 'provide protection of children in peace agreements ..., and *to consider, where possible, the views of children* in those processes'.[42] It further urges efforts to 'consider the views of children in the design and implementation of such policies and programmes where possible'.[43] In addition to these references to children's engagement with peace processes, empowerment of children receives two mentions, both in operative paragraphs of the CaAC resolutions. UNSCR 1882 and UNSCR 1998 call on relevant actors

> to ensure that the protection, rights, well-being and *empowerment* of children affected by armed conflict are integrated into all peace processes and that post-conflict recovery and reconstruction planning, programmes and strategies prioritize issues concerning children affected by armed conflict.[44]

These are important anchors for those advocating for recognition of children's inclusion in peace and protection programming. However, it is important to acknowledge that these references are minimal in comparison to the overall protection ethic, and they are isolated to the early resolutions. These five references across four of the eleven resolutions pales in comparison to the approximately 129 substantial references to the protection of children in the resolutions. Moreover, references to children's agency – passive or active – ends after 2011. The three most recent resolutions contain no reference to children's empowerment, involvement, or views in conflict-related concerns. In

40 S/RES/1314, 11 August 2000, OP 11.
41 Ibid., OP 19.
42 S/RES/1379, 20 November 2001, OP 8e, emphasis added.
43 Ibid., OP 13a.
44 S/RES/1882, 4 August 2009, OP 15; S/RES/1998, 12 July 2011, OP 19.

this sense, while the early acknowledgement of children's agency is important, they are overwhelmingly disproportionate to the number and strength of references to children's protection. Consequently, it provides only light and fleeting relief from the language of protection in the CaAC agenda.

Fourth, the protection ethic with regards to conflict-affected children is persistent across the Security Council's other relevant thematic agendas. While explicitly focused upon the Protection of Civilians, the eight resolutions adopted under the PoC thematic agenda offer no provisions for children's involvement, agency or empowerment in conflict-affected zones. References to children in these resolutions are coupled with women and other vulnerable groups who may be particularly targeted for violence. Similarly, the Council's Women, Peace and Security agenda, while frequently referencing either 'women and girls' or 'women and children', does so predominantly within a protection framework where the focus is upon sexual violence (see, particularly UNSCRs 1820, 1888, 1960) or in the provision of relief and recovery.[45] However, there are four references to the participation and empowerment of girls in the Preambles of four WPS resolutions. UNSCR 1325 (2000) and UNSCR 1889 (2009) note the need to guarantee the 'protection and full participation [of women and girls] in the peace process' while UNSCR 2122 (2013) and UNSCR 2242 (2015) reaffirms 'that women's and girls' empowerment and gender equality are critical to efforts to maintain international peace and security'.[46]

Children and Conflict Outside the Council

Outside of the Security Council, the dominance of the protection discourse in discussing children's experiences of global politics is weaker. In other parts of the UN system there is evidence of attempts to create a balance between protecting and fostering children's agency in global politics. For example, UNICEF (the United Nations Children's Emergency Fund, established in 1946) is mandated by the UN General Assembly to 'advocate for the protection of children's rights, to help meet their basic needs and *expand their opportunities to reach their full potential*' (emphasis added), which promises movement beyond a protection agenda.[47] UNICEF works across a broad agenda, from education,

45 S/RES/1820, 18 June 2008; S/RES/1888, 30 September 2009; S/RES/1960, 16 December 2010.

46 S/RES/1325, 31 October 2000; S/RES/1889, 5 October 2009; S/RES/2122, 18 October 2013; S/RES/2242, 13 October 2015.

47 UNICEF, 'UNICEF's mission statement', 25 April 2003, https://www.unicef.org/about/who/index_mission.html, accessed 28 March 2017.

health care, and children with disabilities, to specific or localised issues such as child marriage. While it does work in sites of humanitarian emergency – both natural and human induced – and works in conjunction with the Office of the Special Representative, it does not have the specific focus upon children in conflict zones as the latter does.

Elsewhere, efforts are being made to streamline the 2016 Sustainable Development Goals (SDGs) across the UN system, including in the implementation of the Children and Armed Conflict agenda. Broadly, the 2030 Agenda for Sustainable Development presents a more nuanced account of children's agency with significant focus upon the empowerment of girls, acknowledgement of the structural obstacles facing children's health and well-being, and an emphasis on the role of boys in efforts to pursue gender equality.[48] This is reflective of the overall attempt by the Agenda to consider diverse – and often vulnerable – constituencies as agents and partners of changes rather than victims and beneficiaries of global politics. It notes, for instance, that 'people who are vulnerable must be empowered. Those whose needs are reflected in the Agenda include all children, youth, persons with disabilities ....'.[49] Furthermore, it notes that 'children and young women and men are critical agents of change and will find in the new SDGs a platform to channel their infinite capacities for activism into the creation of a better world'.[50]

However, despite this progressive language on children's agency and empowerment, the Agenda fails to meaningfully engage with the situation of children affected by armed conflict. Goal 16, which is dedicated to "Promoting Peaceful and Inclusive Societies" provides only one reference to children when it notes an ambition to 'end abuse, exploitation, trafficking and all forms of violence against and torture of children'.[51] The only other reference to children affected by conflict is made in Goal 8 (decent work and economic growth) on the need to eradicate the recruitment and use of children in conflict.[52] The failure to mainstream, or even sufficiently cross-reference the commitment to children's empowerment with, particularly, Goal 16 demonstrates an ongoing blindness to the capacities of children to positively effect change in conflict-affected zones. However, following the release of the SDGs, the Office of the Special Representative for Children and Armed Conflict has attempted to link the two, arguing that:

48 A/RES/70/1, 25 September 2015.

49 Ibid., para. 23.

50 Ibid., para. 51.

51 Ibid., para. 16.2.

52 Ibid., para. 8.7.

> Boys and girls affected by armed conflict are also much more than victims of incredibly difficult circumstances. They are key to building the peaceful, strong societies envisioned by the new development agenda. To fulfil the promise of the SDGs, we must harness the potential of boys and girls affected by war.[53]

The Special Representative justifies these linkages by noting that the SDGs reaffirms children's rights to education, healthy lives, an end to recruitment, and justice for crimes committed against them in conflict. Creating such a link does offer opportunity for an emancipatory practice but there is still no support for this in the Security Council's framework. The resolutions themselves offer no hook upon which to hang children's empowerment in conflict. There are no opportunities to positively connect children's education with peace, for example. In the CaAC resolutions agency is reserved for the enactors of political violence who can deny children education. Thus, for the potential of such linkages to be realised a far more concrete foundation for supporting children's activism is necessary.

This demonstrates a disconnect between the Security Council's approach to children's agency in conflict, and other areas of global politics. While the language of empowerment is evident elsewhere, there is an extremely limited willingness on the part of the UN to acknowledge children's agency *in conflict*. As demonstrated above, both UNICEF and the SDGs drop their emancipatory language in light of the context of armed conflict. Goal 16 highlights only children's protection, while the UNICEF mandate, when directly speaking of 'victims of war' note its commitment to 'ensuring special *protection* for the most disadvantaged children'.[54] Why is there such an unwillingness to afford children agency *in conflict*? There are potentially two reasons that account for this. The first is that affording children agency also arguably affords them accountability. This sits uneasily with the framing of children as victims of conflict, innocent and apolitical. It also suggests that we may need to hold children responsible for their actions in conflict. This is most frequently debated in the issue of violence committed by children as soldiers. Until recently, child soldiers have generally been described as, or assumed to be, forcibly recruited.

53 Leila Zerrougui, 'Harnessing the Potential of Boys and Girls to Fulfil the Promise of the Sustainable Development Goals', April 2016, https://unchronicle.un.org/article/harnessing-potential-boys-and-girls-fulfil-promise-sustainable-development-goals/, accessed 28 March 2017.

54 UNICEF, 'UNICEF's mission statement', 25 April 2003, https://www.unicef.org/about/who/index_mission.html, accessed 28 March 2017.

However, growing evidence has successfully challenged this. The Office of the Special Representative now notes that recruitment occurs for many reasons: 'Many children are abducted and beaten into submission, others join military groups to escape poverty, to defend their communities, out of a feeling of revenge or for other reasons'.[55] The Office continues:

> Regardless of how children are recruited and of their roles, *child soldiers are victims*, whose participation in conflict bears serious implications for their physical and emotional well-being. They are commonly subject to abuse and most of them witness death, killing, and sexual violence. Many are forced to perpetrate these atrocities and some suffer serious long-term psychological consequences.[56]

While there is acknowledgment of the choices children make in conflict, there remains a focus upon their victimisation and it reinforces the need for protection.

The second reason that may account for the unwillingness of the Council to afford conflict-affected children agency is its own paternalistic identity. It has been argued that the protection of children in conflict agenda offers a powerful moral discourse that can be used to indict those states and actors that are thought to behave illiberally in the global rules-based order. Moreover, the victimisation of children can be presented as a moral justification that underpins Western/Global North intervention.[57] Heathcote argues that 'the protection of civilians – and, by this, I am referring to various components including the women, peace and security, as well as the protection of children in armed conflict, resolutions – functions as a form of new justification for the use of force'.[58] This has been further evident in the representation of children's experiences under the Taliban in Afghanistan[59] and the representation of child soldiers in conflicts on the African continent.[60] Similarly, in a post-colonial critique of the UNCRC, Pupuvac argues that the 'moral condemnation of the South through

55 Office of the Special Representative of the Secretary-General for Children and Armed Conflict, 'Child Recruitment and Use', https://childrenandarmedconflict.un.org/effects-of-conflict/six-grave-violations/child-soldiers/, accessed 28 March 2017.

56 Ibid., emphasis added.

57 Heathcote, 'Women and Children and Elephants', p. 80.

58 Ibid.

59 Katrina Lee-Koo, 'Not suitable for children: the politicisation of conflict-affected children in post-2001 Afghanistan', *Australian Journal of International Affairs,* 67/4: 475–490 (2013).

60 Katrina Lee-Koo, 'Horror and Hope: (Re)presenting militarised children in global North–South relations. *Third World Quarterly* 32/4: 725–742 (2011).

concern for the child helps give a sense of mission in the West' through the creation of a paternal adult-North/infant-South relationship.[61] Such critiques position the Council – as a central actor in framing engagement with conflict-affected children – as complicit in these global relationships of power.

Conclusion: Can Children Reform the Security Council?

The UN Security Council's Children and Armed Conflict agenda is animated by the disruption that violence against children causes to peace and security. However, this only tells us half of the story. It is undeniable that violence against children in conflict is unacceptable and constitutes a roadblock to peace. But in creating a narrative that is based upon children's victimisation and passivity we allow our understandings of children's relationship to conflict to be told in simplistic and troubling ways that do not reflect the lived realities of children. Instead this narrative reflects the moral preoccupations of the narrator. Ultimately, this does both a disservice. While this article has been dedicated to detailing the focus upon protection in the Children and Armed Conflict agenda, it has also argued that this focus limits the conceptual, discursive and political possibilities of understanding the multiple subjectivities of children in conflict. It has further argued that the subsequent inability to then interrogate a nuanced understanding of children's relationship to conflict limits creative and inclusive approaches to peace and security.

It is indeed worth asking how a more nuanced approach to considering children's lived experiences would shape the work the Council. As the UN seeks to find both sustainable and preventative approaches to peace and security, the impact of more carefully considering children's agency in conflict is worth further exploration and research. Consideration of the lived experiences of children may focus attention on the preventative roles that empowered children can play in forestalling violence in their communities. In this sense, while focus upon the protection of violence against children remains imperative, there may also be space to consider – as indeed the Youth, Peace and Security,[62] and Women, Peace and Security thematic agendas do – the role that children might play in resisting, preventing, ameliorating and rebuilding after violence. This shifts children's relationship with the Council from one of dependency to partnership.

---

61 Vanessa Pupavac, 'Misanthropy Without Borders: The International Children's Rights Regime', *Disasters*, 25/2: 95–112 (2001), p. 102.

62 S/RES/2250, 09 December 2015.

In his recent acknowledgement of two decades of the Children and Armed Conflict agenda, the UN Secretary-General António Guterres noted that 'while the scale and nature of atrocities committed against children by both state and non-state actors have reached shocking new proportions', 'the best way we can truly protect children is by preventing conflict'.[63] The prevention of conflict is emerging as an imperative for the United Nations, evident across three major reports tabled in 2015 on the Women, Peace and Security thematic agenda, the Peacebuilding Commission Review and Peacekeeping Operations Review. This is reinforced by the founding principle of the 2030 Agenda that notes that sustainable development cannot be achieved without peaceful and inclusive societies. Recognising and supporting the capacity of children to positively impact peace and its sustainability – as children and future adults – will be central to this.

---

63 United Nations Secretary-General, 'Secretary-General's message to Informal Meeting on 20th Anniversary of General Assembly Resolution 51/77 on Children and Armed Conflict', 8 February 2017, https://www.un.org/sg/en/content/sg/statement/2017-02-08/secretary-generals-message-informal-meeting-20th-anniversary-general, accessed 28 March 2017.

R2P and the Prevention of Mass Atrocities: A Child-Centric Approach

Cecilia Jacob
Australian National University, Australia
cecilia.jacob@anu.edu.au

Abstract

Prevention has taken centre-stage in present discussions around both United Nations reform and the R2P implementation agenda. Contemporary humanitarian crises from Myanmar to Yemen reinforce the horrendous atrocities that children face during periods of armed conflict and mass political upheaval to which the prevention agenda is geared. This article considers the atrocity prevention dimension of R2P; it describes changes in both understanding around the dynamics of political violence and strategies for targeting civilians in contemporary conflicts over the past two decades, situates children in the broader social context of mass political violence, and identifies strategies for incorporating a child-centric lens into the existing atrocity prevention toolkit. It argues that while the children and armed conflict agenda strengthens atrocity prevention efforts in relation to children's specific experiences in violent conflict, it does not serve as an adequate proxy for a child-centric approach to atrocity prevention through both structural and targeted measures.

Keywords

atrocity prevention – children – Responsibility to Protect – children and armed conflict

Children hold a unique place in society; families, communities, and political communities at large hold a moral responsibility to ensure children a safe and prosperous future. There is something particularly abhorrent about the killing, maiming, and forced displacement of children during periods of mass political violence. At the time of writing, over half of the 600,000 Rohingya Muslims displaced in the clearing operations conducted by the military campaign in

 | DOI:10.1163/9789004379534_005

Myanmar's Rakhine State are children.[1] As media reports inform us of children being burnt, drowned, and shot in state-sanctioned targeted violence, the international community still grapples with trying to identify the event as potential 'ethnic cleansing', or 'genocide'.[2] The international community fails to protect before it has even determined the nature of the situation to be prevented. In Yemen, nearly a quarter of the civilian population killed in indiscriminate airstrikes are children,[3] a pattern consistent with contemporary urban battlefields.[4] Many more children have been wounded, displaced, recruited into armed forces, and disproportionately affected by the cholera epidemic and food shortages plaguing the country.[5]

Conceptual debates around the distinction between armed conflict, genocide, and mass atrocities may be far removed from the daily lived experience of persecuted populations in which children are integrated. However, these distinctions determine the reality of the international response to crises, and are important for strengthening international protection regimes for children. To date, the focus of the international protection regime for children has centred on children and armed conflict (CAAC) – and in particular on the issue of child soldiering. While an important thematic focus, events such as those in Rakhine State illustrate how the specific thematic framing of protection issues generates a protection gap in contexts of political violence.

A principal value of the Responsibility to Protect (R2P) is its function as the only international framework on atrocity prevention that exists to date. The need to prioritise the preventive dimension of R2P is one area on which the international community has derived substantial consensus in principle, if not in form. The priority of prevention was emphasised in the 2001 International Commission on Intervention and State Sovereignty's report, *The Responsibility*

---

1 Austin Ramzy, 'At Risk in Rohingya Exodus: 230,000 Children, Hundreds All Alone', *New York Times*, 15 September 2017; UN News Centre, 'UN Security Council Calls on Myanmar to End Excessive Military Force in Rakhine State', 6 November 2017, http://www.un.org/apps/news/story.asp?NewsID=58040#.WgKF8GhL-Uk, accessed 20 November 2017.

2 Liam Cochrane, 'Myanmar Could be on the Brink of Genocide, UN Expert Says', ABC News, 6 September 2017.

3 United Nations Human Rights Council, 'Situation of Human Rights in Yemen, Including Violations since September 2014', Report of the United Nations High Commissioner for Human Rights, A/HRC/36/33, 13 September 2017.

4 See the special issue of *International Review of the Red Cross*, 98/1 (2016) devoted to 'War in the Cities'.

5 United Nations Human Rights Council, 'Situation of Human Rights in Yemen'; United Nations General Assembly (UNGA), 'Report of the Special Representative of the Secretary-General for Children and Armed Conflict', A/72/276, 2 August 2017, p. 4, paragraph 11.

to Protect,[6] and reiterated throughout annual United Nations (UN) Secretary-General reports on R2P since 2009. Indeed, under the leadership of António Guterres, prevention has become the central rationale shaping the reform agenda across the UN system.[7]

Prevention is a fraught concept; theoretically it is far more effective in terms of reducing loss of life and the political and financial costs involved in intervention to prevent crises. However, identifying potential or imminent situations of mass atrocity and justifying interventions into the domestic affairs of states has historically been an immense political challenge, one that is intensified by the glaring accountability loopholes for the world's most powerful states that undermine the legitimacy of international human protection efforts. Despite these challenges, the field of atrocity prevention has developed extensively since the early 1990s,[8] and we now have a developed understanding of the specific risk factors, triggers for crisis escalation, and dynamics of mass atrocities to develop tangible strategies for atrocity prevention. As scholars point out, less known today is what prevention tools work at which stages of escalation, and in what combination, to prevent atrocities in the phases of crisis escalation and imminent mass atrocity.[9] As scholarly attention turns its focus to this latter question of successful implementation of atrocity prevention, it is an opportune time to consider how the specific impact of mass atrocities on particularly vulnerable sections of populations fits within overarching prevention strategies.[10]

This article draws three conclusions that can advance the atrocity prevention dimension of R2P in relation to children. First, given mass atrocities involve, by definition, the commission of large-scale systematic violence against a population of which children are a part, there is a need for child-centred

---

6 International Commission on Intervention and State Sovereignty, *The Responsibility to Protect* (Ottawa: International Development Research Centre, 2001).

7 See António Guterres, 'Remarks to the Security Council Open Debate on "Maintenance of International Peace and Security: Conflict Prevention and Sustaining Peace"', 10 January 2017; United Nations Secretary-General, 'Enhancing Performance in the Peace and Security Pillar', memo, 3 January 2017.

8 Barbara Harff, 'Genocide and Political Mass Murder: Definitions, Theories, Analyses' in Michael Stohl, Mark I. Lichbach and Peter Nils Grabosky (eds.), *States and Peoples in Conflict: Transformations of Conflict Studies* (Abingdon: Routledge, 2017), pp. 208–30.

9 Jennifer Welsh, 'The Responsibility to Prevent: Assessing the Gap between Rhetoric and Reality', *Cooperation and Conflict*, 51/2: 216–32 (2016).

10 For a comprehensive survey, see Scott Straus, *Fundamentals of Genocide and Mass Atrocity Prevention* (Washington, DC: United States Holocaust Memorial Museum, 2016), pp. 131–48.

policies within international policy frameworks for the prevention and protection of populations from mass atrocities. To date, the logic of atrocity prevention remains focused on 'populations' writ large; indicators present a monolithic categorisation of populations with a compelling rationale that the mass atrocities target the populace of specific race, ethnicity, religion, political affiliation, or other group identity. Whether or not preventive and protection strategies during imminent or extant mass political violence could be tailored to enhance the protection of particularly vulnerable sections of the population has yet to be demonstrated.

Second, while a noteworthy international protection architecture has developed around the protection of children impacted by armed conflict, it is important to distinguish between armed conflict and mass atrocities as specific manifestations of organised political violence.[11] Current atrocity-prevention frameworks identify specific risk factors that bear on children's physical security and human rights that are relevant in both peacetime and armed conflict, including increased violence and sexual violence targeted at both women and children, birth restrictions such as forced abortion or sterilisation, and the forcible transfer of children.[12] The unique dynamics of atrocity crimes can therefore be disaggregated from the broader enabling context of armed conflict, and consideration needs to be given to whether there is scope to broaden the CAAC agenda to strengthen protection for children in situations of atrocity, or whether a specific protection regime for children should be developed for situations of mass atrocity. Given that the R2P agenda has developed in a unique trajectory that is related to, but independent from, the Protection of Civilians (POC), Women, Peace and Security, and CAAC thematic agendas, developing a child-centric focus within R2P prevention frameworks seems to be the option most consistent with current developments in the international human protection system.

Third and finally, this article surveys the existing R2P prevention toolkit for the prevention of mass atrocities to consider the implications of integrating children's specific protection needs into preventive actions. Whereas the merits of strengthening children's resilience, participation, and ownership of local,

11 Alex J. Bellamy, 'Mass Atrocities and Armed Conflict: Links, Distinctions, and Implications for the Responsibility to Prevent', Policy Analysis Brief (Muscatine, IA: The Stanley Foundation, February 2011).

12 United Nations, 'Framework of Analysis for Atrocity Crimes: A Tool For Prevention' (New York: Joint Office of the Special Advisors to the Secretary-General on the Prevention of Genocide and the Responsibility to Protect, 2014).

bottom-up approaches[13] to early structural prevention strategies are evident in long-term structural prevention efforts, the effectiveness of such strategies decrease as atrocities become imminent. Prevention strategies at the phase of imminent crisis include coercive options for the use of force short of war.[14] Recent examples include airstrikes over Libya in 2011 to halt a violent military repression of civilian protestors, and US airstrikes on Islamic State militants in 2014 to protect Yazidis trapped on Mount Sinjar. The crimes-based approach to atrocity prevention that was advocated by the Special Advisor to the UN Secretary-General from 2013 to 2016 determined that the preventive dimension of R2P transcends all three pillars of R2P. The three pillars include first, state responsibility to prevent and protect populations within its border from atrocities; second, international support to assist states fulfil this responsibility; and third, international responsibility to prevent or halt mass atrocities within states that are unable or unwilling to do so themselves.[15] Conceptually, it is not viable to separate objectives of prevention from protection; coercive interventions under the third pillar entail risk of civilian casualties, particularly in densely populated urban areas, and a destabilisation of the security context. The need to strengthen the protection of civilians – including children that are due special protections through international humanitarian law – in the context of forceful prevention strategies is an area for consideration as international policymakers further clarify and consolidate the atrocity prevention frameworks guiding international collective action to episodes of mass political violence.

Conceptualising Mass Violence and Civilian Targeting

The concept of genocide encapsulates the most extreme form of mass violence known in modern history, and carries with it deep political and moral weight in the international imagination. The 1948 Convention on the Prevention and Punishment of the Crime of Genocide corresponded to the specific experiences of the Holocaust that established the crime of genocide as an artefact of modernity and totalitarianism – a state crime of exceptional violence and the

13 International Committee of the Red Cross, 'Children Affected by Armed Conflict and Other Situations of Violence', Workshop Report (Geneva: ICRC, 14–16 March 2011).

14 Gareth Evans, *The Responsibility to Protect: Ending Mass Atrocity Crimes Once and For All* (Washington, DC: Brookings Institution Press, 2008).

15 United Nations, 'Implementing the Responsibility to Protect', Report of the Secretary-General, A/63/677, 12 January 2009.

ultimate expression of racial discrimination. Given the unique nature of the Holocaust, it was not until the 1970s that historians broke the taboo of comparing episodes of mass violence with the Holocaust in an attempt to recognise other episodes of genocidal violence in modern history.[16]

The prevalence of mass violence against civilians in contemporary conflicts stimulated the development of a new conceptual approach to analysing mass atrocities – episodes of widespread and systematic violence against civilians that could not be defined under the strict definition of genocide. The international criminal tribunals in Rwanda and the former Yugoslavia, and the creation of the International Criminal Court through the 1998 Rome Statute consolidated the international atrocity regime aimed at preventing and prosecuting international crimes of genocide, war crimes, and crimes against humanity. In doing so, the international community extended its capacity to define, identify, and prosecute the more prevalent forms of mass violence manifest in contemporary modes of violent conflict. The recognition that atrocities are crimes committed by individuals against individuals shifts the focus of accountability from the collective responsibility of the state, towards the individual state and non-state perpetrators of violence. International criminal liability and prosecution of the principal orchestrators of mass atrocities through the International Criminal Court serves a preventive function by deterring future perpetrators, and delivering justice for past atrocities.[17]

As Susanne Karstedt argues, the conceptual orientation towards an analysis of mass atrocities teaches us two lessons. First, 'even in the course of these violent decades, genocides are rare events, but mass atrocities are not', and second, 'contemporary mass violence is embedded in macro- and microcontexts that shape particular trajectories of conflict and violence'.[18] Where atrocities manifest as violent peaks in the broader trajectory of long-term patterns of discrimination and reiterated episodes of violence, prevention strategies must entail a responsiveness to the long-term dynamics of violence within a society, rather than abrupt interventions aimed at predicting and preventing a singular, time-bound atrocity 'event'.[19]

Another important conclusion drawn in the atrocity prevention field is the recognition that mass atrocities occur both in periods of armed conflict and in

16 Harff, 'Genocide and Political Mass Murder'.

17 Jennifer Welsh, 'The Individualization of War: Protection, Liability, and Accountability', Lecture, Trudeau Foundation, Ontario, 25 March 2014.

18 Susanne Karstedt, 'Contextualizing Mass Atrocity Crimes: Moving Toward a Relational Approach', *Annual Review of Law and Social Science*, 9: 383–404 (2013), p. 386.

19 Ibid.

peacetime. While armed conflict serves as a crucial enabling context for mass atrocities,[20] and the presence of armed conflict is the single most significant risk factor for potential mass atrocity crimes,[21] the prevention of mass atrocities requires a specific lens that should not be conflated with broad conflict prevention strategies.[22]

Children are constituent actors of the broader social context of contemporary violent conflict and mass atrocities.[23] They are intentional targets of horrendous acts of violence,[24] victims of indiscriminate military assaults, perpetrators of violence, sources of intelligence for armed forces, witnesses to violence, and constitute half of the world's refugees and internally displaced populations.[25] Children are disproportionately affected by the political economies of war, and the legacy of crime, violence, and state-weakness induced by periods of violent conflict. They are also often contributors to these dynamics by filling shortages in resources for combatant and non-combatant roles that sustain state-armed forces and militia.

A starting point for conceptualising children and mass atrocities is to consider the strategic function that the killings and mobilisation of civilians plays during episodes of armed conflict or mass political violence more broadly. The dynamics and strategic logic of violence against civilian populations within episodes of mass political violence – whether armed conflict, revolutions, or mass political upheaval – have long been overlooked within political science and international relations, and therefore little understood.[26] In the decades between the end of the Second World War and the end of the Cold War, political scientists focused their analysis of political violence on the origins of

20 Bellamy, 'Mass Atrocities and Armed Conflict'.

21 Benjamin Valentino, 'Why We Kill: The Political Science of Political Violence against Civilians', *Annual Review of Political Science,* 17: 89–103 (2014), p. 94.

22 Serena K. Sharma and Jennifer M. Welsh, 'Conclusion: An Integrated Framework for Atrocity Crime Prevention' in Serena K. Sharma and Jennifer M. Welsh (eds.), *The Responsibility to Prevent: Overcoming the Challenges of Atrocity Prevention* (Oxford: Oxford University Press, 2015), pp. 368–92, at pp. 369–72.

23 Cecilia Jacob, '"Children and Armed Conflict" and the Field of Security Studies', *Critical Studies on Security*, 3/1: 14–28 (2015).

24 See, for example, Save the Children, 'Unspeakable Crimes against Children: Sexual Violence in Conflict' (London: Save the Children, 2013). The report finds that girls and boys under the age of eighteen make up the majority of survivors of sexual violence in conflict-affected countries. In some cases this figure is as high as 80 per cent.

25 Save the Children International, 'Rising to the Challenge: Save the Children Annual Report' (London: Save the Children, 2016), p. 6.

26 Harff, 'Genocide and Political Mass Murder'.

conflict that had little to say about the specific dynamics of political violence following the onset of hostilities. These analyses failed to disaggregate targeted violence against civilians from the broader theories of the causes of war. Mass violence against civilians was assumed to be either the indiscriminate and unfortunate effects of 'collateral' damage as a by-product of armed conflict, or an irrational manifestation of 'ethnic hatreds'[27] that lacked a strategic function.

Since the 1990s, scholars have opened up the black box of political violence by examining the character, dynamics, and specific strategic logic of political violence following the onset of crisis to explain variation in levels and trajectories of mass violence against civilians during civil conflict and unrest.[28] According to Benjamin Valentino:

> Most significantly, the new research has overturned the once widely held view that large-scale violence against civilian populations was irrational, random, or the result of ancient hatreds between ethnic groups. Instead, most scholars studying political violence now understand it to be primarily, if not exclusively, instrumental and coordinated by powerful actors seeking to achieve tangible political or military objectives. Violence against civilians, once assumed to be a tragic, if virtually inevitable, side effect of wars, is now understood to play a central part in the deliberate strategies of belligerent groups.[29]

Advances in political science have provided invaluable insight into the development of the field of atrocity prevention. Whereas previous generations of scholarship focused on identifying the origins of war and mass violence as a general method for prevention, these strategies were concentrated at the metastructural level of inter-state relations, and failed to capture the localised and internal dynamics of conflicts that have shaped the character of contemporary armed conflict and episodes of mass political violence. As Elisabeth Wood has

27 Robert D. Kaplan, *Balkan Ghosts: A Journey through History* (New York: St. Martins, 1993).

28 Paul R. Brass, *Theft of an Idol: Text and Context in the Representation of Collective Violence* (Princeton, NJ: Princeton University Press, 1997); Barbara Harff, 'No Lessons Learned from the Holocaust? Assessing Risks of Genocide and Political Mass Murder since 1955', *American Political Science Review*, 97/1: 57–73 (2003); Karstedt, 'Contextualizing Mass Atrocity Crimes'; Hugo Slim, *Killing Civilians: Method, Madness and Morality in War* (Oxford: Oxford University Press, 2010); Scott Straus, *The Order of Genocide: Race, Power, and War in Rwanda* (Ithaca, NY: Cornell University Press, 2006); Benjamin A. Valentino, *Final Solutions: Mass Killing and Genocide in the Twentieth Century* (Ithaca, NY: Cornell University Press, 2004).

29 Valentino, 'Why We Kill', p. 91.

argued, understanding why patterns of violence are prevalent in many armed conflicts but *do not* occur in others is also significant, upturning the inevitability thesis of targeted violence against civilians during conflict, and providing a more compelling evidence-base for holding accountable perpetrators that intentionally choose to target civilian populations.[30] Nuanced studies that show how specific relationships between civilian populations and belligerent state or non-state parties that rely on the support or control of populations to fulfil their strategic objectives, determines both the likelihood, pattern, and severity of civilian targeting.[31] These studies confirm that strategic logic for mass violence against civilians during conflict can be identified and incorporated into prevention and protection responses.

The conceptualisation of the dynamics of mass atrocities has radically altered because of research on the micro-dynamics of political violence over the past two decades. These insights have provided hope that early intervention can be deployed in response to the risk factors and early warning signs of mass violence that have been substantially clarified through micro-level research. Atrocity prevention is therefore a new and emerging area of policy and practice,[32] and a number of atrocity prevention toolkits and frameworks that disaggregate structural and dynamic elements of atrocity trajectories have been developed.[33] There is now much greater scope to understand the specific strategic function of children within contexts of violence that facilitates the conceptualisation of a more robust prevention and protection framework for children exposed to risk or extant mass political violence.

---

30 Elisabeth Jean Wood, 'Armed Groups and Sexual Violence: When is Wartime Rape Rare?' *Politics and Society*, 37/1: 131–62 (2009).

31 See, for example, Dara Kay Cohen, *Rape during Civil War* (Ithaca, NY: Cornell University Press, 2016); Stathis N. Kalyvas, *The Logic of Violence in Civil War* (Cambridge: Cambridge University Press, 2006); Jeremy M. Weinstein, *Inside Rebellion: The Politics of Insurgent Violence* (Cambridge: Cambridge University Press, 2007).

32 Straus, *Fundamentals of Genocide.*

33 These include United Nations, 'Framework of Analysis'; the Political Instability Task Force early warning datasets developed by Barbara Harff and Ted Gurr, now maintained by the Center for Systemic Peace, www.systemicpeace.org/, accessed 20 November 2017; the Center for Preventive Action at the Council on Foreign Relations's annual 'Preventive Priorities Surveys'; and the Minority Rights Group International's 'Peoples Under Threat' reports. The European Union (EU) draws on a range of tools and sources for providing country-based data to assess potential risk of mass atrocities. See Task Force on the EU Prevention of Mass Atrocities, 'The EU and the Prevention of Mass Atrocities: An Assessment of Strengths and Weaknesses' (Budapest: Budapest Centre for the International Prevention of Genocide and Mass Atrocities, 2013).

The Relationship between Atrocity Crimes and Children

Children's strategic function in mass violence is a product of their ethnic, racial, or religious identities, intertwined with their socially determined identity based on gender and age. The intimate relationship between children's security and violent conflict is recognised in international humanitarian law; the Fourth Geneva Convention (the Geneva Convention Relative to the Protection of Civilian Persons in Time of War) sets out provisions for special protection for children in situations of armed conflict, and the Optional Protocol identifies children as 'the object of special respect'.[34] The international crimes of genocide, crimes against humanity, and war crimes that constitute international criminal law[35] proscribe specific acts of violence that are committed against civilian populations including children. Legal definitions of genocide also account for violent acts that bear directly on children as a unique identity group, including measures to prevent births and the forcible transfer of children of one group to another group,[36] in addition to the broader acts of killing and physical and mental harm to which children are subjected. The Rome Statute also includes child-specific provisions to include the conscription or enlistment of children under the age of fifteen or their use in hostilities in the definition of war crimes.[37] These legal provisions provide normative and legal justification for including special protections and responsibilities for children at risk of mass political violence – as well as those within contexts of armed conflict with heightened vulnerability to atrocities.

Beyond legal conceptualisations of children and mass atrocities, sociological studies have contributed to our understanding of the different roles that

34 Protocol Additional to the Geneva Conventions of 12 August 1949, and Relating to the Protection of Victims of International Armed Conflicts (Protocol I), 8 June 1977, Article 77(1) (adopted by consensus).

35 Although 'ethnic cleansing' was not included as one of the four international crimes listed in the Rome Statute, the practice is closely associated with genocide and has been incorporated into the four mass atrocities addressed by R2P. The United Nations Commission of Experts report to the Security Council defined ethnic cleansing as 'rendering an area ethnically homogenous by using force or intimidation to remove persons of given groups from the area'. See 'Final Report of the Commission of Experts Established Pursuant to Security Council Resolution 780 (1992)', S/1994/674, 27 May 1994, p. 33.

36 UNGA Res. 260/III, 'Convention on the Prevention and Punishment of the Crime of Genocide', 9 December 1948, Article 2(d),(e).

37 International Criminal Court, *Rome Statute of the International Criminal Court*, A/CONF.183/9, 1 July 2002, article 8.

children play in contexts of political violence. These insights have allowed scholars to view children as not only victims of horrendous acts of violence, but also in more active roles of survivors, perpetrators, post-conflict peacebuilders, and peace activists that are constitutive of the broader social context and processes in which mass violence occurs. That childhood forms a significant dimension of a person's identity, and that children are actors worthy of research in their own right, is an insight from sociological studies of childhood that has arrived relatively late to the field of international relations.[38] Insights from sociology have also contributed to an emergent body of literature in international relations that locates children's presence in global politics and accounts for their roles in key areas such as global security[39] and the international political economy.[40]

When conceptualising children in the context of mass political violence, it is important to view children as central stakeholders in peacemaking and in future peacebuilding processes of their countries to promote justice for populations affected by mass violence,[41] and to prevent future relapse into violent conflict as emphasised in the sociologically informed literature on children's security. The focus within the sociology of childhood literature on children's agency,[42] however, has limitations in the context of mass political violence. The capacity of children to participate and exercise agency within their societies may vary with age, access to information, experience, and opportunity. In contexts of high risk or imminent mass political violence, children's

---

38 Cecilia Jacob, *Child Security in Asia: The Impact of Armed Conflict in Cambodia and Myanmar* (Abingdon: Routledge, 2014), pp. 63–71.

39 J. Marshall Beier (ed.), *The Militarization of Childhood: Thinking Beyond the Global South* (New York: Palgrave Macmillan, 2011); Helen Brocklehurst, *Who's Afraid of Children? Children, Conflict and International Relations* (Farnham: Ashgate, 2006); R. Charli Carpenter, *Forgetting Children Born of War: Setting the Human Rights Agenda in Bosnia and Beyond* (New York: Columbia University Press, 2010); Kim Huynh, Bina D'Costa, and Katrina Lee-Koo, *Children and Global Conflict* (Cambridge: Cambridge University Press, 2015); Cecilia Jacob, *Child Security in Asia;* Alison M.S. Watson, 'Children and International Relations: A New Site of Knowledge?' *Review of International Studies*, 32/2: 237–50 (2006).

40 Alison M.S. Watson, *The Child in International Political Economy: A Place at the Table* (London: Routledge, 2009).

41 Bina D'Costa, 'Children and Justice: Past Crimes, Healing and the Future' in Kim Huynh, Bina D'Costa, and Katrina Lee-Koo, *Children and Global Conflict* (Cambridge: Cambridge University Press, 2015), pp. 212–48.

42 Allison James and Adrian L. James, *Constructing Childhood: Theory, Policy and Social Practice* (Basingstoke: Palgrave Macmillan, 2004); Chris Jenks, *Childhood* (London: Routledge, 1996).

opportunities for productive learning and participation is steeply curtailed. It is also important to address children's specific protection needs with the recognition that children are bearers of human rights regardless of their capacity to exercise agency, and that they are a population to whom the international community owes a special duty to preserve and protect.[43]

The following discussion considers why children become specific targets of mass atrocity violence, and argues that the mobilisation of specific logics employed for targeting children may serve as effective early warning indicators for atrocities. This section first considers the specific logic for targeting children in genocide and ethnic cleansing. It then considers the instrumental logic for targeting children during periods of mass violence that constitute the less restrictive definitional categories of war crimes and crimes against humanity.[44]

The targeting of children in episodes of genocide and ethnic cleansing is primarily strategic and political given the symbolic role of children as reproducers of social and cultural identity of a given nation.[45] For this reason, specific acts of violence against children, or acts that prevent the future births of children, may be indicators of genocidal intent that would distinguish violence as potential mass atrocities. Examples of targeted violence against children through reproduction include rape to forcibly impregnate girls and women as a means of reproducing the hegemonic race,[46] and other forms of sexual violence that would inhibit future procreation (such as castration of men and other forms of genital mutilation),[47] The forced transfer of children, the control of reproduction through sterilisation, abortion, raping women of targeted populations, and mass murder, are examples of strategies of genocide and mass atrocities

43 For a discussion on the limitations of an agency-focused approach to children's security, and the moral status of children as human rights-bearers, see Jacob, *Child Security in Asia*, pp. 56–62.

44 The four atrocities that R2P responds to are genocide, war crimes, ethnic cleansing, and crimes against humanity. United Nations, '2005 World Summit Outcome', A/RES/60/1, 24 October 2005, paragraph 138.

45 Catherine A. MacKinnon, 'Rape, Genocide and Women's Human Rights' in Alexandra Stiglmayer (ed.), *Mass Rape: The War against Women in Bosnia-Herzegovina* (Lincoln, NE: University of Nebraska Press, 1994), pp. 183–96.

46 Carpenter, *Forgetting Children*; Jacob, *Child Security in Asia*, pp. 35–37.

47 Gabrielle Ferrales, Hollie Nyseth Brehm, and Suzy McElrath, 'Gender-Based Violence against Men and Boys in Darfur: The Gender–Genocide Nexus', *Gender & Society*, 30/4: 565–89 (2016).

that have occurred throughout the twentieth century, from the Holocaust,[48] to East Pakistan,[49] Rwanda,[50] and Bosnia.[51]

Children born of wartime sexual violence are particularly vulnerable, as those that survive and grow up in their mother's communities may face severe stigma in post-conflict contexts.[52] In such cases, communities perpetuate a symbolic attachment of national and cultural identity to the child, conferring the 'enemy' identity of the father onto the child. International lawyers have struggled to demonstrate how genocidal rape violates the human rights of children born because of forced impregnation given that the act of violence against the woman was the same act that brought about the child's life. In this case, conceptualising the stigma and denial of human rights after the birth has been the primary lens accepted for conceptualising these children's human rights, rather than the rape itself.[53] Sociologically, the centrality of national and cultural identity that children born of wartime sexual violence embody is central to the logic that underpins genocidal processes, and is perpetuated into the post-conflict period.

Sex-selective killings of children during episodes of genocide and ethnic cleansing follow a similar logic to genocidal rape in seeking to eliminate potential current and future threats from a targeted identity-group. Since the 1990s, the issue of rape and genocide has received extensive treatment in the academic literature, particularly in the wake of prosecutions for rape as acts of genocide and crimes against humanity in the international criminal tribunals in the former Yugoslavia and Rwanda. While predominantly concentrated on females, recent literature has also emphasised the impacts of gendered

48 Brocklehurst, *Who's Afraid of Children?* pp. 49–82.

49 Bina D'Costa, *Nationbuilding, Gender and War Crimes in South Asia* (New York: Routledge, 2011).

50 Straus, *The Order of Genocide.* Straus (pp. 162–69) shows that while there is evidence of mass sexual violence, the decision to kill women and children was embedded in the logic of extermination of the full race and therefore integral to the genocide.

51 Susan Brownmiller, 'Making Female Bodies the Battlefield' in Alexandra Stiglmayer (ed.), *Mass Rape: The War against Women in Bosnia-Herzegovina* (Lincoln, NE: University of Nebraska Press,1994), pp. 180–82; Alexandra Stiglmayer, 'The Rapes in Bosnia' in Alexandra Stiglmayer (ed.), *Mass Rape: The War against Women in Bosnia-Herzegovina,* (Lincoln, NE: University of Nebraska Press, 1994), pp. 82–96.

52 For accounts of the social exclusion and stigma faced by women raped and impregnated during conflict see D'Costa, *Nationbuilding*, pp. 119–36; also Susan Harris Rimmer, *Gender and Transitional Justice: The Women of East Timor* (Abingdon: Routledge, 2010), pp. 123–25.

53 Robin May Schott, 'War Rape, Natality and Genocide', *Journal of Genocide Research,* 13/1–2: 5–21 (2011).

violence on males.[54] The killing of male adult and child populations has been the focus of much of this literature in genocide studies, with sex-selective killings of males now widely understood to constitute a strategy to eliminate the potential military capability embodied in the male population,[55] and to denigrate a population by humiliating and disenfranchising its men.[56] The selective killing of male children *en masse* along ethnic, racial, or religious lines has been a feature of genocidal killings in conflicts such as Bosnia and Herzegovina (notable was the massacre of Srebrenica), Kosovo, Timor-Leste, and Darfur,[57] and serves as an indicator of genocidal and ethnic cleansing processes.

The discussion in this section has so far considered cases of genocide and ethnic cleansing. However, any account of a child-centric atrocity prevention agenda needs to respond to contexts of mass atrocities that occur in both peacetime and conflict, including when genocidal processes are not evident. By their very nature, episodes of mass violence entail the mobilisation and disruption of large population groups; therefore, the character of violent conflict will determine the severity and nature of atrocities committed against children. For example, the formation or rapid strengthening of state-sponsored militia is an early indicator of mass atrocities.[58] Commensurate with the mass mobilisation of populations for fighting forces, the onset of mass atrocities is likely to be preceded by a spike in the recruitment of children into the armed forces to bolster the resources of belligerent parties.[59]

The character of contemporary urban warfare has increased the likelihood that armed conflict will result in mass atrocities, and the use of schools and civilian infrastructure is directly associated with steep increases in the incidence of atrocities committed against children. The widespread use of schools as 'military staging grounds, temporary bases, detention centres, sniper posts and centres for torture and the interrogation of adults and children'[60] by armed groups during urban-based fighting puts large numbers of children at

54 R. Charli Carpenter, 'Recognizing Gender-Based Violence against Civilian Men and Boys in Conflict Situations', *Security Dialogue*, 37/1: 83–103 (2006).

55 Adam Jones, 'Gendercide and Genocide', *Journal of Genocide Research*, 2/2: 185–211 (2000); R. Charli Carpenter, *'Innocent Women and Children': Gender, Norms and the Protection of Civilians* (Farnham: Ashgate, 2006).

56 Ferrales, Brehm, and McElrath, *Gender-Based Violence.*

57 Jones, 'Gendercide and Genocide'.

58 Straus, *Fundamentals of Genocide.*

59 Roméo Dallaire, 'Preventing the Use of Child Soldiers, Preventing Genocide', *UN Chronicle*, 52/1 & 2 (2015).

60 United Nations, 'Children and Armed Conflict', Report of the Secretary-General, A/66/782–S/2012/261, 26 April 2012, p. 23.

risk, both directly in the line of crossfire, and in embedding them in urban spaces subjected to open warfare.[61] Children are caught in sieges where the denial of humanitarian access has become an increasingly difficult challenge for international humanitarian actors who seek to deliver life-saving assistance and protection for vulnerable populations.[62] One of the challenges for incorporating a child-centric lens into atrocity prevention frameworks is to distinguish between the POC and CAAC agendas during armed conflict with an operable concept of prevention that complements existing international protection frameworks. The next section considers these developments in more detail.

The Children and Armed Conflict Agenda

Publication of the 1966 UN report on the impact of armed conflict on children has attracted significant international attention to this problem.[63] Commonly known as the 'Machel Report' after its author Graça Machel, it drew attention to the plight of children worldwide caught up in armed conflicts, that in the mid-1990s were primarily internal and accompanied by large-scale atrocities against civilian populations. The report raised the profile of child soldiering as a phenomenon found in nearly every conflict zone in the world, and identified the horrific physical and psychological impacts of armed conflict on children. The report spurred international advocacy by groups such as Child Soldiers International (formerly the Coalition to Stop the Use of Child Soldiers), and the strengthening of the international architecture of CAAC.

In 1996, the Office of the Special Representative of the Secretary-General for Children and Armed Conflict was created,[64] and in 1999 CAAC was formally added to the UN Security Council (UNSC) as one of the thirteen thematic issues on international peace and security for regular review.[65] The CAAC agenda has strengthened with the identification of six grave violations against children in conflict: killing and maiming of children, recruitment or use of children

61 Save the Children, 'Untold Atrocities: The Stories of Syria's Children' (London: Save the Children, 2012).

62 UNGA, 'Report of the Special Representative of the Secretary-General for Children and Armed Conflict'.

63 UNGA, 'Promotion and Protection of the Rights of Children: Impact of Armed Conflict on Children', A/51/306, 26 August 1996.

64 The mandate for the Special Representative and the new office was established by UNGA Res. A/RES/51/77, 20 February 1997.

65 UNSC Res. 1261, 30 August 1999.

as soldiers, sexual violence against children, abduction of children, attacks against schools or hospitals, and denial of humanitarian access for children. The first five violations can be used to trigger the listing of a state or non-state party onto the UNSC list of concerned parties for international review, and these listings provide an important tool for the UNSC to hold belligerents to a level of accountability through its annual reporting. In 2005, the UNSC created a monitoring and reporting mechanism to monitor, document, and report on violations against children, and to 'name and shame' perpetrators by identifying situations of concern through its annual reporting to the UNSC. In 2009, the UNSC established the Working Group on Children and Armed Conflict to deliver recommendations to states identified as having situations of concern to enhance the protection of children.

International law has also strengthened around the protection of CAAC. In 1998, the Rome Statute included as a war crime the conscription or enlistment of children under the age of fifteen or their use in active hostilities. International Labour Organization Convention No. 182 on the Prohibition and Immediate Action for the Elimination of the Worst Forms of Child Labour in 1999 prohibited the forced or compulsory recruitment of children for use in armed conflict, and in 2000, the Optional Protocol to the Convention on the Rights of the Child on the Involvement of Children in Armed Conflict called on states to raise the age of recruitment and involvement in active hostilities from the age of fifteen (the threshold in the 1989 UN Convention on the Rights of the Child) to the age of eighteen. In addition to the strengthening of the international legal regime around child soldiering, subsequent UNSC resolutions have strengthened international protection for children in hostilities including resolutions to curtail killing, maiming, rape, sexual violence,[66] and attacks on hospitals and schools where children are disproportionately targeted.[67]

Given the specific focus of CAAC on protecting children in situations of armed conflict, what are the implications of this agenda for the protection of children in situations of mass atrocity? The Machel Report identified genocide and ethnic cleansing as among the most egregious effects of armed conflict on children, and made no conceptual distinction between the concept of mass atrocities and armed conflict. Today, the focus of the CAAC agenda at the UN has been on the recruitment and use of children in armed hostilities, as exemplified by the 'children, not soldiers' campaign launched by the Office of the Special Representative of the Secretary-General on CAAC in 2014, signing some

66 UNSC Res. 1882, 4 August 2009.

67 UNSC Res. 1998, 12 July 2011.

twenty-seven action plans with states to end recruitment and procure the release of some 115,000 child combatants.[68] The office maintains a parallel focus on reintegration assistance for children, victims, and perpetrators.[69]

The achievements of the UN CAAC advocacy and protection architecture are laudable. However, there have been significant developments in the conceptualisation of mass atrocities since 1996. In recent years, scholars and policymakers have distinguished between the atrocity prevention agenda and the conflict prevention agenda; this has resulted in a divergence in the political and normative frameworks for protecting children from armed conflict, and for the protection of populations at large through the prevention of atrocity crimes. To date, there has been no articulation of the implications of the atrocity prevention agenda for children, nor the development of a child-centric protection architecture for periods of mass atrocities comparable to the CAAC agenda.

An Agenda for Child-centric Atrocity Prevention

Given that children are embedded in specific political and social contexts, efforts to enhance the human rights and protection of children through preventive action requires inserting a child-centric lens into existing strategies. Existing strategies for atrocity prevention focus on two areas – long-term structural prevention, and short-term operational, or targeted, prevention. Structural prevention relates to long-term efforts to reverse the underlying risk factors for atrocity crimes that include socio-economic inequality, ethnic discrimination, and lack of participatory politics.[70] Preventative strategies at this stage should increase 'support for resilience and inclusiveness', and include activities such as civic education, inter-faith dialogue, and strengthening inclusive domestic institutions.[71]

Opportunities to engage children at the level of structural prevention offer the most promising strategy to ensure that protection mechanisms and

68 Office of the Special Representative of the Secretary-General for Children and Armed Conflict, '20 Years to Better Protect Children Affected by Conflict' (New York: United Nations, 2016), p. 13.

69 Office of the Special Representative of the Secretary-General for Children and Armed Conflict, 'Mandate', https://childrenandarmedconflict.un.org/mandate/, accessed 21 November 2017.

70 Straus, *Fundamentals of Genocide*.

71 Sharma and Welsh, 'Conclusion', p. 377.

social resilience to crises are in place prior to any outbreak of violent conflict or political unrest. Engaging children in peacebuilding and transitional justice mechanisms in societies with a legacy of past atrocity crimes, and with significant risk of political violence, is crucial to strengthening social resilience of societies over the long-term. Efforts may also include developing and integrating peace education and conflict resolution into national curriculum, revising history textbooks to remove discriminatory biases in the retelling of national histories, and encouraging inclusive civic values through the education system. Increasing social resilience to atrocities relies significantly on reconciling inter-group tensions, and strengthening democratic political values of inclusiveness and peaceful resolution of conflicts. Children are valuable sources of cultural reproduction and change through whom long-term resilience can be enhanced.

Experience with child and youth peacebuilding programs through collaborative activities such as music, art, and sport have created opportunities for children to breakdown inter-group barriers, build relationships, and overcome negative stereotypes,[72] and their value for consolidating peace and post-conflict justice needs to be appreciated in the context of long-term atrocity prevention strategies. Peacebuilding strategies require ensuring that sufficient funding and support is available for locally engaged civil society actors and community groups such as religious communities that are best placed to foster these ties.

Potential models that could institutionalise a child-centric prevention focus in national atrocity prevention efforts include the designation of a national R2P focal point,[73] the charging of a government official or respected leader with implementing R2P across relevant national institutions, or the creation of a dedicated national atrocity prevention mechanism.[74] With a broad national focus on mainstreaming atrocity prevention objectives into domestic institutions, these could incorporate specific mandates for promoting children's participation in peacebuilding efforts. Opportunities for partner states and regional or international organisations to strengthen the engagement of children

---

72 See, for example, Heather Elliott (ed.), 'Children and Peacebuilding: Experiences and Perspectives', World Vision Discussion Paper (Melbourne: World Vision, 2002).

73 Mónica Serrano, 'National Focal Points for R2P: Institutionalizing the Responsibility to Protect' in Serena K. Sharma and Jennifer M. Welsh (eds.), *The Responsibility to Prevent: Overcoming the Challenges of Atrocity Prevention* (Oxford: Oxford University Press, 2015), pp. 83–100.

74 Auschwitz Institute for Peace and Reconciliation, 'Pursuing Institutionalization of the Prevention Agenda: National Mechanisms for the Prevention of Genocide and other Atrocity Crimes' (New York: Auschwitz Institute for Peace and Reconciliation, 2017).

as participants and stakeholders in the long-term peacebuilding process of their communities could be supported through areas of development cooperation.

Incorporating a child-centred lens into risk assessment and early warning data-gathering could also provide opportunities to gather systematic data on more general population trends that may indicate an increasing risk that is not available for other population groups. Child-specific early warning indicators of atrocities include rising levels of violence targeted against children and an increase in discriminatory speech and practices.[75] Health and education systems could provide an important source of systematic data to monitor trends if appropriate technical capacity and resource support is in place. National human rights bodies and community-level peace committees are also important institutional sites for gathering data on trends in violence and human rights violations against children. Coordination with international agencies such as the United Nations Children's Fund (UNICEF), the Office of the United Nations High Commissioner for Human Rights, and Save the Children would enhance capacity to assess for atrocity risk through aggregate data and monitor trends where preventive measures could be targeted.

Long-term strategies aimed at strengthening resilience of societies also requires broad national-level reforms. Any child-centred prevention and protection strategies must be developed in the context of nationwide reforms to strengthen democratic norms and human rights, and to promote the rule of law and justice through security sector reform and capacity building of key governance and justice institutions. Dealing with impunity of state authorities and security forces is crucial for rupturing the source of criminalised networks and non-state (as well as state-backed) militia that provide enabling mechanisms for systematic and widespread destruction when violence is triggered.[76] States can adopt constitutional provisions that enhance the protection of vulnerable populations from discriminatory practices and proscribe atrocity crimes through legislation to ensure that domestic legal standards are consistent with international law.

In the event of escalating violence, political space to transform underlying structures diminishes, and the focus of states and the international community must turn towards protecting the human rights of children. Every context of mass violence is unique, but history shows that where social, political, and

75 United Nations, 'Framework of Analysis'.

76 Ward Berenschot, *Riot Politics: Hindu–Muslim Violence and the Indian State* (New York: Columbia University Press, 2011); Paul R. Brass, *The Production of Hindu–Muslim Violence in Contemporary India* (New Delhi: Oxford University Press, 2003); Scott Straus, 'Triggers of Mass Atrocities', *Politics and Governance*, 3/3: 5–15 (2015).

security structures are in place to support impunity, extremist ideologies, and coordinated violence across localities, widespread and systematic violence can escalate rapidly after onset. Incidences of communal violence that appear spontaneous are often tightly planned and orchestrated, and patronage networks can mobilise populations to participate in mass violence in a short timeframe under these conditions. When state forces are complicit or abet this kind of violence, the window for external actors to mobilise protection responses is very narrow, and children are vulnerable to extreme forms of violence through killings, sexual violence, torture, and forced displacement.[77]

Given the short timeframe within which external actors are required to mobilise to effectively prevent and protect vulnerable civilian populations in the event of crisis mobilisation and imminence,[78] investment in early warning systems that can identify indicators of increasing risks and anticipate potential triggers is crucial. The failure of the international community to prevent major humanitarian crises and atrocities has propelled the UN to invest in implementing reforms to enhance the preventive capacity of the organisation. Examples of reform include the improved coordination and sharing of information across field and regional offices, the enhanced role of preventive diplomacy, mediation, and special political missions to diffuse tensions early, and the implementation of the 'Human Rights Upfront' initiative to strengthen system-wide cooperation to respond effectively to mass violence. Importantly, the sustaining peace initiative[79] has emphasised the close relationship between peacebuilding and the prevention of armed violence. These macro-level reforms are still in the early phase, and have had mixed success to date.

Strengthening collective action is vitally important for pooling international resources and generating political will for the international community to support preventive action and human protection where possible. However, as violence escalates, any coercive prevention strategies short of war such as the use of preventive airstrikes generates additional risk to civilians getting caught in crossfire. UN reform is no panacea for the human protection challenges that proliferate across conflict zones and situations of endemic political

77 Cecilia Jacob, 'State Responsibility and Prevention in the Responsibility to Protect: Communal Violence in India', *Global Responsibility to Protect*, 7/1: 56–80 (2015).

78 Reuben Reike, Serena Sharma, and Jennifer Welsh, 'A Strategic Framework for Mass Atrocity Prevention', Policy Paper 03/2013 (Queanbeyan, NSW and Oxford: Australian Civil–Military Centre and Oxford Institute for Ethics, Law and Armed Conflict, 2013).

79 Peter Thomson, 'Building Sustainable Peace for All', Briefing, General Assembly of the United Nations, 20 January 2017, http://www.un.org/pga/71/2017/01/20/building-sustainable-peace-for-all/, accessed 31 May 2017.

violence and instability, and designing targeted protection measures for children caught up in the context of mass political violence becomes fraught with complex strategic and moral considerations.

Conclusion

Is there a place for children within international atrocity prevention frameworks? This article has argued that there is indeed an urgent need to account for children in international atrocity prevention frameworks given the unique experiences that they encounter in mass atrocity situations. Children's experiences in situations of mass political violence are shaped by their identity as children, as boys or girls, and as representatives of the future generations of their specific ethnic, religious, or population group. Children are also caught in the indiscriminate crossfire of increasingly urbanised warfare that characterises today's battlefield, subject to sieges, denied humanitarian access, exposed to disease pandemics and famine when critical infrastructure is destroyed, forcibly displaced, and recruited into armed groups. Furthermore, children are specifically targeted in different ways (for example, rape, killing, abductions, and forced transfer between populations) due to strategic logics in periods of mass violence that are formed through ideologies of nation, race, and religion of belligerent parties.

The CAAC agenda incorporates protections from the six grave violations against children in armed conflict (that relate to situations of armed conflict and mass atrocities), and strengthens atrocity-prevention objectives. However, given that mass atrocities are specific crimes that can occur either in the context of armed conflict or peacetime, the CAAC agenda does not substitute the need for incorporating a child-centric lens into specific atrocity prevention and protection measures. Risk assessment and early warning tools should engage education and health systems to identify both child-specific indicators of atrocity, and to track general trends of human rights violations and violence across populations groups to strengthen early warning data. Children need to be included in community-level peacebuilding and transitional justice initiatives if they are to generate a transformative culture in societies where inter-group tensions and discriminatory behaviours persist. These areas of participation need to be supported at the macro-level through political, security, and human rights reform, which are areas of assistance that partner states, and regional and international organisations, can actively support.

As atrocity risk escalates and security situations deteriorate, the space for tailoring specific strategies to enhance children's protection decreases, and there is a need for state and international community actors to change focus from participation and agency as processes for strengthening resilience of societies to atrocity crimes, to human rights protection. The last resort option of using coercive force short of war as a preventive strategy may be necessary in imminent cases of mass atrocities. Such interventions will invariably generate unintentional loss of life for vulnerable populations, including children. The strategic and ethical costs of making such calculations reinforce the need for the international community to strengthen prevention strategies as early as possible, and to embrace substantial reforms that will improve the effectiveness of early warning systems, communication channels to act on early warning data, and collective action when rapid mobilisation of external preventive action is required.

The Politics of Norm Glocalisation: Limits in Applying R2P to Protecting Children

Jochen Prantl
Australian National University, Australia
jochen.prantl@anu.edu.au

Ryoko Nakano
Kanazawa University, Japan
rnakano@staff.kanazawa-u.ac.jp

Abstract

Two-thirds of the global child population lives in countries affected by violent and high-intensity conflict. International humanitarian law provides broad protection for children in the event of armed conflict. However, as the 2017 report of the UN Secretary-General on children and armed conflict stresses, the scale and severity of grave violations has increased. This paper addresses the central puzzle of why the existing legal and normative frameworks of child protection have achieved so little, in addressing the marginalisation and disempowerment of children in armed conflict. We argue that the contemporary application of R2P in protecting children will be limited unless at least two fundamental challenges are met: (a) taming power politics; and (b) squaring inherent contradictions between the global R2P norm and national and regional normative frameworks of child protection. We highlight the case of Japan to illustrate the limits of the contemporary application of R2P in protecting children.

Keywords

global norm diffusion – glocalisation – feedback loop – power politics – Japan

•••

Where, after all, do universal human rights begin? In small places, close to home – so close and so small that they cannot be seen on any maps of the world. Yet they are the world of the individual person; the neighborhood he

 | DOI:10.1163/9789004379534_006

> *lives in; the school or college he attends; the factory, farm or office where he works. ... Unless these rights have meaning there, they have little meaning anywhere. Without concerted citizen action to uphold them close to home, we shall look in vain for progress in the larger world.*
>
> ELEANOR ROOSEVELT, 'In Our Hands', 1958

Two-thirds of the global child population lives in countries affected by violent and high-intensity conflict. International humanitarian law provides broad protection for children in the event of armed conflict. The Geneva Convention of 1949 and the Additional Protocols of 1977 specify a suite of rules according children special protection. The 1989 Convention on the Rights of the Child establishes limits on children's participation in hostilities. Advancing the goal of child protection, the United Nations Security Council has identified six categories as a reference point for gathering evidence of grave violence against children: killing and maiming; recruitment or use as soldiers; sexual violence; attacks against schools or hospitals; denial of humanitarian access; and abduction. Furthermore, the Security Council established a Monitoring and Reporting Mechanism in 2005 to systematically collect evidence and name parties to conflict who commit violence against children. However, as the 2017 report of the UN Secretary-General on children and armed conflict stresses, the scale and severity of grave violations by parties to conflict has increased in a number of conflict situations. For 2016, the UN recorded at least 4,000 verified violations committed by government forces and more than 11,500 verified violations by non-state armed groups. Compared to 2015, the recruitment and the use of children more than doubled in Somalia and Syria.[1] Reacting to the scale of violations, UN Secretary-General António Guterres called on the conflicting parties 'to abide by their responsibility to protect children, in accordance with their obligation under international humanitarian and human rights law'.[2]

This article addresses the central puzzle of why the existing legal and normative frameworks of child protection have achieved so little in addressing the marginalisation and disempowerment of children in armed conflict. It situates

1 See UN Document A/72/361-S/2017/821, 24 August 2017.

2 UN News Centre, 'UN report reveals shocking levels of grave violations against children affected by conflicts', 5 October 2017, http://www.un.org/apps/news/printnews.asp?nid=57823, accessed 11 October 2017.

the diffusion of global norms such as R2P, Human Security and child protection in their wider systemic context. Understanding the embeddedness of norm diffusion in global, regional, and domestic orders ('the system') is the sine-qua-non for explaining normative traction in global governance. It also forces us to focus on the key nodes that holds the system as a whole together: first, institutional and material power to help or hinder global norm enforcement; and, second, the degree of universal implementation along with the normative buy-in at the global, regional, and domestic levels. Yet, the organising rules and principles of global order are currently undergoing a transformation – driven by the ongoing shifts in the distribution of power from West to East and South. This transformation has a non-linear trajectory that does not proceed in linear life cycles but in feedback loops; the outcome for global order and the underlying rules of the game is open-ended. Normative contestation is the rule rather than the exception. In this context, Japan provides one of the most powerful examples of norm contestation, as it is not considered a usual suspect who would rock the normative boat. As a country of the East, Japan is firmly embedded in liberal order, a norm-taker playing by the rules of the greater liberal West. Yet this conventional narrative is challenged by the coexistence of Japan's long-term embrace of Human Security and its formal adoption of R2P in 2005. This example raises fundamental questions about how global norms travel and how they are received, implemented, and adapted at the regional and domestic levels and fed back into the global arena.

Against this backdrop, we argue that the contemporary application of R2P in protecting children will be limited unless at least two fundamental challenges are met: (a) taming power politics inside and outside the UN Security Council; and (b) squaring inherent contradictions between the global R2P norm and national and regional normative frameworks of child protection. The main argument is substantiated in three sections. The first section sets out the scope conditions of R2P and further develops the analytical framework of the norm diffusion loop, as introduced in an earlier piece.[3] This helps to embed global norms in their wider systemic context and understand better the challenges and opportunities of implementing global protection norms at the regional and domestic levels. The second section applies the analytical framework to R2P and child protection. The third section highlights the case of Japan, which promotes the protection of children through the Human Security rather than R2P agenda. Japan is a particularly pertinent example of the significant differences in dealing with children's issues that have to be taken into account for

3 See Jochen Prantl and Ryoko Nakano, 'Global Norm Diffusion in East Asia: How China and Japan Implement the Responsibility to Protect', *International Relations*, 25/2: 204–223 (2011).

the R2P framework to be effective. The final section offers some conclusions on the potential and limits of contemporary application of R2P in protecting children.

The paper aims to contribute to the literature on International Relations in two ways. First, it highlights the importance for constructivist scholars to view norm diffusion as both top-down and bottom-up processes that are driven by complex dynamics of feedback and contestation unfolding in non-linear ways. Second, it breaks down the domestic-international divide of International Relations scholarship by stressing the crucial and dynamic relationship between global, regional, and domestic levels in norm diffusion.

Conceptualising Norm Diffusion

Any norm is embedded in a wider social context. This is indeed the case for R2P. It is embedded in the social dynamics of global order. In this section, we start by investigating the fundamental relationship between international norms and global order from an English School perspective. Global norms are exposed simultaneously to the forces of solidarism – that is, the widening and deepening normative scope of international society – and pluralism – that is, the recognition of the principles of sovereignty, non-intervention, and restraint with respect to the use of force, as enshrined in Articles 2.1 and 2.4 of the UN Charter. Solidarism and pluralism 'are differently configured frameworks of world order'.[4] They contain multiple layers of mutually agreed upon structural principles that have evolved over time. These principles 'license a particular systemic configuration of political authority (by privileging a particular organising principle), define what constitutes legitimate political agency ... and sanction particular kinds of fundamental institutional practices'.[5] Rather than treating solidarism and pluralism as mutually exclusive conceptualisations of global order, they are better understood as mutually coexisting push and pull factors, setting the normative parameters and bandwidth of international society.[6]

4 Tim Dunne, 'The Responsibility to Protect and World Order' in Ramesh Thakur and William Maley (eds.), *Theorising the Responsibility to Protect* (Cambridge: Cambridge University Press, 2015), p. 88.

5 Reus-Smit, 'The Liberal International Order Reconsidered', p. 170.

6 See Nicholas J. Wheeler, 'Pluralist or Solidarist Conceptions of International Society: Bull and Vincent on Humanitarian Intervention', *Millennium: Journal of International Studies*, 21/3: 463–487 (1992).

The relationship between structural principles and global order is dynamic and non-linear. It is subject to ongoing contestation and re-evaluation. The traction and latitude of any global norm is defined by its contemporary historical context. Changes in the understanding of state sovereignty over the past two decades – both in the security and economic realm – may serve as examples here. Kofi Annan diagnosed in 1999 a decline of state sovereignty and enhancement of personal sovereignty triggered 'by a renewed and spreading consciousness of individual rights'.[7] He argued that '[s]tates are now widely understood to be instruments at the service of their peoples, and not vice versa'.[8] For some, the 1990s reversed the long-standing post-World War II trend that had emphasised state sovereignty at the expense of individual human and civil rights.[9] The 1994 genocide in Rwanda and 1995 ethnic cleansing in Srebrenica bolstered the solidarist case for humanitarian intervention. In this context, the universal adoption of R2P in 2005 seemed to be the logical continuation of a long-term trend. Yet, while the UN Security Council in the 1990s did extend the scope of Article 39 to human security concerns, in particular the protection of civilians in armed conflict, permanent members such as China and Russia were reluctant to embrace a new norm of humanitarian intervention.[10] Taming power politics in the UN Security Council turned out to be the sine-qua-non for any robust UN intervention to protect civilians during war. The far less intrusive Human Security agenda – championed by Japan and universally endorsed by the 2005 World Outcome Document – developed side-by-side the humanitarian intervention debate. In the economic realm, Susan Strange noted in 1996 'The Retreat of the State' caused by the diffusion of power to non-state actors such as global corporations, accounting firms, and mafias.[11] The sovereignty of markets rather than states reflected the *Zeitgeist* of accelerated globalisation and the decentralised world economic order, along with advances in technology that resulted in the shrinkage of distance at a global scale. In sum, state sovereignty not only eroded but became conditional upon meeting certain standards of behaviour.

---

7 Kofi Annan, 'Two Concepts of Sovereignty', *Economist*, 18 September 1999, pp. 49–50.

8 Ibid.

9 See Mark Mazower, *Governing the World: The History of an Idea* (New York: The Penguin Press, 2012), p. 380.

10 See Neil MacFarlane and Yuen Foong Khong, *Human Security and the UN: A Critical History* (Bloomington: Indiana University Press, 2006), Chapter 5.

11 See Susan Strange, *The Retreat of the State: The Diffusion of Power in the World Economy* (Cambridge: Cambridge University Press, 1996).

While the above analysis seems to suggest a significant change of a key structural principle underlying global order,[12] the erosion of sovereignty has never been a linear development. In 2001, the idea of R2P was introduced in the Report of the International Commission on Intervention and State Sovereignty (ICISS), which included specific criteria for determining when military intervention is appropriate and justified.[13] Adopted by the World Summit in 2005, operational paragraph 138 of the Outcome Document emphasised the political commitment towards R2P while avoiding any legally binding elements to enforce the responsibility of the state 'to protect its populations from genocide, war crimes, ethnic cleansing and crimes against humanity'.[14] Any R2P enforcement measures needed to be endorsed by the UN Security Council, including the concurrent vote of its five permanent members. At the same time, operational paragraph 143 entailed the commitment to further discuss and develop the Human Security agenda.[15] The 2009 report on the implementation of R2P introduced a three-pillar structure that effectively deemphasised any potential enforcement measures (Pillar Three). Instead, it emphasised the political commitment of states to protect their populations while re-confirming the UN Charter's bedrock principles of sovereignty and non-intervention (Pillar One) and the political commitment to encourage and assist countries in meeting their responsibilities (Pillar Two).[16] Despite the general understanding that all three pillars enjoy equal strength, subsequent reports have tended to highlight the less controversial capacity-building and conflict prevention aspects of Pillars One and Two rather than the contentious enforcement aspects of Pillar Three.[17]

Global order has undergone significant change after 2005. The adoption of R2P occurred at a time 'when assertive liberalism was at its height, and sovereign equality looked and smelled reactionary'.[18] But this liberal momentum changed with the global balance of power shifting further to the East

12 For example, Dunne argues that the adoption of R2P 'signaled a critically important world order reform'. Dunne, 'The Responsibility to Protect and World Order', p. 95.

13 See International Commission on Intervention and State Sovereignty (ICISS), *The Responsibility to Protect: Report of the International Commission on Intervention and State Sovereignty* (Ottawa: International Development Research Centre, 2001).

14 UN Document A/RES/60/1, 24 October 2005, operative paragraph 138.

15 UN Document A/RES/60/1, 24 October 2005, operative paragraph 143.

16 See UN Document A/63/677, 12 January 2009.

17 See UN Documents A/64/864, 14 July 2010; A/65/877, 28 June 2011; A/66/874, 25 July 2012; A/67/929, 9 July 2013; A/68/947, 11 July 2014; A/69/981, 13 July 2015; A/70/999, 22 July 2016.

18 Jennifer M. Welsh, 'Implementing the "Responsibility to Protect": Where Expectations Meet Reality', *Ethics and International Affairs*, 24/4 (2010), p. 428.

and South, leading to a strong pluralist pullback with normative contraction as a result. The international responses to the crises in Libya (2011) and Syria thereafter amply illustrate how the normative traction and latitude of R2P has been ultimately conditioned by the *power politics* of intervention.[19] Although R2P conditions sovereignty through the language of and political commitment to responsibility and morality, the enforcement of conditional sovereignty does depend on the compliance and *power political* agreement of the five-permanent members of the UN Security Council.

To some, Libya highlighted R2P's coming-of-age, with the UN Security Council for the first time enacting Pillar Three of the principle in Resolution 1973.[20] Others were far more cautious in attributing a decisive role to R2P in providing a UN mandate for NATO's intervention. Morris expresses doubts as to whether R2P – especially the third pillar – had been the primary motive of Council members for adopting the resolution, because it was outweighed by other complex considerations of strategic, political, and operational concern.[21] This became particularly obvious in light of the Gaddafi regime's failure to comply with the Security Council's call for 'an immediate end to the violence'.[22] While Security Council members were united in condemning Gaddafi's suppressive policies and supporting Council action, implementation drove a wedge between key Council stakeholders. Especially Russia stressed that the NATO military operation to protect civilians in Libya had manifestly exceeded the UN Security Council mandate, as provided in Resolution 1973.[23] Responding to 'the growing perception that the concept of R2P might be misused for purposes other than protecting civilians, such as regime change', Brazil sought to re-evaluate and refine the contested R2P norm in November 2011 by proposing the Responsibility while Protecting (RwP) doctrine.[24] RwP aims to establish a

---

19 See Ramesh Thakur, 'R2P after Libya and Syria: Engaging Emerging Powers', *The Washington Quarterly*, 36/2: 61–76 (Spring 2013) ; Nathalie Tocci, 'On Power and Norms: Libya, Syria and the Responsibility to Protect', *Global Responsibility to Protect*, 8: 51–75 (2016). Also Michael Ignatieff, 'How Syria Divided the World', *The New York Review of Books*, 11 July 2012, http://www.nybooks.com/daily/2012/07/11/syria-proxy-war-russia-china/, accessed 1 March 2017.

20 See Alex J. Bellamy, 'Libya and the Responsibility to Protect: the Exception and the Norm', *Ethics and International Affairs*, 25/3: 263–269 (2011).

21 See Justin Morris, 'Libya and Syria: R2P and the Spectre of the Swinging Pendulum', *International Affairs*, 89/5: 1265–1283 (2013).

22 S/RES/1970, 26 February 2011.

23 See the Statement by the Permanent Representative of the Russian Federation in the UN Security Council, S/PV.6627, 4 October 2011.

24 A/66/551-S/2011/701, 11 November 2011, para 10.

suite of criteria to be met prior, during and after an operation with a view to achieve greater normative and institutional accountability of those exercising the delegated authority of the UN Security Council.[25] As such, the doctrine goes back to the drawing board and – similar to the ICISS report – seeks a more principled application of R2P in order to facilitate the practical implementation of the norm.

In the economic realm, the global financial crisis of 2008 reinstated the sovereignty of stakeholders and institutions that make the global economic order hang together: the International Monetary Fund (IMF) and the major global economic powers, as represented in the Group of Twenty (G-20). While this ideological crisis of deregulated Western capitalism[26] put the rules and principles underlying liberal economic order – that is, the Washington Consensus – on the negotiation table, it did not lead to a change of key structural principles. Neither did the global financial crisis produce a clear alternative to liberal economic governance – for example, a hypothetical Beijing Consensus of Eastern capitalism. Yet, the renegotiation of the rules and principles underlying global economic order remains a dynamic and non-linear process with an open outcome.

The above discussion suggests three take-home points that are relevant for conceptualising norm diffusion:

1. Any analytical framework on global norm diffusion must capture the *dynamic* and *non-linear* nature of the process.
2. Norm diffusion is a *continuing* process with *ongoing feedback*.
3. The traction and latitude of norms are *not static* but subject to adaptation in line with the feedback provided.

Keeping those take-home points in mind, how can we conceptualise R2P?

The question of how norms are being implemented, how they travel after formal adoption or institutionalisation, has been understudied thus far in international relations theorising.[27] Constructivist concepts tend to explain norm diffusion as a linear top-down process, missing out key parts that are essential for understanding norm implementation and diffusion: the on-going

25 See Marcos Tourinho, Oliver Stuenkel, and Sarah Brockmeier, '"Responsibility while Protecting": Reforming R2P Implementation', *Global Society*, 30/1: 134–150 (2016).

26 See Joseph E. Stiglitz, 'The Ideological Crisis of Western Capitalism', *Project Syndicate*, 6 July 2011.

27 See Alexander Betts and Phil Orchard (eds.), *Implementation and World Politics: How International Norms Change Practice* (Oxford: Oxford University Press, 2014).

review, re-evaluation, and contestation of a norm. The universal adoption of a norm does not create any automatism for similar implementation across countries and regions.[28] Finnemore and Sikkink usefully disaggregate the life cycle of a norm into three stages – emergence, cascade, and internalisation – using the language of tipping or threshold points to explain the cascading effects of global norms through internal socialisation.[29] Yet, their framework displays limits in capturing the non-linear process of R2P implementation; the trajectory from norm emergence to internalisation stays linear.[30] Also, the life cycle is primarily concerned about the globalisation of norms rather than the regional and local dynamics of norm diffusion. Acharya addresses some of these shortcomings in his concept of norm localisation which looks at the 'active construction (through discourse, framing, grafting, and cultural selection) of foreign ideas by local actors', making the global norm compatible with local beliefs and practices.[31] Success or failure of localisation processes depend in particular on the availability of (institutional) mechanisms, for example advocacy networks, to steer the process of localisation in order to achieve normative compatibility. Yet, as Acharya argues himself, the localisation framework essentially looks inward and exclusively focuses on how the domestic level *reacts* to foreign ideas and norms.[32] As a result, the local audience is relegated to the role of norm taker rather than norm shaper. The dynamic relationship between the global and the local levels remains obscure. Krook and True effectively engage with the challenge of existing constructivist models of norm diffusion that present a static picture of norm content and a dynamic

28 See Prantl and Nakano, 'Global Norm Diffusion in East Asia'.

29 Martha Finnemore and Kathryn Sikkink, 'International Norm Dynamics and Political Change', *International Organization*, 52/4: 887–917 (1998).

30 This is a criticism that has come up in other works on shifting international security norms, for example: Wayne Sandholtz, 'Dynamics of International Norm Change', *European Journal of International Relations*, 14/1: 101–131 (2008); M. Patrick Cottrell, *The Evolution and Legitimacy of International Security Institutions* (New York: Cambridge University Press, 2016); Jeffrey S. Lantis, *Arms and Influence: U.S. Technology Innovations and the Evolution of International Security Norms* (Stanford: Stanford University Press, 2016); also Denise Garcia, *Small Arms and Security: New Emerging International Security Norms* (Abingdon: Routledge: 2006).

31 Amitav Acharya, 'How Ideas Spread: Whose Norms Matter? Norm Localization and Institutional Change in Asian Regionalism', *International Organization*, 58/2 (2004), p. 245.

32 See Amitav Acharya, 'Norm Subsidiarity and Regional Orders: Sovereignty, Regionalism, and Rule-Making in the Third World', *International Studies Quarterly*, 55 (2011), p. 97.

picture of norm adoption and implementation.[33] While they offer a discursive approach – defined 'as sense-making practices'[34] – for theorising the life cycles of global norms, in this article, we situate the emergence, adoption, and implementation of those norms in their wider *systemic* context. Yet, Krook and True also emphasise the importance of *power* 'as integral to the processes of social construction, determining what can and cannot be said – and, as a result, who can and cannot speak'.[35] This directly feeds into our argument that the application of R2P in protecting children is limited unless power politics inside and outside the UN Security Council are tamed. We will build our framework on those useful insights.

In the remainder of this section, we present a dynamic framework able to capture the non-linear processes of R2P implementation and norm diffusion. It starts from the observation that R2P is embedded in a complex adaptive system of rules and structural principles that establish a mutually accepted level of appropriateness in international behaviour. Any new norm triggers a disturbance of the current normative system. A new norm is effective if, to use Finnemore's and Sikkink's terminology, it becomes widely cascaded amongst a critical mass of stakeholders in the system, developing a new 'prevailing standard of appropriateness'.[36] This is important because any evaluation of the potential advancement of child protection within the R2P framework is contingent upon our ability to effectively contextualise the diffusion of the R2P norm thus far, to examine where it sits relative to other key norms and principles, and to establish key parameters that help or hinder further implementation. We situate the traction and bandwidth of R2P on a normatisation continuum with three key properties: (1) *obligation* referring to an ideal-type situation where actors are uniformly treaty-bound by a set of rules; (2) *precision* prescribing a code of conduct for actors that guides and restrains their activities; and (3) *delegation* providing actors with the authority to implement, interpret and apply the rules. The traction and bandwidth of R2P therefore ranges on a continuum of hard and soft ends of obligation, precision, and delegation. While we appreciate that constructivists in recent years have challenged the claim that norms need to be legalised or have precision in order to have traction, we hold that

33 See Mona Lena Krook and Jacqui True, 'Rethinking the Life Cycles of International Norms: The United Nations and the Global Promotion of Gender Equality', *European Journal of International Relations*, 18/1: 103–127 (2012).

34 Ibid., p. 108.

35 Ibid.

36 Finnemore and Sikkink, 'International Norm Dynamics', p. 895.

these three properties still provide a useful benchmark to measure the traction of a norm at a given point of time.[37]

In order to grasp the global-regional dynamics of norm diffusion, we introduce the framework of *norm glocalisation* – the processes of feedback, adaptation, and contestation of globally promulgated norms. These processes occur around the particularities of regional, sub-regional, and domestic circumstances. The Oxford Dictionary of New Words traces *glocalisation* back to the Japanese idiom of *dochakuka*, which essentially means 'making it indigenous'.[38] This would come close to Acharya's understanding of inward-looking localisation. However, Japanese corporations used a different term in the 1980s to master the tide of globalisation, that is *genchika*, which signifies a much shallower level of adaptation than *dochakuka*. It means the clever tailoring and advertising of goods to attract local consumers, which even includes the mimicking of global standards without internalising them. In the process of *genchika*, norms are ameliorated to fit the local normative environment. As a result, *genchika* may either adjust or hollow-out the original contents of the norm, leading to three different potential outcomes. First, *genchika* may enable the application of a norm across a diverse range of local cultures and make it compatible *enough* to generate universal traction. Second, *genchika* may mimic the norm without internalising it.[39] And third, *genchika* may hollow-out the global norm to an extent that both its content and spirit become redundant; what remains is a normative Potemkin façade. Applied to R2P, *genchika* explains how norms can exist and coexist together with other structural principles of global and local orders before (or without) reaching the tipping point of full internalisation by international society. It is a pragmatic response to the pressures of global norm promulgation without committing to regional and domestic norm implementation. As a result, the fewer societies internalise the norm at the regional and domestic levels, the shallower the impact at the global level.

However, both *dochakuka* and *genchika* are not simply top-down processes that diffuse at the regional and domestic levels. They feed back into the global contest over the latitude, bandwidth, and depth of R2P. Those processes are

---

37 In a nutshell, the three properties allow us to measure normative traction as an approximate or average rather than a total value. We greatly appreciate the comments of Reviewer 1 who highlighted this conceptual challenge.

38 Sara Tulloch (ed.), *Oxford Dictionary of New Words* (Oxford: Oxford University Press, 1991), p. 134.

39 This would be similar to Iain Johnston's idea of 'mimicking', which connotes a pattern in which states copy the behaviour of a social group 'prior to any detailed ends-means calculation of the benefits of doing so'. Alastair Iain Johnston, *Social States: China in International Institutions, 1980–2000* (Princeton, NJ: Princeton University Press, 2008), p. 23.

non-linear and driven by feedback loops, providing a mechanism for review, re-evaluation, and self-correction by adjusting the properties of R2P on the normatisation continuum according to differences between the actual and the desired output. Feedback loops are different from norm circulation.[40] Despite Acharya's explicit acknowledgment that 'the creation of international norms is never a *one-source, one-way*, or a *one-step* process', his theory of norm circulation is strikingly linear and largely limited to a situation in which 'the less powerful actors feel marginalised in the norm creation process or feel betrayed by the abuse of the norm by the more powerful actors during the implementation stage'.[41]

By contrast, feedback loops apply to the system as a whole and constitute a sustained process where parts of the output provide new input for the progression, retrogression, or stasis of a given norm. Feedback can be generated through all nodes of the system: state actors, non-state actors, social movements, entrepreneurial individuals. The new input is accumulative and may lead to tipping points or threshold events that tip the balance of the system either way. Cause and effect are disproportionate: small events may generate a tipping point tilting the whole system while large events may have no impact at all. Our glocalisation framework is able to capture the non-linearity and the open-endedness of norm diffusion.

We distinguish between negative and positive feedback loops.[42] *Negative feedback* occurs when the pluralist pull factors of international society *contain* any disturbance of the normative system (caused by the creation of new norms), thereby preserving the system in its original form. *System maintenance* is the outcome. *Positive feedback* occurs when the solidarist forces of international society *amplify* any disturbance of the normative system, thereby altering the system in its original form. *System change* is the outcome, usually triggered by tipping points and threshold events.

In sum, the glocalisation framework offers important comparative advantage in capturing the dynamic and non-linear process of R2P implementation and diffusion. Norm diffusion is a complex adaptive system that is subject to on-going feedback that may take form of review, re-evaluation, or contestation as evidenced in the simultaneously evolving Human Security discourse. Norm

40 See Amitav Acharya, 'The Responsibility to Protect and a Theory of Norm Circulation' in Ramesh Thakur and William Maley (eds.), *Theorising the Responsibility to Protect* (Cambridge: Cambridge University Press, 2015), pp. 59–77.

41 Ibid., p. 73.

42 On the challenges of operating in a complex system, see Robert Jervis, *System Effects: Complexity in Political and Social Life* (Princeton: Princeton University Press, 1997).

diffusion occurs in feedback loops – negative and positive – at the global, regional, and domestic levels. The traction and latitude of R2P are not static but range on a normatisation continuum; it is subject to adaptation in line with the feedback provided. This is the operational environment of R2P that needs to be clarified before we can address the question of whether the protection of children in armed conflict could be effectively dealt with under the R2P framework.

The remainder of this article will apply the concept of norm glocalisation. It substantiates our main argument: that integrating normative frameworks of child protection into the R2P framework is bound to be limited unless (a) power politics – especially, but not exclusively, in the UN Security Council – will be tamed, and (b) inherent contradictions between R2P and national and regional normative frameworks of child protection can be reconciled.

R2P and Child Protection

The protection of children in armed conflict is firmly embedded in international humanitarian law. Article 1 of the nearly universally ratified 1989 UN Convention of the Rights of the Child (UNCRC) defines a child as 'every human being below the age of eighteen years unless under the law applicable to the child, majority is attained is earlier'.[43] The four Geneva Conventions of 1949 and the two Additional Protocols of 1977 attribute special protection to children, given their vulnerable status. Article 77 of Additional Protocol I imposes specific obligations on combatants stipulating that '[c]hildren shall be the object of special respect and shall be protected against any form of indecent assault. The Parties to the conflict shall provide them with the care and aid they require, whether because of their age or for any other reason'.[44] Furthermore, the Additional Protocols, for the first time, sought to regulate the participation of children in hostilities ranging from the aiding of combatants – for example the supply of arms and ammunition or assistance in carrying out reconnaissance missions – to their actual recruitment as combatants in national armed forces. Protocol I obligates state parties to undertake all feasible measures to

43 The UNCRC has been ratified by all UN member states with the exception of the United States, South Sudan, and Somalia.

44 Protocol additional to the Geneva Conventions of 12 August 1949, and relating to the protection of victims of international armed conflicts (Protocol I), Chapter II, Article 77, adopted at Geneva on 8 June 1977, available at https://treaties.un.org/doc/publication/unts/volume%201125/volume-1125-i-17512-english.pdf, accessed 5 December 2017.

prevent children under the age of 15 from direct participation in international armed conflict. Article 4, paragraph 3c, of Protocol II extends this provision further by prohibiting both the recruitment and the participation – direct or indirect – of children under 15. Article 38 of the UNCRC further extends the application of Protocol I to non-international armed conflict.

The UN Security Council, since 1999, adopted a series of resolutions to address the plight of children affected by war.[45] Resolution 1261 (1999), operative paragraph 2, identifies six grave violations that affect children most in armed conflict, that is: killing and maiming; recruitment or use as soldiers; sexual violence; abduction; attacks against schools or hospitals; and denial of humanitarian access. Resolution 1314 (2000), operative paragraph 11, requests 'parties to armed conflict to include … provisions for the protection of children, including the disarmament, demobilisation and reintegration of child combatants, in peace negotiations and in peace agreements and the involvement of children … in these processes'. It also sets out a suite of arrangements which regional, sub-regional, and domestic institutions should put in place for the protection of children affected by armed conflict (operative paragraphs 16–18). Resolution 1674 (2006), for the first time, directly connected the agendas of R2P and child protection. It condemns 'in the strongest terms' (operational paragraph 5) violence against children and the recruitment of child soldiers while at the same time reaffirming paragraphs 138 and 139 of the 2005 World Summit Outcome Document that stipulates the responsibility of UN member states 'to protect population from genocide, war crimes, ethnic cleansing, and crimes against humanity' (operational paragraph 4). The parallel references to R2P and violence against children in armed conflict create *political* (rather than legal) space to forge a diplomatic response in implementing the child protection norm along R2P objectives. In effect, the R2P and child protection norm agendas have become intertwined.

More than 20 years after the publication of the influential 1996 Machel Report[46] that drew global attention to the devastating consequences of armed conflict experienced by children, the Security Council has developed a normative framework, including tools, to meet its responsibilities under international law vis-à-vis the protection of children. Over 115,000 children have been

45 See UN Documents S/RES/1261 (1999), 30 August 1999; S/RES/1314 (2000), 11 August 2000; S/RES/1379 (2001), 20 November 2001; S/RES/1460 (2003), 30 January 2003; S/RES/1539 (2004), 22 April 2004; S/RES/1612 (2005), 26 July 2005; S/RES/1882 (2009), 4 August 2009; S/RES/1998 (2011), 12 July 2011; S/RES/2068 (2012), 19 September 2012; S/RES/2143 (2014), 7 March 2014; S/RES/2225 (2015), 18 June 2015.

46 See UN Document A/51/306, 26 August 1996.

released from armed forces since 2000; 25 action plans have been signed with parties to conflict in order to stop violations against children.[47] In 2005, the Security Council established a formal mechanism to monitor, review, and report on abuses of children in armed conflict based on the aforementioned six grave violations, which is effectively a naming-and-shaming tool to hold state parties accountable for their responsibilities under international law. The Monitoring and Reporting Mechanism identifies the parties to a conflict who commit one (or several) of the six violations as stipulated above.

However, the 2016 report of the UN Secretary-General on children and armed conflict 'highlights the increased intensity of situations of armed conflict' which are 'directly related to the denigration of the respect for international humanitarian and human rights law by parties to conflict'.[48] For example, in Syria, the year of 2016 was 'the worst year ... since child casualties have been formally documented', with six million children now formally depending on humanitarian assistance and almost three million displaced.[49]

This brings us to the central puzzle of this paper. Why is it that, despite rather elaborate legal normative frameworks of child protection and after the UN International Decade for a Culture of Peace and Non-Violence for the Children of the World (2001–2010), we have made only limited progress in addressing the marginalisation and disempowerment of children in armed conflict?

Three observations are in order. First, the current international legal framework of child protection 'is far removed from the complex processes that shape, rupture and reshape global conflict'.[50] Situating the child protection norm on the normatisation continuum with the key properties of obligation, precision, and delegation, child protection seems to be a robust global norm. As far as obligation is concerned, the state parties are bound by treaty to a suite of rules that guides and restrains the treatment of children in armed conflict. The prescribed code of conduct is fairly precise. Delegation to implement, interpret and apply the rules is left to the state parties, which constitutes one obvious weak point. In sum, looked at from a legal point of view, the child protection norm ranges at the hard end of the obligation and precision continuum, while

47 See *Concept note: Security Council open debate on children and armed conflict*, UN Document S/2016/662, 29 July 2016, p. 2.

48 See UN Document A/70/836, 20 April 2016, paragraph 4.

49 UNICEF, *Hitting Rock Bottom: How 2016 Became The Worst Year for Syria's Children*, March 2017, p. 2.

50 Bina D'Costa, Kim Huynh and Katrina Lee-Koo, 'Introduction: Why Children Matter to Global Conflict' in Kim Huynh, Bina D'Costa and Katrina Lee-Koo (eds.), *Children and Global Conflict* (Cambridge: Cambridge University Press, 2015), p. 5.

the delegation of enforcement stays at the soft end.[51] However, the universalism and abstraction of child protection in many respects is a Potemkin façade concealing the fundamental differences – regional, cultural, religious – and tensions between global and domestic understandings of childhood. Multiple (legitimate) understandings of childhood co-exist across societies and cultural traditions.

Second, underlying the global child protection norm is an arbitrary age-contingent construction of childhood that is prominently framed by Western liberal legal ideas. This is compounded by the circumstance that many domestic societies conceptualise childhood through a social rather than legal lens.[52] There are clear limits to which the globally very diverse social dimension of childhood has been glocalised. What is missing thus far are the feedback loops necessary to produce a child protection norm that has enough bandwidth and traction across the global, regional, and domestic levels. Amongst the international instruments on child protection, the UNCRC is the most glocalised convention, with a fairly deep engagement between state parties, intergovernmental organisations and NGOs representing a vast range of regional, cultural, and religious stakeholders across the globe. Yet, some have argued:

> ...that the keen interest that states showed to sign the treaty had more to do with the perception that the UNCRC was a 'soft' treaty based on various values that are fundamental to cultures across the globe rather than a genuine commitment to children's rights.[53]

Third, despite the solidarist push to develop fairly elaborate global child protection standards, strong pluralist pullback makes the uniform application of the norm very difficult. It is not only the power constellation *within* the UN Security Council that makes advances in the protection of civilians in armed conflict difficult; power politics outside the Council exacerbate this situation. For example, the 2016 report of the UN Secretary-General on Children and armed conflict listed a Saudi Arabia-led (and U.S. backed) military

51 This is further complicated by the circumstance that the vast majority of parties to a conflict committing violations against children are non-state armed groups rather than state armies. See *Concept note for the Security Council open debate on children and armed conflict: child victims of non-State armed groups*, UN Document S/2015/168, 6 March 2015.

52 Katrina Lee-Koo, 'Children and Armed Conflict: Mapping the Terrain' in *Children and Global Conflict*, p. 11.

53 Bina D'Costa, 'The Rights of the Child: Political History, Practices and Protection' in *Children and Global Conflict*, p. 105.

coalition in Yemen amongst a list of armies that had undertaken attacks on schools and hospitals, killing children.[54] However, the coalition was removed from the list 'pending review' shortly after the publication of the report.[55] According to the Secretary-General, Saudi Arabia threatened to discontinue funding for humanitarian operations in the Palestinian territories, South Sudan, and Syria, if he did not take the coalition off the list.[56] Under the new UN Secretary-General, António Guterres, the Saudi-led coalition was added again to Annex I of the latest report in August 2017.[57] In sum, any effective universal norm implementation requires the proactive engagement with the power politics of global norms.

As this section has demonstrated, the normative agendas of R2P and the protection of children are legally separable but not politically separate. While Resolution 1674 (2006) formally linked the prevention of violence against children in armed conflict to R2P objectives, there are serious questions about whether R2P would be the most obvious avenue to pursue the protection of children and the prevention of violence against them. In both the R2P and child protection cases, taming power politics – inside and outside of the UN Security Council – imposes considerable constraints in advancing the norms. Furthermore, without squaring the inherent contradictions between global protection frameworks and domestic norms of child protection, the traction of the child protection norm stays limited. Hence, the bulk of social work needs to be done behind the Potemkin façade of universal norms, a bottom-up rather than top-down process that would need to be driven by careful intervention of civil society, globally, regionally, and domestically.

In light of the above, even with the most elaborate normative framework in place, the protection of children in armed conflict remains a *diplomatic* rather than legal challenge. References to the norm create *political* space and legitimacy for those with the commitment to act.

Japan and the Promotion of Child Protection

Japan is a powerful case to illustrate the limits of the contemporary application of R2P in protecting children. While the country formally endorsed R2P at

54 See UN Document A/70/836-S/2016/360, 20 April 2016.

55 See UN Document A/70/836/Add. 1-S/2016/360/Add. 1, 24 June 2016.

56 See 'United Nations Chief Exposes Limits to His Authority by Citing Saudi Threat', *The New York Times*, 9 June 2016.

57 See UN Document A/72/361-S/2017/821, 24 August 2017, p. 40.

the World Summit in 2005, it never internalised the norm. As the global legal framework of the protection of children has evolved, Japan has taken several measures to promote the child protection norm both internally and externally. After ratifying the 1989 Convention of the Rights of the Child in 1994, the most significant efforts that Japan made were amendments to the Enforcement Regulation on the Self-Defense Forces Law and the Instruction Concerning the Recruitment of Youth Cadets, allowing Japan to ratify the 2002 Optional Protocol to the Convention of the Rights of the Child on the involvement of children in armed conflict.[58] Other measures to localise the spirit of the Convention have included the establishment of the Education Rebuilding Council and the development of National Youth Development Policy.[59]

Internationally, the Japanese government has promoted Human Security as the master framework for the protection of children in armed conflicts. In the 2008 report to the Committee on the Rights of the Child, the Japanese government argued that 'Based upon this concept [Human Security], Japan has been reinforcing its support in response to the growing needs for relief of children around the world who have been affected by conflicts and/or natural disasters.'[60] Japan recognises the need to tackle the root causes of children's problems. Koichi Haraguchi, Japan's Ambassador to the UN, stated in 2003 that protection and empowerment should go side by side,[61] Assuming that the background of child soldiers is, in most cases, poverty and social exclusion, Professor Yasushi Katsuma of Waseda University further argues that 'empowerment' is required to make children resilient to downside risks.[62] Provision for

58 Article 1 of Optional Protocol to the Convention on the Rights of the Child on the involvement of children in armed conflict demands that States ensure that members of their armed forces who have not attained the age of 18 years do not take a direct part in hostilities. See Ministry of Foreign Affairs of Japan, 'The first report of Japan under the Optional Protocol to the Convention on the Rights of the Child on the involvement of children in armed conflict', April 2008, p. 2, http://www.mofa.go.jp/policy/human/child/report_a8.pdf, accessed 17 October 2017.

59 Ministry of Foreign Affairs of Japan, 'The third report of Japan under article 44, paragraph 1 of the Convention on the Right of the Child', April 2008, http://www.mofa.go.jp/policy/human/child/report_a44.pdf, accessed 17 October 2017.

60 Ibid.

61 Ministry of Foreign Affairs of Japan, 'Statement by H.E. Ambassador Koichi Haraguchi, Permanent Representative of Japan to the United Nations on the Protection of Civilians in Armed Conflict', 9 December 2003, http://www.mofa.go.jp/announce/speech/un0312-3.html, accessed 17 October 2017.

62 Yasushi Katsuma, 'Buryoku Funso ka no Eikyo wo Uketa Kodomo no Anzen Hosho wo meguru Kokusaiteki na Torikumi' [A Search for the Security of Children Affected by Armed Conflicts], *Ajia Taiheiyo Tokyu*, 17: 125–126 (October 2011).

education, and other social services, is essential to the prevention of children from returning to combat. United Nations International Children's Emergency Fund (UNICEF), a major international organisation for the assistance of children, used the UN Trust Fund of Human Security, which was founded with Japan's initial contribution of about 500 million yen, to assist children in post-conflict situations, ranging from the reconstruction of primary education and the introduction of a new integrated curriculum in Kosovo (2002–2005) to humanitarian programs for internationally displaced and unsettled populations in Somalia (2003–2005), and to victim assistance and landmine risk education in Sudan (2006–2008). The wellbeing of children born and living within armed conflicts requires a wide range of support. Japan regards Human Security as the most practical tool to address not just physical violence but also mental health problems that would threaten the lives of children.

Japan's strong preference for using the framework of Human Security to implement the child protection norm derives from its domestic normative context that makes the government very cautious vis-à-vis R2P. First and foremost, Japan's post-war constitution limits the use of force to self-defense as a matter of principle. This constitutional constraint is supported by a deep-seated culture of antimilitarism in Japan.[63] Although the majority of the Japanese recognise the importance of US military power for their national security, their opinions over the use of military action to suppress terrorism and promote democracy overseas are far more critical.[64] Second, Japan is hesitant to confer authority for unilateral military intervention to any states or organisations. As the cases of Libya and Syria have shown, intervention without consensus drives a wedge inside and outside UN Security Council. With its own historical baggage of invading Asia, Japan is hesitant to support military enforcement even for the aim of protecting civilians during war. Through *genchika*, Japan has been able to fulfil the commitments arising from the formal endorsement of R2P in 2005, without abandoning the predominant local norm of Human Security.[65] In particular, obligations under Pillar Two of R2P are broadly compatible with the Human Security agenda. In this context, *genchika* turned R2P

63 See Glenn D. Hook, *Militarization and Demilitarization in Contemporary Japan* (London and New York: Routledge, 1996); Thomas Berger, *Cultures of Antimilitarism: National Security in Germany and Japan* (Baltimore, MD: The Johns Hopkins University Press, 1998).

64 Paul Midford, *Rethinking Japanese Public Opinion and Security* (Stanford: Stanford University Press, 2011).

65 This especially refers to the international commitment to provide assistance to states in building capacity to meet their obligations under R2P, a goal that is broadly compatible with the Human Security agenda.

into a domestic Potemkin façade that allows Japan to appear compliant with R2P commitments without internalising this norm. As a result, R2P coexists with Human Security without generating normative traction.

Prior to the emergence of R2P in the international arena, Japan had internalised Human Security as a new concept of humanitarian assistance. Although conceptual and practical concerns about Human Security have been raised and discussed in Japan as in other countries, the focus on 'human' assistance sounds more acceptable to a public whose concern is caring and helping the weak and vulnerable.[66] Internationally, the Japanese government has enthusiastically promoted this concept based on a multilateral, consensus-based approach. After the Outcome Document of the World Summit 2005 mentioned both R2P and Human Security, Japan accelerated its drive to clarify the Human Security concept and to develop consensus over its definition. Prior to Japan's efforts, Canada and Norway had initiated the Human Security Network (HSN) to tackle a wide range of agendas including the protection of civilians in armed conflicts. However, Japan started a separate platform, the Friends of Human Security, with Mexico in 2006, assuming that Human Security does not have a military enforcement component whereas R2P does. While the HSN was dominated by Western, mostly European, states, the Friends forum increased the membership, from the initial 24 countries and 7 UN institutions to more than 100 countries (including China, Russia, and Pakistan) and 11 UN institutions in 2009.[67] While Canada and other HSN participants later withdrew their language of Human Security,[68] Japan and Mexico introduced the Human Security agenda to the General Assembly, which led to the opening of the Informal Thematic Debate on Human Security in 2008. By pushing the Human Security envelope internationally and forming a global issue coalition, Japan fed its concerns vis-à-vis R2P back to the UN level and effectively introduced Human Security as an alternative – and far less controversial – security norm.

To mainstream Human Security within the UN, it was necessary to achieve normative compatibility on a global scale. Such an effort started at an earlier

66 With a firm recognition that Human Security is the right concept to develop a more humane global society in future, a Graduate Program on Human Security and other related programs were established in Tokyo University and other leading universities in Japan.

67 Takahiro Shinyo, 'Nihon no Ningen Anzen Hosho Seisaku to Sono Gaikoteki Jissen' [Japan's Policy on Human Security and Its Implementation], *Kokusai Kokyo Seisaku Kenkyu*, 13/1: 39–52 (2008–2009).

68 Robert J. Bookmiller and Kirsten Nakjavani Bookmiller, 'Canada and the Human Security Network (1998–2010): RIP?', *British Journal of Canadian Studies*, 23/2: 246–271 (2010).

stage of addressing Human Security in the late 1990s. To attract the interests of African diplomats, Yukio Sato, then Japanese ambassador to the UN (1998–2002), referred to the life, living and dignity of 'community' instead of 'individual,' and raised poverty reduction as a key agenda of Human Security.[69] Japan also moved the ideas of 'self-help' and 'national ownership' to the fore. The 2003 ODA White Paper attributes the importance of 'self-help' to Japan's own experience of modernisation after the Meiji Restoration, and its successful postwar economic recovery and development while receiving loans from the World Bank from 1953 to 1966.[70] This official narrative of Japan's own 'self-help' story assumes that both the governments and the people are engaged in the development of national economy, and it creates the image that aid to the government is equivalent to empowerment of the people.[71] This image allows the Japanese government to portray its aid program as a more interactive, two-way process while the concept of 'national ownership' fits well in the local normative framework of aid recipient countries that resist forceful intervention. In other words, the rhetorical and conceptual manoeuvring of Human Security allows it to better fit within the local normative frameworks both in Japan and beyond.

Japan's approach to distinguishing Human Security from R2P was incorporated into the 2010 Secretary-General's follow-up report. This report defined Human Security as 'comprehensive, people-centred, context-specific and prevention-oriented' and made it clear that Human Security differed from R2P since 'the use of force is not envisaged in the application of the human security concept'.[72] In 2012, the General Assembly also adopted a draft resolution jointly submitted by Japan and Jordan that confirms that 'Human Security is distinct from the responsibility to protect and its implementation' as it 'does not entail the threat or the use of force or coercive measures'.[73] Both documents ensure the importance of national ownership in dealing with the Human Security agenda. This understanding allows Human Security to address broader agendas of protecting and empowering vulnerable people and widens the *political* space for action by integrating various humanitarian projects and

69 Yukio Sato, 'Nihon no Kokuren Gaiko to Ningen no Anzen Hosho', *Kokusai Mondai*, 530 (March 2004), p. 7.

70 Ministry of Foreign Affairs of Japan, ODA White Paper, 1993, http://www.mofa.go.jp/mofaj/gaiko/oda/shiryo/hakusyo/03_hakusho/index.htm, accessed 17 October 2017.

71 Mitsuhiro Udagawa, 'Nihon no Enjo Rinen to shite no Jijodoryoku Shien no Kokusai Seijiron teki Kosatu' [The Study of Self-help as Japan's ODA Philosophy in International Politics], *Kokusai Seiji*, 186: 113–128 (January 2017).

72 UN Document A/64/701, 8 March 2010.

73 UN Document A/Res/66/290, 22 October 2012.

related agendas into the Human Security framework while avoiding the power political constraints on implementation that have been the case for R2P.

Japan's comprehensive Human Security approach simultaneously pushed R2P to the preventive and capacity-building focus of R2P, described as Pillar Two in the 2009 report of the Secretary General on Implementing the Responsibility to Protect s.[74] This is the outcome of the *genchika* process (clever tailoring to attract locals), which enables the application of R2P in Japan, but is remarkably shallower than the *dochakuka* (making it indigenous) of Human Security. Japan is unwilling to engage in the implementation of R2P due to a fear of damaging the legacy of Japan's consensus-based approach. In contrast to R2P, Human Security is also an arena where Japan can develop independently and does not have to change the preexisting local normative frameworks of Japan and other countries.

In sum, the Japanese case illustrates that there are limitations in applying R2P to child protection that go well beyond the constraints of power politics. Even if power politics inside and outside the UN Security Council can be tamed, the inherent contradictions between the global R2P norm and national and regional normative frameworks of child protection, strongly suggest a suite of different entry points to strengthen the protection of children in armed conflict. These will be highlighted in the following section.

Conclusions: Moving Forward Sideways

In this paper, we addressed the puzzle of why existing normative frameworks of child protection are limited in coping with the extremely complex role that children play in armed conflict. Children are marginalised, disempowered, and vulnerable to the destruction of armed conflict that turns the everyday life of their childhood upside down. They are also central actors and perpetrators in armed conflict. Hence, children operate far from the ideal-type global legal conceptions of child protection that portray them as pre-political human beings without political consciousness and without the capacity to contribute to the development of societies. The dilemma of child protection is particularly evident in societies where 50% or more of the total population is under the age of eighteen.[75] The child protection norm in those cases must be embedded

74 This is further examined in Prantl and Nakano, 'Global Norm Diffusion in East Asia'.

75 This is, for example, the case in Angola (52%), Ethiopia (53%), Ghana (51%), Liberia (50%), Mozambique (51%), Sierra Leone (50%), and Uganda (56%). Quoted in D'Costa, 'The Rights of the Child', p. 91.

into the wider context of a country's complex processes that promote, derail, and reform transitions from war to peace.

This paper also stressed that great power management is one of the key nodes that holds the normative system together, and must be part and parcel of any successful norm implementation. Those are the necessary conditions to shape and implement the underlying rules and principles of global normative order. The solidarist push of international society that has led to the expansion of the universal human rights regime and the pluralist pull that causes its contraction have created a manifest tension that states and societies must address through diplomatic rather than legal channels. So far, the UN Security Council's parallel references to R2P and violence against children in armed conflict have widened the *political* space to forge a diplomatic response in implementing the child protection norm along R2P objectives. However, while the R2P and child protection norm agendas have become intertwined, this article has expressed doubts as to whether this avenue ought to be pursued under a new Responsibility to Protect Children in Armed Conflict (R2PCAC). The language of responsibility is deliberately chosen 'for conferring authority and allocating powers rather than [...] for imposing binding obligations and commanding obedience'.[76] Yet it may find different expressions across regions, cultures, and languages, like Japan's adoption of Human Security rather than R2P. The R2P and the child protection norm need to be glocalised in order to find their way into the contest over the principles that shape the code of conduct in global order. A global child protection norm with traction ought to have enough semantic bandwidth and flexibility to generate authority in a wide range of audiences. This is what 'moral globalisation' is about, 'the steady enlargement of the audiences before which we feel we must justify ourselves'.[77] Glocalisation is the process that constantly reviews, contest, and adapts the content of a norm through feedback loops to advance norm promulgation and implementation.

Ultimately, the careful calibration of local, regional, and global interventions of civil society – that is, advocacy – appears to be the most promising entry point in strengthening the child protection norm.[78] Encouraging further commitments by UN member states to provide safeguards for children

---

76 Anne Orford, *International Authority and the Responsibility to Protect* (Cambridge: Cambridge University Press, 2011), p. 26.

77 Michael Ignatieff, 'Human Rights, Global Ethics, and the Ordinary Virtues', *Ethics and International Affairs*, 31/1 (2017), p. 15.

78 Bina D'Costa, 'Who Speaks for Children? Advocacy, Activism and Resistance' in *Children and Global Conflict*, pp. 249–281.

in armed conflict, especially by adhering to the principles of *distinction* and *proportionality* under international humanitarian law appears to be another.[79]

Eleanor Roosevelt's dictum posed in 1958, ten years after the adoption of the Universal Declaration of Human Rights, still holds that universal human rights – be it R2P or child protection – start at home.

---

79 See UN Document A/72/361-S/2017/821, 24 August 2017, para 236.

Representing Children

∴

Responsibility to Protect the Future: Children on the Move and the Politics of Becoming

Jana Tabak
PUC-Rio, Brazil
jtabak@gmail.com

Letícia Carvalho
PUC Minas, Brazil
leticiacarvalho@pucminas.br

Abstract

Protection, development, progress: this is the trilogy of promises carried by the international framework for protecting young people. Based on the analysis of the UNICEF *Unfairy Tales* project videos, this article aims to unveil the fierce battle over the meaning of children for the international arena. Specifically, how the compelling claim for an international responsibility to protect children contains a promise of a progressive future to global politics. The focus is on the discursive manoeuvres that articulate the so called 'children on the move' as the epitome of vulnerability, positioning them as requiring protection; and, at the same time, as the image of a future at risk, threatened by violence and the prospects of an uncivilised becoming. We intend to discuss how this ambivalent understanding of childhood might produce limits to contemporary application of child protection practices.

Keywords

children on the move – protection – UNICEF – *Unfairy Tales*

* The authors would like to thank Capes and CNPq for funding part of this research and both anonymous reviewers for their comments, suggestions and criticisms.

 | DOI:10.1163/9789004379534_007

The contemporary migration crisis is shedding light on many challenging features of international politics. However global the world may have become, our political imagination remains limited by the imaginative geography of the sovereign state,[1] which is informed by a relatively fixed connection between territory, population and maintenance of security.[2] Within this framework, human movement between sovereignties – especially when these humans are uninvited, unwanted and undocumented as is the case for most forced migrants – arouses contrasting reactions. They range from xenophobic demonstrations and concern with negative impacts of population flows over national economy and security, to claims about the responsibility of international society to protect and promote human rights.

The movement of children is possibly the most shocking face of the flows of internally displaced persons, asylum seekers, refugees and migrants. According to the UNICEF, nearly 1 in 200 children in the world today is a child refugee and 1 in 8 migrants is a child.[3] In 2015 and 2016, at least 300,000 unaccompanied and separated children moving across borders were registered in 80 different countries, becoming easy prey for human trafficking and many forms of abuse and exploitation.[4] More than any other present problem, 'children on the move'[5] – especially when these children are unaccompanied and unprotected – pose a challenge to our[6] future. This is so because we associate the biological immaturity of children with the lack of a series of properties and capacities that are still to be developed. Children's path of social development is understood as a process of *human becoming*, a repository of hope and wishes for the future. According to our orthodox accounts of normality, physical, psychological or social deviations in this path from child to adulthood represent a risk to our ideal(ised) future.

1 Michael Shapiro, *Reading the Postmodern Polity: Political Theory as Textual Practice* (Minneapolis: University of Minnesota Press, 1992).

2 Michel Foucault, *Security, Territory, Population: Lectures at the Collège de France 1977–1978* (New York: Picador, 2009).

3 UNICEF, *Uprooted: The Growing Crisis for Refugee and Migrant Children*, 30 October, 2016.

4 UNICEF, *A Child is a Child: Protecting Children on the Move from Violence, Abuse and Exploitation*, 3 May, 2017.

5 Jacqueline Bhabha, *Child Migration & Human Rights in a Global Age* (Princeton: Princeton University Press, 2014).

6 In this article, 'Our/We' refers to the general modern western-based category that informs most protection practices unfolded by international organisations, non-governmental organisations and states.

In September 2015, the body of a three-year-old boy found on a beach in Turkey reached the front pages of newspapers all over the world. The story of Aylan Kurdi and his family has revived the debate about the tens of millions of people that are on the move globally and the possible deleterious effects of present circumstances on future prospects. In January 2016, the French satirical magazine Charlie Hebdo published a cartoon with the question 'what would little Aylan become if he'd grown up?' The image depicted what would be a grown-up Aylan as a sexual molester, alluding to sexual assault incidents allegedly caused by migrants in Germany on New Year's Eve.[7] A few days later, Jordan's Queen Rania hit back at the magazine sharing another cartoon in her Facebook page. In the image, we could see the boy completing his development cycle, playing and learning until becoming an adult. In her message, she said that little Aylan could have become 'a doctor, a teacher, a loving parent …'[8]

In both cartoons what is at stake is not who Aylan really was, but who he might have become, raising the question of how discursive battles over our perception of people on the move shape national, regional and international action. Taking part in the dispute, in March 2016, UNICEF has launched a series of animated films and an interactive e-book telling true stories of children who fled conflict zones in order to help framing positive perceptions towards them.[9] According to their press release, 'the *Unfairy Tales* are part of an initiative, #ActOfHumanity, emphasizing that children are children, no matter where they come from, and that every child has rights and deserves a fair chance'.[10]

Based on the analysis of the UNICEF *Unfairy Tales* project videos, this article aims to unveil the fierce battle over the meaning of children and children

7 Amanda Meade, 'Charlie Hebdo cartoon depicting drowned child Alan Kurdi sparks racism debate', *The Guardian*, 14 January 2016, https://www.theguardian.com/media/2016/jan/14/charlie-hebdo-cartoon-depicting-drowned-child-alan-kurdi-sparks-racism-debate, accessed 10 August 2016.

8 Will Worley, 'Queen Rania of Jordan commissions Aylan Kurdi cartoon in response to Charlie Hebdo', *The Independent*, 17 January 2016, http://www.independent.co.uk/news/world/middle-east/charlie-hebdo-receive-backlash-by-queen-rania-of-jordan-over-aylan-kurdi-cartoon-a6817166.html, accessed 20 January 2017.

9 UNICEF, 'UNICEF launches "Unfairy Tales" of refugee and migrant children', 29 March 2016, https://www.unicef.org/media/media_90760.html, accessed 7 June 2016.

10 Ibid.

forced migrants for the international arena. Specifically, how the compelling claim for an international responsibility to protect children contains a promise of a progressive future to global politics. The focus is on the discursive manoeuvres that articulate the so called 'children on the move' as the epitome of vulnerability, positioning them as requiring protection; and, at the same time, as the image of a future at risk, threatened by violence and the prospects of an uncivilised becoming.

In order to do so, the article is divided into four sections, besides this introduction. The first section analyses three short animations produced by the UNICEF as part of the *Unfairy Tales* Project. Informed by the perspective of childhood studies, the second section analyses and problematises how the so-called children's rights milestones authorise and normalise a particular notion of the child and childhood. Then, the third section shows how the UNICEF videos reproduce this interplay between norm and deviation, while highlighting the necessity of protecting children on the move. Finally, the last section discusses how our ambivalent understanding of childhood produces limits to contemporary application of child protection practices.

Unfairy Tales

Sweet and happy music accompanies the title written in a cute and colourful font style that *introduces* us to three stories of three forced migrant children. The titles of each story: 'Mustafa Goes for a Walk', 'Malak and the Boat' and 'The Story of Ivine and Pillow'[11] are ordinary ones and would not be out of place on any children's book (Figure 1). But, suddenly, when the story begins, there is no 'once upon a time' and these 'childish' aspects of each animation give room to elements of war that invade children's daily lives. The colours, together with (normal) ingredients of childhood – happiness and safety – disappear as darkness, monsters, loneliness and tears take over, transforming those children's lives into nightmares – or 'unfairy tales'. The message through the three short animations is very clear: although these stories are not unusual – at least 30 million children and young people globally are on the move trying to escape from conflict, poverty and extreme weather[12] – they are also not what we imagine a normal childhood should be. At the end of the day, these children on the move are *out of place*.

11 All three videos are available at UNICEF's *Unfairy Tales* project page, https://www.unicef.org/emergencies/childrenonthemove/unfairytales/en, accessed 7 June 2016.

12 UNICEF, *Uprooted: The Growing Crisis for Refugee and Migrant Children*, 30 October 2016.

FIGURE 1 Unfairy Tales *project homepage.*[13]

The borders of this particular *place* called *childhood*, from which these children should never have left, are carefully drawn throughout these three animations. The 13-year-old Mustafa tells us the horror behind why he fled his home: in virtue of the war in Syria, he was always afraid and his family was completely destroyed – in the video, one by one they are blown up and disappear from the dining table – so he left carrying his toys that he 'loved very much'.[14] However, it was very long and tiring walk so that Mustafa had to leave his toys

13 UNICEF, *Unfairy Tales* project homepage.

14 UNICEF, 'Mustafa goes for a Walk: a Journey from Syria', UNICEF video, 2:16. 29 March 2016, https://www.unicef.org/emergencies/childrenonthemove/unfairytales/en, accessed 7 June 2016.

behind. The joy of his childhood turned into sadness, a change illustrated by the boy's robot crying when it sees his friend leaving. Sadness, loneliness and fear are the only possible feelings when Mustafa departs from the 'childhood place'.

Also fleeing from Syria but in a different kind of journey, 7-year-old Malak, the youngest of the three children, tells us about her voyage in a leaky boat across the Mediterranean. There, she is the only child and the adults, except for Malak's mother who wears a purple scarf, look all the same: colourless, faceless ghostly figures that are incapable of protecting her. In Malak's words: 'Once it moved, water started getting onto the boat (…) I was very, very, very cold. After I got cold, I was very, very, very scared'.[15] Then, a different music emerges, transitioning viewers to a tense moment in which storm takes over and Malak's fears materialise in the form of a giant sea monster that pushes the small crowd in the boat to the limits between life and death. When morning finally comes, it brings hope to the story. Amid celestial chords and calm waves, Malak is still alive in her tiny leaky boat and, although the loss of family and friends will certainly haunt her for years to come, she will have a chance to grow old and complete her development cycle from child to adulthood.

The third video starts with a 'very afraid' 14-year-old Ivine and her pillow hiding in the living room while bombs explode all around her house. Rescued by her mother, Ivine escapes from Syria, running through streets covered with blood and getting in an inflatable boat full of terrified people. After a storm, Ivine and her mother reach a desert beach, only to walk day and night searching from help. Hungry, unsheltered and exhausted, Ivine is haunted by phantoms of war. The only comfort to her tears is her polka dot pillow, a fragile link to the years of innocence that are now far behind her. As she is forced out of childhood, Ivine asks herself: 'Why life is so hard?'[16]

The unsettling endings of Mustafa, Malak and Ivine's journeys are clearly not fairy tale finishes. Although daylight eventually finds these children in more stable environments – calm seas and refugee camps – they are bleak places, like a poor canvas that is permanently missing its colours. This lingering feeling that there is something forever lost in these children's stories is put in words at the end of the videos with a simple statement – 'some stories were

---

15 UNICEF, 'Malak and the Boat: a Journey from Syria', UNICEF video, 1:57. 29 March 2016, https://www.unicef.org/emergencies/childrenonthemove/unfairytales/en/video/malak-and-the-boat, accessed 7 June 2016.

16 UNICEF, 'The Story of Ivine and Pillow', UNICEF video, 2:35. 29 March 2016, https://www.unicef.org/emergencies/childrenonthemove/unfairytales/en/video/the-story-of-ivine-and-pillow, accessed 7 June 2016.

never meant for children' – and a compelling call for action: you can change the story for children like Mustafa/Ivine with an '#ActOfHumanity'.[17]

Through the animations and this particular message by UNICEF at the end of each video, Mustafa, Malak and Ivine are articulated – rightly or wrongly, for better or worse – as carriers of our world's future and, because of that, helping them is not only an act of humanity, but it is surely an act *for* humanity. In light of this, the next section relies on the perspectives of childhood studies to critically reflect on children's rights milestones and to challenge the limits that articulate a norm about childhood and its children. Our idea is to discuss the complexities, silences and power relations that permeate and are authorised by supposedly ordinary concepts – child, childhood, child forced migrants. Furthermore, we explore how these ideas participate in the establishment and maintenance of the promise of a better future for international politics.

Hoping for a Better Future: Protecting Children, Producing 'the' Child

In 1924, long before the establishment of the rights of *human beings* in 1948 through the adoption of the 'Universal Declaration of Human Rights' (UDHR), children's special international status was formally defined by the League of Nations when it adopted the 'Geneva Declaration of the Rights of the Child'.[18] In five short sentences, the document called mainly for the national and international provision of children's economic, social and psychological needs. Its provisions are premised on what the Declaration calls the 'duty' that 'mankind owes to the Child'.[19] In this sense, although the title suggests that the child was already conceived of as having individual rights, the language of the Declaration evokes certain moral imperatives for adults in their behaviour towards children who are (re)produced as vulnerable and weak objects incapable of carrying any legal entitlements.[20]

Since then, various child-specific and general human rights treaties have been adopted internationally, reflecting the gradual recognition of children

17 UNICEF, 'The Story of Ivine and Pillow'; 'Mustafa Goes for a Walk'.

18 In terms of the protection of children at the national, domestic level, the concerns with child-saving activities for the enjoyment of childhood became central in the political agenda of modern states in late nineteenth century. See Hugh Cunningham, *Children and Childhood in Western Society Since 1500* (United Kingdom: Pearson Education Limited, 2005).

19 John Wall, 'Human Rights in Light of Childhood', *International Journal of Children's Rights*, 16/4: 523–554 (2008), p. 534.

20 Anna Holzscheiter, *Children's Rights in International Politics: The Transformative Power of Transnational Discourse* (New York: Palgrave Macmillan, 2010).

as a separate social group as particularly defenceless, innocent and worthy of protection as the representatives of a future generation who is entitled to standards different from those for adults.[21] Of global appeal, the special status of children as the potential promise of a better future has rendered them, thus, in a particular position: uniquely vulnerable and relegated to an innocent and happy phase of human existence, still undeveloped, and thus uniquely targeted and subjected to new forms of control.[22]

Considering these children's rights milestones,[23] the focus of this section is on the discursive manoeuvres that articulate children as the epitome of vulnerability, positioning them as requiring protection; and, at the same time, as the image of a future at risk, when children, like the ones on the move, by having experienced episodes of violence and loss, transit between the notion of victim and the notion of the child as a threat, who did not follow the 'natural' stages into becoming a 'normal' adult. More specifically, we investigate how an ensemble of statements and narratives about childhood is articulated internationally, normalising what a child is supposed to be and authorising practices of protection, care and control. In turn, these practices discipline children's journeys towards becoming full modern adult citizens, forging a model that contains a promise of a progressive future to international relations.

According to the 'Declaration of the Rights of the Child', children should enjoy a happy childhood.[24] Although, there is nothing wrong about being happy, our focus here is on shedding light on the difference between this formulation and the 'Universal Declaration of Human Rights',[25] the goal of which is to promote everyone's right to 'life, liberty and security', but not specifically a happy life. Furthermore, according to this Declaration, in order to be happy, amid many recommendations, children must specifically play, grow up within a loving family atmosphere and go to school.

---

21 Ibid.

22 Jacqueline Bhabha, 'The Child: What Sort of Human?', *PMLA*, 121/5: 1526–1535 (2006).

23 The children's rights milestones, which are analysed here, include: League of Nations, *Geneva Declaration of the Rights of the Child*, 26 September 1924; UNGA, *Universal Declaration of Human Rights*, A/RES/ 217 A, 10 December 1948; UNGA, *Declaration of the Rights of the Child*, A/RES/1386 (XIV), 10 December 1959; UNGA, *International Year of the Child*, A/RES/34/4, 18 October 1979; UNGA, *Convention on the Rights of the Child*, Treaty Series, vol. 1577, 20 November 1989; UNGA, *World Summit for Children*, A/RES/45/217, 21 December 1990; UNICEF, *World Declaration on the Survival, Protection and Development of Children*, 30 September 1990; and UNGA, *World Fit for Children*, A/RES/S-27/2, 11 October 2002.

24 UNGA, *Declaration of the Rights of the Child*, Preamble.

25 UNGA, *Universal Declaration of Human Rights*.

Specifically regarding the family context, the 'Universal Declaration of Human Rights'[26] established the family as a fundamental group in society and the natural environment for the growth and well being of all its members and particularly children. This same idea is reproduced in the preamble of the United Nations 'Convention on the Rights of the Child' (UNCRC). Within this approach, the 'Declaration of the Rights of the Child' states: 'he [the child] shall, wherever possible, grow up in the care and under the responsibility of his parents, and, in any case, in an atmosphere of affection and of moral and material security'.[27] It is interesting to note through these documents how the family environment is naturalised as a safe and loving place – fundamental aspects for the development of a still-dependent, vulnerable and innocent being. Following on this same message, 'The World Fit for Children' affirms that 'The primary responsibility for the protection, upbringing and development of children rests with the family'[28] and because of that the family should be strengthened and entitled to receive comprehensive protection and support.

From such a particular understanding, the family as an environment marked by happiness and love, where the child should grow up and develop, operates as a social mechanism and space par excellence for producing not only this model of childhood, but also a particular conception of an entire social system, which makes this normalised child possible. As Lee-Koo aptly captures, 'The treatment of children becomes a key battleground which assists in constituting a broader social identity and, potentially, a marker of difference between one society and another'.[29] While the nuclear family is naturalised as a safe place for children so they can be raised properly and be protected against any harm coming from the outside world, schooling is articulated as fundamental because it is the space where children are prepared for the future. As the 'Declaration of the Rights of the Child' says, education will:

> (…) promote his [the child's] general culture and enable him, on a basis of equal opportunity, to develop his abilities, his individual judgment, and his sense of moral and social responsibility, and to become a useful member of society.[30]

---

26 Ibid., Article 16.3.

27 UNGA, *Declaration of the Rights of the Child*, Principle 6.

28 UNGA, *World Fit for Children*, para. 15.

29 Katrina Lee-Koo, 'Horror and Hope: (Re)presenting Militarised Children in Global North–South Relations', *Third World Quarterly*, 32/4: 725–742 (2011), p. 739.

30 UNGA, *Declaration of the Rights of the Child*, Principle 7.

In addition, the UNCRC, in Article 29, refers specifically to children's rights to education and affirms that it shall be directed to 'The development of the child's personality, talents and mental and physical abilities to their fullest potential' (Item A) and, in this sense, to the child's preparation for a responsible life in a free society (Item D).[31] At the same time that some spaces are normalised as places for children, such as their homes and the recreational institutions and schools that circumscribe children's daily lives and shape their social experiences,[32] others are articulated as places *not* for children. Within this approach, phrases like, 'child labour', 'child marriage', 'child prostitution', 'street child', 'child forced migrants' and 'child-soldiers' evoke a profound sense of incompatibility and of commiseration. In the three short animations analysed above, for example, the *safe places* for children are destroyed by the armed conflict in Syria while Malak, Mustafa and Ivine are portrayed in *risky* spaces, calling our attention to children whose childhood was *lost* by virtue of their war experiences. For UNICEF, in its report 'The Progress of Nations', the places of the '*lost* children' – or 'children at risk' – are already known: 'They are in the tents and barracks of Africa. In the brothels of Asia, the slums of Europe and North America, the sweatshops of Latin America'.[33] We could add to this list the hazy pathways populated by those who are *on the move* to other countries aspiring to a future that is more secure and rights respecting than the past they left behind.

What is distinctive about the protection rights of the child is how they are justified and strongly demanded. The *World Declaration on the Survival, Protection and Development of Children*, for example, clearly states the preoccupations over children's development and their formation, in the future, as useful members – or citizens – of the society:

> The children of the world are *innocent*, *vulnerable* and *dependent*. They are also curious, active and *full of hope*. Their time should be one of *joy* and *peace*, of *playing*, *learning* and *growing*. Their future should be shaped in harmony and co-operation. *Their lives should mature, as they broaden their perspectives and gain new experiences.*[34]

Within this approach, because children are conceived as a different sort of human – a dependent, immature and irrational being – they are *naturally* in

31 UNGA, *Convention on the Rights of the Child.*

32 Kim Rasmussen, 'Places for Children – Children's Places', *Childhood*, 11/2: 155–173 (2004).

33 UNICEF, *The Progress of Nations*, 2000, p. 29.

34 UNICEF, *World Declaration on the Survival, Protection and Development of Children*, p. 1, emphasis added.

need of forms of protection. This 'children's needs' formulation is, thus, a very powerful one in the sense that it articulates a specific conception of children as passive, to be serviced, protected and provided for, rather than to be engaged with as active participants.[35]

Both the 'Declaration of the Rights of the Child'[36] and later the UNCRC[37] state that: 'Whereas the child, *by reason of* his physical and mental immaturity, needs special safeguards and care, including appropriate legal protection, before as well as after birth'. Prompted by the *vulnerability* and *incapacity* of children, the children's rights regime institutionalises the need for advocacy *on behalf of* the child.[38] In this sense, Archard suggests that the 'by reason of' here has a double meaning.[39] First, the child needs special rights and protection against harms insofar (and possibly only insofar) as he/she is naturally 'the' child. Second, these rights impose responsibilities on those entrusted with the care of children to ensure that 'in the best interest of the child',[40] international mechanisms of protection and practices of care must be implemented in order to exclude any form of neglect, cruelty or exploitation of children.

Even when contemplating the UNCRC efforts in adding the so-called 'participation' rights, the idea of protection of the vulnerable child – the 'in formation' being – still prevails, limiting the possibilities of considering children's perspectives and contributions in a meaningful way. Within this approach, Article 12.1 from the UNCRC would be the best example:

> States Parties shall assure to the child who is *capable* of forming his or her own views the right to express those views freely in all matters affecting the child, the views of the child being given *due weight in accordance with the age and maturity of the child.*[41]

At the same time that Article 12 from the UNCRC opens room for children's participation, it still emphasises that it should vary according to their age and maturity, which traces us back to the particular conception of childhood that establishes children's development as a progressive graduation through stages

35 Erica Burman, *Deconstructing Developmental Psychology* (New York: Routledge, 2008).

36 UNGA, *Declaration of the Rights of the Child*, para. 3.

37 UNGA, *Convention on the Rights of the Child*, Preamble, emphasis added.

38 Vanessa Pupavac, 'Misanthropy Without Borders: The International Children's Rights Regime', *Disasters*, 25/2: 95–112 (2001), p. 100, emphasis added.

39 David Archard, *Children: Rights and Childhood* (New York: Routledge, 2004), p. 61.

40 This expression appears both in the UNGA *Declaration of the Rights of the Child*, and in the United Nations *Convention on the Rights of the Child.*

41 UNGA, *Convention on the Rights of the Child*, Article 12.1, emphasis added.

to ever greater competence and maturity. This slippery – and even ambiguous – conception of the child's right to participation is articulated very well in the Convention as it attaches, as Archard notes, a conditionality to the right of the child to participate. First, the capability condition is that the right is assured only to a child 'who is capable of forming his or her own views'.[42] Because children are constantly referenced to their future potential and possibilities, not all children can exercise this right and their present actions are downplayed. The word 'due' articulates this idea even clearer as it makes the weight associated to children's views proportionate to their age and maturity. Thus, from this formulation, it is simply assumed that the older the child, the more developed, mature and capable he/she is in terms of participating in social life.

The central importance of the duty to protect the child against any harm or violence is reflected in the fact that all the child's rights agreements reproduce the idea that children are naturally immature and, because of that, they should be cared for, in very similar terms. The 'Geneva Declaration of the Rights of the Child', for example, says: 'The child must be put in a position to earn a livelihood, and must be protected against every form of exploitation'.[43] The 'Universal Declaration of Human Rights', in turn, affirms: 'Motherhood and childhood are entitled to special care and assistance. All children, whether born in or out of wedlock, shall enjoy the same social protection'.[44] Then, the 'Declaration of the Rights of the Child' states: 'The child shall be protected against all forms of neglect, cruelty and exploitation'.[45] Finally, the UNCRC says:

> States Parties shall take all appropriate legislative, administrative, social and educational measures to protect the child from all forms of physical or mental violence, injury or abuse, neglect or negligent treatment, maltreatment or exploitation, including sexual abuse, while in the care of parent(s), legal guardian(s) or any other person who has the care of the child.[46]

Through these statements, it is possible to identify the four main aspects pointed out by Hockey and James, which gave form to a particular, but prevailing, conception of childhood: (i) the child is set apart spatially and temporarily as

42 Archard, *Children: Rights and Childhood*, p. 65.

43 League of Nations, *Geneva Declaration of the Rights of the Child*, 26 September 1924, Article 4.

44 UNGA, *Universal Declaration of Human Rights*, Article 25.2.

45 UNGA, *Declaration of the Rights of the Child*, Principle 9.

46 UNGA, *Convention on the Rights of the Child*, Article 19.

different and childhood is a time of 'joy and peace, of playing, learning and growing'; (ii) the child is naturally distinct and associated with nature; (iii) the child is inherently innocent; and therefore (iv) the child is dependent and vulnerable, so he/she need to mature, broad their perspectives and gain new experiences in order to become a productive adult.[47] For this conception of the child to be convincing, children and adults are understood to be fundamentally different types of humans. While 'modern children are supposed to be segregated from the harsh realities of the adult world and to inhabit a safe, protected world of play, fantasy and innocence',[48] adults are assumed to be mature and rational beings who must work in order to provide for children.

Childhood appears then as a transitional stage and is represented by expectations as to child's futurity as an adult.[49] Once constituted as 'a human *becoming*',[50] 'the' child is essentialised as a tabula rasa, dependent and incomplete, while childhood is understood as the phase of life that lays down the foundations and shapes the individual in order to prepare him/her for the future, or to enter the adult world. The age criterion is, thus, itself significant for defining and constituting 'the' child since it marks these 'processes of temporality'.[51] Under the terms of the UNCRC,[52] which may be considered the main document for defining and (re)producing the child internationally, eighteen is the temporal limit – or the age border – that marks the transition from human *becoming* to human *being*.

In this sense, children are forced into a *waiting position*: precisely by being *excluded* in the present time, children are *included* in the social realm as potential citizens of the future society. Children are waiting to become adults; to mature; to become competent; to acquire rights; to become useful.[53] Furthermore, through this dichotomy between beings/becomings, 'the' adult,

---

47 Jenny Hockey and Allison James, *Growing Up and Growing Old: Ageing and Dependency in the Life Course* (London: Sage Publications, 1993), p. 60.

48 Sharon Stephens, 'Introduction' in Sharon Stephens (ed.), *Children and the Politics of Culture* (Princeton: Princeton University Press, 1995), p. 14.

49 Hockey and James, *Growing Up and Growing Old.*

50 Jens Qvortrup, 'Varieties of Childhood' in Jens Qvortrup (ed.), *Studies in Modern Childhood: Society, Agency, Culture* (New York: Palgrave Macmillan, 2005), p. 5.

51 Allison James, Chris Jenks, and Alan Prout, *Theorizing Childhood* (Cambridge: Polity Press, 1998).

52 UNGA, *Convention on the Rights of the Child*, p. 3.

53 Nick Lee, *Childhood and Society: Growing Up in an Age of Uncertainty* (Maidenhead: Open University Press, 2001); Jens Qvortrup, 'Editorial: The Waiting Child', *Childhood*, 11/3: 267–273 (2004).

with connotations of stability and completeness, functions as a kind of standard model of a person that the child should become in the future. In this sense, this binary relation that articulates 'the' child as 'the citizen to be' and 'the' adult as the 'full citizen' is bound up in a 'gradualist dualism' between time of development/ time of accomplishment, which resonates in other related dualisms, such as vulnerable versus competent, dependent versus autonomous and protection versus participation.[54]

Children's process of development towards adulthood should be understood in its broadest sense as a holistic concept, embracing the child's physical, mental, spiritual, moral, psychological and social development.[55] This idea was first introduced by the 'Geneva Declaration of the Rights of the Child' when it says in its second point:

> The child that is hungry must be fed; the child that is sick must be nursed; the child that is backward must be helped; the delinquent child must be reclaimed; and the orphan and the waif must be sheltered and succored.[56]

Thus, in order to ensure the 'normal development' of the child, biological needs – such as those associated to feeding and illness –, psychological issues – like those related to being 'backward' in relation to some kind of norm – and moral aspects – such as treating the 'delinquent' – must all be addressed.[57] Without problematising what is meant by a 'normal development', a specific set of boundaries delimits the spaces and times of the child so he/she can be 'fully prepared to live an individual life in society'.[58]

For the purpose of this article, it is worth noting how these delimitations on both 'where' children should be and 'when' not only authorise what are supposed to be *normal* experiences of children in society, but also articulate the child as the principle of hope on which the modern promise of the progressive future depends, and also a universalising (but not universal) standard of purity as related to an 'original' state of innocence.[59] Like this, children's destiny

---

54 Jana Tabak, *In the Best Interest of Whom? Rethinking the Limits of the International Order through the (Re)constructions of the World Child and Child-soldiers*, Ph.D, Pontifícia Universidade Católica do Rio de Janeiro, 2014. Print.

55 'General measures of implementation of the Convention on the Rights of the Child', General comment no. 5, CRC/GC/2003/5, 27 November 2003.

56 League of Nations, *Geneva Declaration of the Rights of the Child*, p. 1.

57 Ibid.

58 UNGA, *Convention on the Rights of the Child*, Preamble.

59 Tabak, *In the Best Interest of Whom?*

is not only to wait to become adults, but also to wait for 'economic prosperity, social justice and peace permitting everyone to live a joyful childhood and thriving adulthood without poverty, exploitative labour or discrimination'.[60] Within this formulation, at the same time that children are (re)produced as the symbol of the promise of a progressive future, they are taken to display for the adult society its own state of once untutored and undeveloped difference. Erica Burman points that out: '(...) childhood becomes a site of multiple emotional as well as political investments: a *repository of hope* yet a site of *instrumentalization* for the future, but with an *equal* and *opposite nostalgia* for the *past*'.[61] In turn, children's high profile in modern society as the epitome of goodness and knowledge linked to the *risks* associated with their *un*developed, or still *uncivilised* stage has rendered them susceptible to different forms of regulation and training based on modern ideas of their development, protection, conditioning and innocence.[62]

This ambivalent approach to childhood is clearly expressed by the former Prime Minister of Norway, Jens Stoltenberg, in an article published by one of the main medical journals in the world, *The Lancet*: 'Children are our best investment (...) *Protecting our children is a moral and political imperative.* It is also essential for socioeconomic development'.[63] In other words, improving children's opportunities is seen as the essential way to make the world's development possible. In this way, the cause of children is regarded as capable of transcending national, political and social divisions and enlisting people globally to counter social problems and militate against disorder and conflict.[64]

Within this discursive formulation, childhoods and their children, in their process of being, inescapably signify and embody futurity[65] and, consequently,

60 Karl Hanson, 'Embracing the Past: "Been", "Being" and "Becoming" Children', *Childhood*, 24/3: 281–285 (2017), p. 281.

61 Erica Burman, *Developments: Child, Image, Nation* (New York: Routledge, 2008), p. 11, emphasis added.

62 Chris Jenks, *Childhood* (London: Routledge, 2005); Patrick Ryan, 'How New Is the "New" Social Study of Childhood? The Myth of a Paradigm Shift', *Journal of Interdisciplinary History*, 38/4: 553–576 (2008).

63 Jens Stoltenberg, 'Our Children: the Key to Our Common Future', *The Lancet*, 368/9541: 1042–1044 (2006), p. 1042, emphasis added.

64 Vanessa Pupavac, 'The International Children's Rights Regime' in David Chandler (ed.), *Rethinking Human Rights: Critical Approaches to International Politics* (New York: Palgrave Macmillan, 2002).

65 Daniel Cook, 'A Politics of Becoming: When "Child" is Not Enough', *Childhood*, 22/1: 3–5 (2015), p. 4.

the *risks* associated with this ambivalent approach to the child are always present. In this way, not only is it 'morally' right to protect and care for children, especially those in poor circumstances, but also not doing so could lead us to an instable future. To use Bigo's classification, protecting children may evoke the idea of *tutore*,[66] which has the sense of looking after. The protector as a tutor, thus, organises the life of the protected and channels the corridor of its freedom – for children, freedom would equate to their transition to adulthood.

At the end of the day, the children's rights milestones define, promote and reproduce a model – a norm – of childhood, that not only authorises the delimited spaces where children must be placed, but also monitors their experiences and silences potential sources of disruption in the present as preparing them for the future, creating new visible forms of being (or becoming). Potential deviations in relation to the norm of the child are not excluded or extinct. Rather the opposite, notions of normality are extrapolated from our attention to those children who deviate from the 'normal' course of development. The questions that remain are how diverse these visible forms of being are or can be, and what 'we' should do when confronted with *normal* – in the sense of being common – childhood experiences that deviate from the norm. Maybe, invisibility is not the fundamental problem when dealing with child forced migrants. Twum-Danso Imoh,[67] for example, argues that no matter how hard children's experiences may be to swallow, there is a need to problematise these simplistic dichotomies. Consequently, spaces may be opened for children who live their lives in shades of grey and whose interest is not necessarily to be sacralised or to be presumed to inhabit innocence.[68]

When the Child Meets Its (Potential) Deviations: Children on the Move and the Ambivalent Approach to Childhood

In her book 'Children's Rights in International Politics', Anna Holzscheiter summarises the various discursive strands that together form what she calls the 'discursive ecology' of childhood: child images as the 'irrational child',

66 Didier Bigo, 'Protection: Security, Territory and Population' in Jef Huysmans, Andrew Dobson, and Raia Prokhovnik (eds.), *The Politics of Protection: Sites of Insecurity and Political Agency* (New York: Routledge, 2006).

67 Afua Twum-Danso Imoh, 'Children's Perceptions of Physical Punishment in Ghana and the Implications for Children's Rights', *Childhood*, 20/4: 472–486 (2013), p. 484.

68 Daniel Cook, 'When a Child is Not a Child, and other Conceptual Hazards of Childhood Studies', *Childhood*, 16/1: 5–10 (2009).

'immanent child', 'innocent child' and the 'evolving child'[69] are complemented and (re)produced by particular norms that have articulated this particular conception of childhood. Considering specifically the first three images and the discourse elements that articulate them – such as immaturity, irresponsibility, and irrationality for the 'irrational child'; children as future and valuable contribution to society for the 'immanent child'; and vulnerability, victim, apolitical and happiness for the 'innocent child' – it is possible to glimpse some of the borders that (re)produce children as an object of protection *per se*.

Table 1, extracted from Holzscheiter's book, systematises this discursive ecology of childhood, showing how different child images have appeared in international politics in the last 100 years or so. We've added one line to the table in order to show how elements of the discourse about children and childhood related to normality and deviation are articulated and organise the stories being told in the *Unfairy Tales* videos, hinting at an ambivalent approach to children on the move, involving vulnerability and risk, that both authorises and informs protection practices.

Based on Table 1, it is possible to say that the norm of the child operates in four guises: as that which is natural and healthy; as that against which children are judged and labelled as deviations; as that which is to be produced by (developmental and protection) programs; and as that which provides the rationale for intervention when 'reality' and 'normality' fail to coincide.[70] The *Unfairy Tales* videos reproduce this interplay between norm and deviation, representing Mustafa, Malak and Ivine as children like the children we know – immature, irrational, developing – facing situations we could hardly imagine ourselves in – exposed to violence, alone, helpless. The more their stories are described as deviations from a normal childhood, the more vulnerable they become, which, in the videos, turns them into children at risk and reinforces the need (human obligation) to protect them. The problem of having protection practices authorised and informed by the norm, especially in the case of children, is that once the natural sequence of development stages leading from child to adulthood is broken, children are not only at risk, but may represent a risk to our imagined future. As a shadow is cast over their future prospects, dealing with these children entails, at the same time, care and control.

69 Holzscheiter, *Children's Rights in International Politics*, p. 137.

70 Nikolas Rose, *Governing the Soul: The Shaping of the Private Self* (London: Free Association Books, 1999).

TABLE 1 *Fairy and unfairy child images in international politics.*[71]

Images	Unruliness / Irrationality	Immanence	Innocence	Evolving
Discourse elements	- Immaturity - Irresponsibility - Irrationality - Child as object of parental and State intervention - Child as object of international intervention[72]	- Children as future - Valuable contribution to society - Education as the means for personal development - From immaturity to maturity - Childhood as transitory phase to adulthood - Teleological - Progress - Standardization of childhood - Uniform developmental stages	- Vulnerability - Misery, Suffering - Happiness - Playfulness - Victim - Apolitical neutral zone - Immaturity - Children as a 'carefree zone'	- Individuality - Political - Child's autonomy - Right to speak - Child as social agent
Linguistic code	Protectionist, educative	Developmental, psychological, economistic	Emotional, protectionist	Legalistic, political language
Reflection in international politics	**Paternalism** Principle of the best interests of the child. Traditional view of the child	**Development** Personal and collective development, education, nurturing	**Peace and civilization** Children as a zone of peace, treatment of children as indicator for 'civilization'	**Emancipation/ Human Rights** Child's rights (especially civil and political) empowerment

71 Based on Ibid.

72 This discourse element does not appear in the original table. We have added it in order to make more explicit that children are seen as objects of intervention not only to particular states, but to international actors, such as international organisations, especially when states and families are incapable of protecting and/or systematically violate children's rights.

(Re)production of normal and deviant elements of the discourse about children and childhood (*Unfairy tales*)[73]	- Difficulty to understand what is going on around them - Need to translate situations in terms that would belong to children's universe: fairly or unfairly tales (toys and special objects that come to life, darkness, monsters, emotions reflected or transferred to toys) - By the end of the videos, they are still in the process of making sense of what happened to them and unable to think clearly about the future - Children's homes, families and country are destroyed – the only hope left to them is international action - The story of these children can only be changed with international action - Helping children is an act of humanity[74]	- Videos highlight the 'human condition' of those children – biological needs (like hunger and cold) and ordinary feelings (fear, sadness, loneliness) – in spite of any particularities related with the environment in which they were born or grew up - Attempt to reproduce what would be children's language: animation, lots of colors, straightforward narratives, fantastic elements and journeys - Children from the videos all have similar reactions – perplexity, difficulty to understand, fear, helplessness, loneliness - Stories that have not reached an end yet – the end can be changed	- Children exposed to violence and danger of physical harm (bombs, tiny and fragile boats, stormy seas, cold, hunger, exhaustion, lack of shelter) - Loneliness and helplessness (family and friends are dead or gone and the children have to go on their journey alone through long desert paths, uncertainty about the future) - In the beginning of Mustafa's story, the family is sharing a meal in a loving and happy environment. - The videos highlight the special connection between children, toys and stories - Trauma (fear, tears, nightmares) - Adults around the children, who are fleeing just like them, are threats or unable to protect them - 'Some stories were never meant for children'[75] - 'For every child, an #ActOfHumanity'[76]	- Malak, Mustafa and Ivine tell their own stories (voice of the child) - Children making decisions for themselves (Mustafa is alone during his journey and is able to reach a refugee camp. Malak fled with her mother, but is the only survivor on the boat after the storm and is represented finishing her journey alone). - The target audience includes children

73 This line has been added to the original table in order to systematise the argument developed throughout this article.

74 'You can change the story for children like Mustafa/Ivine with an act of humanity'. This sentence appears in the end of Mustafa and Ivine's *Unfairy Tales*.

75 Ibid.

76 Ibid.

As the UNICEF report 'A Child is a Child' states,

> when children on the move are left unprotected, the consequences for their long-term development can be dire. Violence, abuse and exploitation can compromise children's physical and mental health and make it harder for them to learn, which can curtail their opportunities for the future.[77]

According to the same report, the increasing number of people on the move often happens against a backdrop of rising xenophobia and intensely politicised debate. 'Popular fears over newcomers changing the culture, committing crimes and competing for jobs and benefits complicate efforts to integrate refugee and migrant children, who very much depend on people's willingness to welcome them'.[78]

Many governments respond to this by reinforcing restrictive measures and mechanisms of control. As a result, states make it increasingly difficult for asylum seekers and migrants to enter their territories or to resettle once they have done so. According to the 'New York Declaration for Refugees and Migrants', the situation is usually worse for child migrants, especially when they are unaccompanied and separated from their families, who do not qualify for international protection as refugees, and who may need assistance.[79] Some of these children, unlike the ones from the *Unfairy Tales* videos, leave their countries searching for work and better education conditions, running from family breakdown, domestic violence, forced marriage or conscription and even harsh climate conditions, sometimes to reunite with family members that are already abroad. Today, over 100 countries are known to detain, arrest and deport children for migration related reasons and the number of children who have their rights violated worldwide because of their migration status is unknown.[80] In 2015 and 2016, around 200,000 unaccompanied and separated children applied for asylum in about 80 countries with available data, while about 100,000 were apprehended at the border between Mexico and the United States during the same period.[81]

It is clear that barriers to legal migration and aggressive border enforcement do not stop people from moving, just push them underground. To UNICEF,

---

77 UNICEF, *A Child is a Child*, p. 18.

78 Ibid., p. 29.

79 UNGA, *New York Declaration for Refugees and Migrants*, A/RES/71/1, 3 October 2016.

80 UNICEF, *A Child is a Child*.

81 Ibid.

'most children who are on the move do not interact with existing social services, which leaves official mechanisms in the dark about where children are going and what they are going through as they migrate'.[82] They are trapped in a limbo in poor conditions, and frequently resort to petty crime, selling themselves for sex, hiring smugglers or they may even end up in the hands of organised criminal networks, where the laws, policies and services meant to protect children simply do not reach them.[83]

In many senses, our understanding about children on the move is trapped in the discourse about the risk, which limits our ability to engage more meaningfully with them. Whether if children on the move are seen as at risk or a risk, our efforts are still not oriented towards the beings we claim need protection, but towards the norm. These efforts are designed to control the risk to the category 'child' as it is imagined and with all it represents to international politics: civilisation, progress, a better future. If we think about why the stories of most children on the move must be changed, the answer is pretty straightforward. The problem here is related to how it should be done. This 'how' has to be reexamined bearing in mind the individuals we are trying to protect: children who might not be wrapped in the childish packages we are used to and have life stories more common than we imagine, even though they are not 'normal' ones.

When 'Child' is not Enough: Fairy and Unfairy Tales of Modern International Life

The main argument of this paper is that the limits of contemporary application of human rights apparatuses in protecting children start with an ambivalent approach to otherness. Our *responsibility to protect* is trapped between identification with *humans like us* and our need to be protected from *unknown outsiders* and their potentially disruptive effects on our daily lives.[84] Policies targeting children have especially confusing reflections of this ambivalence, since they are seen as bearers of hopes and dreams for a better future – a responsibility most people are not willing to leave in the hands of what they see as little unknown outsiders with a troubled past. Therefore, on the one hand there is an idealised image of childhood that evokes sacredness, caring, universality, and the idea that every child deserves a fair chance of living a good life. On the other hand, however, beyond any empathy they might have towards children in search for a better life, what most states and citizens see is the threat

82 UNICEF, *In Search for Opportunities: Voices of Children on the Move in West and Central Africa*, July 2017.

83 UNICEF, *A Child is a Child.*

84 Bhabha, *Child Migration & Human Rights in a Global Age.*

posed by the possibility that something might go wrong in the path leading from childhood to adulthood – and the multiplier effects of those problems.

Their line of thought is a straightforward one: if helping children on the move that eventually reach our shores already is a costly and complex commitment in the present, what about having to deal with the delinquent juveniles, sexual molesters and even terrorists that they might become in the future? At the end of the day, the potential disruptive effects associated with children who are not experiencing what is considered to be a normal childhood are not only present, but also future. Based on that understanding, people feel responsible for and interested in protecting only a very specific kind of Aylans: those who will spend the next years playing, learning, growing, and becoming an ideal citizen, a docile and productive body,[85] ready to play its part in preserving the coherence of our modern existence. People want the boy in Queen Rania's story, not in the Charlie Hebdo's.

The point being made here is that the ambivalent understanding of others, particularly of children on the move, leaves us trapped between these two images, disputing which of them will better describe the future of millions of children that reach beaches and borders every year. And while we discuss the nobility of protecting future teachers, doctors, and loving parents, or the risk of welcoming future sexual molesters, hundreds of Aylans die or grow up in camps created to contain population flows. In our ambivalent understanding of children and childhood, the *becoming* often overwhelms the *being*.[86] Even international organisations do not escape ambivalence towards children. Protection apparatuses are designed to assure a process of development informed by a universalised image of children and a very clear *telos* to their development. Perhaps most importantly, they aim at correcting potential deviations in children's development process, preventing ruptures that might jeopardise our future.

What we see in the UNICEF animations is a narrative that highlights that universalised image of children – as humans like us. Mustafa, Malak and Ivine are all innocent children, incapable of fully realising what is going on in the world around them, and having to rely on someone else for protection. The need to protect them is constructed around the biological needs of any child – they are hungry, cold, unsheltered – and the ideal social environment imagined for them – they have lost their homes, families, friends, toys, and schools and should have all of these things back. The stories that were never meant for children are stories of children without childhoods. In other words, a kind of

85 Michel Foucault, *Discipline and Punish: The Birth of the Prison* (New York: Vintage Books, 1995).

86 Cook, 'A Politics of Becoming: When "Child" is Not Enough'.

imaginary of childhood is set up. That is, a configuration of 'truths' (narratives, images, questions, assertions and speculations) guided by ideas related to the notions of what/where a child should or should not do/be, sticks to – or glues to – the concept of childhood and it is thus (re)produced as innate to childhood itself. As biological development is understood as coinciding with social development, children who have lost childhood are at risk of becoming a *lost generation*. And if every child has the right to a fair chance in life, 'you can change the story for children like Mustafa/Ivine with an act for humanity'.[87]

In many senses, an act *of* humanity is also an act *for* humanity – as we know and imagine it. While protecting their future, we are also protecting ours.[88] Furthermore, the child to be protected with this act of humanity is one of a very specific kind. It is a norm of child, not any child. It is precisely the possibility of rupture of the developmental process that authorises external interventions, so its linearity can be restored and a normal irrational, innocent and immanent child[89] can be produced.

> One cannot speak of, speak to, gaze upon, consider or analyze any particular child, or various childhoods, without entering into and becoming entangled with morally infused vocabularies concerning the rightness and wrongness, appropriateness or inappropriateness of one's actions and, indeed, one's thoughts. Every decision made on behalf of a child favors some aspects of the world over others. No word or deed directed at a child, no object intended for a child's possession or space crafted for children's use, no image fabricated for their eyes or sound made resonant for their ears, no amount of attention or inattention paid their activities, voices or perspectives—in none of these can neutrality reside.[90]

As we act to avoid a lost generation, we engage in a 'politics of becoming' in which, sometimes, a child is simply not enough. Giving visibility to the stories of forced migrant children, turning them into Mustafas, Malaks and Ivines will not be enough if we do not engage in problematising this ambivalent feeling that states and citizens have towards them: we feel obliged to protect them, but we also blame them for the risk they pose to our social fabric.[91] Our modern,

---

87 UNICEF, 'The Story of Ivine and Pillow'.

88 Erica Burman, 'Innocents Abroad: Western Fantasies of Childhood and Iconography of Emergencies', *Disasters*, 18/3: 238–253 (1994).

89 Holzscheiter, *Children's Rights in International Politics*.

90 Daniel Cook, 'Childhood as a Moral Project', *Childhood*, 24/1: 3–6 (2017).

91 Bhabha, *Child Migration & Human Rights in a Global Age*.

globalised world urgently needs to discuss this tension between equality (as human beings) and the multifaceted differentiation mechanisms embedded in our conception of citizenship. While we remain trapped in ambivalence, our responsibility to protect is undermined by the idea that 'not all children are 'our' future because not all children are 'ours' and because not all children promise or portend a desired future'.[92] Furthermore, as Daniel Thomas Cook brilliantly puts it, 'no invocation of innocence or sacredness – let alone appeals to children's perspective or voice – could overcome the threat of these children's becomings in the minds of these 'patriots'. It is a threat that they might … maybe … perhaps … become us'.[93]

When we engage in discussing ambivalence, we can start to think about children in their diversity, considering the multiple capacities and limitations that they do – and not only might – have. We can start to see that recognising and assuring their right to be protected and to participate in the society as subjects in the present and in the future, should be added together, not mutually exclusive. This is not to say that the protection programs that we have today are bad or irrelevant. They are simply not enough. Agencies like UNICEF and so many others that work daily to improve life conditions for children around the world are undoubtedly important and play a significant role in calling people's attention to the challenges faced by children on the move. Projects such as *Unfairy Tales*, an award-winning initiative with hundreds of thousands of views on YouTube, are certainly effective as a way to create awareness of forced migration and many other problems that affect children. They also raise the question of how important it is for us to show solidarity with these children. However, we cannot rely only on compassionate responses. The limits of our responsibility to protect rest exactly on those children who do not necessarily fit in the stories like Mustafa, Malak and Ivine's. Repoliticising ambivalence may allow us to think also about other children with complex life stories and agendas. Not necessarily forced migrants, but children who search for a better life, for a place where their rights are respected. Between victims, good citizens-to-be, and children excluded in the name of whatever risk they might represent to our future, is a great number of the children on the move. While the *Unfairy Tales* invite humanity to open the doors to children, we have to consider that if those doors are opened only to a specific kind of imagined child, we are actually building walls to so many others. These are children that our responsibility to protect must, but does not always, reach.

92 Cook, 'A Politics of Becoming: When "Child" is Not Enough', p. 3.

93 Ibid., pp. 4–5.

R2P and the Novel: The Trope of the Abandoned Refugee Child in Stella Leventoyannis Harvey's *The Brink of Freedom*

Erin Goheen Glanville
Simon Fraser University, Canada
egoheeng@sfu.ca

Abstract

The abandoned refugee child is a powerful yet simplistic cultural trope that can inspire intense, sympathetic reactions to asylum seekers but cannot sustain that sympathy in more complex contexts. In contrast, literary novels unpack the intricacies, details, and nuances of refugee children's experiences, serving as a reliable representation of reality and a winsome pedagogical tool for increasing curiosity and attention to refugee children. As cultural pedagogy, refugee fiction promotes public discussions around the complex situations of vulnerable children, educates readers about sovereignty as responsibility, and thus mobilises and nuances the political will to fulfill a nation's responsibility to protect. Literary novels leverage a rhetoric that is concrete, polyphonous, interlocking, and intimate. This paper uses the example of Stella Leventoyannis Harvey's Canadian novel *The Brink of Freedom,* which embeds complex, even contradictory, representations of R2P issues into the particular details of a displaced child's perspective. The pedagogical work of this example of literary fiction is accomplished through the differing perspectives embodied concurrently by sympathetic characters, the concrete details of one child's deeply intimate moments, the central metonym of the child/caregiver as the citizen/nation, and the contrasting first person child narrator. In a highly polarised global context that appears to be moving towards protectionist policies, this kind of local, creative cultural intervention can feed an alternative social imaginary that prioritises interdependence over independence for the health of everyone.

Keywords

Canadian literature – child refugee – forced migration narratives – metonym – refugee representation – refugee trope – culture and political will

 | DOI:10.1163/9789004379534_008

At a popular level, the political will to be responsible to and for refugee-ed[1] children has been activated in the past two years by the circulation of images, videos, and stories on social media. When the photograph of Alan Kurdi, a drowned Syrian child, went viral online in September 2015, a groundswell of interest in the discussion of what Canada's responsibility is to refugee-ed children took place largely at the level of popular culture. Only months later, that international swell of compassion—a compassion gathered and fed by the singular and simple representation in a viral photo—was sorely tested by reports of sexual assaults by migrant youth in Cologne. The about-face of public sentiment, from mourning the loss of innocent lives to protesting the presence of migrant youth in the EU, points to the need for more complex and thoughtful representations of migrants and migrant children. Clearly the viral photograph did not produce a will broad or deep enough to encompass the complexities of crime in migrant populations. The interrelated reality of our world requires creative representations that can broaden public imaginings of refugee-ed children and that can appeal to emotions more complex than pity.

Fiction, and in particular, literary novels are prized for their ability to represent complex realities; novels embed a multiplicity of perspectives and experiences in concrete and interrelated details. Using the example of Canadian author Stella Leventoyannis Harvey's 2015 novel, *The Brink of Freedom*, this paper examines the potential for literary novels to reshape social imaginaries of refugee-ed children and to strengthen the political will for supporting the pillars of R2P. In this novel, the varied perspectives embodied by sympathetic characters, the concrete details of one child's deeply intimate moments, the central metonym of the child/caregiver, and the contrasting first person child narrator all serve to round out the simplistic cultural trope of the abandoned refugee child.

The first section of this article looks at aesthetic and cultural representational tropes in relation to political will. The second section gives a broad description of the simplified cultural trope of the abandoned refugee child in globalised Western cultures with attention to the novel's ability to re-narrate such tropes. The final section will offer examples from *The Brink of Freedom* in which an abandoned refugee child is the main character and the novel's only first-person narrator and in which the child/parent relationship serves as a metonym for the citizen/state relationship. I offer eight examples of how this

1 For an explanation of this term, see Daniel Coleman, Erin Goheen Glanville, Agnes Kramer-Hamstra, and Wafaa Hasan 'Introduction', in *Countering Displacements: The Creativity and Resilience of Indigenous and Refugee-ed Peoples* (Edmonton: University of Alberta Press, 2012), XLII.

novel re-narrates simplified tropes of the abandoned refugee child, by embedding the discourse and principles of R2P within the complex and contradictory material reality of a refugee child. I finish by describing the rhetoric of the literary novel as particularly suited to round out simplistic cultural tropes. Collectively, these stories add breadth to the deeply buried root system of stories evoked by single and simplistic images gaining momentum in social media and news media.

Political Will and Culture in R2P

The problem of political will, or lack thereof, and the importance of public opinion for operationalising R2P principles is a recurring theme in R2P discussions.[2] As the concept of 'legitimate humanitarian intervention' suggests, an intervention should be representative of the opinions of the intervening state's citizens. The 'should' of legitimate humanitarian intervention has as much to do with efficacy as with idealism: lack of mass support makes it 'difficult for decision makers to intervene in the first place and sustain support for that intervention over the longer period'.[3] Presently, in first world nation-states there exists a crisis of political will to fulfill human rights obligations, let alone to assent to their responsibility to protect. Lack of public support for enacting sovereignty as responsibility is arguably one of the root causes of the current, so-called refugee crisis.[4]

At the 2016 International Association for the Study of Forced Migration conference in Poland an emerging theme was the need for a conceptual shift,

2 See, S. Neil Macfarlane, Carolin J. Thielking and Thomas G. Weiss, 'The responsibility to protect: Is anyone interested in humanitarian intervention?', *Third World Quarterly*, 25/5: 977–992 (2004); Alex Bellamy, *Massacres and Morality: Mass Atrocities in an Age of Civilian Immunity* (Oxford: Oxford University Press, 2012); Tom Keating, 'Mobilising the troops: generating the political will to act', in W. Andy Knight and Frazer Egerton (eds.), *Routledge Handbook of the Responsibility to Protect* (Abingdon: Routledge, 2012); Graeme A.M. Davies and Robert Johns, 'R2P from Below: Does the British public view humanitarian interventions as ethical and effective?', *International Politics*, 53/1: 118–137 (2016).

3 Davies, 'R2P from Below', p. 3.

4 The connection between the principles of asylum rights and the principles of R2P cannot be adequately explored here but have been established by others. See, Susan Martin, 'Forced Migration, the Refugee Regime and the Responsibility to Protect', *Global Responsibility to Protect*, 2: 38–59 (2010); Susan Harris Rimmer, 'Refugees, internally displaced persons and the "responsibility to protect"', *New Issues in Refugee Research*, 185 (UN High Commissioner for Refugees, 2010).

articulated first by plenary speaker Heaven Crawley and then circulated in various panel sessions: that is, the shift to label the refugee crisis more appropriately as a political crisis. As Crawley and others pointed out, the crisis faced by governments and non-governmental activists alike is the lack of will at a popular level to see the EU as responsible for the displaced citizens of other countries. The language of 'refugee crisis' evokes the desire to protect nation states from refugees, overturning that nation state's responsibility to protect refugees whose states of origin are unwilling or unable to protect them. The relationship between widespread resistance to responsibility for refugees and the politicians who are setting and implementing policy is symbiotic: politicians respond to the fear of refugees among their constituents, and constituents become further convinced of a crisis as they hear it affirmed by politicians. This discursive ecosystem of established patterns enables 'reactive policy and administrative approaches which are fuelled by political leaders attuned to 'reactive' populations ... at times playing on xenophobic attitudes'.[5] Popular resistance to the responsibility of nations to one another and one another's citizens often drives the policy agendas of politicians, but the fear driving that resistance originates and resides in the circulation of images, phrases, and narratives in the cultural realm. Yet, the discussions of R2P principles and implementation largely have taken place in academic and policy spheres.

The infrequent focus on cultural spheres has resulted in very little being written on aesthetic production in R2P scholarship, a lacuna addressed by Thomas G. Weiss and Rama Mani. Their analysis of culture in relation to R2P includes understanding culture as a sustaining resource: cultural and aesthetic practices have the potential to create 'committed citizens and strong cultural institutions' necessary for 'preventing mass atrocities'.[6] While they acknowledge the limitations of culture's contribution to the R2P conversation, they provide a modest assessment of culture as valuable knowledge. 'In scholarly terms, such knowledge is valuable; in more utilitarian terms, it also should provide a means to design and implement more effective, appropriate, and culturally acceptable means, both internal and external, to protect affected populations'.[7] At a minimum, they suggest that 'nonviolent civic movements [in culture] should be acknowledged and supported, and their non-verbal artistic expressions and

5 Claudia Tazreiter, *Asylum Seekers and the State: The Politics of Protection in a Security-Conscious World* (Aldershot, England: Ashgate, 2004), p. 16.

6 Rama Mani and Thomas G. Weiss, 'R2P's Missing Link, Culture', *Global Responsibility to Protect*, 3/4: 451–472 (2011), p. 469.

7 Rama Mani and Thomas G. Weiss (eds.) *Responsibility to Protect: Cultural Perspectives in the Global South* (Abingdon: Routledge, 2011), p. 8.

peaceful alternatives to war heeded and pursued vigorously' and, importantly, that cultural institutions function in a nation as a bulwark against mass atrocities.[8] In other words, aesthetic production can both provide warning signs of a nation-state en route to genocide and also produce alternatives to violent intervention. Weiss and Mani acknowledge 'the considerable ignorance or misgivings about R2P in some circles' and call for R2P theorists to 'better understand the sources of support and sustenance for effective human protection and the responsibility to provide such protection among a variety of cultures and traditions'.[9] This paper is, in answer to that call to holistic prevention, a consideration of the sustaining role of refugee fiction in producing stories and nuancing tropes that will influence culture in support of R2P.

Culture is a notoriously slippery concept and subject for study. In a globalised world, culture is never static and cultures are never discrete, so an analysis of the role of aesthetic production in shaping a culture will have to allow for mutual influence and overlap. A more fluid, globalised understanding of culture, such as that proposed by Arjun Appadurai, potentially highlights the interdependence of nations at all levels, interdependence being a key supporting presupposition of R2P principles. Appadurai's work on the digital circulation of images in a globalised world points to the larger reality of imagination as a social practice. 'The image, the imagined, the imaginary ... are no longer mere fantasy .... Imagination is now central to all forms of agency, is itself a social fact, and is the key component of the new global order'.[10] His analysis of cultural phenomena helps us to understand imagination and imaginative narratives as social practices with agency in the formation of global relationships. Charles Taylor, whose historical analysis works toward an understanding of how discrete polities work, coined the term 'social imaginary' to describe the way 'ordinary people "imagine" their social surroundings, how they fit together with others'.[11] Contrasting a social imaginary with a social theory, Taylor gives the social imaginary a three-fold definition: '(i) ... the way ordinary people imagine their social surroundings', '(ii) ... shared by large groups of people, if not the whole society', and '(iii) ... the common understanding that makes possible common practices and a widely shared sense of legitimacy'.[12]

---

8 Mani and Weiss, 'R2P's Missing Link', p. 470.

9 Mani and Weiss, *Responsibility to Protect*, p. 8.

10 Arjun Appadurai, *Modernity at Large* (Minneapolis: University of Minnesota Press, 1996), p. 31.

11 Charles Taylor, *Modern Social Imaginaries* (London: Duke University Press, 2004), p. 23.

12 Ibid.

The social imaginary is both a limiting and a generative phenomenon, and it is held and expressed in a confluence of images, stories, legends, and other cultural tropes that create the conditions for social interaction and shared values. Cultural tropes shape social imaginaries through patterned repetition and easy recognition.

I use the term cultural trope here to mean the representation of something or someone that is repeated in various cultural and aesthetic texts, such as news media, political speeches, advertising, and popular films, becoming readily recognisable to its readers/viewers. An example of a cultural trope might be the resilient refugee who gives back, which invokes a predictable, larger narrative of a person from what was once referred to as the third world who has, against all odds, arrived in a place of safety in the first world and become economically successful enough to participate in charity work. Tropes are effective because they become shorthand for communicating, materialising stereotypes. Readers, or viewers as the case may be, can more efficiently and easily make meaning out of the narrative. For the purposes of this volume, consider the cultural trope of the abandoned refugee child. In Western, globalised countries, such as Canada, this trope has become shorthand for the failure of other nations and other nations' parents to protect their most vulnerable. For many Canadians it also triggers the trope of the peacekeeping nation, with its accompanying narrative of Canada's unique international responsibility for humanitarian action.[13] Yet even this sympathetic response perpetuates a simplistic understanding of refugee children as innocent victims of a corrupt kinship group in need of a new 'family' and does not open up curiosity, neither about the myriad avenues by which displaced children come to be designated as abandoned nor the way resources and individuality shape a child's response to abandonment. Images work to consolidate cultural tropes, because a single image 'suggests a long list of stories and myths that are buried inside of us .... Pictures that evoke these deep memories can be very powerful'.[14] The need to nuance and ground cultural tropes in the material lives of those represented by such tropes brings us to the role of literary fiction in shaping a more complex and informed social imaginary that can open up the possible responsibilities and abdications of nations to stateless, refugee, and abandoned children.

---

13 For a critical look at the Canadian peacekeeper mythology, see Paulette Regan, *Unsettling the Settler Within* (Vancouver: UBC Press, 2010).

14 J. Francis Davis. 'The Power of Images: Creating the Myths of Our Time', *Impact of Images: Life and Culture in the Media Age*, 57 (1992), http://www.medialit.org/reading-room/power-images-creating-myths-our-time, accessed 3 December 2017.

The Trope of the Refugee Child in Social Imaginaries

The child is a particularly evocative trope in the social imaginary, standing in variously for an idealised past, the possibilities of the future, innocence, and vulnerability.[15] Partial credit must go to international movements supporting children's rights that have been highly successful in positing childhood as a 'symbolic common denominator underlying global divisions'.[16] The child as a symbolic common denominator is spread and solidified through cultural production: portrayals of children in advertising, legends, films, and images present them as innocent, pre-cultural blank slates, dependent on provision, protection, and education. Joanne Faulkner's historical analysis of cultural representations of children shows that as far back as the Romantics, 'the child [has been] represented as the human in its "purest" form—that is, as pre-social humanity'.[17] Innocence is linked to vulnerability because innocence is an 'empty trait'.[18] Figuring the child as a blank, pre-cultural slate impacts forced migration reality in many ways, not the least of which is that receiving countries consider child refugees more desirable than adults. That which is pre-cultural and vulnerably empty presents no threat but is rather an invitation to influence. Studies of representations of refugees in Canadian news media have shown that, where adults are portrayed as fraudulent threats, children of those same adults are represented as wise investments since they are straightforward recipients of education and care.[19] Thus the abandoned child has become the ideal migrant, because she evokes the desire to protect and is perceived as

---

15 See Zoe Anderson, 'Borders, Babies, and "Good Refugees": Australian Representations of "Illegal" Immigration, 1979', *Journal of Australian Studies*, 36/4: 499–514 (2012); Claudia Castaneda, *Figurations: Child, Bodies, Worlds* (Durham, NC: Duke University Press, 2002); Joanne Faulkner, 'Vulnerability of "Virtual" Subjects: Childhood, Memory, and Crisis in the Cultural Value of Innocence', *SubStance* #132 42/3: 127–147 (2013); Kent A. Ono and John M. Sloop, *Shifting Borders: Rhetoric, Immigration and California's Proposition 187* (Philadelphia, PA: Temple University Press, 2002); Margaret Steffler, 'The Production and Use of the Globalized Child: Canadian Literary and Political Contexts', *Jeunesse: Young People, Texts, Cultures*, 1/2: 109–124 (2009); Charles Watters, *Refugee Children: Toward the Next Horizon* (London: Routledge, 2008).

16 Lisa Hermine Makman, 'Child Crusaders: The Literature of Global Childhood', *The Lion and the Unicorn*, 26: 287–304 (2002), p. 296.

17 Faulkner, 'Vulnerability of "Virtual Subjects"', p. 132.

18 Ibid., p. 129.

19 Laura di Tomasso, 'More Equal than Others: The Discursive Construction of Migrant Children and Families in Canada', *International Journal of Child, Youth and Family Studies* 3/2–3: 331–348 (2012).

having the potential to eventually give back to her hosts in ways that will not destabilise cultural norms.

As is evidenced by the Canadian response to the photograph taken of Alan Kurdi's lifeless body on the beach, public opinions about sovereignty as responsibility and global interdependence are capable of shifting quite rapidly when the powerful social trope of the abandoned child is triggered. Consider the evocative power of that photo and Canadian responses during the 2015 national elections and following. Justin Trudeau's promise to welcome 25,000 refugees in contrast to then-Prime Minister Stephen Harper's promise to keep refugees out is popularly credited for clinching Justin Trudeau's landslide victory. One of the factors that made that image particularly effective in Canada was the narrative that accompanied it, of Alan's aunt, Tima Kurdi, in British Columbia whose application to sponsor her brother to come to Canada had been denied. Canadians felt a sense of their particular responsibility in having denied protection to the Kurdi family and wanted to make up for it.[20] The narrative of Canadians denying asylum to vulnerable children linked into a narrative of national identity in which Canadians are a multicultural mosaic at home and thus uniquely suited to be peacekeepers abroad.

While critics have dismissed this burst of compassion as short-lived, a sense of responsibility for those seeking protection in the international refugee system has been sustained. This is evidenced by the decision in December 2016 of Canada's federal government to establish a quota on the number of refugees that come to Canada through Group of Five sponsorships.[21] Following the freeze on refugee resettlement put in place by Donald Trump in The United States, protesters in Canada, recognising the power of the social imaginary, re-circulated Alan's photo to remind people of the abandoned refugee child. Though Alan was not abandoned and though, contrary to popular misinformation, his father had not previously applied for refugee status in Canada, his photographed body has come to represent children abandoned first by their own nation and second by Canada, joining and presenting a challenge to the larger narrative of national identity. The photo galvanised people without connections to refugee-ed people to prove their participation in a more benevolent national narrative. This joining of narratives partially explains how the energy produced by that photograph has been sustained. The image of an abandoned

20 The denied applicant was mistakenly reported to have been Abdullah, Alan's father, but was later discovered to have been Mohammed, Alan's uncle.

21 Group of Five is a stream in Canada's private sponsorship program that allows a group of five citizens to sponsor a refugee and a program that has not needed capping since 1979 when it was established.

refugee child triggers a lifetime of cultural tropes about the innocence of childhood destroyed, the hope of the future jeopardised, and, as can be seen more concretely in news media responses, nations who closed their borders during WWII to refugee children who subsequently died in concentration camps. The circulation of the Alan Kurdi photograph and the accompanying narrative on social media was undoubtedly more significant for public opinion on Canadian responsibility to child refugees than the latest policy document, in-depth journalistic analysis, or academic publication, in part because it was able to evoke a long history of entrenched stories and myths about the trope of the Canadian nation and the trope of the abandoned refugee child. Clearly, if they are to be relevant, efforts to influence the political will (that is, the 'genuine commitment to support') of 'agents of civil society' towards R2P policy initiatives must include dialogue about cultural narratives.[22]

As has been mentioned, the trope of the vulnerable or abandoned child is particularly potent for connecting people to their own desire to protect.[23] But the effectiveness of a trope is precisely its weakness: the simplicity and predictability of the vulnerable, abandoned refugee child leads to simple and predictable responses, and a political will grounded in this singular trope will be uprooted easily when faced with the complexity of, for example, instances of violence among unaccompanied minors in the EU. Cultural tropes are powerful mobilisers but can also do a disservice to the complex theory and policy of R2P by weakening the robustness of political will. One possible strategy for bringing the nuance of R2P objectives and discussion regarding children into the social imaginary is to put stories into cultural circulation (or highlight stories already in circulation) that do not shy away from the complex subjectivity of displaced children. Such stories nuance or round out what is represented by the abandoned refugee child trope; creating a broader root system of stories that can be quickly referenced through popular written and visual tropes.

The influence, specifically, of literary production on public opinion and political will are difficult factors to quantify because a literary narrative's mode of consumption is generally private and because a particular novel's engagement

22 Keating, 'Mobilising the Troops', p. 117.

23 I acknowledge the danger of desire as sole motivator, but also recognise its pragmatic importance, so long as it retains the possibility of nuance and encourages continued knowledge gathering. A particular danger in bringing together the abandoned child trope and the desire of citizens to protect is that it can turn the abandoned child into a metonym for displacement and result in infantilising all displaced people. However, most novels make links between children and their adult iterations, providing a holistic, narrative context for the trope in question.

with current events is one step removed from the direct names, places, and events being discussed. Even so, evidence for society's dependence on fictional narratives for explaining current events and thus for shaping the social imaginary can be found. For example, consider the spike in sales for George Orwell's *1984* and other dystopian novels immediately following Donald Trump's presidential election in the United States.[24] Or, consider the 2017 protest that took place in Texas, where women dressed up in red robes and white bonnets to bring Margaret Atwood's novel *The Handmaid's Tale* into the conversation around proposed anti-abortion laws.[25] In an interview, Paul Ricoeur describes fiction's interaction with lived reality in this way:

> Narrative is a redefining of what is already defined, a reinterpretation of what is already interpreted. The referent of narration, namely human action, is never raw or immediate reality but an action which has been symbolized and resymbolized over and over again. Thus narration serves to displace anterior symbolizations on to a new plane, integrating or exploding them as the case may be. If this were not so, if literary narrative, for example, were closed off from the world of human action, it would be entirely harmless and inoffensive. But literature never ceases to challenge our way of reading human history and praxis.[26]

Fiction participates in shaping the 'social imaginary', to borrow the Taylor term, but does so by constantly displacing the known symbols with fresh ones. Thus the images, phrases, metaphors, and narratives found in several recent bestselling Canadian novels that narrate the realities of forced displacement become part of the reader's shared social imaginary or individual imaginative landscape in myriad ways.[27]

---

24 Brad Tuttle, 'Sales of Dystopian Novels Have Been Spiking on Amazon Since the Election', *Money*, 25 Jan 2017, http://time.com/money/4648774/trump-1984-dystopian-novel-sales-brave-new-world/, accessed 30 March 2017.

25 Lindsay Pulse, 'Women dress in tribute to *The Handmaid's Tale* to protest new Texas abortion bills', *Newsy*, 21 March 2017, https://www.aol.com/article/news/2017/03/21/women-dress-in-tribute-to-the-handmaids-tale-to-protest-new-t/21904437/, accessed 30 March 2017.

26 Paul Ricoeur, 'Interview with Richard Kearney', in Lucy Burke, Tony Crowley, Alvin Girvin (eds.), *The Routledge Language and Cultural Theory Reader* (London: Routledge, 2000), p. 343.

27 In the last decade, Canadian authors have published at least ten novels and numerous volumes of poetry and short stories narrating refugee experiences, most of which involve child characters and/or child narrators. For example, bestselling author Lawrence Hill

While human-interest news stories share similarities with novels and short stories, in the current culture of suspicion and the rhetoric of 'fake news', any news story meant to garner empathy is suspect. The power of literary fiction in this cultural milieu is that it is based in rigorous research yet makes no claims to accuracy or reality. The harmlessness of made up stories is precisely what makes them 'dangerous' to entrenched cultural tropes, as Paul Ricoeur writes: 'Literary narrative involves a creative use of language often ignored by science or by our everyday existence. Literary language has the capacity to put our quotidian existence into question; it is *dangerous* in the best sense of the word'.[28] Results are slow and intangible for academic and community educators who use literary texts to shift the political will of those closed to political dialogue about forced migration. Yet the method of re-narration enacted by the rhetoric of the novel can be rigorously analysed and defended. The following section offers examples from one recently published Canadian novel of how the rhetoric of fiction engages readers in a nuanced understanding of R2P themes related to the abandoned refugee child trope.

Telling the Story of a Refugee Child in *The Brink of Freedom*

Addressing the R2P pillar of prevention, one of the recommendations for civil society in Canada put forward in the Will to Intervene Project's 2009 policy report was to 'leverage new information and communications technologies to educate the public and government' followed by the recommendation to 'initiate public discussions on the prevention of mass atrocities'.[29] This paper is arguing for the importance of literary narratives that can nuance entrenched cultural tropes and contribute to a broader root system of 'buried' stories. To switch metaphors, the poet Lisa Robertson writes, 'when pushed to the wall, art is too slow'. However, behind the wall (that is, the need for urgent, immediate action) room exists for preparatory and preventative work in this same

wrote *The Illegal*, which won Canada Reads 2016. His novel was defended in a debate on national television for asking 'Canadians to imagine the humanity of one refugee, and thus all refugees', http://www.cbc.ca/books/2016/03/lawrence-hill-wins-second-canada-reads-title-with-the-illegal.html, accessed 3 December 2017.

28 Paul Ricoeur, 'Interview with Richard Kearney', in Lucy Burke, Tony Crowley, Alvin Girvin (eds.), *The Routledge Language and Cultural Theory Reader* (London: Routledge, 2000), p. 343.

29 Will to Intervene (W2I), 'Mobilizing the Will to Intervene: Leadership and Action to Prevent Mass Atrocities', 2009, p. xi. https://www.concordia.ca/research/migs/projects/will-to-intervene/about-w2i/report.html, accessed 6 January 2018.

direction. Refugee fiction is an old technology that is adept at leveraging new information for such work.

Stella Leventoyannis Harvey's novel *The Brink of Freedom* is an excellent example of how a novel can engage people at a popular level with the intricacies of the international responsibility to protect. Her novel embeds themes relevant to R2P and productively rounds out the trope of the abandoned refugee child to create an understanding of refugee-ed children that can both provoke political will and stand up to complicated, negative representations of refugee-ed children. Leventoyannis Harvey's writing of this novel, which was published earlier in 2015, foreshadowed the events of September 2015, to the extent of including a toddler that was drowned as his parents sought asylum. Reading the novel, one encounters—though indirectly—the pillars, complications, and possibilities of R2P embedded in the particular and the ordinary, that is, the ordinary, everyday details of a particular child's story. Again and again, in different ways, the characters and the narrators ask the question, 'who is responsible for this refugee child?' Harvey's novel effectively resymbolises the principles and discourse of R2P through creative narrative, focusing on a single, silent child. The child's need for protection is affirmed by a series of related and unrelated adults, but he is abandoned in various ways by all those same adults and ends up dying.

Before we address the rhetoric of the novel allow me to first contextualise the novel's production and then provide a synopsis of the plot for those unfamiliar with this novel. Stella Leventoyannis Harvey is a well-known writer and founder of the Whistler Writers Festival, based on the west coast of Canada. She was born in Cairo, but her family lives in Greece. Much of her research for the novel was done in detention centres in Greece, and the novel is informed by her years spent living in Italy and Spain during asylum crises. As a Greek citizen and public figure in Canada, Leventoyannis Harvey intends the production and distribution of her book to have direct human impact: she interviewed migrants during her research who asked her to tell their stories in her book, and part of the proceeds from its sales go to the Red Cross to support their efforts to help refugees in Greece. This novel has achieved significant recognition in Canada, including being highlighted at a panel on forced migration at the Vancouver Writers Festival in 2015. Leventoyannis Harvey's training as a social worker makes her especially concerned with the tug of the 'saviour complex' exemplified in the Canadian character, Shelby. A woman Leventoyannis Harvey interviewed in Greece told her, 'the ones who talk the most are the ones furthest removed from the people they are talking about'.[30] Leventoyannis

30 Stella Harvey Leventoyannis, 'Halt, who goes there?', *BC Booklook*, 5 November 2015, http://bcbooklook.com/2015/11/05/halt-who-goes-there/, accessed 1 September 2017.

Harvey tells the story of a silent child by following the noisy efforts of those trying to help him, showing her Canadian and Greek audience alike the danger of action based on a cultural trope rather than curiosity about the expressed needs of people.

In *The Brink of Freedom*, the main character is Sanjit, the abandoned, stateless child. In Chapter Two we are introduced to Vijay and Saphal, who are discussing the next leg on their journey from Greece to Germany, and the possibility of leaving their child, Sanjit behind. He is an asset to them when they are stable and when he can work to provide for the family, but when they are moving across national borders seeking protection, he is a liability. The dilemma that sets the plot in motion is that Sanjit's parents, unable to provide for Sanjit's basic needs let alone the medical procedures he requires, choose to abandon him in pursuit of the protection of citizenship. They decide after much conflict to entrust him to other adults and travel on their own because his presence will slow them down and make their irregular border crossing more risky. Significantly, their analysis of the risk to Sanjit is that he will likely receive better provision if he is 'abandoned'.

During the course of the events that follow, Sanjit's multiple sclerosis and lack of legal status put him in significant need of both provision and protection, a delicate balance of interrelated needs that take turns displacing and exacerbating each other. A group of unrelated adults from around the world—a veritable representation of the global community in a dance of independence and interdependence—uniformly give up their responsibility for Sanjit, each choosing their own wants over the child's needs. The adults who interact with Sanjit include the well-meaning Canadian aid worker, Shelby, who has an unhealthy saviour complex and a lack of boundaries. Her passionate over-involvement has more to do with her need to fix situations that seem simple and to avoid issues she is embroiled in closer to home. The next characters on the scene are Kem and Mirella, the non-status Roma couple who offer to care for Sanjit. Kem and Mirella have the least resources, sacrifice the most for the child, but also treat him the most brutally. Eventually they have to sell him to survive and are punished as adults in a brutal law enforcement system, though they turn out to be mere children themselves. Ted is the alcoholic businessman whose friends watch and wait for an appropriate time to stage an intervention. He is forced to fly in from North America because of familial and business entanglements, but he uses his money to pay off foreign courts and to stay uninvolved relationally with the child. Christos, the powerless Greek law enforcement officer, seems the most promising as a protector for Sanjit, but his friendliness and desire to help are thwarted once by the political careers of his superiors and then a second time by his wife. She kindly reminds him to prioritise responsibility for the feelings of his own racist children ahead of keeping Sanjit in their home. Finally, Kefalas, Christos's boss, the police commander, shows complete disinterest in the child in his attempts to penalise the child's parents for lacking legal status; he makes policy based on the political atmosphere of hostility towards migrants and determines the department's priorities according to what will save his career and keep the peace. Unaware the child has died, he makes a public statement claiming responsibility both for the reunification of the child and his mother and also for the crackdown on illegal immigrants, a statement rife with internal incoherence given the preceding narrative.

The Brink of Freedom grounds the abandoned refugee child trope in a specific example, which gives the trope complex historical, cultural, political, and personal narrative roots. So for example, in this narrative, the reader notices that the abandoned child is never actually alone but rather is shifted from place to place, person to person in a landscape dominated by self-interest and limited responsibilities. His parents' lack of choices demonstrates the need for protection and provision *before* abandonment of a child; the prior abandonment enacted by a nation on the adult caregivers is what makes it necessary for them to put him into someone else's care. Further, the interrelation of protection and provision make clear the importance of provision and not only protection in preventative policies. This last point is a contentious one, highlighted by academic critiques of the UNHCR Convention's strict definition of a refugee in distinction from an economic migrant.[31] Because the novel follows an individual child rather than outlining the logic of legal definitions or answering the demand for useful news, artificially separated concepts, such as provision and protection, are reintegrated as experiential realities for refugee children.

In the following list I have aggregated some of the salient ways the novel materialises the complex conditions surrounding the subject of the refugee-ed child, thereby rounding out the cultural trope of the abandoned refugee child. In this way, Harvey informs the imaginations and expands the curiosity of those who read with an integrated picture of complex human realities:

1. The abandoned refugee child dies because everyone he comes into contact with chooses to value their independence over their interdependence. Interdependence is shown to be a human reality.
2. Even though everyone is responsible in some way, the abandoned refugee child's death cannot be blamed on a single institution nor is the follow-up action of shaming helpful. Responsibility is clearly shared.

31 Peter Nyers, *Rethinking Refugees: Beyond States of Emergency* (New York: Routledge, 2006).

3. The abandoned refugee child needs practical provision as much as he needs legal protection, and his need for provision comes prior to his need for protection. Provision is both a preventative measure and an emergency intervention.
4. The death of the abandoned refugee child clarifies the importance of the logic of sovereignty as responsibility: the effects of abdication play out to the detriment of everyone. Thus, interdependence is shown to be integral at the global level as well.
5. Concomitantly, the abandoned refugee child is also let down by the characters that intervene unilaterally and without consulting anyone else. Their reactions are sloppy and serve their own interests, negatively demonstrating the importance of communal preventative action.
6. The abandoned refugee child carries and lives within a confluence of personal, familial, cultural, political, national, and global narratives. His needs and capabilities are best understood when all of these are taken into account and acknowledged as relevant.
7. The abandoned refugee child has wisdom and a perspective that, if centralised, could have prevented much of the turmoil, including his own death. Testing policy against the expressed needs of the individual human most affected by those policies would have made for more accurate knowledge.
8. The abandoned refugee child is both the most vulnerable person in the story and also the most reliable interpreter of reality, insofar as his limited perspective provides concrete descriptions of events along with unaffected emotional responses. When a refugee child can be understood not as a blank slate but as human in the same way as adults, their own resources can contribute to their thriving.

The Rhetoric of the Literary Novel

This integrated picture of a refugee child's experience and the responses of those surrounding him is powerful because of the form or genre within which it is presented. Harvey writes *The Brink of Freedom* in the tradition of the literary novel and draws on the novel's generic rhetoric. The rhetoric of the novel is well suited to present the experiences of and responses to refugee children as concrete, polyphonous, interlocking, and intimate. As such, the rhetoric of the novel creates an aesthetic representation that can elicit human feeling and political will without repeating the simplified cultural tropes that are easily uprooted by opposing negative tropes.

Concrete

One of the values of fictional narratives for shifting public opinion and political will in non-academic communities lies in a story's ability to be an inductive learning experience that is at once particular and varied. Because novels focus on an individual's embodied experience in a particular context, they can remind their readers of the specificity and uniqueness of every refugee situation and so contribute to a broader framework for understanding statelessness without reverting to the stereotypes produced by collective representation. Yet, that particularity is usually accompanied by a variety of supporting and conflicting characters. Fictional narratives expose readers to a complex community of individuals in relation to one another, embodying a variety of opinions and ideologies in response to the plot conflicts created by forced migration. Creative narratives can simultaneously individuate and differentiate refugee experiences without removing an individual from their contexts. Creative narratives are expected to give multi-faceted contextual information so that the reader can be immersed in the characters' material world. Thus the individual character can be both individual and embedded. When refugees are represented as undifferentiated masses without social, political, or historical detail, those representations elicit fear and suspicion, while refugees represented as individuals in complex communities within particular contexts provide the reader with empathetic connection, short-circuiting anxiety in order to provide the opportunity to learn. What was, in the reader, a vague fear or moral panic about the unknown can become concrete knowledge or an ethical imperative regarding the life of an individual human being.

Polyphonous

Novels are able to disarm reactive, politically entrenched readers with a non-confrontational invitation to imagination and curiosity. This is in part due to the apparently non-political motives of fiction writing and also in part due to the variety of perspectives that can be held in tension within a story. The novel genre is peculiar in its ability to immerse readers in multiple perspectives, either through a third person narration describing the actions and motivations of various characters or through multiple first person narrators. For novels that are written to interrogate a real-life situation or issue, the effect of multiple viewpoints is that the novel cannot be dogmatic or singularly ideological about an issue without losing its integrity as a novel. Nuance, tension, and believability—all of which can increase empathy—are a necessary component of character development for the rhetoric of the novel. In narrating a complex entanglement of subjectivities, public contexts, and personal motivations, Harvey allows the reader to encounter and observe a variety of policy responses to abandoned refugee children. The narrative makes clear the external pressures that make it possible for every single observer to abdicate their responsibility for the displaced child. The reader is left with the question of whether, given the same situation, they would similarly push the responsibility for an abandoned child onto another organisation or take responsibility, and if they would take responsibility, what would need to be different from those characters whose protection was unwelcome or harmful. The abandoned refugee trope is not the only simplified subjectivity addressed: the novel also complicates the voices of the humanitarian with a saviour complex, the heartless law enforcer, and the protectionist mercenary. Harvey gives each of these characters a human story to make sense of their responses. Having their oversimplified cultural tropes challenged, the reader of this novel finds their own voice in the final line of the novel: 'What does that mean, *one of those*?'

Interlocking

The child/caregiver relationship is at the centre of the novel, serving as a metonym for the citizen/nation relationship and for the refugee/international community relationship. The complicated nexus of relationships among parents, children, nation-states, irregular migrants, and citizens that the novel uncovers moves beyond the realm of metaphor. While the relationship of a child to a parent may seem to operate in a different sphere to the interactions of nation-states and international agreements, this individual story because of its attention to detail demonstrates the conceptual and material links among international, national, and familial systems. Metonymy is classically defined as an attempt 'to convey some incorporeal or intangible state in terms of the corporeal or tangible'.[32] In contrast to metaphor, which attributes meaning to a concept through overlapping domains, metonym produces mutual influence among domains that are already in contact in the material world. Put in other words, metonymy is 'a conceptual projection whereby one experiential domain is partially understood in terms of another experiential domain included in the same experiential domain'.[33] As the novel progresses, the reader is lead to realise that the parents' responsibility to protect a child is related to a nation's responsibility to protect a citizen, is related to a global community's responsibility to one another's citizens. The novel uses metonym to explore abandonment and responsibility, insecurity and security at all these levels

32 Kenneth Burke, *A Grammar of Motives* (Berkeley: University of California Press, 1945), p. 506.

33 Antonio Barcelona (ed.), *Metaphor and Metonymy at the Crossroads: A Cognitive Perspective* (Berlin, DE: De Gruyter Mouton, 2003).

(familial, national, global) simultaneously. The only child that can trigger the political will towards R2P is a child without their family. Yet, as this novel shows evocatively in the death of Sanjit, not only is protection of an abandoned child too little, too late, but the view that a child needs protection when she is abandoned and is otherwise the responsibility of her parents ignores the way interlocking systems work. As one character says in frustration, 'where was their compassion before the newspaper headline?'[34]

Intimate

Harvey strategically employs a combination of third person and first person narration to explore Sanjit's situation. All but five of the thirty-five chapters cycle through the adult main characters, focusing on the experience of a different character each chapter. The chapters are narrated from a limited third person point of view with internal focalisation through a single character, allowing the character's knowledge to limit what the reader knows while maintaining a layer of mediation and distance. In order to highlight the perspective of Sanjit, the child at the centre of the controversy, Harvey has scattered throughout the novel six short chapters narrated in the first person by Sanjit, chapters 3, 4, 11, 17, 24, and 30. Each of the chapters narrated by Sanjit comes as a surprise, a decisive narrative shift that requires adjustment from the reader. The adult actions we have just been reading about and been worried about for the sake of the child suddenly feel powerfully imminent. One of the effects of contrasting third person adult narrators with a first person child narrator is the reader's ability to see how adult decisions impact the child and are interpreted by the child. Sanjit's childlike witnessing presence serves the adult reader, like many child narrators, as an 'affective index of the appalling'.[35] First person narration is designed to increase the intimacy between the character and the reader and to create a sense of immediacy in the narrative. While a child is a classic example of an unreliable narrator, that is, a narrator whose limitations make their perspective untrustworthy, the simplicity of Sanjit's expressions and his half-knowledge of adult motivations make him the most trustworthy narrator in the novel. Giving Sanjit the sole privilege of first person narration emphasises that the novel is most concerned with how the plot affects this child and that the decisions of various adults have a more direct and intense impact on him than on anyone else. Nevertheless, Sanjit is not only vulnerable. Importantly,

34 Stella Leventoyannis Harvey, *The Brink of Freedom*, (Winnipeg: Signature Editions, 2015), p. 268.

35 Annie Gagiano, '*Ice-Candy-Man* and *In the Country of Men*: The politics of cruelty and the witnessing child', *Stellenbosch Papers in Linguistics*, 39/1: 25–39 (2010), p. 32.

Sanjit plays a role in his own abandonment, leaving the one safe place he finds in order to search for his parents, an action that leads to his death. If any of the adults around him had been courageous enough to centralise his perspective and recognise their own dependence on him, they could have prevented Sanjit's death.

Conclusion

The ability of specific literary novels, like *On the Brink*, to complicate received cultural tropes such as the abandoned refugee child is rooted in their rhetorical effectiveness. They need to unpack the intricacies, details, and nuances of experience and avoid didacticism in order to serve as a reliable presentation of reality and a winsome pedagogical tool. As cultural pedagogy, refugee fiction promotes public discussions around the complex situations of vulnerable children, educates readers about sovereignty as responsibility, and thus mobilises and nuances the political will to fulfill a nation's responsibility to protect. While *On the Brink* is still a modestly circulated publication, it has, like many local cultural productions, effectively conveyed the complexity of the refugee condition, an efficacy valuable far beyond its local audience. Many other recent novels similarly have narrated the stories of young refugees and/or make use of fictional refugee children as narrators. Creating zones of creative engagement and even internal disagreement, these novels have the potential to springboard respectful local, public conversations about sovereignty as responsibility and the potential to contribute to nuanced, non-polarising cultural narratives about the relational nexus of children, parents, citizens, and nation states. Complex, even contradictory, representations of R2P issues, embedded in the concrete, intimate details of a displaced child's perspective can broaden and strengthen the roots of political will among readers. In a highly polarised global context that appears to be moving towards protectionist policies, these kind of creative cultural interventions can feed an alternative social imaginary that prioritises interdependence over independence for the health of everyone.

Ultimate Tests: Children, Rights, and the Politics of Protection

J. Marshall Beier
McMaster University, Canada
mbeier@mcmaster.ca

Abstract

Whether in the rhetorical strategies of the campaign to ban landlines, appeals for famine relief, or the present historical apex of mass refugee migration, deployed images of abject childhood are central to the visual economies of humanitarian crisis. As the quintessential innocents deemed in need of protection, children are constructed outside of meaningful subjecthood and objectified as the evocative 'scenery' of the politics of protection. As such, children's place in these visual economies together with their relative voicelessness are particularly revealing of how the concept of protection is beset by a paradox it cannot resolve: simultaneously imperative in consequence of diminished political subjecthood and itself demeaning of that same subjecthood. Tracing the problematique of children's agency and subjecthood through the UN Convention on the Rights of the Child and applicable aspects of legal regimes in Canada both beholden to the Convention and charged with care and protection of children, this article offers insights relevant to but perhaps less immediately apparent in the context of the R2P regarding the tricky and fraught intersections of childhood, subjecthood, and protection.

Keywords

children – security – subjecthood – rights – victimhood – spectacle

• • •

> 'The ultimate test of a moral society is the kind of world that it leaves to its children.'
>
> DIETRICH BONHOEFFER (n.d.)

 | DOI:10.1163/9789004379534_009

Introduction: Testing Ourselves[1]

Dietrich Bonhoeffer's 'ultimate test' of moral society reflects a prevailing view of vulnerability and dependency in childhood that locates responsibility in the adult world and informs a corresponding politics of protection. Amongst the starkest arousals of this inclination, images and, though with perhaps somewhat more mediated effect to pathos, accounts of horrors visited on children, can manifest powerful affective responses, activating an impulse to extend protection that is at once constitutive of some subject positions and effacing of others. Half a decade ago, the U.S.-based organisation, Invisible Children, inadvertently provoked a moment of critical reflection along these lines after its 'Kony 2012' viral video – a call to emancipatory action against child abduction and enslavement by the central African Lord's Resistance Army – drew sharp criticism for locating meaningful oppositional political subjecthood in the Global North. In his response to 'Kony 2012', Teju Cole inveighed against this pretension to define and dictate the terms of others' emancipation and the requisites of their wellbeing, highlighting how, all best intentions notwithstanding, resulting protector/protected juxtapositions reproduce colonial ascriptions and relations of power whilst deflecting responsibility for all manner of humanitarian disasters in which societies of the North might themselves be directly implicated.[2] This marks a key feature of what, for Jean Baudrillard, is 'the last phase of colonialism: the New Sentimental Order', in which we in the North, positioned as bearers of global political subjecthood, 'are the consumers of the ever delightful spectacle of poverty and catastrophe, and of the moving spectacle of our own efforts to alleviate it'.[3] Critical interventions of the sort brought by Cole, Baudrillard, and others[4] alert us to how the pretension to protect may all too often be complicit in domination and the erasures

1 Research for this article was supported by an Insight Grant from the Social Sciences and Humanities Research Council of Canada.

2 Teju Cole, 'The White Savior Industrial Complex', *The Atlantic*, 21 March 2012, http://www.theatlantic.com/international/archive/2012/03/the-white-savior-industrial-complex/254843, accessed 14 July 2016.

3 Jean Baudrillard, *The Illusion of the End*, trans. by Chris Turner (Stanford: Stanford University Press, 1994), p. 67.

4 See, for example, Shereen Razack, *Dark Threats and White Knights: The Somalia Affair, Peacekeeping and the New Imperialism* (Toronto: University of Toronto Press, 2004); Shereen Razack, 'Stealing the Pain of Others: Reflections on Canadian Humanitarian Responses', *Review of Education, Pedagogy, and Cultural Studies*, 29/4: 375–394 (2007); Ananya Roy, 'Praxis in the Time of Empire', *Planning Theory*, 5/1: 7–29 (2006); Heike Härting, 'Global Humanitarianism, Race, and the Spectacle of the African Corpse in Current Western Representations of

of advanced colonialism. Less acknowledged, however, is what may further be revealed about – and learned from – hubris of this sort where it intersects both childhood and the politics of protection.

Protection, in its barest essentials, has likely always been closely tied to notions of responsibility. What is novel about the global Responsibility to Protect (R2P) agenda has, in this sense, less to do with the forging of that connection than with its application in limiting sovereign right. That is not to say that protection must necessarily be born of responsibility or that other constellations of interests and motivations are not determinate in some circumstances. It is simply that the connection has a long lineage, often coupled with affinities that are viscerally felt. It inheres perhaps most uncontentiously in the widely-held sense of (at least ideally) a duty of care to children, whether in familial and small in-group settings or in broader societal and even global contexts. But the very idea of protection also summons the positioning of a 'protector' and a 'protected' and, thus, an acting subject vis-à-vis an acted for (or upon) object. Of course, each may still be recognised as agents in important, if unequal, senses. Those in need of protection might, for example, be called on or expected to play a part in its facilitation by varied means of retreat, resistance, or resilience. All three of these have been recurrent in reportage of the circumstances of civilians caught in the indiscriminate violence of the Syrian civil war, expressed in, among other things, refugee migration, ad hoc neighbourhood defence efforts, and myriad other practices ranging from the formation of volunteer rescue groups to the documentation of atrocity via social media. Notwithstanding what may oft-times be quite conspicuous performances of agency, however, inscriptions of victimhood have an inherently objectifying effect, reducing those so inscribed to passive skin on which the centred subjecthood of the perpetrators of violence is performed and, in consequence of which violence, the imperative subjecthood of would-be protectors is mustered.

With this in mind, there is an important distinction to be made between agency and subjecthood, the former being the capacity to act and the latter the condition of being the autonomous or, at least, relatively autonomous author of one's own actions or agential choices.[5] Like victimhood, childhood brings this distinction into relief. In its currently hegemonic, Western-derived renderings, childhood is understood as, perforce, a time of innocence and vulnerability during which deferred autonomy is the enforced norm. Subjecthood may

the Rwandan Genocide', *Comparative Studies of South Asia, Africa, and the Middle East*, 28/1: 61–77 (2008).

5 J. Marshall Beier, 'Shifting the Burden: Childhood, Resilience, Subjecthood', *Critical Studies on Security*, 3/3: 237–252 (2015), p. 240.

be contingent on others' recognition of it in the context of unequal relations of power, as exemplified where young people are concerned inasmuch as they tend not to hold the power resources requisite to having their claims to bona fide or legitimate subjecthood prevail against the adult world's withholding such recognition. If, in light of this, critiques like those made of 'Kony 2012' and of 'White Saviors'[6] haughtily setting about to resolve the ills of the Global South go only so far as problematising these (neo)colonial knowledges and relations of power, this leaves unchallenged the analogously – and, in many instances, coeval – marginalising relations of adult-protector and child-protected. The co-constitution of subject/object, perpetrator/victim, protector/protected, and adult/child positions enjoins us to closely interrogate the politics of protection and the circulations of power that operate, in particular, through its various inscriptions and erasures of subjecthood.

In examining these issues, my aim is to move beyond the usual and expected association of the R2P with zones of conflict or in the context of mass atrocity and, with children's security, rights, and wellbeing in mind, to inquire into practices and conditions requisite to promoting and sustaining the prevention pillar of the R2P agenda. In what follows, I draw from two recent instances of horror suffered by young children, each in its own way manifesting spectacle. Though unrelated and separated from one another by great distance, each nevertheless presented a kind of ultimate test of Canada's self-image as a moral society. Both cases activated the impulse to protect and both prompted considerable deliberation upon the nature, extent, and location of responsibility. But despite Canada's long experience with and leading role in framing and sustaining the global R2P agenda since the formation of the International Commission on Intervention and State Sovereignty, both of these solitary instances of horror turn out to have challenged – and, indeed, continue to challenge – operant practices and understandings of protection and of responsibility in quite profound ways. In both cases, the impulse to protect was activated only after the failure of responsibility permitted horror to unfold unchecked, and this despite ample advance opportunity to intervene. Taken together, these discrete spectacles of horror reveal much about what is at stake in the politics of protection and for whom. They are likewise revealing of key impediments to a less hubristic framing of responsibility and protection – one proceeding from an orientation toward young people that takes them seriously as meaningfully possessed of autonomous subjecthood. As such, they give valuable content to a cautionary tale of the thorny ethical issues inherent

6 Cole, 'The White Savior Industrial Complex'.

in thinking about the responsibility to extend protection, in particular where young people are concerned.

Human Objects and the Spectacle of Horror

Within hours of his death on 2 September 2015, the abject, diminutive figure of Alan Kurdi was transformed into, among other things, an iconic figuration taken up and mobilised across a broad spectrum of political subject positions, none of them of his own making. The viral spread of shocking images of the drowned three-year-old's lifeless body, facedown on a Turkish beach and in the arms of the sombre police sergeant who carried him from the water's edge, came almost instantaneously to dominate the semiotic field attending the dramatic 2015 surge of refugee and migrant arrivals in southern Europe. Though his own story began in flight from the Syrian civil war, Alan's personal tragedy has since become visually and metonymically symbolic of the ongoing human tragedy of perilous Mediterranean transits from a multiplicity of origins, as far from Europe and from each other as Senegal, Somalia, and Afghanistan. At the same time, he has been discursively appropriated and semiotically deployed in support of, among other things, new initiatives to crack down on human smuggling, demands for humanitarian intervention, provision of foreign aid, calls to wage war against a host of groups and actors implicated in or deemed responsible for the refugee crisis, and even rallying of xenophobic political movements. Such is the evocative effect and broad purchase of dominant renderings of childhood innocence and of children as properly objects of protection which resonated strongly in everything from genuine grief to rhetorical feints attending these many and varied responses.

Half a world away, this resonance was felt in the federal election campaign then underway in Canada.[7] As the fuller story of Alan Kurdi was revealed in the days following his death, a Canadian connection came to light: efforts had been made to have the Kurdi family accepted into Canada as refugees and, were it not for difficulties encountered in the immigration process, at least this one tragedy might never have unfolded as it did. It turned out that Alan's father had a sister living in Canada who had wanted to sponsor the family's resettlement and who had appealed directly to then-Citizenship and Immigration

7 See CBC, 'Refugee Crisis, Drowned Syrian Boy Shift Focus of Election Campaign', *CBC News*, 3 September 2015, http://www.cbc.ca/news/politics/syria-migrants-canada-drowned-migrants-leaders-respond-1.3213878, accessed 11 July 2016.

Minister Chris Alexander on her brother's behalf months earlier.[8] What consequently emerged, literally overnight,[9] as a major election issue prompted a swift response from the Conservative government of Prime Minister Stephen Harper and the announcement that changes would be made to the process for adjudicating refugee claims, which opposition parties had previously charged was moving too slowly. Meanwhile, Justin Trudeau's Liberal Party reiterated its campaign promise to admit 25,000 Syrian refugees to Canada if elected – a commitment seen through, to much initial fanfare, after the Liberals won the 19 October 2015 election and Trudeau assumed the office of prime minister with a comfortable parliamentary majority.

Images of children once again figured prominently in both mainstream and social media coverage as the first of the 25,000 Syrians to arrive in Canada were greeted personally by the newly-elected Prime Minister Trudeau in December 2015. Trudeau, who had assigned to himself the cabinet role of Minister for Youth in the new government, later tweeted out photos in which he was seen welcoming young children specifically. But even as Canadians were becoming acquainted with the new federal government and a popular new prime minister, and as their making good on granting safe haven to Syrian refugees garnered considerable and sustained attention from Canadian media and an attentive – Baudrillard might say consumptive – public, new horrors were unfolding. Children from Syria and other counties continued to lose their lives in sinkings of overcrowded boats bound for southern Europe. In fact, 2016 saw a one third increase over 2015 in drownings of refugees and other migrants en route to Europe by way of inherently treacherous clandestine transits of the Mediterranean in dangerously overloaded and/or unseaworthy vessels, sometimes no more than inflatable rafts.[10] In the same period, the number of unaccompanied children who arrived in Italy by boat doubled.[11] And, as

8 Jillian Kestler-D-Amours, Peter Edwards, Tonda MacCharles, and Jacques Gallant, 'Tima Kurdi's Pleading Letter to Allow Brother to Enter Canada Revealed', *Toronto Star*, 3 September 2015, http://www.thestar.com/news/world/2015/09/03/canada-rejected-request-to-take-in-family-of-drowned-syrian-boy.html, accessed 12 July 2016.

9 See Aaron Wherry, 'Life, Death and Politics: The Death of Alan Kurdi and the Federal Election Campaign of 2015', *Maclean's*, 3 September 2015, http://www.macleans.ca/politics/life-death-and-politics/, accessed 11 July 2016.

10 Nick Cumming-Bruce, 2016. '"Worst Annual Death Toll Ever": Mediterranean Claims 5,000 Migrants', *New York Times*, 23 December 2016, http://www.nytimes.com/2016/12/23/world/europe/migrant-death-toll-mediterranean-europe.html, accessed 26 December 2016.

11 Deutsche Welle, 'Child Migrants Face Risks from Cold Weather, Boat Crossings, Says UNICEF', 13 January 2017, http://www.dw.com/en/child-migrants-face-risks-from-cold-weather-boat-crossings-says-unicef/a-37126510, accessed 13 January 2017.

Syrian refugee families were arriving in Canada, an unrelated coroner's inquest was underway in Toronto on the matter of the failure to extend protection to a child who was brutalised and murdered by her caregivers some three years before the start of the civil war in Syria.

Though it did not galvanise the same global circuits of reaction as that which Alan Kurdi came to signify, the horror inflicted on seven-year-old Katelynn Sampson bears in similar ways on intersections of childhood and the politics of protection. When her body was found in a west Toronto apartment on 3 August 2008, Katelynn had already suffered months of horrific abuse at the hands of her court-appointed guardians. An autopsy revealed that she had endured beatings so severe that her liver had ruptured. Among her many other injuries, she had multiple broken ribs and a laceration on one of her fingers reached the bone. Katelynn had not died in direct consequence of any of her many injuries but, rather, from toxic shock that set in from untreated injuries that were sustained over an extended period of time.[12] Officially, the cause of death was listed as 'complications from multiple blunt force injuries' and the death itself was ruled a homicide.[13] Police found Katelynn's blood in every room of the apartment where she had lived with the guardians whose brutality eventually killed her.[14] Disturbing evidence of protracted emotional and psychological torment was also found, including handwritten lines of text that Katelynn had been forced to transcribe repeatedly: 'I' am A awful girl that's why know one wants me'.[15] There was much more to the abuse, all revealed in an agreed statement of facts read in court and all just as appalling.[16]

12 Paola Loriggio, 'Toronto Girl Murdered by Guardians Was Once Struck So Hard Her Liver Ruptured, Pathologist Tells Inquest', *National Post*, 10 November 2015, http://news.nationalpost.com/toronto/toronto-girl-murdered-by-guardians-was-once-struck-so-hard-her-liver-ruptured-pathologist-tells-inquest, accessed 12 November 2015.

13 Ontario, Office of the Chief Coroner, 'Inquest Touching the Death of Katelynn Sampson: Jury Verdict and Recommendations', 29 April 2016, Toronto.

14 Catherine Porter, 'Katelynn Sampson Tragedy Shows We Forget Children Are People: Porter', *Toronto Star*, 30 April 2016, http://www.thestar.com/news/gta/2016/04/30/katelynn-sampson-tragedy-shows-we-forget-children-are-people-porter.html, accessed 1 May 2016.

15 Megan O'Toole, 'Guardians Get Life for Killing 7-Year-Old Girl', *National Post*, 1 May 2012, http://news.nationalpost.com/posted-toronto/two-accused-in-killing-of-7-year-old-girl-plead-guilty-to-second-degree-murder, accessed 26 November 2015.

16 Betsy Powell, 'Katelynn Sampson: Guardians Sentenced to Life in Prison For Murdering 7-Year-Old Toronto Girl', *Toronto Star*, 1 May 2012, https://www.thestar.com/news/crime/2012/05/01/katelynn_sampson_guardians_sentenced_to_life_in_prison_for_murdering_7yearold_toronto_girl.html, accessed 26 November 2015.

As did the spectacle attending Alan Kurdi's death, the horror that came to light following the murder of Katelynn Sampson moved subjects to action and prompted considerable introspection on the related dispositions of responsibility and protection. Questions of responsibility and protection were very much at issue in the 2012 trial of Katelynn's former guardians – both of whom entered guilty pleas for second-degree murder and were sentenced to life in prison with no chance of parole for fifteen years – and, even more, in the coroner's inquest that ran from November 2015 through April 2016. The inquest was confronted with the disquieting situation of a child having been murdered at the hands of the very persons explicitly charged with ensuring her wellbeing and protection. In May of 2007, care and custody of Katelynn had been voluntarily delegated to her eventual killers – Donna Irving and Warren Johnson – by Katelynn's mother, who was struggling to overcome addiction at the time. In 2008, an Ontario Court of Justice judge granted formal custody to Irving, who had a criminal history that included violence and who had told the Children's Aid Society some months earlier that she was unable to care for Katelynn and wanted her removed from her home.[17]

Importantly, the critical lapse that had left Katelynn to a lingering death at the hands of her appointed guardians could not be put down to the court alone. In fact, the Ontario Judicial Council – the public body charged with investigating the conduct of judges appointed in the province of Ontario – moved quickly to dismiss a formal complaint that was brought against the judge who granted Donna Irving full and final custody of Katelynn in June 2008, less than two months before the seven-year-old's death. Though court transcripts showed that the judge had asked few questions before granting custody to Irwin, the Judicial Council issued its dismissal of the complaint on the basis that the judge had not, in any event, been presented with anything to suggest Katelynn might be in danger or that her best interests were not being met.[18] But whatever the court did or did not glean from the process, by the time of the final decision as to custody Katelynn was already suffering abuse. Significantly, however, Katelynn's voice was not heard in order that her own assessment of her circumstances and of what would be in her best interests might be weighed. Even more troubling, the inquest into her death heard that both the Toronto Children's Aid Society and Native Child and Family

17 Jacques Gallant, 'Coroner Announces Inquest Into Death of Katelynn Sampson', *Toronto Star*, 13 August 2015, http://www.thestar.com/news/crime/2015/08/13/coroner-announces-inquest-into-death-of-katelynn-sampson.html, accessed 26 November 2015.

18 Joanna Smith, 'Judge Cleared in Katelynn Complaint', *Toronto Star*, 19 December 2008, http://www.thestar.com/news/gta/2008/12/19/judge_cleared_in_katelynn_complaint.html, accessed 5 December 2015.

Services – oversight of Katelynn's case was referred from the former to the latter because of her Indigenous heritage – as well as school officials had missed and/or let pass opportunities to intervene. The lawyer representing Katelynn's mother, Bernice Sampson, told the inquest jury that Katelynn was ignored; counsel for the coroner said Katelynn was 'unseen and unheard'.[19]

Several common threads recommend considering the otherwise separate and discrete tragedies of Alan Kurdi and Katelynn Sampson alongside one another. Most immediately apparent is horror. In its own way, each wrought an encounter with horror in which attentive publics were abruptly confronted with stark images and accounts of vulnerability and, ultimately, death under shocking conditions of abjection and suffering. As the broader narrative of his short life and tragic death unfolded, images of the living child, Alan, circulated with and were juxtaposed to the photos of his body on the beach. Similarly, photos of the living child, Katelynn, accompanied print and electronic media reports of the violence and abuse she suffered. Recognisable and relatable as representations of childhood innocence, the photos of the living Alan and the living Katelynn functioned to give further points of affective reference to the grave and terrible circumstances of their deaths. And, in both cases, this foregrounded horror was answered with much deliberation and debate on issues of responsibility and protection.

The question of responsibility can be accessed along two main lines. The first, responsibility in the sense of culpability for the dire human consequences visited on Alan and Katelynn, speaks to the acting subjects of the violences suffered by them and the assignment of blame. In each case, however, this is rather more complicated than it might at first appear. Although Katelynn Sampson's abusers-cum-killers were quite rightly held criminally responsible, both the trial judge and, later, the inquest jury were highly critical of the failure of public agencies and institutions to meet their duty to protect her. Likewise, while responsibility for Alan Kurdi's death was placed, variously, on human smugglers, warring factions in Syria, and the government of Bashar al-Assad, among others, many also laid blame with the inadequacy of international humanitarian responses to what had, by the time of his death, already been recognised for some time as a refugee crisis. This hints at the second sense in which responsibility is at issue in these cases, which is in the commitment to the view that there exists a responsibility to protect. And here protection

19 CBC, 'Katelynn Sampson Inquest: Institutions Too Slow to Assess Case, Says Children's Aid Lawyer', *CBC News*, 29 February 2016, http://www.cbc.ca/news/canada/toronto/katelynn-sampson-inquest-last-day-1.3468286, accessed 1 March 2016.

itself emerges as another central issue common to the cases of both Alan and Katelynn – one deserving of much closer examination.

Just as the abject circumstances and eventual deaths of Alan and Katelynn drew notice to intersecting sites of responsibility, so too both became bound up in the complicated and often fraught politics of protection. In the horror they laid bare, they prompted tangible and programmatic remedial action, from accelerated efforts to settle Syrian refugees in Canada to a new requirement for criminal background checks prior to reassignment of child custody in Ontario. But, in each case, despite the profundity of the sense of horror that was evoked and which was widely felt, it came too late to move any remediation to the benefit of either Alan or Katelynn. Thus, in the subsequent political action undertaken in their names, both were transmogrified into metonyms of vulnerable childhood (and, in Alan's case, a metonymic figuration of vulnerable refugees also). Each was objectified, then, in the sense that they were made iconic representations of an imperative to extend protection that could neither be of their making nor to their benefit. Instead, the whetted sense of a responsibility to protect which the horrific renditions of their respective stories brought about looked to other, living referents of protection to whom the benefits of that responsibility might yet be extended. Still critically at issue, however, are the subject/object relations of protector/protected that continue to cast a particularly long shadow in the context of adult/child relations. And this recommends a closer look at the operation of subjecthood in dominant cultural practices where our consumption of horror intersects childhood and the politics of protection.

Iconography of the Child Victim

More than mere artefacts or reportage, images can bear in significant ways on areas of social life such as the politics of protection, constituting key subjects and objects and situating them vis-à-vis one another in contexts of stability, crisis, security, capacity, responsibility, and more.[20] Judith Butler draws attention to how images that appear simply to have been found are, by way of framing, selection, and more – none of which need be immediately apparent to the

20 See Michael C. Williams, 'Words, Images, Enemies: Securitization and International Politics', *International Studies Quarterly*, 47/4: 511–531 (2003); Lene Hansen, 'Theorizing the Image for Security Studies: Visual Securitization and the Muhammad Cartoon Crisis', *European Journal of International Relations*, 17/1: 51–74 (2011).

viewer – products of composition that may involve the purposeful management of the viewer's sentiments.[21] For Butler, the photograph does not simply await our interpretation but is an interpretation in itself – one that encodes a political perspective in its very composition. Of course, there remains an important interpretative moment in consumption also. Composition relies on our bringing the relevant cognitive and affective competencies to the image if we are to see from its managed perspective. Something of this crucial element of intersubjectivity is evident in the ways war photography draws on affect. Analysing iconic war images dating from the early twentieth century to more recent years, Lilie Chouliaraki maps photojournalism's accent on emotional impact with the shift toward 'humanitarian' wars of intervention undertaken with the ostensible aim of reducing human suffering.[22] It is in these and similar visual economies that children and childhood take on particular saliency as reliable evocative scenery.

The presence or absence of recognisable markers of childhood in an image of violence or its aftermath can function as an implicit form of what Roland Barthes termed 'anchorage', directing the viewer 'through the signifieds of the image' so as to ensure – or, at least, urge the viewer toward ensuring – that the intended interpretation is drawn from the field of possible readings.[23] Though Barthes referred specifically to textual notations added to images, dominant renderings of childhood are so widely and deeply held that they can be counted on to direct interpretation in an analogous way and, being less conspicuously placed for the purpose of direction, possibly even more compellingly so. Constructed outside of political subjecthood and therefore outside of political life, children are positioned as the quintessential innocents in need of protection when the political projects of others turn to violent means. Accordingly, images of child victims of violence call on prevailing norms and predispositions concerning political subjecthood and may thus play a significant part in determining how the violence is understood. Our understandings of and approach to children and childhood, then, are key among the requisite competencies we bring to our interpretive encounters with images of horror.

We gain a clearer perspective on this if we consider the relative ambiguity of images of violence perpetrated against adults, especially adult men. The corpse of a man, no matter how thoroughly brutalised, is not automatically

21 Judith Butler, 'Photography, War, Outrage', *PMLA*, 120/3: 822–827 (2005).

22 Lilie Chouliaraki, 'The Humanity of War: Iconic Photojournalism of the Battlefield, 1914–1912', *Visual Communication*, 12/3: 315–340 (2013).

23 Roland Barthes, *Image, Music, Text*, trans. by Stephen Heath (New York: Hill & Wang, 1977), p. 40.

dissociated from political subjecthood in the same manner as that of a child. Though divested of it in death, the figure of the adult corpse will still sustain an imputation of active subjecthood in life. For this reason, the death may yet derive social meaning as, for example, a noble sacrifice in the manner of a warrior acting on behalf or in defence of others. Conversely, the same corpse might be taken to signify an erstwhile danger, perhaps an attacker justly and properly dispatched by another subject unseen in the image frame, and may thereby evoke a cathartic sense of the violence. Which of these diametrically opposed subject positions – or yet some other – may be read from the same image is contingent on some form of anchorage, but subjecthood itself is not held in question. Where the framing captures child victims, however, it is wont to delegitimise the violence represented and accentuate the sense of horror derived from it, no matter what the broader context, and pains may therefore be taken in image composition either to include or exclude child victims as befits the political purpose at hand.[24]

In this way, childhood itself provides the stable anchor, issuing unambiguous interpretive cues in the moment of an image's consumption. In their framing and given the broader contexts of their consumption, some affect an iconic figuration of vulnerable childhood that, in its capture of individualised horror, lends to political mobilisation against a broader unfolding of horror for which it is a metonymic representation. The famous photo of a young boy in short pants, his hands raised in surrender and with a look of fear on his face as he and others were rounded up in the 1943 Nazi liquidation of the Warsaw ghetto, is one such iconic figuration. So too the 1972 Pulitzer Prize winning photograph of nine-year-old Kim Phúc running naked from her village of Trang Bang, Vietnam following a napalm attack. In some instances, inanimate objects might serve as metonyms for childhood itself: a doll or other toy in the rubble of a building destroyed in an air raid; a small shoe left on the ground in the aftermath of a terror attack. In the campaign for a ban on landmines, a child-sized prosthetic limb was placed near the podium at some meetings. The prosthesis functioned as metonym of the singular child victim who, in turn, was metonymic of the aggregate category of 'victim' – objects of violence made objects of protection.[25]

It so happens that of the three aforementioned images of Syrian refugee arrivals which Justin Trudeau tweeted out in December 2015, the two that

24 J. Marshall Beier, 'Grave Misgivings: Allegory, Catharsis, Composition', *Security Dialogue*, 38/2: 251–269 (2007).

25 J. Marshall Beier, 'Dangerous Terrain: Re-Reading the Landmines Ban Through the Social Worlds of the RMA', *Contemporary Security Policy*, 32/1: 159–175 (2010), p. 168.

pictured Trudeau personally showed him welcoming Syrian children to Canada. Whether this was an intentional framing of the arrivals or merely coincidental, the images nevertheless encode vulnerability and protection in a manner that is arguably much more favourable to the Trudeau government's policy of welcome than to the position espoused by some voices in Canada to the effect that Syrian refugees were being admitted too abruptly and/or that they might pose a security threat. Extending refuge is fundamentally a matter of protection. Images and accounts of child refugees bespeak vulnerability in a way that implores and beseeches such protection. The upshot is that a politics betraying reluctance to extend protection to children is apt to be located on a spectrum running from callousness to iniquity. Illustrative in this regard was the resounding condemnation in January 2016 of a cartoon published by French magazine *Charlie Hebdo* suggesting Alan Kurdi, had he lived, would have grown to be a sexual predator. Despite its reputation for what many regarded as deeply offensive content, the magazine had drawn considerable sympathy and even vocal support from many quarters after it was targeted in a terrorist attack that left twelve dead a year earlier, but debasement of Alan Kurdi's innocence seemed a transgression few were willing to defend.

This is instructive as to how children constituted outside of political life, besides enabling projects that claim alignment with apposite aims of protection, present as potent discursive and semiotic resources for the delegitimisation of political opponents also. With reference to rhetorical flourishes by both sides in the Israeli-Palestinian conflict, as well as key interlocutors such as the United States and the United Kingdom, Robbie Duschinsky notes the Abrahamic traditions' deeply entrenched cultural norms of protecting children together with the view of innocent childhood and how this also enables metonymy such that the 'child is used to represent the persecuted nation, lending it a moral legitimacy in the face of criticism'.[26] Childhood is thus a terrain of engagement in its own right in the ongoing political violence in the region. Together with rhetorical appeals to innocent and vulnerable childhood as referent object of protection, children are cast as the intended beneficiaries of imagined futures in a manner reminiscent of Bonhoeffer's ultimate test. Political violence as the means to secure a future for children works to the fulfilment of the test and, thereby, is constitutive of moral society. Childhood so deployed functions once again as a device enabling political projects – including but not limited to war-making – of the adult world.

26 Robbie Duschinsky, 'Slaughtered Innocents: Child Victims in Political Discourse During the Second Intifada and Gaza Conflict', *Social Semiotics*, 21/1: 33–51 (2011), p. 33.

It is childhood's association with innocence and vulnerability that is critically at issue in these and other such projects, relying as they do on stable renderings of victimhood and the imperative blamelessness that sustains it.[27] Even where children might have some measure of acknowledged agency, recognition of autonomous subjecthood runs counter to hegemonic understandings of childhood. Despite its historical contingency as a distinctly late modern commitment, innocent childhood nevertheless has deep cultural purchase. Child soldiers, for example, who are undeniably actors of consequence, are not imagined to be the authors of their actions. Subjecthood and, with it, responsibility – or blame – for the violent acts in which they engage is usually located instead in some guileful and controlling figure of the adult world, erasing the subjecthood of child soldiers who may have adopted the role as an autonomously reasoned survival strategy[28] but also holding them blameless – in fact, preserving their victimhood – in respect of the political violence in which they participate.

This contrasts sharply with the possibility of assigning blame even to the corpse of the adult, though here too metonymy of innocent childhood can provide important anchorage to spectacles of horror. In September 2000, the world was shocked by a video broadcast on French television showing twelve-year-old Muhammad al-Durrah and his father, Jamal, caught in the crossfire between Israeli and Palestinian forces in Gaza. A dispute which later arose as to whether Muhammad had actually been killed as the video seemed to confirm only served to underscore the enormity of the political stakes for both sides in the Israel-Palestine conflict where issues of childhood, responsibility, and protection intersected the spectacle of horror. Writing in *The Guardian* just days after the tragedy, Susan Goldenberg noted that Muhammad had already 'become a potent symbol of one of the world's most bitter and enduring conflicts'.[29] Three years later, French photographer Jean-Marc Bouju captured another iconic image of a father and son in abject circumstances of insecurity when he photographed a hooded Iraqi man comforting his four-year-old son at a U.S. Army holding centre for prisoners of war in the early days following the U.S.-led invasion of Iraq in March 2003. As testament to its discursive reach,

27 Kieran McEvoy and Kirsten McConnachie, 'Victims and Transitional Justice: Voice, Agency and Blame', *Social & Legal Studies*, 22/4: 489–513 (2013).

28 Beier, 'Shifting the Burden', pp. 241–242.

29 Susan Goldenberg, 'Making of a Martyr', *The Guardian*, 3 October 2000, http://www.theguardian.com/world/2000/oct/03/israel6, accessed 12 August 2016.

the Dutch photojournalism organisation, World Press Photo, awarded Bouju's photo first prize in its annual World Press Photo of the Year competition.[30]

Much in the way of the poignancy of these images inheres in the presence of the child in each case. Countless images of adult men in similar circumstances but without their children (though they too might be fathers) fail to register the same notice, much less sympathy. In both cases, the anticipated acting subject of protection, the father, is palpably compromised in his ability to extend protection to the presumptive object of protection, his child. Perhaps what is so unsettling – and, for that reason, so evocative – about these images is that responsibility lacks for an imaginable subject position, unless it is ours. Alan Kurdi's father's expressions of grief and anger at the loss of Alan, his older brother, and their mother operate along the same register such that we come to see the images of Alan, alive and in death, implicitly and explicitly in terms of failure/inability to protect. In Canada, this renewed both popular and official dialogue on the aims, ethos and, ultimately, the workability of the R2P. Tina Jiwon Park, executive director of the Canadian Centre for Responsibility to Protect – based at the University of Toronto's Munk Centre and with an advisory board that includes early contributors to the R2P agenda – made the connection as clear as any could, highlighting the urgency, as signaled in the tragedy of Alan Kurdi, of progress on R2P on behalf of imperiled people everywhere, but 'especially women and children'.[31] Park also astutely cautioned that care must be taken to be mindful of unintended consequences of acting on a sense of responsibility to intervene in defence of others. Among these, I would like to suggest, are problematic renderings of subjecthood that bedevil the politics of protection.

Seen But Not Heard

Though not as readily reconciled to the R2P agenda as the case of Alan Kurdi, the tragedy of Katelynn Sampson is illuminating nonetheless for what it tells us about the relationship between subjecthood and protection. Security and rights frequently evince an uneasy coexistence, particularly in utilitarian

30 See World Press Photo, 'People in the News, First Prize Singles', 2004, http://www.worldpressphoto.org/collection/photo/2004/people-news/jean-marc-bouju, accessed 12 August 2016.

31 Tina Kiwon Park, 'From Promise to Practice, UN Marks 10 Years of R2P', *Open Canada*, 16 September 2015, http://www.opencanada.org/features/from-promise-to-practice-un-marks-10-years-of-r2p, accessed 20 June 2016.

framings that posit a hierarchy of needs or values.[32] Certainly, our present historical rendition is one in which rights claims are routinely subordinated to the declared requisites of security. Security – or, more precisely, insecurity – was very overtly at issue in Katelynn Sampson's case, but so too were rights. Specifically, the coroner's jury in the inquest into her death included first among its recommendations a call for 'all decision-making affecting children' as well as associated agencies, policies, and legislation, to operate on the basis of what it identified as 'Katelynn's Principle'.[33] Referred to the inquest jury for consideration by the provincially appointed Advocate for Children and Youth, 'Katelynn's Principle' drew directly from Article 12 of the United Nations Convention on the Rights of the Child (UNCRC) in its call for, among other things, giving effect to the recognition that 'children are individuals with rights, whose voices must be heard on matters effecting them, and their views must be given due weight in accordance with the age and maturity of the child'.[34]

The fly in the ointment remains the complicating factor of subjecthood, signaled already in the proviso, originating in the UNCRC, that weight be given to children's views on matters affecting them 'in accordance with the age and maturity of the child'. Here the adult world seeks to retain its regulatory function in respect of the extent of autonomy accorded to child/youth subjecthood. And it is in this connection that the hegemonic knowledges and commitments about childhood which provide critical anchorage for the decoding of images of children place their subjecthood in deferment once more. Dominant ideas about childhood hold it as a time of innocence and vulnerability but also of incapacity and deferred autonomy. It is for reason of these same knowledges and commitments, underwriting our cultural competencies so that we know how to 'see' children, that we do not know how to 'hear' them. To be a rights bearer is, in some imperative measure, to be a bearer of subjecthood also. 'Katelynn's Principle' makes this implicit link in its appeal to UNCRC Article 12. But it is undercut at the same time by the operant politics of protection that continue to position adult others as arbiters of the tension between children's rights and security.

Of course, and as Cecilia Jacob persuasively argues, this is in some senses as it must be, owing to the possibility of investing too much in children's

32 See, for example, Abraham H. Maslow, 'A Theory of Human Motivation', *Psychological Review*, 50/4: 370–396 (1943).

33 Ontario, Office of the Chief Coroner, 'Inquest Touching the Death of Katelynn Sampson'.

34 Ontario, Office of the Provincial Advocate for Children and Youth, 'Suggested Recommendations for Jury Consideration: Inquest into the Death of Katelynn Sampson', 26 February 2016, p. 3.

subjecthood given their usually significant and, in many cases, extreme position of disadvantage in social relations of power.[35] It is precisely this which calls for the intervention of more privileged and empowered subjects where children are in peril. That said, this is not wholly unique to the circumstances of children but is the case in respect of all those who may be similarly imperiled. It is characteristic of victimhood writ large that the ability to autonomously satisfy security needs is somehow compromised. Where this is not the case, there is no role for the exogenous protector. And it is consequently an irresolvable paradox of protection itself that it becomes necessary for reason of the diminished subjecthood of victims, which it simultaneously functions to diminish. The danger we are confronted with is that unsettling the constructions of childhood that efface children's subjecthood is simultaneously to disturb the very commitments that may be drawn upon to activate a sense of responsibility to extend protection to children. But this must be balanced with the pathological effects of being too readily disposed to appoint ourselves arbiters of the tension between rights and security.

It is useful here to recall critiques of protector/protected relations drawn along global North/South lines. Beyond bare hubris, the pretension to protect on the global level is not rendered benign by good intentions. In their metonymic figurations, children and childhood are deployed to facilitate political projects arising from a full spectrum of interests and intentions. This has been the case from the earliest days of the civil war in Syria[36] which is by no means unique in the marshalling of imagery of children.[37] Helen Brocklehurst shows how children are essentialised and sentimentalised in support of political projects premised on their protection and wellbeing but in respect of which they are denied independent political subjecthood.[38] Relying upon and reproducing 'common senses' and commitments about vulnerability and, with it, the subject/object inscriptions of protector/protected, machinations can be at work behind even the more benignly-conceived of the strategic discursive and

---

35 Cecilia Jacob, *Child Security in Asia: The Impact of Armed Conflict in Cambodia and Myanmar* (London: Routledge, 2014).

36 Cecilia Jacob, '"Children and Armed Conflict" and the Field of Security Studies', *Critical Studies on Security*, 3/1: 14–28 (2015), pp. 15–16.

37 Helen Brocklehurst, *Who's Afraid of Children? Children, Conflict and International Relations* (Aldershot: Ashgate, 2006); R. Charli Carpenter, *'Innocent Women and Children': Gender, Norms and the Protection of Civilians* (Aldershot: Ashgate, 2006).

38 Helen Brocklehurst, 'The State of Play: Securities of Childhood – Insecurities of Children', *Critical Studies on Security*, 3/1: 29–46 (2015).

visual deployments of childhood.[39] At the same time, the overwhelming focus on the global South works to (re)constitute North and South along (neo)colonial lines[40] reminiscent of the worst excesses of the 'White Man's Burden' and framing the North's obligation to the South in terms not only of aid but also armed intervention.[41] Epitomised by children in need of protection, pathology is located in the troubled South and solutions – together with the wherewithal to see them through – in the secure and developed North.

The fact is, children's insecurity and the myriad pathologies that exacerbate it are found in the North and the South. Jacob's detailed research on Cambodia's legacy of conflict and genocide and the social impacts that has had with respect to mental illness as well as family and community dysfunction shows how these endogenous conditions accentuate children's vulnerability.[42] Importantly, she reveals how child protection initiatives operate to the satisfaction of adult-centered political interests in ways that create the appearance of functioning practices oriented to the protection of children. Significant threats to children's – and especially girls' – security arise in the domestic context, exacerbated by the historical and cultural circumstances of everyday life in post-conflict Cambodia. This is elided, however, by the predominant focus on trafficking and other exogenous threats toward which protection regimes are oriented.

Though operating in different ways, all of these factors are present also, to greater or lesser extents, in contexts of the (post)industrial global North. In Canada in 2015–16, Indigenous suicide epidemics were overshadowed only by increased attention to the appalling recent (and ongoing) history of missing and murdered Indigenous women and girls. Unexplained deaths of Indigenous boys attending school in Thunder Bay, Ontario have occurred amidst complaints of virulent racism by some in that community directed toward these students from chronically under-served northern reservations. Numerous Indigenous communities face crises of insufficient, overcrowded, and woefully substandard housing. Domestic violence and chronic substance abuse plague many families, perpetuating cycles of trauma suffered by their adult members

39 R. Charli Carpenter, '"Women, Children and Other Vulnerable Groups": Gender, Strategic Frames and the Protection of Civilians as Transnational Issue', *International Studies Quarterly*, 49/2: 295–334 (2005).

40 Erica Burman, 'Innocents Abroad: Western Fantasies of Childhood and the Iconography of Emergencies', *Disasters*, 18/3: 238–253 (1994); Lorraine Macmillan, 'The Child Soldier in North–South Relations', *International Political Sociology*, 3/1: 36–52 (2009).

41 Katrina Lee-Koo, 'Horror and Hope: (Re)presenting Militarized Children in Global North–South Relations', *Third World Quarterly*, 32/4: 725–742 (2011).

42 Jacob, *Child Security in Asia*, pp. 104–108.

in a residential school system that endured well into the latter part of the twentieth century and whose legacies include the devastation of families and communities as some 150,000 children were severed from home and tradition (the latter having been an explicit aim of Canadian colonial authorities) and subjected to systemic violence, deprivation, and widespread sexual abuse.[43] More broadly, Canada is to a very significant extent an immigrant society with both newer and established refugee communities that include many people who will have experienced conflict with all of its traumatic effects in a full range of global contexts. Generally, Canada is no less prone than comparator countries to the gamut of more mundane social ills and the challenges they raise for children's security and well-being.

A further instructive point to be taken from the cases of Alan Kurdi and Katelynn Sampson, then, is that both came to embody and stand for a defined category of victim, Katelynn's case more readily inferred as the exception and Alan's as the rule. The qualitatively different approach to protection moved by each offers a glimpse into this distinction. That is to say, Alan's tragedy lends to the reading of an irredeemable status quo from which all for whom he comes to stand metonymically can only be offered refuge or intervention. Without minimising the humanitarian disaster that is the broader context of Alan's death, it is still the case that his is much more the exception than popular imaginaries – and purposeful deployments – might hold it to be. The death of Katelynn Sampson, on the other hand, has been constructed and engaged as a focal point for adjustment and redemption of a different status quo, here the institutionalised child protective regime in Ontario. And this has been so despite the fact that Katelynn's case was less exceptional than popular imaginaries might appreciate. This, then, suggests a further basis upon which to curb the hubristically outward gaze that characterises dominant framings of the R2P.

Resubjecting Security and Protection

In the meantime, childhood continues to circulate through the visual economies of humanitarian disaster in predictable ways, reinforcing the hubristic mappings of North/South, protector/protected, subject/object, and adult/child. On 28 January 2017, in response to the Trump Administration's announcement

---

43 See Truth and Reconciliation Commission of Canada, *Honouring the Truth, Reconciling for the Future: Summary of the Final Report of the Truth and Reconciliation Commission of Canada* (Winnipeg: National Centre for Truth and Reconciliation, 2015).

of a U.S. ban on refugees from Syria together with sweeping travel restrictions affecting seven Muslim-majority countries in all, Justin Trudeau retweeted one of the three images he first tweeted out more than a year earlier as Syrian refugees were arriving in Canada. Unsurprisingly, the retweeted image was the one that, of the three, most clearly bespoke the intersection of childhood and protection, framed around the Prime Minister crouching to welcome a newly arrived young girl at her eye level. Anchorage for the retweeted photo was furnished in the accompanying hashtag '#WelcomeToCanada' and in a separate tweet from the Prime Minister which read, 'To those fleeing persecution, terror & war, Canadians will welcome you regardless of your faith. Diversity is our strength'. The ways in which childhood itself also functions as anchorage here reminds us that, however laudable its exercise, there is an ineluctable dimension of protection that is, at base, paternalistic. Acknowledging this is not a call to foreswear the protective impulse but, rather, urges us to do the oft-times difficult work of reflecting on the problematic and, at times, pathological implications of even the best conceived intentions and projects.

In accessing the power circulations that simultaneously rely upon and reproduce the subordination of women as referent objects of protection, feminist contributions on vulnerability and the gendered logics of masculinist protection[44] are especially helpful in beginning to think beyond this. Carol Cohn proposes a move away from protection and toward preservation – an orientation that 'recognizes the agency of vulnerable humans and sees that it is the support of that agency that is crucial [and] … also asks not just how to protect against a danger, but how to prevent it, how to transform the circumstances that create it'.[45] Similarly, Jacob carefully demarcates child *security* from child *protection* and persuasively argues that '[l]ocating the *politics that determine children's insecurity* as a site for intervention is as important … [as] the political influence or agency exerted by children'.[46] These moves suggest means by which we might begin to ply the difficult interstices between subject

44 See, for example, V. Spike Peterson, 'Security and Sovereign States: What is at Stake in Taking Feminism Seriously?' in V. Spike Peterson (ed.), *Gendered States: Feminist (Re)Visions of International Relations Theory* (Boulder: Lynne Rienner Publishers, 1992); Iris Marion Young, 'The Logic of Masculinist Protection: Reflections on the Current Security State', *Signs: Journal of Women in Culture and Society*, 29/1: 1–25 (2003); Sara E. Davies, 'Addressing the Gender Gap in R2P', in Alex J. Bellamy and Tim Dunne (eds.), *The Oxford Handbook of the Responsibility to Protect* (Oxford: Oxford University Press, 2016).

45 Carol Cohn, '"Maternal Thinking" and the Concept of "Vulnerability" in Security Paradigms, Policies, and Practices', *Journal of International Political Theory*, 10/1: 46–69 (2013), p. 64.

46 Jacob, *Child Security in Asia*, p. 47; emphasis in original.

and object, protector and protected, adult and child, and Alan and Katelynn. However, it is essential that we guard against collapsing Jacob's important distinction into a public/private dichotomisation of violence and deprivation. Much turns on how 'politics' is delineated. If confined to hegemonic circuits of governance or even, more broadly, to include civil society actors and opposition groups, diminution of children's subjecthood – a politics in its own right – remains beyond the reach of intervention.

The greater significance of the horror suffered by Katelynn Sampson is in the lens it brings to bear on systematically engendered child insecurity, even in environs relatively 'peaceful' and privileged in terms of global registers. Here too, dominant ideas and assumptions about children and childhood are deeply implicated. Katelynn's is not a matter of domestic(ated) abuse operating in isolation from broader societal norms and merely indicative of 'failings' of a social regime of child protection – rather, it reveals highly problematic dispositions *in the name of child protection* that are both systemic and deeply imbricated with prevailing social norms and practices that are inimical to child security. It is important to bear in mind that while his most certainly was not an isolated case, neither was Alan Kurdi's iconically tragic fate exemplary of that of the majority of Syrian children, or even the majority of Syrian refugee children for that matter. Noting this is neither to deny the appropriateness of bringing his case under a child security rubric nor to engage in profoundly unhelpful relative weightings of violence. Much to the contrary, it is to resist the creeping re-insinuation of essentialised secure and insecure childhoods imagined into association with the global North and South, respectively.

Jonathan Wadley puts succinctly the gravitas of our engagements with protection, saying it is 'less about what is provided than it is about the effects of the performances undertaken in its name'.[47] It is well to remember, then, that just as abject childhood is effective in activating sympathy, child victims are no less effective in spurring outrage. The emotionally evocative framings that result may as readily summon retribution as respite. Responses of both sorts have been seen in the cases of Alan Kurdi and Katelynn Sampson, albeit in different ways but drawing on the same hegemonic ideas about childhood that work to constitute subject/protector and object/protected relations across multiple valences. Foregrounded in representations and reportage of violence visited on noncombatant groups, images and accounts of children's victimisation draw on markers of innocent childhood to function as metonym for

47 Jonathan D. Wadley, 'Gendering the State: Performativity and Protection in International Security', in Laura Sjoberg (ed), *Gender and International Security: Feminist Perspectives* (New York: Routledge, 2010), p. 52.

groups – victims and perpetrators alike – in aggregate and thereby lend easily to the mobilisation of state violence.[48] In all its dimensions, this affirms children's thorough objectification. They are pervasively acted upon, but no quarter is left within which to imagine that they may meaningfully act. Politics of protection or security engaged in their name simultaneously work to exclude them.

In what might be taken as a hopeful sign, in December 2015 the UN Security Council adopted a resolution calling for recognition of youth as active contributors to local and global peacebuilding efforts and, thus, their engagement as acting subjects of security, not merely its referent objects.[49] This sits well with a growing body of scholarly research that works to recover child/youth political subjecthood.[50] Doing so in respect of the politics of protection, though, demands a rethinking not only of childhood but also of the requisites of security and the manner of its provision. Though it is beyond the scope of this article to sketch even the barest outlines of a program of action, an approach that seeks to balance protection with 'bodily integrity' derived from an assumption of agency rooted in capabilities[51] suggests one such possible reconceptualisation. In addition to material requisites of wellbeing and safety from physical harm, bodily integrity requires broader freedom from restrictive control and/or regulation over young people's bodily autonomy. The very denial of children's subjecthood in this formulation is rendered inimical to a condition of security. The point here is not to resolve the irresolvable paradox of protection's effacing of subjecthood but to hold subjecthood and protection visibly in tension. Perhaps the ultimate test of the R2P inheres most fundamentally in the extent to which the requisites of a formulation such as bodily integrity are promoted. Moreover, it is imperative that this be on a global register, not merely in zones of conspicuous conflict or sites of mass atrocity for, as we have seen, the same relations of power work violences of erasure in other contexts also.

---

48 See Lorraine MacMillan, 'Children, Civilianhood, and Humanitarian Securitization', *Critical Studies on Security*, 3/1: 62–76 (2015), p. 64.

49 United Nations, 'UN Security Council Adopts First-Ever Resolution on Youth, Peace and Security', *UN News Center*, 9 December 2015, http://www.un.org/apps/news/story.asp?NewsID=52773#.WIukZBgZM_U, accessed 15 August 2016.

50 See, for example, Jacob, *Child Security in Asia*; Helen Berents, 'Children, Violence, and Social Exclusion: Negotiation of Everyday Insecurity in a Colombian Barrio,' *Critical Studies on Security*, 3/1: 90–104 (2015); Alison M.S. Watson, 'Resilience is its Own Resistance: The Place of Children in Post-Conflict Settlement', *Critical Studies on Security*, 3/1: 47–61 (2015).

51 See Martha C. Nussbaum, 'Capabilities as Fundamental Entitlements: Sen and Social Justice', *Feminist Economics*, 9/2–3: 33–59 (2003); Mar Cabezas and Gottfried Schweiger, 'Girlhood and Ethics: The Role of Bodily Integrity', *Girlhood Studies*, 9/3: 37–53 (2016).

Conclusion

Protection is beset by a paradox it cannot resolve. It is at one and the same time imperative in consequence of diminished political subjecthood, and yet, is itself demeaning of that same subjecthood. Where children are concerned, however, the paradox turns all the more swiftly to pathology. Bonhoeffer's 'ultimate test' of moral society locates children at its margins, as the eventual beneficiaries but not the builders of a just order. As such, it encodes a certain solipsism of the adult world not only in the presumption of an adult monopoly over political subjecthood but also in centering the adult world as the real referent of action: it is, after all, the adult world whose achievement – or forfeiture – of morality is at stake. Children in Bonhoeffer's formulation function in the manner of a literary device, the intelligibility of which derives, I would suggest, from hegemonic ideas about childhood vulnerability and childhood incapacity. There is thus a certain narcissism to this inasmuch as there is subject production at work here also, constituting adult-protectors as bearers of moral subjecthood.[52] A first step toward redress of this is to cultivate an ethic of responsibility *to* young people rather than *for* them.

The coroner's jury in the inquest into Katelynn Sampson's death lamented that Katelynn was not heard. The critically important question, however, is *why* hear Katelynn? Perhaps more to the point, why listen to the next child who finds herself in a situation of acute insecurity? Is she to be heard merely as a witness to what has played out or is likely to play out on her corporeally as an object of violence, abuse, or neglect, or is she to be respectfully engaged as a bona fide subject? Is she to be heard and taken seriously as a bearer of rights with meaningful input into what her circumstances will be going forward? These questions are more than rhetorical. In December 2015, a change to legislation in Ontario mandated that the province's Child and Youth Advocate would thenceforth be notified of serious injury or death suffered by children in care.[53] This is an indisputably vital measure – so much so that it is, in its own right, an indictment of the system that such a measure was not already in place. But it needs to be accompanied by equally clear measures to ensure

52 See Helen Berents, 'Hashtagging Girlhood: #IAmMalala, #BringBackOurGirls and Gendering Representations of Global Politics', *International Feminist Journal of Politics*, 18/4: 513–527 (2016).

53 Ashley Csanady, 'Children Who Die in Care in Ontario Will Get a New Voice Under Bill to Expand Advocate's Powers', *National Post*, 3 December 2015, http://news.nationalpost.com/news/canada/canadian-politics/children-who-die-in-care-in-ontario-will-get-a-new-voice-under-bill-to-expand-advocates-powers, accessed 5 December 2015.

children are heard as subjects with a valid perspective on their own rights, security, and requisites of wellbeing, not merely as sources of reportage as to the conditions of their care. Though seemingly remote from the usual terrain of the R2P, much is brought to light in Katelynn Sampson's case about the power relationships, subject/object configurations, and prevailing views on childhood that confound child security in local and global contexts alike. A final, ultimate test will be of our ability to make the connection.

Case Studies

Children on the Front Lines: Responsibility to Protect in the Israeli/Palestinian Conflict

Timea Spitka
Hebrew University, Israel
timea.spitka@gmail.com

Abstract

Children are disproportionally affected in violent conflict, are vulnerable to exploitation and lack protection when a state is failing in its responsibility to protect. In the Israeli/Palestinian conflict, children, particularly those living in Gaza, East Jerusalem, parts of the West Bank are not only vulnerable during escalations but are subject to exploitation, detentions and severe security measures. Divisions over culpability have made the local representatives and the international community incapable or unwilling to take collective action to protect this most vulnerable population. Given the divisive international context, are there R2P tools that can be used effectively to enhance protection for children and teenagers in the Israeli/Palestinian conflict? The focus on the protection of children demonstrates: Firstly, the need to closely analyse current protection tools particularly under Pillar III of R2P, Secondly, the importance to eradicate unintended effects of protection efforts, and finally the potential contribution of focus on children towards reaching a consensus on a protection regime.

Keywords

Responsibility to Protect – atrocity crimes – Israeli/Palestinian conflict – children and teens – protection

 | DOI:10.1163/9789004379534_010

Children and teens are disproportionally affected in violent conflict, are vulnerable to exploitation and as young activists, can be targeted by soldiers or in-prisoned. Children lack basic protection mechanisms when a state or other authorities are failing in their responsibility to provide protection. Pillar III of the Responsibility to Protect (R2P) norm gives responsibility to the international community to take timely and decisive action when the state or relevant authorities are manifestly failing in providing protection from atrocity crimes. Fear of misuse of measures, particularly under Pillar III, combined with a lack of international consensus in divided conflicts, has placed protection tools on hold in the most difficult contexts. Currently, there are few intersections between R2P and the prioritisation of protection of children. While the UN agenda prioritises prevention and the strengthening of state capacities under Pillar I and II, the most vulnerable population, children living in conditions with no state protection, continue to be exposed to ongoing atrocity crimes.

There has been much debate among scholars and practitioners on the importance and application of the R2P norm. According to supporters of the norm, R2P may be the most dramatic normative development of our time since it managed to finesse the tensions between sovereignty and protection from atrocity crimes.[1] Skeptics, however, point to R2P as being applied selectively and only when the interests of the great powers align.[2] Although R2P has failed to prevent atrocities in some of the most volatile and divisive conflicts, the concept that civilians have a right to protection has gained widespread international support.[3] An effective operationalisation of protection under R2P, however, is dependent on international consensus on the realities of the conflict, culpability for atrocity crimes and a construction of a collective framework for a protection regime. While R2P has become integrated into the international agenda, the operationalisation of the norm is indeed difficult when the interests of the great powers do not align. Pillar III of R2P in particular raises much concern among states and scholars about potential abuse and unintended effects. The use of sanctions and military tools to protect children, raises many red flags, however, lack of any action to protect this most vulnerable population, is also unconscionable.

Children are not only vulnerable in situations of violent conflict; they are also susceptible to exploitation and recruitment by extremists or the state. The

1 Ramesh Thakur and Thomas G Weiss, 'R2P: From Idea to Norm – and Action?', *Global Responsibility to Protect*, 1/1: 22–53 (2009).

2 Mahmood Mamdani, 'Responsibility to Protect or Right to Punish?', *Journal of Intervention and State Building*, 4/1: 53–67 (2010).

3 Jon Western and Joshua S. Goldstein, 'R2P after Syria, To Save the Doctrine Forget Regime Change', *Foreign Affairs*, 13 March 2013.

effectiveness of a protection regime for children can be difficult in complex and divided settings and runs the risk of unintended effects. The contentious military intervention in Libya and the lack of consensus among key interveners in Syria, point to the challenges of international intervention when a state is failing in its protection responsibility. Children whose homes, families and lives have been devastated by conflict, commonly lack agency and are vulnerable to exploitation, which gives the international community an increased responsibility. Children are not only vulnerable during a conflict, they commonly represent half of the displaced population and are at high risk of exposure to violence and exploitation.[4]

The Israeli/Palestinian conflict is one of the most divisive and politicised conflicts in the world. It is a conflict that has generated the highest number of vetoes in the Security Council and is commonly perceived as too contentious for the emerging R2P norm.[5] It is also a conflict that has provoked accusations of bias and unfair application against the UN by both Israel and the US, and against the US, which is perceived as shielding Israel from international repercussions. Protection issues, particularly related to children living in Gaza, East Jerusalem and parts of West Bank are fundamental, since all relevant authorities can be argued to be failing in their responsibility to protect. Given the divisive local and international context, East Jerusalem and parts of West Bank are there R2P tools that can contribute to providing protection for children and teenagers in the Israeli/Palestinian conflict? Can tools under R2P contribute towards a consensus on providing protection for children within the most divisive conflicts?

The Israeli/Palestinian conflict provides a good case for an examination of the relevance of Pillar III and protection tools under the umbrella of R2P in a divided context. The killing and exploitation of children, divisions on culpability, and a lack of basic protection measures are especially evident in Gaza, East Jerusalem and parts of the West Bank, where the failure of a protection regime exposes the fundamental challenges of the operationalisation of R2P in a divided context. While the Israeli-Palestinian conflict is admittedly one of the most divisive conflicts in the world, it exposes the vulnerability of children to war crimes and highlights an urgent need for a construction of a protection

4 Samira Sami, Holly A Williams, Sandra Krause, Monica A Onyango, Ann Burton, Barbara Tomczyk, 'Responding to the Syrian Crisis: the Needs of Women and Girls', *Viewpoint*, 8 November 2013, http://dx.doi.org/10.1016/S0140-6736(13)62034-6, accessed 23 November 2017; 'Global Trends, Forced Displacements in 2015', UNHCR, http://www.unhcr.org/576408cd7.pdf, accessed 23 November 2017.

5 Interview with political advisor, Office on Genocide Prevention and Responsibility to Protect, United Nations, 29 June 2016.

regime. Although consensus among key interveners is difficult to come by in many conflicts, the protection of children can also be used as a common consensus tool. For example, in Columbia, the protection of children was used as an entry point to negotiate the peace agreement.[6]

Outlined in the 2005 UN World Summit outcome document, the three pillars of R2P form the conceptual framework of Responsibility to Protect (R2P).[7] R2P norms outline that: first, the state is responsible to protect its population from war crimes; second, the international community (IC) is responsible to assist states to meet this obligation; and third, it is the responsibility of IC to take timely and decisive collective action when a state is 'manifestly' failing in meeting this obligation.[8] As noted by UN Secretary-General, and reiterated by Alex Bellamy, R2P applies everywhere and all the time.[9] This article examines Pillar III, which embodies a focus on the most vulnerable population, children under no state protection. Currently, there is little consensus on appropriate tools under Pillar III when a state, or responsible authorities, are failing in protecting their own population from war crimes.

This article will examine the tools under R2P when it comes to the protection of children in a divided context. Subsequent to an analysis of the challenges of protection of kids under Pillar III, when the relevant authorities are failing in their responsibilities; the article will examine the applicability of the tools under R2P in the context of the Israeli/Palestinian conflict. The focus will be on exploitation of children and examination of areas where there is little to no protection. Although protection is of concern for all children and teens affected by the conflict, in the case of Gaza, East Jerusalem and parts of the West Bank under Israeli Military Authority, no state or authority can be said to be providing protection. The article will look at the complexities of the responsibility of the various authorities in providing protection, examining whether R2P can be a constructive tool for enhancing protection for children in a divided context. The article will examine the current local and international protection efforts and tools. As in Syria, the UN Security Council has been deadlocked and attempts to reach a consensus on accountability and

---

6 'Vital efforts to protect children 'an entry point' for wider peace in Colombia – UN child rights envoy', UN News Centre, 25 October 2016, http://www.un.org/apps/news/story.asp?NewsID=55393#.WGJEHyN96oo, accessed 23 November 2017.

7 A/RES/60/1, World Summit Outcome, 2005, p. 30, paras. 138–140.

8 Alex J. Bellamy, 'The Three Pillars of Responsibility to Protect', http://www.cries.org/wp-content/uploads/2015/09/006-bellamy.pdf, accessed 23 November 2017.

9 Alex J. Bellamy and Tim Dunne (eds.), 'R2P in Theory and Practice', *The Oxford Handbook of Responsibility to Protect* (Oxford: Oxford University Press, 2016), p. 8.

sharp protection tools have been met with vetoes. Security Council vetoes are not new to the Israeli-Palestinian conflict where divisions among interveners have longevity predating R2P.

Examining the protection and lack of protection of children in a violent conflict suggests three fundamental elements. First, the focus on children evokes a need to analyse the appropriateness and effectiveness of current protection tools. Second, emphasis on children highlights the importance of protection tools with no unintended effects. Third, in a divided context, the protection of children can potentially serve as a bridge between the warring parties on constructing a protection regime. The article will proceed as follows: the first section will examine the challenges and appropriateness of R2P tools under Pillar III for the protection of children. The second section will examine the realities under current protection regimes for children in the Israeli-Palestinian conflict. The final section will examine hazards and potential opportunities toward the construction of a protection regime for the most vulnerable children within the Israeli/Palestinian context. The article will conclude with implications for protection of children under R2P in other divided conflicts.

R2P and Protection of Children: Appropriateness of Protection Tools

Since 2009, the emphasis of R2P has been on early warning, early engagement, assessment and preventative measures. The first Special Advisor for R2P Edward Luck noted that the key goal of the 2005 Outcome Document: 'should be prevention, prevention, prevention'.[10] Subsequent Special Advisor on R2P Jennifer Welsh placed her main focus on Pillar II, emphasising strengthening state capacities.[11] The activation of Pillar III is the source of most contention due to fears of breaches to sovereignty and the potential abuse of military tools. The range of potential tools under Pillar III, however, is vast and includes: diplomacy, mediation, public advocacy, conciliation, arbitration, judicial settlement, economic, political and strategic inducements, political support,

10 Edward C. Luck, 'Informal interactive dialogue on early warning, assessment, and the Responsibility to Protect', United Nations General Assembly, 9 August 2010, p. 2.

11 Jennifer Welsh, 'Remarks of the Special Advisor to the Secretary General on Responsibility to Protect', 11 September 2013, http://www.un.org/en/preventgenocide/adviser/pdf/Special%20Adviser%20Jennifer%20Welsh%20remarks.GA%20Dialogue%202013.pdf, accessed 8 January 2018.

peacebuilding, and consensual peacekeeping.[12] 2009 UN Secretary-General Report outlined a basket of tools under Pillar III including: on-site investigations and fact-finding missions; monitoring of hateful speeches and rallying international support to discourage public incitement; diplomatic sanctions; arms embargoes; financial and trade embargoes and military force.[13]

Although a consensus on Pillar III of R2P was reached in Libya, the subsequent military intervention, conducted by NATO, become a source of much discord.[14] NATO's operations and drones caused panic, killing and displacing children during the air strikes.[15] The ensuing chaos, lack of political progress and preparedness for post Gadhafi Libya, left the country as a failed state. There has been a rise in the abduction of children by armed groups, reported ISIS training camps of kids under 16, sexual violence by armed groups as well as summary executions of children.[16] These atrocities are in addition to the casualties as a result of shelling, suicide bombings and destruction of schools and hospitals.

Subsequent to the enactment of R2P in Libya, there has been little enthusiasm towards the use of Pillar III in other conflicts. Countries including the BRICS (Brazil, Russia, India, China and South Africa) noted that NATO intervention in Libya abused the good faith of emerging powers and overstepped UN's mandate.[17] In the case of Syria, UNSC resolutions that advocated the use of tough measures were vetoed by either Russia or China. The 11 resolutions that were passed avoided coercive measures or actions that would compromise Syrian sovereignty.[18] Non-intervention in conflicts where a population is vulnerable to ongoing war crimes is a failure of a different type.

The well-being of children comes from construction of a protection regime without unintended effects. The Child Protection Working Group (CPWG)

12 Alex J. Bellamy, 'The First Response: Peaceful Means in the Third Pillar of the Responsibility to Protect', The Stanley Foundation, December 2015, http://www.stanleyfoundation.org/publications/pab/Bellamy3rdPillarPAB116.pdf, accessed 23 November 2017.

13 'Implementing the Responsibility to Protect: Report of the Secretary-General', A/63/677, 12 January 2009, pp. 22–28.

14 Nathalie Tocci, 'On Power and Norms Libya, Syria, and the Responsibility to Protect', *Global Responsibility to Protect*, 8/1: 51–75 (2016), p. 68.

15 Lere Amusan, 'Libya's Implosion and its Impacts on Children', *Journal of International Women's Studies*, 14/5: 66–79 (2013), p. 74.

16 Office for the Special Representative for Children in Armed Conflict, A/70/836–S/2016/360, 20 April 2016.

17 Oliver Stuenkel, 'The Bricks and the Future of R2P: Was Syria or Libya the Exception?', *Global Responsibility to Protect*, 6/1: 3–28 (2014), p. 18.

18 Tocci, p. 63.

set up the minimum standards for child protection in humanitarian action in line with human rights law, humanitarian law and refugee law.[19] The UN Convention on the Rights of the Child (CRC) highlighted four key principles: protection rights, survival and development, non-discrimination and child participation.[20] Protection rights include safeguarding from all forms of violence, exploitation, trafficking and sexual exploitation, detention and child labor. Survival and development rights emphasise the basic right to life and the development of one's full potential. Non-discrimination emphasises a fair treatment of child regardless of background. Finally, child participation rights outlines that children have the right to be heard and their opinion taken into account.[21]

An examination of tools is fundamental for noting their effectiveness and unintended effects, especially on children. Monitoring, investigation and fact-finding missions can be useful tools to shed light on atrocity crimes and shame the perpetrators. Diplomatic sanctions, halting public incitement, naming and shaming and referring violations to the International Criminal Court (ICC) can be effective tools without unintended effects on children. Ban Ki-moon's 2009 report noted that leadership responsible for atrocity crimes should not be welcomed among their peers.[22] Findings have noted the effectiveness of Human Rights Organisations targeting a regime in the popular press, mobilising others to take actions to protect a repressed population.[23] Combating incitement and hate speech is another tool without negative effects and one of the priorities for UN Special Advisor for the Prevention of Genocide.[24] Due to its public and explicit character, it is relatively easy to identify incitement and rally international support for efforts to discourage it.[25]

Children living within a violent conflict are easy targets for exploitation by militants or the state. Militancy can be attractive to children because it can

19 Child Protection Working Group, 'Minimum Standards for Child Protection in Humanitarian Action', 2012, https://www.unicef.org/iran/Minimum_standards_for_child_protection_in_humanitarian_action.pdf, accessed 23 November 2017.

20 Ibid., p. 15.

21 Ibid., pp. 27–32.

22 Ban Ki-moon, *Implementing the Responsibility to Protect* (New York: United Nations, A/63/677), 12 January 2009.

23 Amanda Murdie and Dursun Peksen, 'The Impact of Human Rights INGO Shaming on Humanitarian Interventions', *Journal of Politics*, 76/1: 215–228 (2014).

24 H.E. Adama Dieng, Special Advisor for the Secretary-General on the Prevention of Genocide, United Nations, INoGS Conference, Keynote Speech, 'Preventing Genocide Today: Applying the Lessons of the Past to Protect Future Generations', Jerusalem, 26 June 2016.

25 A/63/677, 12 January 2009, p. 24.

provide meaning, group identity, and options that civilian life does not afford.[26] Social media has made it easier to reach and recruit pre-teens and teens. Radical groups stand to benefit from exploiting children as it is convenient and cheap.[27] Recruitment of children by armed groups exposes the children to exploitation and engagement in paramilitary activities. The need to protect children is seldom officially disputed among states or belligerents since most are held to account by their support base.

Children's protection has become a priority for many UN missions and this has delivered some results. UN led dialogue with national armed forces and armed groups since 2000 has resulted in the release and rehabilitation of more than 115,000 child soldiers.[28] Dialogue with perpetrators in the Central African Republic, Colombia, Mali, Myanmar, the Philippines, Sudan and South Sudan in 2015, resulted in the release of over 8,000 children.[29] Exploitation of children can also be at the hands of the protectors. A 1996 UN study highlighted that the arrival of UN peacekeeping troops had been associated with a rapid rise in child prostitution.[30] The appointment of Special Representative of the Secretary General on Children and Armed Conflict (SRSGCAC) and monitoring of grave violations against children has led to more concrete actions and safety measures focused on children. The UN has deployed child protection staff and set up child protection units in many missions including: United Nations Mission in South Sudan (UNMIS), United Nations Mission in Darfur (UNAMID), United Nations Organization Stabilization Mission in the DR Congo (MONUSCO), United Nations Stabilization Mission in Haiti (MINUSTAH), United Nations Assistance Mission in Afghanistan (UNAMA), United Nations Mission in Liberia (UNMIL), and United Nations Operation in Côte d'Ivoire (UNOCI).[31]

26 Michael Wessells, *Child Soldier: From Violence to Protection* (Cambridge, US: Harvard University Press, 2009), p. 4.

27 Ibid., p. 2.

28 'Impact of Armed Conflict on Children Twenty Years of Action Following the Publication of Graça Machel Report to the General Assembly', Office for the Special Representative of the Secretary General for Children and Armed Conflict, 25 August 2016, https://childrenandarmedconflict.un.org/graca-machel-report-20th/, accessed 2 January 2017.

29 Department of Peacekeeping Operations, 'Child Protection in the United Nations Peacekeeping', (United Nations: Spring 2011).

30 'Promotion and Protection of the Rights of Children, Impact of Armed Conflict on Children', A/51/306, 26 August 1996.

31 Ibid., p. 18.

The safety and wellbeing of children is a yardstick that can assist in measuring effective protection mechanisms for the civilian population. SRSGCAC identified 6 categories of grave violations against children including: killing and maiming of children; recruitment or use of children as soldiers; sexual violence against children; attacks against schools or hospitals; denial of humanitarian access for children and abduction of children.[32] Children and teens in conflict are vulnerable to intended and unintended killings, maiming, exploitation, detentions, recruitment by extremists as well as other abuses such as child labor, lack of access to basic human needs, domestic violence, sexual exploitation and child marriage.

R2P, however, addresses only the most serious atrocity crimes related to: genocide, ethnic cleansing, war crimes and crimes against humanity. This article examines war crimes and crimes against humanity as these are arguably the most relevant to the Israeli/Palestinian case. War crimes include crimes that are committed in times of war and violate international humanitarian and human rights law such as proportionality in war, exploitation, and use of child soldiers.[33] Crimes against humanity include degradation or humiliation of human beings based on their culture or religion such as deportation, imprisonment, apartheid, and torture.[34] The office of SRSGCAC has expressed many concerns to both Israel and the relevant Palestinian authorities regarding violence and killing of children by Israeli Defense Forces (IDF), exploitation of children by Islamic extremist groups and overall lack of security for children in the Israeli/Palestinian conflict.[35] This article's examination of the Israeli/Palestinian conflict will consider the intersections of R2P and protection of children in two key areas potentially related to war crimes and crimes against humanity: firstly, proportionality in the Gaza wars and use of children as human shields and secondly, exploitation, killing, maiming and detention of children.

---

32 Office for the Special Representative for Children and Armed Conflict, 'The Six Grave Violations Against Children during Armed Conflict: The Legal Foundation', October 2009 (Updated November 2014), https://childrenandarmedconflict.un.org/publications/WorkingPaper-1_SixGraveViolationsLegalFoundation.pdf, accessed 2 January 2018.

33 Prevent Genocide International, 'Rome Statue of the International Criminal Court', 17 July 1998, https://www.icc-cpi.int/NR/rdonlyres/ADD16852-AEE9-4757-ABE7-9CDC7CF02886/283503/RomeStatutEng1.pdf, accessed 2 January 2018.

34 Ibid., articles 5–9.

35 Report of the Secretary-General, 'Children and Armed Conflict', A/70/836–S/2016/360, 20 April 2016.

Children in the Israeli/Palestinian Conflict

Children within the Israeli/Palestinian conflict are subject to significantly different conditions and protection mechanisms depending on their place of residence and their ethno-religious identity, making steps towards a R2P regime more complex. The children of Gaza are subject to the most volatile and harsh conditions stemming from the Gaza wars, Israeli military incursions into Gaza, living under radical Islamic regime, being subject to harsh economic sanctions and limited mobility. Although children living in Gaza have the least protection and are the most vulnerable to alleged atrocity crimes, only focusing on the children in Gaza leaves out the interconnectedness of the conflict and potential common solutions. Children living within Israel are subject to sequences of rocket attacks, terrorist attacks and cycles of violence, which traumatise kids and serve as the justification for security measures which infringe on the protection of Palestinian children. Living under harsh conditions of Israeli military occupation, Palestinian children living in the West Bank are subject to cycles of violence, exploitation, detentions, shootings and collective punishment including searches, closures and the demolition of homes.

Local protection measures for children are extensively different depending on the location and ethno-religious identity of the child. Most Israeli homes and buildings are equipped with safe rooms and Israeli children have access to adequate policing and social protection mechanisms. Most vulnerable within Israel are those residing next to Gaza, Palestinian-Israelis (Israeli-Arabs), Bedoin communities and visible minorities. Palestinian children and youth living in East Jerusalem are vulnerable not only because they are frequently subject to harsh security measures and lack citizenship, but also since most families do not accept Israeli institutional jurisdiction, children and teenagers have a contentious relationship to the Israeli police and other institutional services. The escalation in the summer of 2017 triggered by the change of status quo at the Al Aqsa mosque, demonstrates the lack of protection measures for Palestinians living in East Jerusalem. In order to disperse Palestinian demonstrators, the security forces used tear gas, stun grenades, skunk spray, rubber bullets and live fire. As noted by B'tselem, the Israeli police and security 'treated the Palestinian residents as if they were enemy soldiers rather than as a civilian population for whose wellbeing and security it is responsible'.[36] The escalation resulted in

36 'Playing with fire: Israel's sweeping disregard for the wellbeing and security of East Jerusalem residents has led to four fatalities and dozens of injuries, and disrupted the lives of tens of thousands of residents', *B'TSELEM*, 24 July 2017, http://www.btselem.org/press_releases/20170724_playing_with_fire_in_jerusalem, accessed 30 November 2017.

hundreds of injuries and the deaths of 3 young Palestinian protesters at the hands of Israeli security, as well as 3 Israeli settlers killed in their home by a young radicalised Palestinian attacker.

For decades, Israeli and Palestinian armed groups have been engaged in cycles of violence contributing to a lack of security for the civilian population. Children have been on the front lines of this conflict subject to harsh realities, political manipulation, violence and severe security conditions. The state-centric focus on security has contributed to the justification of security measures that prioritise the protection of its own groups while infringing on the security of others. Measures that were designed to be temporary and transitional under Oslo Agreement, such as dividing the West Bank into Areas A (under Palestinian authority), Area B (Joint Israeli/Palestinian Control) and Area C (under Israeli Military Authority), have become a permanent reality for a generation of Palestinian children growing up with checkpoints, violence, walls, and lack of law and order. The children and youth most vulnerable in the West Bank are those living in rural areas near Israeli settlements and in Area C where there are no Palestinian police.

Children, or those under the age of 18, are commonly not viewed as children when they are suspected of being perpetrators in the conflict. Children are considered to belong to the enemy making the difference between adults and minors almost irrelevant.[37] Palestinian Islamic groups such as Hamas as well as Israeli Military Authorities in the Occupied Territories officially consider children over 16 as adults. Palestinian children as young as 12 can be jailed by Israeli authorities and suspects are commonly labeled as terrorists in the Israeli media.

Palestinian children living in Gaza, have minimal access to protection since neither Israeli authorities nor the current Hamas-led Palestinian Authority prioritises the protection of children. Children have been used as human shields by the IDF, and exploited and recruited for terrorism by Palestinian extremists. Since Gaza is under effective Israeli control and under the governing authority of Hamas and Palestinian Authority, a fundamental question is whether any authority is providing protection for the civilian population in Gaza. Palestinian-ruling Hamas has prioritised fighting Israel and the arming of militants over providing protection. Israel perceives its bombardment of Gaza and other security measures as necessary to protect its own civilians. Palestinian

---

37 Piet Van Reenen, 'Children as Victims in the Israeli/Palestinian conflict, Policing Realities and Police Training', in Charles W. Greenbaum, Philip E. Veerman and Naomi Bacon-Shnoor (eds.), *Protection of Children During Armed Political Conflict, A Multidisciplinary Perspective* (Oxford: Intersentia, 2006), p. 375.

Authority has been unable to govern Gaza, and its current measures of controlling Hamas, such as limiting electricity, only impacts on the hardship of the population.

The current international divisions hinder the application of R2P tools that could be implemented in the Israeli/Palestinian conflict. Since 2000, US has vetoed more than 18 UN Security Council resolutions including: sending unarmed monitors to the West Bank and Gaza (2001), condemning Israel for acts of terror against civilians in the Occupied Territories (2001), immediate cessation of Israeli settlement activities (2011), and condemning Israel for its massive violations of international law in Gaza and the West Bank (2015). Although US did not veto the recent UNSC resolution 2334 on settlements, this was the first resolution to pass since 2009, and was a final act under Obama administration that is unlikely to be repeated under the new Trump administration. US has also blocked other initiatives. In 2015, US placed pressure on UN Secretary-General Ban Ki-moon to drop Israel from the list of offenders in the report on Children and Armed Conflict.[38] Although the pressure was successful in removing Israel and Hamas from the list, the report included detailed list of incidents that later incited accusations of bias from the Israeli representative.

Gaza Wars

Children are most vulnerable in Gaza, where they make up close to 40% of the 1.8 million people living under cycles of violence that include bombardment, harsh conditions of the occupation and a Hamas-led militant regime. Gaza is one of the most densely populated areas of the world, cut off from outside and almost entirely dependent on foreign aid. Since 2007, the Gaza Strip has been under a tightly controlled land, sea, and air blockade. The economic blockade, severe fuel and water shortages, and Israeli restrictions on many items including basic construction materials have left much of the population vulnerable to not only violence but also natural elements.[39] A 2015 report by UN

38 'UN: Ensure Integrity of Children's "List of Shame"', *Human Rights Watch*, 4 June 2015, https://www.hrw.org/news/2015/06/04/un-ensure-integrity-childrens-list-shame, accessed 2 January 2018.

39 At the time of writing, Gaza has electricity for 3–5 hours per day and most of the water is considered undrinkable. See 'Gaza energy crisis: limited improvement in water and sanitation indicators; concerns over waterborne diseases remain', OCHA United Nations Office for the Coordination of Humanitarian Affairs, Occupied Palestinian Territory, 10 November 2017, https://www.ochaopt.org/content/gaza-energy-crisis-limited-improvement-water-and-sanitation-indicators-concerns-over, accessed 2 January 2018;

Conference on Trade and Development warned that Gaza Strip under current trends would become uninhabitable by 2020.[40]

The 2008/9, 2012 and 2014 Gaza wars resulted in many civilian deaths, destruction of homes, schools, hospitals that ensued in accusations of war crimes perpetrated by Hamas and IDF, threats of sanctions, and bringing those responsible to justice. Ten-year-old children living in Gaza would have lived through 3 wars in their lifetime and due to the blockade, most children would have not been able to exit Gaza. Even prior to the 2008 Gaza war, 83% of youth living in Gaza reported witnessing a shooting and 82% of children reported moderate or severe levels of Post Traumatic Stress Disorder (PTSD).[41] Since Gaza is closed and there are few shelters or safe areas, children are exposed to violence during escalations, as well as within schools and their homes. Palestinian children living in Gaza reported that 82% were exposed to tear gas attacks, 74% were exposed to night raids, and 53% had a family member imprisoned.[42] UNICEF has estimated that 95% of children between the age of 1 and 14 living in Gaza, also experience psychosocial aggression or physical punishment.[43]

In December 2008, Israeli Operation Cast Lead launched massive Israeli airstrikes killing hundreds of people in Gaza within the first four minutes. Around 1,400 people, including up to 431 children, were estimated killed in the 22 days of the war.[44] The attack was a response to the increasing number of Qassam rockets launched from Gaza targeting southern Israeli towns, killing or maiming dozens of Israeli civilians. The subsequent UN inquiry, headed by Richard Goldstone, accused IDF of war crimes, crimes against humanity and serious violations of international law, recommending further investigation and the bringing of those responsible to justice.[45] The report documented many atrocity crimes against children including the killing of children, the launching of

---

'With Only Three Hours of Electricity a Day, Gaza Is "On Verge of Explosion"', *Haaretz*, 4 January 2017, https://www.haaretz.com/middle-east-news/palestinians/.premium-1.763586, accessed 2 January 2018.

40 'Gaza could become uninhabitable in less than five years due to ongoing "de-development"', UN Conference on Trade and Development, *UN News Centre*, 1 September 2015.

41 Samir Quota and Eyad El Sarraj, 'Prevalence of PTSD Among Palestinian Children in the Gaza Strip', *Arabypsynet Journal*, 2: 8–13 (2004).

42 Ibid.

43 UNICEF, 'Protecting children from violations and abuse in Gaza', 25 October 2016 https://www.unicef.org/infobycountry/oPt_92946.html, accessed 23 November 2017.

44 Amnesty, 'Operation Cast Lead: 22 Days of Death and Destruction', *Amnesty International*, MDE 15/015/2009.

45 UN Human Rights Council, Fact Finding Mission, 'Human Rights in Palestine and Other Occupied Arab Territories' (Geneva: Human Rights Council, A/HRC/12/48, Sep 24, 2009).

attacks from within civilian areas, the use of white phosphorus, and using children as human shields. The UN Human Rights Council endorsed the report and the UN General Assembly urged Israel and Palestine to conduct an independent investigation into the alleged war crimes. The EU Parliament also endorsed the report, noting that the report's recommendations should be carried out with accountability for all violations. On the other hand, US Congress voted the Goldstone report to be 'irredeemably biased' and called on President Obama to maintain his opposition to the report.[46] In response to the criticism from Israel and US, Goldstone noted that the report would have looked different had the Israeli government cooperated with the investigation and toned down criticism of Israel in the final report. There has been little accountability for the alleged atrocity crimes of 2009. In one case that did go to the courts, two Israeli soldiers were convicted of using a 9-year-old Palestinian boy as a human shield to open bags that were suspected of containing explosives, however, their sentences were suspended.[47]

The 2014 Gaza War resulted in more civilian deaths, external investigations and accusations of war crimes and once again little accountability or repercussions for perpetrators. Israeli justification for the military campaign was the kidnapping and murder of 3 Israeli teens and the ongoing rocket fire launched by armed groups from Gaza. In the 2 month escalation leading up to the Gaza war, Israeli forces fatally shot two 15 and one 17-year-old unarmed Palestinian teens, Palestinian men killed three Israeli settler teens (16, 16 and 19) and Israeli settlers kidnaped and burned alive a 15-year-old Palestinian teen.[48] None of the teens killed were suspected of doing anything inappropriate but were victims of indiscriminate targeting or revenge attacks. The killings of the teens sparked public outrage and led to massive Israeli retributions.

Israeli bombardment of Gaza destroyed residential buildings, hospitals, schools and much of the infrastructure, and displaced close to a third of the population.[49] Two universities, 7 UN schools and 141 local schools suffered

---

46 US Congress, 'Opposing any endorsement or further consideration of the Report of the United Nations Fact Finding Mission on the Gaza Conflict', *Congressional Record*, 3 November 2009.

47 'Israeli soldiers who used Palestinian boy, 9, as a human shield avoid jail', *The Guardian*, 21 November 2010, https://www.theguardian.com/world/2010/nov/21/israeli-soldiers-human-shield-avoid-jail, accessed 23 November 2017.

48 Defense for Children International, Palestine, 'Child Fatalities', http://www.dci-palestine.org/child_fatalities_statistics, accessed 23 November 2017.

49 United Nations Office for the Coordination of Humanitarian Affairs (OCHA), 'Fragmented Lives: Humanitarian Overview 2014', 26 March 2015.

severe damage.[50] A UN Human Rights Council report noted that of the 2,251 people killed in Gaza, about 1,462 were civilians.[51] The war also resulted in the death of 551 Palestinian children and 1 Israeli child.[52] At least 2,955 Palestinian children were injured in Gaza with up to one-third (1000) disabled permanently.[53] During the July and August period, Palestinian militants indiscriminately fired 4,881 rockets and 1,753 mortars towards Israel, killing 6 civilians.[54] Alarms, safe rooms and the air defense system (Iron Dome) prevented the loss of more Israeli lives, however, many civilians were under the threat of bombardment and unable to move freely. Studies have shown that children, especially younger children exposed to missile attacks, suffered from posttraumatic stress symptoms.[55]

An investigation by the UN Human Rights Council found serious violations of international humanitarian and human rights law by both Israel and Palestinian militants that were investigated as potential war crimes.[56] Defense for Children International reported at least 7 cases where Palestinian children, aged 9 to 17, were used as human shields by the IDF during the 2014 Gaza Conflict.[57] The kids were forced at gunpoint to search buildings and tunnels, and were held in captivity for days in dire conditions without the knowledge of their families.[58] The UN Secretary-General noted that he was deeply alarmed

50 Rasha Faek, 'Educational Toll of Gaza War: At Least 2 Universities, 148 Schools', *Al Fanar Media*, 3 August 2014.

51 'Report of the detailed findings of the independent commission of inquiry established pursuant to Human Rights Council resolution S-21/1', A/HRC/29/CRP.4, Human Rights Council, 23 June 2015.

52 'Fragmented Lives: Humanitarian Overview 2014', 26 March 2015, p. 6.

53 'Children and Armed Conflict', Report of the Secretary-General, A/69/926-S/2015/409, 5 June 2015.

54 UN Human Rights Council, *Report of the Independent Commission of Inquiry Established Pursuant to Human Rights Council Resolution S-21/1*, 2015, www.ohchr.org/Documents/HRBodies/HRCouncil/CoIGaza/A-HRC-29-52_en.doc, accessed 23 November 2017.

55 L.E. Miller-Graff and E.M. Cummings, *Developmental Review*, 43: 1–47 (2017).

56 'Report of the detailed findings of the Commission of Inquiry on the 2014 Gaza Conflict', A/HRC/29/CRP.4, 23 June 2015.

57 'Palestinian Children Being Used as Human Shields', Defense for Children International, 1 February 2015, http://www.dci-palestine.org/palestinian_children_being_used_as_human_shields, accessed 25 November 2017.

58 'Operation Protective Edge, War Waged on Gaza's Children', Defense for Children International, April 2015, https://d3n8a8pro7vhmx.cloudfront.net/dcipalestine/pages/530/attachments/original/1436292897/OPE_A_War_Waged_on_Children.pdf?1436292897, accessed 2 January 2018.

at the extent of grave violations suffered by children as a result of the Israeli military operation:

> The unprecedented and unacceptable scale of the impact on children in 2014 raises grave concerns about Israel's compliance with international humanitarian law, notably the principles of distinction, proportionality and precaution in attack, and respect for international human rights law, particularly in relation to excessive use of force.[59]

According to Alex Bellamy, there were at least four principles of acceptable war conduct that IDF violated; targeting (when the target is not clearly military), the principle of due care (minimising civilian harm), the principle of proportionality (proportionate to the military objective) and the use of indiscriminate weapons in civilian areas.[60] As noted by Bellamy, 'whilst Israel has a right – and a responsibility – to protect its citizens from war crimes against humanity, it also has a responsibility to do the same for the Palestinians in Gaza'.[61] The protection of civilian populations was essentially non-existent or completely ineffective in Gaza. The United Nations Relief and Works Agency for Palestine Refugees in the Near East (UNRWA) schools were used as shelters for internally displaced women and children, however, many were directly hit by missiles or artillery. An UNRWA school in Beit Hanoun was struck by several missiles, which killed 11 people including 7 children. A school in Jabalia was also struck by artillery killing 15 including 4 children.[62] The targeting of schools was blamed on Israel as well as Hamas. The UN found evidence that Hamas deliberately used Gaza's civilian population including children to shield military assets.[63] UNRWA announced the discovery of approximately 20 rockets hidden in one of its vacant schools.[64]

IDF claimed that measures such as leaflets recommending evacuation and a small blast on the roof were intended as warnings for people to evacuate

59 'Children and Armed Conflict', A/69/926-S/2015/409, 5 June 2015.

60 Alex J. Bellamy, 'The Responsibility to Protect and the 2014 Conflict in Gaza', *E-International Relations*, 22 July 2014, http://www.e-ir.info/2014/07/22/the-responsibility-to-protect-and-the-2014-conflict-in-gaza/, accessed 25 November 2017.

61 Ibid., p. 2.

62 OCHA, 'Fragmented Lives', p. 20.

63 UN Human Rights Council, A/HRC/29/52, 24 June 2015.

64 'UNRWA strongly condemns the placement of rockets in school', 17 July 2014, https://www.unrwa.org/newsroom/press-releases/unrwa-strongly-condemns-placement-rockets-school, accessed 2 January 2018.

residential buildings targeted for bombardment. However, civilians had nowhere to flee; no location in Gaza was considered safe, and even those areas that were designated as 'safe' such as UN schools were targeted. In densely populated areas, the 'small blasts' created confusion as individuals did not realise their building was targeted, or were hurt or killed while escaping the building.[65] In addition, children, the elderly and those providing for their care found escape especially challenging.

In some cases, armed groups including Hamas purposely fired from built-up areas and prevented civilians from evacuating.[66] Hamas authorities recommended to the civilian population to ignore IDF instructions and remain in their homes. The IDF considered all those who were warned to leave but remained in areas designated to be targeted, as voluntary shields. According to interviews with IDF soldiers who took part in the operation, the rules of engagement in 2014 were quite lax.[67] Discussing the operation in Bureij, an IDF soldier interviewed note:

> I asked my commander: "Where are we firing at?" He told me: "Pick wherever you feel like it." And later, also, during talks with the other guys – each one chose his own target, and the commander, on the two-way radio, called it "Good Morning al-Bureij".[68]

The Hannibal Directive, which gives leeway to Israeli soldiers for shooting at all targets in order to prevent abduction of soldiers, was reportedly activated in Rafah and Shujaija.[69] In Rafah, where two Israeli soldiers were killed and one was suspected of being kidnapped, every person and moving vehicle became a potential target.[70]

The 2014 Gaza war had an unprecedented negative effect on children's sense of wellbeing and security. UNICEF estimates that about 373,000 children

65 UN Report, A/HRC/29/CRP.4, 23 June 2015, p. 65.

66 UN Human Rights Council, A/HRC/29/52, 24 June 2015.

67 'This is How We Fought in Gaza: Soldiers' Testimonies and Photographs from Operation "Protective Edge"', *Breaking the Silence*, 2014, Testimony 43, p. 110, http://www.breakingthesilence.org.il/pdf/ProtectiveEdge.pdf, accessed 2 January 2018.

68 'This is How We Fought in Gaza: Soldiers' Testimonies and Photographs from Operation "Protective Edge"', *Breaking the Silence*, 2014, Testimony 29, p. 80, http://www.breakingthesilence.org.il/pdf/ProtectiveEdge.pdf, accessed 2 January 2018.

69 Human Rights Council, A/HRC/29/52, 24 June 2015, p. 13.

70 Ibid., p. 14.

in the Gaza strip required specialised psychosocial support.[71] – The psychological impact on children subsequent to the war include: excessive nervousness, difficulty in concentrating, sleep disturbances, eating problems, fear, withdrawal and violent behaviour.[72] The high levels of exposure to political violence have also been linked to higher rates of family, school and interpersonal violence.

Human Rights Council report noted; 'impunity prevails across the board' and recommended an inquiry into war crimes by the International Criminal Court (ICC).[73] Israel and the US rejected the UN investigative report and have remained steadfast against the ICC. Israel, like the US, has not ratified the Rome Statute for fear it may be used to persecute its own citizens. However, the Government of Palestine accepted the jurisdiction of the ICC and opened a formal investigation. The ICC is currently investigating over 3,000 reported incidents and crimes that occurred during the 2014 Gaza conflict.[74] The ICC's preliminary investigation into alleged crimes noted that the conflict had a significant impact on children.[75]

Exploitation, Killing, Maiming and Detention of Children in the Israeli/Palestinian Conflict

Within the Israeli/Palestinian conflict, children and youth participating in actions such as demonstrations, throwing stones or attempted assaults are subject to maiming, arrests, detention and extrajudicial killings. Children and youth are also vulnerable to being exploited by members of their families, the community, in schools, and manipulated though cultural activities and social networks by paramilitary organisations. While Palestinian paramilitary groups have been accused of recruitment of children, the IDF have been accused of intentional or unintentional killing of children and teens and as well as military detentions of children. Some of the attacks by Palestinian youth have

71 'Gaza two years on: the psychosocial impact on children', UNOCHA, 6 September 2016, https://www.ochaopt.org/content/gaza-two-years-psychosocial-impact-children, accessed 25 November 2017.

72 Laura E. Miller-Graff and E. Mark Cummings, 'The Israeli-Palestinian Conflict: Effects on Youth Adjustment, Available Interventions, and Future Research Directions', *Development Review*, 43: 1–47 (2016), p. 27.

73 UN Human Rights Council, A/HRC/29/52, 24 June 2015, pp. 19–22.

74 Ibid., p. 30.

75 Office of the Prosecutor, 'Report on Preliminary Examination Activities', International Criminal Court, 14 November 2016, https://www.icc-cpi.int/iccdocs/otp/161114-otp-rep-pe_eng.pdf, accessed 25 November 2017, p. 27.

been attributed to suicide attempts by frustrated teens, lacking opportunities or having personal problems, knowing they will likely be swiftly killed if they take out a knife or scissors in front of Israeli soldiers.[76] Children and teens may also lack appropriate skills or coping mechanisms for passing though strict military checkpoints and searches, and unarmed Palestinian teens have been killed for suspicious behaviour or not following instructions. In some areas, especially around Israeli settlements, Palestinian youth engaged in regular activities such as walking home from school are subject to harassment by settlers, border police and private security guards.[77]

Since the 2014 Gaza war, dozens of children have been killed in demonstrations, crossing checkpoints or while involved or suspected of being involved in attacks against Israelis. In 2015, heightened tensions resulted in cycles of violence, demonstrations and individual attacks by Palestinians, killing more than 20 Israelis. During 2015, 14 Palestinian youths were shot dead while involved in or suspected to be involved in stabbing attacks against Israelis. Children found to be holding knives or scissors as young as 14, have been killed on the spot by Israeli security or vigilante civilians. In 2015, 30 Palestinian children (25 boys and 5 girls) were killed and at least 1,735 injured (1,687 boys and 48 girls) in the West Bank and East Jerusalem.[78] The IDF was responsible for the killing of most of the children in the West Bank. The number of Palestinian children killed in the West Bank went up in 2016 with 33 minors killed under the age of 17.[79]

Palestinian children living under the Occupation in Gaza and the West Bank are subject to military rule, where the current age of responsibility is 12 years. According to UNICEF, the majority of children on trial in Israeli military courts have been charged with throwing stones.[80] In 2016, the Israeli Knesset (Parliament) passed amendments to the penal code increasing the maximum sentence for throwing stones to 20 years. While a child between the age of 12 and 13 can receive a maximum sentence of 6 months, a teen between the ages of 14 to 15 charged with throwing stones can receive a maximum penalty of 20 years. The Knesset also approved a new bill that allowed a child 'terrorist' as

---

76 Gideon Levy and Alex Levac, 'Israeli Police Help Palestinian Girls Commit Suicide', *Haaretz*, 3 June 2016.

77 'Settlers' presence in Batan al-Hawa results in local minors being arrested and detained by security forces', *B'Tselem*, 28 December 2016, http://www.btselem.org/jerusalem/20161228_batan_al_hawa_minors, accessed 25 November 2017.

78 A/70/836-S/2016/360, 20 April 2016.

79 Defense for Children International, 'Child fatalities'.

80 UNICEF, 'Children in Israeli Military Detentions: Observations and Recommendations', February 2013, p. 8.

young as 12 to be jailed within Israel. The justification for the new legislation noted:

> The seriousness that we attach to terror and acts of terror that cause bodily injury and property damage, and the fact that these acts of terror are being carried out by minors, demands a more aggressive approach including toward minors who are convicted.[81]

Anat Berko, a member of Benjamin Netanyahu's Likud party, said that the law is borne of necessity: 'A society is allowed to protect itself. To those who are murdered with a knife in the heart it does not matter if the child is 12 or 15'.[82]

General escalation in violence, political incitement, influence of social media, and vigilantism has all contributed to the killing of teens. Several members of the Israeli government praised extrajudicial killings by police, private security guards and vigilante civilians. Interior Security Minister Gilad Arden stated that 'every terrorist should know that he will not survive the attack he is about to commit'.[83] Knesset Member Yair Lapid declared that 'you have to shoot to kill anyone who pulls out a knife or screwdriver'.[84] In 2015, the Major of Jerusalem suggested to all Jewish residents with gun permits to carry their weapons. Senior IDF officers took a more moderate tone to the politicians. IDF Chief of Staff, Lieutenant-General Gadi Eisenkot emphasised that 'I don't want to see a soldier empty a magazine [to shoot] a young girl with scissors'.[85] In one of many instances of questionably proportional responses, 14 and 16-year-old girls armed with scissors were shot repeatedly after they stabbed and lightly wounded a man in West Jerusalem.[86] Human rights organisations noted that instead of acting in a manner consistent with the nature of each incident, police officers and soldiers are quick to shoot to kill, and criticised political and

81 Lizzie Dearden, 'Israel approves new law to jail child "terrorists" as young as 12', *Independent*, 3 August 2016, http://www.independent.co.uk/news/world/middle-east/israel-approves-new-law-to-jail-palestinian-child-terrorists-as-young-as-12-human-rights-stabbings-a7170641.html, accessed 25 November 2017.

82 Ibid.

83 'Human Rights Organizations in Israel: Politicians' calls to police and soldiers to shoot rather than arrest endorse the killing of Palestinians', *B'Tselem*, 14 October 2015.

84 Ibid.

85 Noam Amir and Maariv Hashavua, 'IDF Chief: No Need To Pump Bullets Into Palestinian Girl With Scissors', *Jerusalem Post*, 17 February 2016.

86 'Palestinian teens armed with scissors shot in Jerusalem', *Al Jazeera*, 23 November 2015, http://www.aljazeera.com/news/2015/11/israeli-palestinian-violence-151123101833511.html, accessed 6 January 2018.

public support for such actions. 'Politicians and senior police officers have not only failed to act to calm the public climate of incitement, but on the contrary have openly called for the extrajudicial killing of suspects'.[87]

Shooting rubber and live ammunition at Palestinian youth while they are demonstrating has also resulted in many serious injuries. In 2016, there were 3215 known injuries of Palestinians by Israeli Forces in the Occupied Territories, many of them to children and youth.[88] There is seldom investigation even though some of the injuries result in permanent damage. The Israeli Army has recently been accused of a 'shoot to cripple' campaign due to a sharp rise in shooting injuries directly to the knees. A security officer, referred to by youth as 'Captain Nidal', has been said to be behind a campaign that targets demonstrators with a bullet to the knees with an alleged intent to cause permanent damage. Youths in the Dheisha refugee camp in the Bethlehem area said that 'Captain Nidal' on visits to the camps and to their homes has threatened to cripple them. According to youth living in the camp, the officer tells the young people that 'there will be no martyrs in the camp but all of you will end up on crutches'.[89]

The 2014 Gaza War and its coverage in social media had a strong impact on especially the young population in the West Bank, East Jerusalem and within the Israeli-Arab community in Israel. Unedited photos and videos of violence and atrocities were shared in social media such as Facebook, affecting and radicalising populations already sympathetic to the Palestinian suffering. East Jerusalem Facebook sites such as Bab Al-Amud Al-A'n called for solidarity with the Gaza people, punishment for the perpetrators of the violence, protests and a violent uprising.[90] For example:

> The social network sites of Palestinian boys invite you to many angry marches in the West Bank and in the security zones and the Mukataa headquarters [the headquarters of the Palestinian Authority] – burn

87 'Human Rights Organizations in Israel: politicians' calls to police and soldiers to shoot rather than arrest endorse the killing of Palestinians', *Adalah*, 14 October 2015, https://www.adalah.org/en/content/view/8659, accessed 25 November 2017.

88 OCHA, 'Protection of Civilians Report', 7–20 March 2017.

89 Amira Hass, 'Is the IDF Conducting a Kneecapping Campaign in the West Bank?', *Haaretz*, 27 August 2016.

90 Maya De Vries, Asmahan Simry, Ifat Maoz, 'Like a Bridge Over Troubled Water: Using Facebook to Mobilize Solidarity Among East Jerusalem Palestinians During the 2014 War in Gaza', *International Journal of Communication*, 9: 2622–2649 (2015), p. 2637.

> them because they are the reason for the Mahmoud Abbas betrayal of our brothers in Gaza. "Fight, victory or death".[91]

For Hamas and Palestinian Islamic Jihad, recruitment of children particularly in Gaza but also within the West Bank and inside Israel is an ongoing phenomenon. Inside the Palestinian territories, Hamas runs mosques, schools, orphanages, summer camps, sports leagues, student unions and cultural activities which are used to socialise young children and youth.[92] Other radical Islamic groups have been linked to NGOs and schools, and pictures of martyrs are commonly displayed in schools and other public areas. A graduation ceremony at a kindergarten run by al-Jam'iya al-Islamiya, featured 1,600 preschool age children wearing uniforms and carrying pretend rifles.[93] In 2015, the Izz el-Deen al-Qassam Brigades ran a military camp in Gaza for 25,000 children and young people between 15 and 21 years of age.[94] The Popular Front for the Liberation of Palestine reportedly held a graduation ceremony during a camp for girls, which included training in weapons.[95]

Harsh security measures and fear of recruitment of Palestinian teens by radical groups has made them one of the primary targets for arrest. Approximately 7,000 Palestinian children have been detained, interrogated, prosecuted and/or imprisoned within the Israeli Military Justice System in the past 10 years.[96] According to UNICEF, this is an average of 700 kids per year or 2 children per day and has been one of the focal points of concern for protection for humanitarian organisations. Many arrests take place at night and children report being blindfolded, painfully hand-tied, strip-searched and subject to physical violence. A 2014 working group on *Grave Violations Against Children* gathered 208 affidavits from children: 162 reported being blindfolded, 189 being painfully hand-tied, 171 subjected to physical violence and 148 reported being strip-searched.[97] Since October 2015, the numbers have risen. UNICEF has identified practices 'that amount to cruel, inhuman or degrading treatment or

91 Ibid., p. 2638.

92 Matthew Levitt, 'Hamas from Cradle to the Grave', *Middle East Quarterly*, Winter: 3–15 (2004).

93 Ibid.

94 'Children and Armed Conflict, Report of the Secretary General', A/70/836-S/2016/360, 24 August 2017, p. 14.

95 Ibid.

96 'Children in Israeli Military Detention, Observations and Recommendations', *UNICEF*, February 2013.

97 Ibid., p. 4.

punishment according to the Convention on the Rights of the Child and the Convention against Torture'.[98]

According to UNICEF, in no other country are children systematically tried by juvenile military courts, which fall short of providing the necessary guarantees to ensure respect for their rights.[99] The Committee on the Rights of the Child expressed 'its deepest concern about the reported practice of torture and ill-treatment of Palestinian children arrested, prosecuted and detained by the military and the police'.[100] Human rights groups have also requested that Israel end the practice of night-arrests and solitary confinement for children. Although the impact of the conflict on the lives of children has been the source of external investigation and criticism launched against Israeli authorities and Palestinian Paramilitary groups, there has been little action towards construction of a protection regime.

Palestinian and Israeli representatives have utilised the dim realities of children affected by the conflict to hurl accusations against the opposing side. Israel's representative to the UN Amit Heumann publicly pointed out that in Gaza, Hamas uses young boys to dig terror tunnels, children as human shields and it embedded its terror infrastructure in schools, hospitals and civilian neighborhoods. 'For the sake of peace, for the sake of the children on both sides, the international community must send a clear message to the Palestinian leadership' he said.[101] Nadya Rasheed, UN observer for the State of Palestine, said that Palestinian children continue to be killed, injured and terrorised by the occupying power with impunity and pressed the Council to provide protection to Palestinian children and hold accountable violators of international law.[102]

Children and R2P in the Israeli-Palestinian Conflict: Towards a Protection Regime

Invoking R2P within the Israeli/Palestinian conflict is a complex process given the deep external divisions, existing realities, and the question of appropriate protection tools under the relevant authorities. Currently there is little

98 Ibid., p. 9.

99 Ibid.

100 Children in Israeli Military Detention, Observations and Recommendations', *UNICEF*, February 2015, p. 4.

101 'Children's Rights Violations during Armed Conflicts on Rise despite National Action Plans to End Abuse, Security Council Told in Day-long Debate', SC/12470, 2 August 2016.

102 Ibid.

protection of children and teens, particularly those living in Gaza, East Jerusalem or parts of the West Bank. The first challenge is the potential of reaching a consensus among local and international interveners on prioritising the protection of children. The second challenge is constructing a protection regime within the current complex reality. The third challenge is discerning appropriate protection tools given the differing authorities and the potential of unintended effects on children.

Political solutions, namely a final status peace agreement, would be the ideal step towards the creation of a protection regime, but this is far from a realistic option given the current local and international political context, heightened tensions and lack of an acceptable external broker. One can outline three different categories of protection tools: those that are likely to cause more harm to children such as military solutions or collective economic sanctions; those that are helpful and do not cause harm but may not alleviate or prevent war crimes and crimes against humanity such as humanitarian solutions and monitoring, observing and fact finding missions; and those that may contribute to preventing war atrocities and are less likely to cause unintended effects on children such as monitoring hate speeches, international policing missions, justice tools such as International Criminal Court (ICC) and targeted sanctions.

The use of an external military force is clearly inappropriate or impossible in the Israeli/Palestinian context. If one prioritises the protection of children, it is difficult to perceive any type of military intervention that would contribute to the protection of the civilian population in densely populated areas. Financial and trade embargoes can have unintended effects on children and are unlikely to work effectively in the context of international disunity. Sanctions against Hamas since 2005 have only served to harm the civilian populations in Gaza without contributing to a political solution or protection. Hamas in Gaza have managed to smuggle in weapons and goods while the general population has become more vulnerable. Boycott, Disinvestment and Sanctions (BDS) against Israel has caught the attention of the international community as well as Israel but international divisions on its application has thus far resulted in only marginal impact. The US administration at the time of writing would also likely block any sanctions against Israel.

Operationalisation of a protection regime under R2P is challenging given the complex context. The realities and vulnerability of children and youth are significantly different depending on the location and identity of the kids. The most serious protection issues for the children living within Israel are the rocket attacks that indiscriminately target the civilian population and the cycles of violence and incitement by both Islamic organisations and members of the Israeli government. Under Pillar I of R2P, the Israeli state is responsible for providing protection, however, the current security measures, such as the policy of shooting-to-kill civilians suspected of terror attacks is deadly for teenagers. For the most part, young teenagers armed with scissors, screwdrivers or knives do not pose a serious risk to soldiers or armed civilians, and force should be used proportionally to the threat. Israeli politicians and senior police officers have not only failed to calm the public, but on the contrary have openly called for extrajudicial killings regardless of age or the level of threat of the suspect.

On-site investigations and fact-finding missions are tools without harm to children and are already conducted in the Israeli/Palestinian conflict. Conclusions of investigations have been used to bring atrocity crimes to the attention of the International Criminal Court (ICC). Although the ICC is free from unintended effects on children, it is a challenging tool given the opposition from the US, Israel and the divided international context. However, as noted by Ercan, if successful in pressuring local investigation of atrocity crimes or persecuting individuals responsible for war crimes, ICC investigations may indeed be a game changer in the Israeli/Palestinian conflict.[103] Although the ICC may be the most powerful preventative tool, it is yet to be seen whether the international judiciary body is powerful enough to withstand opposition from Israel and the US. In 2002, the US government threatened to veto every UN peacekeeping operation on the ground if its personnel did not receive a blanket amnesty from prosecution by the ICC.[104] Subsequent to the 2016 UN Security Council Resolution 2334, Trump questioned the value of the UN, and cut US funding to UNWRA.

In Area 'A' of the West Bank, it is the Palestinian Authority, Palestinian security and police, who are responsible for providing protection. The protection issues of most concern are in areas under no local Palestinian authority, namely in Area C, where Palestinian civilians live under Israeli military rule without access to Palestinian police or any protection. Similarly, in East Jerusalem kids and teens are vulnerable since they do not have full Israeli rights, their families do not accept Israeli authority, and are cut off from Palestinian institutions including police and the judiciary. Thus, Area C of the West Bank

103 Pinar Gözen Ercan, 'Responsibility to Protect and Inter-state Crises: Why and How R2P Applies to the Case of Gaza', *The International Journal of Human Rights*, 19/8: 1018–1111 (2015), p. 1106.

104 Ariela Blatter and Paul D. Williams, 'The Responsibility Not To Veto', *Global Responsibility to Protect*, 3/3: 301–322 (2011), p. 310.

as well as East Jerusalem arguably falls under the category of Pillar III of R2P, since currently no authority is providing protection for the population. The role of international policing missions such as the EU Coordinating Office for Palestinian Police Support (EU COPPS), which currently mentors, trains and advises Palestinian police, can also be expanded deployed in Areas B and C. This could serve as a transitional phase towards transference of full authority under the Palestinian security and state.

Monitoring of hateful speeches in local media and rallying international support to discourage public incitement are tools without unintended effects on children provided the information is not used to detain children. Monitoring of media and hateful speeches for public incitement is particularly important to prevent children and teens from being recruited into terrorist activities. Israeli authorities are focused on monitoring of hate speech, and are one of the leading countries in favor of this R2P tool. However, in 2016, five Palestinian children were placed in Israeli administrative detention following accusations of inciting or threatening to commit violence in Facebook posts.[105] The arrest of children living under the military occupation and the treatment of Palestinian minors in detention, is of special concern, and needs to conform to international law.

Currently, all relevant authorities are arguably failing in providing protection to children living in Gaza, which makes Gaza also a prime case for Pillar III of R2P. The civilian population, in particularly the children, are vulnerable not only to alleged war crimes committed by both Israel and Islamic militant groups, but also to lack of basic human needs due to the harshness of the occupation and economic sanctions. Evoking Pillar III in the Gaza context is a challenge both from the perspective of appropriate tools and reaching an international consensus. The deployment of a regional or international police force in Gaza would contribute towards law and order, which is currently in short supply. However, reaching an international consensus in a divisive context is not a simple task.

Reforms of the UN machinery such as Responsibility while Protecting (RwP), restraints on the use of veto and shifting the role of executor from the Security Council to the General Assembly have been recommended as potential roadmaps towards improved operationalisation of R2P. Ercan noted that R2P's dependency on the Security Council is arguably the greatest handicap

105 Defense of Children International, 'Year in Review, Worst Abuses against Palestinian Children in 2016', 1 January 2017, http://www.dci-palestine.org/year_in_review_2016, accessed 8 January 2018.

for an effective global implementation of R2P.[106] The veto rights of the five permanent members of the UNSC (US, China, Russia, France and UK) have been noted to be obstructive in many conflicts including Israel/Palestine. The Responsibility Not to Veto (RN2V) in response to atrocities has been seen as a mechanism to improve the implementation of R2P. Sixty-three states as well as the EU have so far called for reform of the Security Council outlining restraint on the use of veto in mass atrocity situations.[107]

The R2P norm has ascended as a mechanism for reaching a consensus on the appropriateness of international intervention in a sovereign state. Alex Bellamy noted that R2P is a label that can be tagged to a conflict in order to generate the will and consensus necessary to mobilise a decisive international response.[108] Focusing on the protection of children in the Israeli/Palestinian conflict is a potential uniting point for initiating the construction of a protection regime. Tools without unintended effects such as investigations by the ICC, or supportive policing missions in Gaza that could assist to establish rule of law, prevent firing rockets against Israel, and work with local and international authorities to prioritise protection, could contribute towards protection of the most vulnerable. Using appropriate tools without unintended effects especially on children, R2P can become as it was intended, a mechanism for reaching consensus in conflicts where the population is vulnerable to atrocity crimes.

Conclusion

The legitimacy and effectiveness of R2P is entwined with providing protection for the most vulnerable populations. Children and teens are commonly the most vulnerable not only because they are victims but also because they may challenge existing realities and be easily exploited by extremists or incarcerated by authorities. Pillar III of R2P raises particular concerns due to the possibility of military intervention and unintended effects on children. Even as a last resort, military intervention, particularly the use of bombing campaigns, is an inappropriate protection tool if one prioritises the welfare of children. However, Pillar III of the R2P norm has a wide array of tools and gives responsibility to

106 Ercan, 'Responsibility to Protect and Inter-state Crises', p. 1108.

107 Simon Adams, 'Failure to Protect: Syria and the UN Security Council', *Global Centre for Responsibility to Protect*, March 2015, pp. 1–32, p. 20.

108 Alex. J. Bellamy, 'The Responsibility to Protect – Five Years On', *Ethics and International Affairs*, 24/2: 143–169 (2010), p. 159.

the international community to take timely and decisive action when the state is manifestly failing to provide protection. Operationalising R2P in divided settings such as the Israeli/Palestinian conflict is challenging given the divisions about culpability for war crimes and accusations of bias, however, if one prioritises the welfare of children, it can be used to construct a consensus.

There are several implications for the protection of children under Pillar III of R2P that would be relevant to other conflicts. First, protection of children is a good yardstick with which to predict and measure the effectiveness of protection tools. Unintended effects, such as killing of children under the guise of protection, are simply unacceptable. The international community would be well advised to unpack tools under Pillar III and use protection mechanisms which enhance protection for the most vulnerable. Policing missions that emphasise law and order, human rights and working with local authorities and civil society would be far more effective in contributing to a protection regime than those that solely punish the perpetrators. Protection can be in parallel with empowerment since children and teens are not without resilience. The 2018 incarceration of 16-year-old Palestinian activist Ahed Tamimi for slapping a soldier has made her into a symbol of Palestinian resistance. A focus on protection with children in mind can also emphasise the importance of zero tolerance on unintended effects such as exploitation. Pillar III of the R2P norm, however, should not be left on the shelf, since it addresses the needs of the most vulnerable. Rather, if one prioritises the protection of children, Pillar III of R2P could be a useful tool to construct a consensus in the most divisive conflicts.

Post-War Stigma, Violence and 'Kony Children': The Responsibility to Protect Children Born in Lord's Resistance Army Captivity in Northern Uganda

Myriam Denov
Professor, Canada Research Chair, McGill University. Canada
myriam.denov@mcgill.ca

Atim Angela Lakor
Founder, Watye Ki Gen, Uganda
atimsekpatience@gmail.com

Abstract

The R2P framework underscores the responsibility to protect populations caught up in the maelstrom of war and armed conflict, and as such, holds relevance for children born of conflict-related sexual violence. This paper explores the role and framework of R2P in relation to children born of conflict-related sexual violence in northern Uganda, a population largely overlooked in the post-war period. Drawing upon the direct experiences and perspectives of a sample of 60 children born in Lord's Resistance Army (LRA) captivity, the paper highlights the significant stigma and violence that these children continue to face in the post-war context. The post-war lives of these children not only demonstrate the multiple hardships they face as a result of the fallout of war, but also highlight the situation of these children as secondary and intergenerational victims of war that would benefit from the protection of the R2P framework and subsequent support.

Keywords

Northern Uganda – children born of war – R2P – Lord's Resistance Army – sexual violence – stigma

* This paper is dedicated to the children and youth whose lives are featured in this paper. In the face of great adversity, these young people continue to exude profound strength, insight and courage, and their stories embody extraordinary resilience and capacity. We are deeply grateful to them for sharing their lives and stories with us. Special thanks to the Pierre Elliott Trudeau Foundation for their generous support of this research.

 | DOI:10.1163/9789004379534_011

•••

Life is hard here because people stigmatise us ... they have turned their hate against us ... In my family, they hate the three of us who were born in captivity ... My uncle beats us and said he would kill us. He doesn't want rebel children, Kony children, at home (girl).

Introduction: War and Sexual Violence in Northern Uganda

Northern Uganda has slowly been emerging from a twenty-year civil war that lasted from 1986 to 2007. Led by Joseph Kony, the rebel Lord's Resistance Army (LRA) was formed to counter the abuse and oppression that the Acholi experienced at the hands of the Ugandan government.[1] And yet, the LRA itself was responsible for brutal war crimes, atrocities and gross human rights violations against civilians. During the two decades of war, the region endured brutal violence characterised by mass killings, sexual and physical assaults, abductions, and the torture of civilians by rebel and government forces. Over 1.7 million people were displaced by the war, and an estimated 60,000–80,000 children were abducted and forced to become child soldiers and forced wives.[2] The violence ultimately tore at the social and cultural fabric of families and communities, and led to the erosion of economic infrastructure, and cultural, health and education systems.[3]

The abduction, forced marriage and impregnation of females was a key military strategy of the LRA. As a critical part of his military and ideological operations, LRA leader Joseph Kony organised and implemented a forced wife system.[4] Abducted girls – with a preference for those who had reached age 12–13 – were forced to 'marry' male commanders and were victims of repeated sexual violence. While girls and women abducted into the LRA held multiple

1 Sverker Finnström, *Living with Bad Surroundings* (Durham, North Carolina: Duke University Press, 2008).

2 Fiona Shanahan and Angela Veale, 'How Mothers Mediate the Social Integration of Their Children Conceived of Forced Marriage Within the Lord's Resistance Army', *Child Abuse & Neglect*, 51: 72–86 (2016).

3 Khristopher Carlson and Dyan Mazurana, *Forced Marriage Within the Lord's Resistance Army* (Medford, MA: Feinstein International Center, Tufts University, 2008).

4 Carlson and Mazurana, *Forced Marriage Within the LRA*.

and complex roles as soldiers, commanders, porters, cooks, and spies, forced marriage and motherhood represented key functions within the LRA's war machine. The forced wife system had among its objectives to produce a new clan and the next generation of LRA fighters.[5] Roughly 10,000 abducted girls became pregnant from sexual violence, giving birth to two or more children each.[6] While not all of these children survived war, hunger, violence and deprivation, thousands of children born in LRA captivity (CBC) are currently living in northern Uganda.[7]

Children Born of Conflict-Related Sexual Violence: An Invisible Population

Incidents of sexual violence have been documented with increasing regularity in contemporary wars, transcending countries and contexts, serving as a weapon of war to intimidate the enemy, terrorise local populations, as a form of gendered power relations, ethnic cleansing, and genocide.[8] A growing literature has addressed the powerful and long-term implications of conflict-related sexual violence.[9] As the UN Secretary-General has noted: 'systematic sexual violence, without a doubt, can be every bit as destructive to communities as more conventional weapons'.[10]

While the realities and impact of conflict-related sexual violence have been studied extensively, its intergenerational effects remain largely unexplored. In particular, the reality of children born of conflict-related sexual violence has received minimal attention, and the issue is often cloaked in silence, shame, and denial.[11] And yet the issue deserves far greater scrutiny and research.

---

5 Myriam Denov and Atim Angela Lakor, 'When War is Better Than Peace: The Post-Conflict Realities of Children Born of Wartime Rape in Northern Uganda', *Child Abuse and Neglect*, 65: 255–265 (2017).

6 Grace Akello, 'Experiences of Forced Mothers in Northern Uganda: The Legacy of War', *Intervention*, 11/2: 149–146 (2013).

7 Watye Ki Gen, *Documentation of Children Born in Captivity* (Unpublished Report: Gulu, Uganda).

8 Patricia A. Weitsman, 'The Politics of Identity and Sexual Violence: A Review of Bosnia and Rwanda,' *Human Rights Quarterly*, 30: 561–578 (2008).

9 Dara Kay Cohen, 'Explaining Rape During Civil War: Cross National Evidence (1980–2009)', *American Political Science Review*, 107: 461–477 (2013); Megan Mackenzie, 'Securitizing Sex? Towards a Theory of the Utility of Wartime Sexual Violence', *International Journal of Feminist Politics*, 12/2: 202–221 (2010).

10 UN General Assembly, *Implementing the Responsibility to Protect: Report of the Secretary-General*, A/63/677, 12 January 2009, p. 16.

11 Myriam Denov, 'Children Born of Wartime Rape: The Intergenerational Complexities of Sexual Violence and Abuse', *Ethics, Medicine and Public Health*, 11: 61–68 (2015); Elisa Van Ee

Carpenter notes that since the mid-1990s, tens of thousands of children have resulted from wartime mass rape campaigns, sexual violence, and forced pregnancy in conflicts around the globe.[12] However, few studies have elicited the voices and direct experiences of the children themselves – to understand the realities of their situations from their unique perspectives.

The silence surrounding the issue of children born of conflict-related sexual violence is not only reflected in research, but also policy-making. Scholars have emphasised that children born of conflict-related sexual violence have been largely invisible when it comes to the development of national and international policies to assure their protection and well-being.[13] Studies have shown that these children are marginalised as subjects of human rights law and that there is a tendency to identify them with the perpetrators, rather than the victims, of war and genocide.[14] Policy and protection efforts have centred largely on women as the victims/survivors of sexual violence and not their children born of rape. This focus has often been regarded as an intentional advocacy strategy, or is implemented with the assumption that the benefits of programs designed for women will inevitably trickle down to their children.[15] Some humanitarian actors have argued that the invisibility of children born of conflict-related sexual violence is important as it ensures the anonymity of these children who may face stigma – ultimately representing an important protection mechanism. However, other researchers and advocates have noted the potential harm of this silence and denial, arguing that neglecting to pay attention to the specific dimensions of these children's vulnerabilities, may result in further marginalisation and discriminatory treatment.

Concrete examples of this policy-oriented silence exist in multiple contexts around the world. In Rwanda, during the three and a half months of genocide, an estimated 350,000 women and girls were raped or gang-raped, subjected

---

and Rolf J. Kleber, 'Growing Up Under a Shadow: Key Issues in Research on and Treatment of Children Born of Rape', *Child Abuse Review*, 22/6: 386–397 (2013).

12 Charli Carpenter, *Forgetting Children Born of War: Setting the Human Rights Agenda in Bosnia and Beyond* (New York, NY: Columbia University Press, 2010).

13 Ibid.

14 Karmen Erjavec and Zala Volčič, '"Target", "Cancer", and "Warrior": Exploring Painful Metaphors of Self-Presentation Used by Girls Born of War Rape', *Discourse & Society*, 21/5: 524–543 (2010).

15 Virginie Ladisch, *From Rejection to Redress: Overcoming Legacies of Conflict-Related Sexual Violence in Northern Uganda,* International Centre for Transnational Justice, October 2015, www.ictj.org/sites/default/files/ICTJ-Report-Uganda-Children-2015.pdf, accessed 1 December 2017.

to sexual mutilation and torture, or taken as sex slaves by the *Interahamwe*.[16] While the precise number of children born of genocidal rape in Rwanda remains unknown, some estimates place it at 25,000.[17] Children born of genocidal rape – who are now young adults – continue to live with the lasting consequences of sexual violence and the genocide, and continue to face profound forms of stigma, socio-economic marginalisation and rejection.[18] While these children live with the fallout of their biological origins and conception which are directly linked to the genocide, these children have, for the most part, been excluded from the country's genocide 'narrative', as well as systems of support. As evidence of this, they are ineligible to receive compensation or support from the Rwandan government's Fund for the Neediest Survivors of Genocide in Rwanda (FARG), which supports genocide survivors born prior to 1994.

During the war in Bosnia-Herzegovina, forced impregnation carried out by the Serb militias was a deliberate policy dictated by the Serbian government. In the aftermath of the war, Carpenter (2010) notes that in Bosnia-Herzegovina, UN agencies attempting to explore the issue found it difficult to operate because 'an official policy of denial seemed to be in place with respect to children born of wartime rape'.[19] Carpenter argues that orphanages and government-run Centers for Social Work were generally reluctant to cooperate with UNICEF and that UNICEF 'found no evidence that the government was addressing the children's vulnerabilities'.[20]

In northern Uganda, the context that is the focus of this paper, to date, there has been minimal government programs or policies to acknowledge and recognise victims of the conflict or provide them with adequate redress.[21] In the aftermath of the war, the Ugandan government instituted an amnesty for all formerly abducted persons, which was accompanied by 263,000 Ugandan Shillings (approximately $75 USD). However, beyond the amnesty, no law exists that protects the rights and freedoms of formerly abducted persons and

16 Lisa Sharlach, 'Rape as genocide: Bangladesh, the former Yugoslavia, and Rwanda', *New Political Science*: 22(1), 89–102 (2000).

17 Jemma Hogwood, Christine Mushashi, Stuart Jones and Carl Auerbach, '"I learned who I am": Young People Born from Genocide Rape in Rwanda and their Experiences of Disclosure', *Journal of Adolescent Research*, 1–22. doi: 10.1177.0743558417713302.

18 Myriam Denov, Leah Woolner, Jules Pacifique Bahati, Paulin Nkusi, and Obed Shyaka, 'The Intergenerational Legacy of Genocidal Rape: The Realities & Perspectives of Children Born of the Rwandan Genocide', *Journal of Interpersonal Violence*, 1–22 (2017). doi: 10.1177/0886260517708407.

19 Carpenter, *Forgetting Children Born of War*, p. 178.

20 Ibid.

21 Ladisch, *From Rejection to Redress*.

their children. Programs of support have existed, including government development programs for recovery. However, in practice, multiple barriers, including lack of information, stigma, restrictive criteria, and gender norms have precluded women's and children's access.[22] According to a study conducted by Apio, programs that focused on the reintegration of children affected by armed conflict were inadequate as they did not focus on the specific needs of children born of conflict-related sexual violence.[23] Moreover, there is very limited compliance and enforcement of the Children's Act, the Local Government Act, and other government policies that protect the rights and welfare of children. The Probation and Social Welfare Officers and Community Development Officers, who are responsible for protecting the rights of children, are said to be limited in their ability to support these children due to a lack of financial support and corruption.[24]

The R2P framework – meant to provide an effective approach to managing conflict and mass violence – underscores the responsibility to protect populations caught up in the maelstrom of war and armed conflict, which holds relevance for children born of conflict-related sexual violence and more specifically, children born in Lord's Resistance Army captivity. This paper explores the role and framework of R2P in relation to children born of conflict-related sexual violence in northern Uganda, a population largely overlooked in the post-war period. Drawing upon the experiences and perspectives of a sample of 60 children born in Lord's Resistance Army (LRA) captivity, the paper highlights the significant stigma and violence that these children continue to face in the post-war context. The post-war lives of these children not only demonstrate the multiple hardships as a result of the fallout of war, but also show the situation of these children as secondary and intergenerational victims of war that would benefit from the protection of the R2P framework and subsequent support.

Methodology

Funded by the Pierre Elliott Trudeau Foundation, this research was a collaboration of the authors, who are researchers at McGill University and *Watye Ki Gen* ('We Have Hope'), a local community-based organisation of women formerly

22 Ibid.

23 Eunice Apio, 'Uganda's Forgotten Children of War' in Charli Carpenter (ed.), *Born of War: Protecting Children of Sexual Violence Survivors in Conflict Zones* (Bloomfield, CT: Kumarian Press, 2007).

24 Ladisch, *From Rejection to Redress.*

abducted into the LRA, based in Gulu, Uganda. Data collection was carried out between June and September 2015. Qualitative in-depth interviews were conducted with 60 children born in LRA captivity (CBC), 33 males and 27 females. Interviews were primarily conducted in Acholi, with English translation for the non-Acholi speaking researcher. All interviews were audio-recorded with permission and translated and transcribed into English. The study also included interviews with 27 mothers of CBC (formerly abducted into the LRA), 21 extended family members of these children, and 4 primary school teachers, for a total of 112 participants. However, only the data from children born in captivity is addressed and reported in this paper.

This study received ethical approval from two research ethics boards: the first from the Uganda National Council for Science and Technology/Office of the President (Uganda), and the second from the Research Ethics Board of McGill University, Canada.

Our sample of 60 children and youth who were born in LRA captivity were identified and approached through *Watye Ki Gen*, who had ongoing contact with these children as a result of their ongoing work and advocacy for women and children born in LRA captivity. The child and youth participants, who were between the ages of 12 and 19 at the time of interview, were living in the districts of Gulu (20), Pader (20), and Agago (20) districts of northern Uganda, representing both rural and urban contexts. Participants were included in the study if they had been born in captivity and were currently living in one of the three aforementioned districts. Informed consent was attained from all participants. For those under age 18, assent forms were signed by the child participants, and the consent of a parent/guardian was acquired.

Participants spent formative years in LRA captivity, ranging from a few months to 7 years. During interviews, the child and youth participants were asked questions about their lives during captivity, and post-conflict realities including mental and physical health, education, identity and heritage, stigma and community belonging, inheritance/land issues/marriage, and their future goals and dreams.

The data collected from the participants was invariably affected by their willingness to disclose sensitive information. The limitations of memory must also be taken into account, especially for those children who were very young during their time in captivity. The potential flaws of memory and self-disclosure should be taken into account when considering the children's narratives. Moreover, as a result of the small sample size, the study cannot be generalised to the experiences of all CBC.

Data was analysed using an iterative process involving the continual analysis of qualitative data. Transcribed interviews were studied at length and prominent and recurring themes in the data were identified and coded using N-Vivo qualitative software. This process enabled significant themes and patterns to emerge. To facilitate analysis, a conceptual coding tree was created, allowing patterns and the relationship between themes to be visually mapped. A recurrent theme within the interview data was the stigma and violence that CBC faced in multiple areas of their lives. The following section outlines the realities of stigma and violence, and importantly, its implications in relation to R2P.

Children Born in LRA Captivity: Post-War Stigma and Violence

Born within a context of war and captivity, the children born in LRA captivity (CBC) interviewed for this study all survived extreme adversity in the bush. They lived and survived in a context of war, sexual violence, militarised 'families', and ongoing fear. During their captivity, CBC reported experiencing and witnessing severe forms of violence including people being beaten, burned to death, and killed, including close family members such as parents or siblings. Participants reported enduring starvation, sleeping in the rain, the constant threat of violent ambushes by government forces, as well as walking long distances. While the focus of this paper is to address the post-war context, it is nonetheless important to take into consideration the violence that children endured during captivity, given its impact on CBC:

> I asked her when we were still in the bush that, 'Mother, is this our home?' She replied, 'This is not our home.' [What made you to ask her such a question?] It is because I saw my mother being beaten several times. Whenever she was to receive any beatings, she would first remove me from her back. She would be beaten and later she would carry me back on her back. That's when I asked her, 'Mother, don't we have a home? Who are these people?'(girl).

> Yes, I remember [the bush]. When we were arrested by the rebels at the time there was fighting between rebels and the UPDF [government forces]. The rebels ran with us away and they said they were going to kill one of the children among us. They separated the old people from the children. They picked a child and they killed that child while we were watching (girl).

> A helicopter appeared all of a sudden ... [it was] flying low and started shooting at us. My mother was shot dead ... Then my father ran for us and removed us forcefully from the government soldiers. But we were still taken away (girl).

> Yes, I remember [the bush] because long ago when both my father and mother were all together and we were penetrating thick bushes, we found a big tree in a homestead ... Little did we know that the government soldiers were trailing us. The soldiers came and began shooting at us (boy).

Following their rescue, escape, or release from LRA captivity, most CBC transitioned through one of northern Uganda's reception/rehabilitation centres before entering into civilian life – a life they had never before known. The length of time spent in a rehabilitation centre varied from a couple of weeks, to several months, to a year. At the rehabilitation centres, CBC received medical care, food, shelter, and counselling. As these participants remembered:

> Life was easy because we had enough food and clothes and we were given good beds and blankets. Using them was nice compared to the things our father used to raid from the bush and take to us to use (girl).

> We began feeling some relief with life. We were given food to eat. We were also having regular baths. We were given enough water to drink and we were sleeping where it was warm (boy).

Following their time in a reception centre, most mothers and their children born in captivity returned to the home or village of their maternal family. Others returned to IDP camps, where living conditions were cramped and inhospitable. Camp services and infrastructure frequently lacked the resources to meet people's basic needs and importantly, people were restricted from engaging in traditional occupations, particularly agriculture.[25]

New Family Structures and Post-War Realities: Living with Stigma

As in most post-war contexts, returning to 'civilian' life was not simple or straightforward and the notion of 'family' was significantly and permanently altered. Within the LRA, children produced through rape and forced marriage were understood to belong first and foremost to their fathers and these children represented an important status symbol within the LRA.[26] Whereas CBC often perceived and experienced their family unit during LRA captivity as 'strong' – with a loving, protective father – upon return to civilian life, their

25 Theresa McElroy, Herbert Muyinda, Stella Atim, Patricia Spittal, and Catherine Backman, 'War, Displacement and Productive Occupations in Northern Uganda', *Journal of Occupational Science*, 19/3: 198–212 (2012).

26 Denov and Lakor, 'When War is Better Than Peace'.

sense of family was no longer intact. In the post-war period, participants reported missing and longing for the protection and care of their (commander) father.[27] These participants explained:

> When I was in the bush, we were all living together with my, mother, father and I. We were all living as one … My father loved me (boy).

> [During the war] I did not think about anything. I thought that was home … I felt I loved staying in the bush because I felt that was home. I had both parents … I remember [my father's] love for me. How he talked, prayed. He was a catechist. He was a joke maker (girl).

Moreover, the relational dynamics between mothers and their child(ren) born in captivity was reported to be complex. After the war, ninety per cent of our sample of CBC continued to live with their biological mothers, while 9% lived with their grandmother. The remaining 1% were living with their biological father. In a minority of cases, mothers, who were still very young when they returned from the bush, left their CBC with relatives to pursue new marriages and a new family. According to participants, for those whose mothers were in new relationships and marriages, the new husband rarely accepted the CBC, and some refused to allow the mother to keep the CBC living in the family home. In these cases, mothers visited their children occasionally, or not at all. CBC who were unable to live with their biological mothers held out hope that their situations would change and they one day they would be able to live with their mothers. For the CBC whose mothers left them to live with relatives, living apart from their mother while siblings born from home continued to live with her was experienced as deeply hurtful and confusing:

> Sometimes [my mother] comes to visit me, but whenever she comes to visit me, the husband quarrels with her. He tells her 'Why do you go to visit that useless child?' So she does not visit me often (girl).

> I think if my mother loved me she wouldn't have accepted to go live at the other man's place. She would have just stayed with me at home … She shouldn't have chosen to go to the other man who is so rude and abusive to me (boy).

> I only visited her [mother] once. Her husband is so fierce. He warned me not to go his place. He told me he would beat me if I stepped foot in there

27 Ibid.

> again. He always questions me about what I want at his place. I told him I only go to his place to visit my mother. So, I have never visited them again ... I feel hurt because a child should live with his mother so that he learns good ways (boy).

In addition to feelings of abandonment and rejection, interviews revealed that stigma and marginalisation, based on their biological origins and identity as children born in LRA captivity, was a pervasive factor that extended into every aspect of the lives of CBC. Participants reported that within and outside the family, they were commonly perceived to be violent, psychologically disturbed, dangerous 'rebel children', who had brought 'bad spirits' from the bush. These CBC described the stigma that they faced within the home, school, and in the larger community as a result of their former LRA affiliation:

> Some teachers still humiliate us in class. They use insensitive words like 'be careful with that girl, she was in the bush and she may be possessed with evil spirits and she may harm you.' They say this especially ... if you are stubborn in class (girl).

> For me, I am not wanted by both my stepfather and my mother's side [of the family] ... My mother gave birth to the two of us from the bush .... But they keep abusing me that I will grow up a rebel like my bush father ... they stigmatise me and tell other children not to play with me and say that I would kill them like my father did in the bush. They keep reminding me that I have no home with them. I have to look for where I belong ... (boy).

> Neighbourhood children never mix with us. We [CBC] always play alone. They keep mentioning that we are from the bush. This has made it very difficult for us to associate with other children because their fear was that we could decide to kill them or even they thought we had a gun and we could shoot them at any time or even burn their houses down. This affects us. We live in fear (girl).

The effects of stigma were described as pernicious and cumulative, with implications for their physical, psychological, and social well-being. The stigma they endured had profound social, economic and educational consequences, and according to participants was intrinsically linked to material deprivation, exploitative labour, discrimination and social exclusion. These themes are addressed further below.

Material Deprivation

Material deprivation – being denied food, medication, health care and clothing – within the family unit was reported by the vast majority of participants. CBC reported that if they did receive such items, they typically received them last, after their siblings' (born from home) needs were provided for. CBC were told they did not deserve to eat, or were served last after the meat or most nutritious part of the meal has already been eaten. This deprivation of food, so linked to survival and nurturance, was particularly hurtful to children. In addition, perceived as a financial burden on the family, CBC reported having to work to raise money to provide for their own material needs:

> First of all when my stepfather buys things, he only gives to my siblings leaving me out. Then I also struggle to do work like burning charcoal to raise my school fees. I raise my own money to pay my school fees (boy).

> She would make harsh statements like: 'You children [born in captivity] have become a very big burden to me. I wish you had died in the bush.' My grandmother is also fond of discriminating against me as compared to the other children who were born at home. Normally on market days, she picks the other children to go with her and buys for them clothes, while we [CBC] are left behind. She goes ahead to tell us that we should look for our own money because she is not the one who killed our mother. She buys clothes for her daughter, but for me, I have to raise money by myself to buy my clothes (girl).

Denial of Education

A source of great anguish for CBC was the denial of or the disruption to their education. In most families, poverty made it difficult to send all the children in the home to school. Stepfathers almost universally refused to contribute to the education of CBC. Within the family, CBC reported that if their primary school fees were paid, they were often paid for last, after the other children in the household. CBC also reported that if they were able to attend school, they were sent to low quality primary public schools, while the children born from home were sent to better quality private schools.

> My parents do not love me. They discriminate against me as compared to my siblings who were born from home. Right now I am not in school. They are not paying my school fees, while my siblings' school fees are being paid (boy).

> In my mother's home, they treated me differently. They refused to pay my school fees but they did it for other children. I am paying for myself in school (boy).

CBC viewed education as their hope for the future, their chance to escape their difficult circumstances, and a way to challenge stigma by becoming self-sufficient and productive citizens. For CBC, the inability to attend school led to profound disillusionment, and even suicide attempts:

> I wouldn't be here now. I would have been dead. Because one time I had decided that I wanted to go back to school and my [step]father said I will not go to school. I was so hurt. I decided to get a rope to hang myself. My mother found me and grabbed me down and untied me from the rope. She then comforted me and gave me advice not to commit suicide. On that day, I cried so much. I had made up my mind to die because I found life so harsh. So it is my mother who saved my life (boy).

Exploitative Labour

As a result of stigma and resentment, CBC reported that they were required to perform more household chores, and more physical labour, and caregiving duties than children born from home. As a result, CBC reported being frequently late or absent from school, and having little time for leisure or socialising activities:

> I feel my stepfather discriminates against me. First of all, when we go [to work in the field], I am given the biggest portion of the field to dig, while my brothers [born from home] are given a smaller portion to dig. So, because of that my siblings complete their work before me and take a rest early. I continue digging up to late into the night sometimes until 10pm. Sometimes I am left alone in the field (boy).

> I do not attend school regularly. For example, if I attend school on Monday and Tuesday, I am told to skip the rest of the days because of too much work to do at home – like digging and weeding in the field. Meanwhile at school the rest of the children would be studying. As much as I copy class notes from my friends who attended, I find it hard to understand the notes because I did not attend the lesson in person (girl).

> I skip school sometimes when my grandmother wants me to help with work at home. But when I make a mistake or disobey her words, she beats me and she even denies me meals (boy).

Social Exclusion and Marginalisation

Social exclusion and isolation reportedly permeated the lives of CBC. Neighbours and relatives prevented their children from socialising with CBC. Participants reported that their peers avoided playing with them once they discovered that they were born in LRA captivity. These children described the realities of social exclusion and its profound impact:

> They [siblings born from home] keep segregating me. When it comes time to eat, they don't want to eat with me because they say something will come in my mind and I might do something [violent] to them ... They don't want to play with me. When it comes time to sleep, they don't want to share a sleeping room with me. They say something may come to my mind and I may strangle them at night (girl).

> They [community] speak ill of us, they tell their children not to associate with us because we have bad behaviours and that we are violent and will harm their children (girl).

> It affects my life a lot from the school because no one wants to socialise with me. Sometimes when I join a group where students have gathered, they start disappearing and leave me alone. And sometimes when I had nightmares, they would tell their friends that I was dreaming such and such a thing and those students should not stay around me because I may strangle them. So those students fear living with me [in the boarding school]. And it is very difficult for me to borrow things from the [other] students at school because they say if I or another CBC borrows their things, when I return their things I will return it with the demons that I got from the bush (girl).

In the home, this exclusion is often played out in the family's sleeping arrangements. CBC reported that they were forced to sleep apart from other children born from home in less comfortable conditions, or were even locked out of the family home at night and required to roam the streets to find a place to sleep. Similarly, CBC reported being relegated to a small portion of land isolated from the rest of the family. One male participant reported that he was forced to build his own hut on the far border of his family's land, isolated from the rest of the family, where he cooked, ate, and slept alone. These participants explained:

> When I find [my cousins] already sleeping, I ask them if I can spread my blanket to sleep. That cousin of mine gets up and goes to my grandmother to report me. My grandmother then comes and begins insulting me saying that I should go away from her house. Some days I sleep away from home (boy).

> I sleep outside in the bush just behind the home. [My grandmother] always locks herself inside her house with all my clothes and blanket. I sleep naked, outside, without any blanket or anything to cover me up (boy).

The stigma and exclusion often led CBC to isolate themselves from others, out of shame and humiliation:

> Some people stigmatise me and use inappropriate language against me. Stigma against me is common in areas where people are gathered drinking or where children are playing. When they see me they say: 'Look at that boy, he is badly behaved because he was born in captivity.' Such statements come out even when I have not insulted them or provoked any of them or quarreled with any of them ... that is why I now choose to stay home most of the times and reduce my movements (girl).

Living in Fear: Post-War Violence against Children Born in Captivity

In addition to stigma, CBC reported experiencing violence and chronic abuse at the hands of their caregivers, and family members. Perpetrators of the violence were reported to be the stepfather, or other caregiver relative, and in a minority of cases the child's mother. According to participants, even in extreme cases, the perpetrators of violence – whose abuse was reportedly linked to their identity as a CBC – committed their acts of violence with impunity, as local authorities failed to intervene. For example, one female participant reported that she been beaten unconscious by her uncle and thrown into a latrine. However, when her mother and grandmother reported it to the police, no action was taken. These participants provided examples of the violence they endured:

> It [the beating] happens if I do not run away from him [stepfather] ... Sometimes, I stay away during the night, and when I return in the morning I find he has gone away to drink ... He beats especially us who have returned from the bush.

> The problem is my stepfather drinks a lot, and when he is drunk, he becomes very abusive to the extent that he will send the two of us [CBC] away. So for those days when he is drunk we spend the night elsewhere. Even for some of the days when he is sober, we still find it difficult to stay there with him around (girl).

CBC also reported that their mothers experienced stigma as a result of the former LRA affiliation, and continued to be targets for post-war cruelty and violence. A substantial number of CBC reported having regularly witnessed violence against their mothers. One participant reported that his mother was shot and killed in her field by a neighbour who declared that her mother was an LRA 'rebel', which justified shooting her. Constant hostility and the persistent threat of violence added to CBC profound sense of insecurity:

> She [mother's co-wife] insults my mother telling her to go back to her husband who is in the bush. She threatens my mother that if she disobeys her, she will cut my mother with a panga [machete] (boy).

While the violence and exclusion CBC experienced was reported as a constant source of hardship, fear and sadness, many respondents developed their own insights into the reasons they, as a group, were so widely targeted within their communities in the post-conflict period. These participants explained:

> Some people sympathise with me and they say my brother should have taken care of me until I am an adult, while those who hate me say that I am useless and that my brother should not have accepted me in that home in the first place. They have it in their mind that my father was among the people committing atrocities on them. They said that I should also be made to suffer [...] They say it was the fathers of those children who were born in captivity who were causing havoc on the civilians during LRA insurgency. So that is why. Because we are connected to them, they have turned their hate against us (boy).

> I think it's because they imagine what the LRA used to do to them and their families and friends and they want if possible to retaliate on us. But it was not our wish to be abducted and to make them unhappy. Sometimes they think we have carried all what we have done or seen from the bush at home and we may do it to them. Yet they don't know that it is the environment that makes people behave differently (boy).

Invoking R2P: Protecting Children Born in LRA Captivity

The data derived from interviews with CBC have demonstrated the ways in which the lives and experiences of these children represent a form of secondary victimisation. Their mothers – abducted into the LRA barely as adolescents, raped, and forced into marriage and pregnancy – were primary victims of the LRA's brutality and violence. Yet their children born of rape, as secondary victims, continue to carry the burden of being born in LRA captivity, and their identity, paternal heritage and their affiliation with the LRA has led to profound and debilitating forms of stigma and violence in the post-war period. These children are, in fact, illustrations of the intergenerational realities of conflict-related sexual violence, as well their profound effects.

For CBC, while the crisis of war and captivity has ended, in fact, the post-war period has become a prolonged crisis – where stigma and violence have become endemic and chronic – and shapes and configures all aspects of their psycho-social life. As Vigh notes in his discussion of crisis and chronicity in post-war situations:

> Instead of being a passing period of chaos, [crisis] settles as a social state. Rather than seeing social processes implode and disintegrate, what we see in situations of prolonged crisis is that the state of emergency becomes a 'situation of emergence' whereby social life is made sense of and unfolds within a terrain of risk and uncertainty.[28]

In this sense, for CBC, crisis has now become context, and these children must continually adjust and readjust to the ever-changing and volatile social environment.

Under R2P, in response to armed conflict and genocide, the international community has three core pillars of responsibilities.[29] Pillar One – the protection responsibility of the state – ensures that every state has the responsibility to protect its populations from four mass atrocity crimes: genocide, war crimes, crimes against humanity and ethnic cleansing. This responsibility includes the prevention of such crimes, including their incitement. Pillar Two – international assistance and capacity building – asserts that the wider community has the responsibility to encourage and assist individual states in meeting that responsibility. Pillar Three – timely and decisive response – maintains that if a state is manifestly failing to protect its populations, the

28 Henrik Vigh, 'Crisis and Chronicity: Anthropological Perspectives on Continuous Conflict and Decline,' *Ethnos*, 72/1: 5–24 (2008), pp. 12–13.

29 A/63/677, 12 January 2009.

international community must be prepared to take appropriate collective action, in a timely and decisive manner and in accordance with the UN Charter. Yet how do the post-war lives and realities of CBC 'fit' within the R2P pillars and framework? What are the international community's core responsibilities in relation to children born in LRA captivity?

With regard to Pillar One and the protection responsibilities of the state, CBC are currently living with ongoing violence and stigma within their families, schools and communities, and with substantial physical, psychological, and socio-economic impacts on their lives and their futures. This state of affairs constitutes a warning sign in terms of these children's short and long-term well-being and security. In relation to R2P, the UN Secretary General calls upon societies to reflect upon and potentially derail current social realities and systems of intolerance and injustice, given their potential implications for future violence.[30] The intolerance and discrimination directed at CBC and the potential for this violence and stigma to degrade and deteriorate further, calls for greater attention by both State and international bodies. As the UN has indicated in relation to R2P:

> The duty to prevent and halt genocide and mass atrocities lies first and foremost with the State, but the international community has a role that cannot be blocked by the invocation of sovereignty. Sovereignty no longer exclusively protects States from foreign interference; it is a charge of responsibility where States are accountable for the welfare of their people. This principle is enshrined in article 1 of the Genocide Convention and embodied in the principle of 'sovereignty as responsibility' and in the concept of the Responsibility to Protect.[31]

As Whitman has aptly noted in relation to children affected by armed conflict and R2P, there is an urgent need to ensure that children who survive war and political violence have the opportunities, skills, and coping mechanisms to overcome the cycle of violence and that this cycle of violence must be halted as these children represent future leaders and parents.[32] In this sense, protection responsibilities not only apply to the prevention of violence *against* CBC, but also, supporting and protecting CBC will help to ensure the prevention

30 Ibid., p. 13.

31 'Peace and Security', http://www.un.org/en/sections/issues-depth/peace-and-security/index.html, accessed 14 January 2017.

32 Shelly Whitman, 'The Responsibility to Protect and Child Soldiers' in W. Andy Knight and Frazer Egerton (eds.), *The Routledge Handbook of the Responsibility to Protect* (London: Routledge, 2012), p. 161.

of violence *by* CBC, who may be at risk of re-recruitment into armed groups should their social exclusion and marginalisation continue unabated. This is especially true given that previous research on CBC in northern Uganda has uncovered that due to post-war stigma, violence, and marginalisation, many of these children view their wartime experiences as *better* than their peacetime realities.[33]

In relation to Pillar Two and international assistance and capacity-building, the insecurity and precarious well-being of CBC calls for the policy and practice attention of both the State and the international community. Yet as noted in the introduction, not only do current policies on war-affected children not easily apply to children born of war and conflict-related sexual violence, but also, given the complex identities of these children, there has been a notable silence with regard to creating policies and services on their behalf. Governments have typically ignored, resisted, refused and even denied the very existence of this important population of children. In following the R2P framework, international assistance and building the capacity of states to protect this population seems evident, with the international community encouraging and assisting states to meet their responsibility to children born of conflict-related sexual violence.

Finally, Pillar Three – timely and decisive response – stands for a commitment to take appropriate collective action in decisive manner. It requires an early and flexible response and one that is tailored to the situation and fully in accordance with the UN Charter. A consolidated, thoughtful, and timely response is needed in relation to CBC specifically, and children born of conflict-related sexual violence more generally. Given that there are innumerable and multiple victims of war and its after-effects, many might argue that the focus and attention should remain with only 'urgent' cases, and that CBC stigma, violence, intolerance and discrimination does not yet warrant a systematic response. Here we draw directly upon the words of the UN Secretary General in relation to R2P:

> Even in relatively stable, developed and progressive societies need to ask themselves whether they are vulnerable to such events; whether the seeds of intolerance, bigotry and exclusion could take root and grow into something horrific and self-destructive; and whether their social, economic, and political systems have self-correcting mechanisms in place to discourage and derail such impulses. Candid self-reflection, searching dialogue among groups and institutions, both domestically and internationally, and periodic risk assessment are needed in both fragile and

33 Denov and Lakor, 'When War is Better Than Peace'.

> seemingly healthy societies in all regions of the world. We are all at risk if we believe that it could not happen to us.[34]

Schnabel notes that the Responsibility to Rebuild has been largely dropped from the R2P agenda and that rebuilding 'has slowly been sacrificed in order to secure member states' commitment to the first and second legs of R2P: prevention and reaction'.[35] However, the case of CBC, and the need to alleviate the multiple forms of violence and stigma that they face in order to prevent the recurrence of conflict, violence and social exclusion speaks volumes in terms of the importance of rebuilding in the post-war period. A lack of commitment to rebuilding would mean failing to protect the rights and lives of CBC born of war and captivity who have already been subjected to gross human rights violations, abuse and neglect.

Conclusion: Addressing the Needs of Children Born in Captivity

The scholarly literature on children born of conflict-related sexual violence, while small, has rarely drawn upon the perspectives and voices of the children themselves. Children's views on the mother/father/caregiver-child relationship, experiences of community belonging and stigmatisation in the post-conflict context, and the meaning and implications for social identity have remained largely unexplored. Prioritising the voices and perspectives of CBC provides an opportunity to ascertain their daily lives, post-war realities and experiences, their reflections on stigma, belonging and their perceived needs. As part of this project, our research team inquired directly with CBC as to what they believed was critical to their protection and long-term security and well-being. They identified education and training, access to land and livelihood, sensitisation and protective laws as the key pathways to protection, prevention and well-being. These themes, addressed further below, can be drawn upon extensively in the creation and implementation of the R2P framework in a systematic way.

Access to Education and Vocational Training

The most pressing need the youth identified is the need for support for accessible education. Education was the top priority of all CBC, whether formal

34 A/63/677, 12 January 2009, p. 13.

35 Albrecht Schnabel, 'The Responsibility to Rebuild' in W. Andy Knight and Frazer Egerton (eds.), *The Routledge Handbook of the Responsibility to Protect* (London: Routledge, 2012), p. 50.

education or vocational schooling. Education was viewed by CBC as the path to a bright future, as finding employment is extremely difficult without completing both primary school and senior school. CBCs highlighted, however, that when other children see that they are being sponsored, it may expose them as having been born in captivity, and lead to further stigmatisation and jealousy. As a solution, they suggested that sponsorship programs should be geared towards vulnerable children more generally, so as not to single them out. Among youth who are unable to attend school, they expressed the need for vocational training programs for hopes of future employment, including tailoring, mechanic, and computer training programs.

A further pertinent finding in the data is the CBC desire to attend a boarding school. Almost every CBC said they would prefer to attend a boarding school to a day school. They explained that at a boarding school where no one would know of their identity or LRA affiliation, they would have the chance to distance themselves from stigma and constant harassment, and be free to focus on their studies. Some participants stated that this would help them 'forget the past'. Moreover, at a boarding school, they would have less household chores, labour, and caregiving responsibilities to perform, allowing them to concentrate solely on school.

Access to Land and Livelihood

In Acholi culture, land inheritance and access is normally patrilineal in descent. For CBC, given the absence of their fathers, access to land is a significant barrier. CBC identified the need to access land to cultivate, as well as livelihood opportunities to help them and their families generate income for food, healthcare and school fees. CBC suggested support in the form of start-up capital, such as goats, chickens or oxen for each child born in captivity, in order to help them raise money for school and other requirements through livestock farming. The youth also suggested the formation of a farming group that communally cultivates a piece of land, which could not only help with food, but also any surplus could be sold to raise money for school fees. Some CBC's requested they be given land far away from their current living place where their identity would be unknown, and they along with their mothers would be free to go about their lives without land-disputes and the constant stigma, abuse and threat of violence by family and neighbours and community.

Sensitisation: Family, School and Community

Participants emphasised that sensitisation at all levels – home, school, community, government – would benefit them and fight stigma. According to participants, sensitisation should include programs and workshops with school administration and with students, as well as targeted workshops for their mothers, caregivers, family members (including stepfathers), as well as local leaders and community members. Sensitisation should centre on a) the history of CBC and formerly abducted persons and to inform them that it was not their mother's choice to be abducted and forced into marriage, nor their choice to be born in the bush, and b) the challenges faced by CBC. They suggested radio talk-shows, music, drama and dance as effective ways to engage and sensitise the community regarding their plight.

Protective Laws

CBC suggested that the Government could institute bylaws to protect them from stigma and violence, as well as teach people in the community the effects of stigmatisation. CBC desired equality, to be treated like other children in the community, and to be treated with dignity and respect. They wanted to be afforded protection from harm when their right to physical and psychological harm was threatened. As such, participants called for the creation of official policies or bylaws against CBC discrimination, affording them some security and the possibility for recourse when their rights are being violated. The expressed needs of children born in LRA captivity are well aligned with the UN's own suggested ways forward in terms of R2P:

> Expanding development assistance to the 'bottom billion' would undoubtedly have a net positive effect on preventing crimes and violations relating to the responsibility to protect if such assistance is targeted to give the poor and minority groups a stronger voice in their societies, enhances equality and social justice, raises their education levels and increases their opportunities for meaningful political participation. However if additional assistance is distributed in a way that exacerbates, rather than narrows, differences in the status and living conditions of rival ethnic, religious or cultural communities within these societies, then the effect would be destabilising and could fuel existing tensions and resentments. Aid programmes therefore need to be sensitive both to conflict and to the responsibility to protect.[36]

All of these initiatives, whether social and/or economic in nature, require substantial political will, commitment and investment at multiple levels of family, community and government. However, these are essential to ensuring the long-term protection, health and well-being of this unique and vitally important population of children.

36 A/63/677, 12 January 2009, pp. 19–20.

Prevent to Protect: Early Warning, Child Soldiers, and the Case of Syria

Dustin Johnson
The Roméo Dallaire Child Soldiers Initiative, Canada
dustin@childsoldiers.org

Shelly Whitman
The Roméo Dallaire Child Soldiers Initiative, Canada
shelly@childsoldiers.org

Hannah Sparwasser Soroka
The Roméo Dallaire Child Soldiers Initiative, Canada
hn448982@dal.ca

Abstract

The war currently raging in Syria is without a doubt the most serious failure of the R2P paradigm. Hundreds of thousands of civilians have been brutally killed while the world has looked on, largely unable to affect events on the ground. The use of child soldiers by all sides in the conflict has been well documented, and the authors' previous work has demonstrated the importance of the recruitment and use of child soldiers as an early warning indicator. Yet, the world has consistently failed to act preventatively, and this is most notable in the case of Syria. This paper takes the Syrian war as a case study to examine how the recruitment and use of child soldiers can serve as an early warning indicator of mass atrocities and be used to help prevent conflict escalation.

Keywords

child soldiers – Responsibility to Protect – Prevention – early warning

Since the failures of the international community to prevent mass atrocities in the 1990s, there has been an increased focus, at least rhetorically, on taking early action to prevent such losses of life from ever happening again. Yet, this

 | DOI:10.1163/9789004379534_012

decade has seen an uptick in violence around the world and new and escalating wars in Syria, Iraq, Yemen, Libya, South Sudan, and elsewhere. These wars are marked by atrocities, lack of respect for international humanitarian law, and the immense suffering of civilians. All of these wars involve the extensive use of child soldiers, who often form a key component of fighting forces.

Looking at the example of the war in Syria that began with the revolution in 2011, this paper asks if the international community could have responded in a more preventative manner to the crisis if it had seen and taken action on the abuses against children that occurred in Syria from the very start. It argues that violations committed against children, especially the recruitment and use of child soldiers, are a reliable and early indicator that a conflict is likely to produce mass atrocities due to this disregard for children's rights, and therefore the international community should be vigilant for the recruitment of child soldiers and not hesitate to take preventative action when it occurs to forestall atrocities.

The paper begins with a brief history of the Responsibility to Protect and the role of prevention within it, especially with regard to the crises in Libya and Syria. It then discusses the use of child soldiers in current wars, and provides an overview of how children have been targets and agents of violence in the Syrian war since the very beginning of the revolution. It concludes with a discussion of the implications for prevention and Responsibility to Protect of this attention to the use of child soldiers.

The Responsibility to Protect and Prevention

The Responsibility to Protect is an evolving global norm, endorsed by the United Nations and the international community, but lacking the binding character of international law. The failure of the international community to first prevent, and then adequately respond to, the genocide in Rwanda and the mass atrocities committed in the former Yugoslavia and other crises of the 1990s led to calls for a new framework for both preventing such events in the future, and allowing for interventions when states commit atrocities against their own citizens. To answer this call, the Canadian government established the International Commission on Intervention and State Sovereignty (ICISS) in 2000 to examine this issue. In December 2001 they published their final report.[1]

1 ICISS, *The Responsibility to Protect*, December 2001, http://responsibilitytoprotect.org/ICISS%20Report.pdf, accessed 10 January 2017.

The ICISS report advocated for the adoption of the concept of the Responsibility to Protect: in addition to having a right to sovereignty, states have a responsibility to their people. States bear the primary responsibility for protecting their citizens from harm—an inability or unwillingness to do so reveals a fundamental instability at the heart of the state. In such cases, the international community has a responsibility to protect the state's people which overrides the right of non-intervention. The commission envisioned the Responsibility to Protect as being built upon three pillars: the responsibility to prevent, the responsibility to react, and the responsibility to rebuild. Even at the time, prevention was identified as the most important component: 'prevention options should always be exhausted before intervention is contemplated, and more commitment and resources must be devoted to it'.[2]

While discussion of the Responsibility to Protect has customarily been located in the context of military intervention for humanitarian purposes, the ICISS report makes it quite clear that proper application of the Responsibility to Protect involves 'less intrusive and coercive measures being considered before more coercive and intrusive ones'.[3] The ICISS report stipulates that invoking the Responsibility to Protect ought to involve as little force as possible except to prevent the commission of atrocities, and only after non-military solutions have been unsuccessful.[4]

The Responsibility to Protect was officially endorsed by the international community at the 2005 World Summit. The version articulated in the World Summit Outcome (WSO) document differed somewhat from the ICISS report. The most significant difference is that the WSO document specifies that Responsibility to Protect can only be invoked in four situations: genocide, war crimes, ethnic cleansing, and crimes against humanity. States bear the responsibility to protect their populations from these crimes, and 'the international community should, as appropriate, encourage and help States to exercise this responsibility and support the United Nations in establishing an early warning capability'.[5]

To help prevent these crimes, the international community is prepared 'to use appropriate diplomatic, humanitarian and other peaceful means'.[6] Only if a state's authorities 'manifestly fail' to protect their population, can collective

2 Ibid., p. XI.

3 Ibid.

4 Ibid., pp. XI–XIII.

5 '2005 World Summit Outcome', A/60/L.1, 15 September 2005, http://responsibilitytoprotect.org/world%20summit%20outcome%20doc%202005(1).pdf, accessed 11 January 2017, ¶p. 138.

6 Ibid., p. 139.

action under Chapter VII of the UN Charter become a possibility, given that all attempts at peaceful resolution fail. Finally, the international community 'intend[s]' to aid states to prevent these crimes via capacity building.[7] These principles have since been reaffirmed in a number of Security Council and General Assembly resolutions.[8]

The Responsibility to Protect has, from its inception, clearly been framed primarily as a preventative mechanism. However, much of the most vociferous debate over the principles of the Responsibility to Protect over the past few years has focused on the military intervention component, and its application—or lack thereof—in the Libyan and Syrian crises.

The conflict in Libya began in February 2011 as part of the widespread Arab Spring movement. Almost immediately the Gaddafi regime responded by cracking down on protest and threatening civilian lives.[9] On February 22, 2011, the UN Security Council (UNSC) condemned the actions of the regime. The UNSC passed Resolution 1970 on February 26, 2011, which called upon the regime to fulfill its obligation to its people and imposed an arms embargo and other sanctions. On March 17, 2011, Gaddafi directly threatened the city of Benghazi and its inhabitants; on the same day the UNSC passed Resolution 1973 which invoked the Responsibility to Protect to establish a no-fly zone and authorised all necessary measures to protect civilians. Military action began on March 19, 2011, and by the end of August Gaddafi had been toppled.[10] The Responsibility to Protect was, in the Libyan crisis, invoked at an early stage and moved quickly through attempts at non-intervention to the ultimate decision to intervene militarily. Garwood-Gowers cites three crucial factors in the expedient manner in which the Responsibility to Protect was invoked: first, the clarity of the threat against civilians; second, the strong regional consensus on the need for external intervention; third, defections from within the Gaddafi regime.[11]

However, the intervention in Libya is viewed by many scholars including Garwood-Gowers, Kelly, and Cronogue[12] as a tipping point in the application

7 Ibid.

8 See A/RES/63/308 and S/RES/1674 (2006).

9 Lyndsey Kelly, 'The Downfall of the Responsibility to Protect: How the Libyan and Syrian Crises Secured the Fate of the Once-Emerging Norm', *Syracuse Journal of International Law and Commerce*, 43/2: 381–409 (2016), p. 396.

10 Andrew Garwood-Gowers, 'Thematic: The Responsibility to Protect and the Arab Spring', *UNSW Law Journal*, 36/2: 594–618 (2013), pp. 602–603.

11 Ibid., pp. 604–605.

12 Graham Cronogue, 'Responsibility to Protect: Syria: The Law, Politics, and Future of Humanitarian Intervention Post-Libya', *International Humanitarian Legal Studies*, 3/1: 124–159 (2012).

of the Responsibility to Protect. All of these scholars point to the decision by NATO forces to arm anti-government rebels and target high-ranking members of the Libyan regime as a defining moment in the conflict. The decision to support Libyan rebels is, arguably, an overstep of the UNSC mandate to maintain a no-fly zone and protect civilians while calling for a ceasefire, and the Responsibility to Protect's stipulation that only the minimum amount of force necessary to protect human lives may be exerted. Kelly writes, 'Though the U.N. mandate explicitly outlined a humanitarian mission designed to protect Libyan noncombatants, the North Atlantic Treaty Organization ('NATO') officials decided to engage in a regime change operation that would force Gadhafi from power'.[13] Garwood-Gowers, Cronogue, and particularly Kelly point to the NATO forces' interference as the cause of a loss of faith in the Responsibility to Protect on the part of non-NATO governments, and a fracture in the UNSC that remains a major impediment to intervening in the Syrian crisis.

The Syrian crisis began in March 2011, like the Libyan crisis, with a series of crackdowns on anti-government protest. The UNSC has only been able to pass resolutions on humanitarian access, investigating chemical weapons attacks, calling for a political settlement to the conflict, and addressing terrorist organisations like the so-called Islamic State and the al-Nusra Front.[14] Multiple attempts at passing a resolution condemning or sanctioning the Syrian government have been vetoed by Russia and China.[15] Garwood-Gowers identifies two tensions between NATO member states and Russia and China that help explain the reasons for these vetoes. First, where Western powers tend to see an instance of government forces violently suppressing democratic protest, Russia and China identify a legitimate attempt by a government to combat attacks on the state. More importantly, Garwood-Gowers points to fear about misuse of the Responsibility to Protect as a reason for China and Russia's continual vetoes of resolutions on Syria. The overreach in the Libyan intervention has caused mistrust on the part of Russia and China regarding the Responsibility to Protect.

The intervention in the Libyan crisis and its ramifications are a crucial part of many criticisms of intervention in the context of the Responsibility to Protect. As mentioned earlier, the majority of scholarly sources interpret

13 Kelly, 'The Downfall', p. 397.

14 Security Council Report, 'UN Documents for Syria: Security Council Resolutions', http://www.securitycouncilreport.org/un-documents/search.php?IncludeBlogs=10&limit=15&tag=%22Security%20Council%20Resolutions%22+AND+%22Syria%22&ctype=Syria&rtype=Security%20Council%20Resolutions&cbtype=syria, accessed 7 July 2017.

15 Garwood-Gowers, 'Thematic', p. 610.

NATO forces' decision to arm rebels and target government commanders, in addition to targeting utilities such as the electrical grid, as an example of overstep in an intervention.[16] This sort of overstep, most critics agree, weakens the Responsibility to Protect. Kelly goes so far as to say that it renders the Responsibility to Protect ineffective.[17] Garwood-Gowers not only suggests that concerns about motivations for intervention external to the desire to protect human lives stand as a real impediment to future implementations, but makes the pertinent point that any military intervention entails a serious amount of rebuilding.[18] The responsibility to rebuild following military intervention is inherent to military intervention—the present state of affairs in Libya is compelling evidence that an insufficient amount of rebuilding took place. The uniting theme in these critiques is the notion that the Responsibility to Protect was improperly applied in the context of the Libyan crisis.

A number of scholars have focused on the importance of prevention as the primary element of the Responsibility to Protect. For instance, Hubert and Blätter argue that in the Responsibility to Protect framework, prevention is best addressed from the angle of international crimes prevention. The four types of mass atrocities falling under the Responsibility to Protect can all be classified as crimes against humanity under international law, and therefore are amenable to approaches targeting these crimes. They focus on the operational level of prevention, in the immediate run-up to the commission of crimes. This includes a focus on:

> Potential perpetrators, what are their motivations or intentions, are plans or policies in place or in the process of being developed, how strong are command and control structures between leaders and those who might carry out the criminal acts, and which specific target groups may be vulnerable to attack.[19]

As elaborated on later in this piece, such a focus works well with early warning indicators in the immediate run up to the commission of mass atrocities such as the recruitment of child soldiers.

---

16 Spencer Zifcak, 'The Responsibility to Protect After Libya and Syria', *Melbourne Journal of International Law* 13/1: 1–35 (2012), p. 5.

17 Kelly, 'The Downfall', pp. 403–406.

18 Garwood-Gowers, 'Thematic', p. 597.

19 Don Hubert and Ariela Blätter, 'The Responsibility to Protect as International Crimes Prevention', *Global Responsibility to Protect*, 4/1: 33–66 (2012).

Prevention, however, is most effective if it addresses the root causes of conflict and instability, rather than the most proximate causes of violence. Tackling poverty, income inequality, environmental degradation, under-education, weak civil society, and other aspects of fragile states that contribute to instability not only prevent conflict, but benefit society at large.[20]

Children, Child Soldiers, and R2P

When it comes to children, especially children recruited and used as soldiers, and the Responsibility to Protect, there are few mentions in the core documents, and little focus in the literature so far. When discussing children and child soldiers in this paper, it is important to be specific. We use the words child and children based on the definition in the Convention on the Rights of the Child, which considers all people under the age of 18 to be children.[21] The definition of child soldier is that from the Paris Principles:

> Any person below 18 years of age who is, or who has been, recruited or used by an armed force or armed group in any capacity, including but not limited to children, boys and girls, used as fighters, cooks, porters, spies or for sexual purposes.[22]

Since the end of the Cold War, child soldiers have become a defining feature of many conflicts around the globe, particularly in civil wars. There are various tactical and strategic benefits to using child soldiers that lead to their recruitment by both armed forces and armed groups: the comparative ease of abducting, coercing, or indoctrinating children; the ability of a group lacking popular support to rapidly increase its ranks through abduction (such as the LRA); the minimal amount of training that children require to become effective fighters; their fearlessness and lack of adult reasoning skills; and the moral dilemmas that arise when professional security sector actors confront them.[23] As will be

---

20 Alex J Bellamy, 'Conflict Prevention and the Responsibility to Protect', *Global Governance*, 14/2: 135–156 (2008).

21 *Convention on the Rights of the Child*, GA/RES/44/25, 20 October 1989, Article 1.

22 UNICEF, *The Paris Principles: Principles and Guidelines on Children Associated with Armed Forces or Armed Groups*, February 2007, http://www.refworld.org/docid/465198442.html, accessed 11 January 2017, 2.1.

23 Shelly Whitman, Tanya Zayed, and Carl Conradi, *Child Soldiers: A Handbook for Security Sector Actors* (Halifax, NS: The Roméo Dallaire Child Soldiers Initiative, 2014), pp. 20–23.

discussed in greater detail later, the use of child soldiers can also be used to intentionally prolong a conflict.

There are three main avenues by which child soldiers are recruited: abduction, coercion, and volunteering. Abduction involves the forcible seizure of children, often followed by the use of indoctrination, intimidation, and extreme punishments to keep children in line. Forcible recruitment is often used when groups lack the popular support to recruit by other means, or need to rapidly increase their manpower. Coercion involves the use of deceit, manipulation, or threats to recruit. This can include making false promises of food, clothing, and education; paying parents to surrender their children; or tricking children into thinking they are volunteering.[24]

In many cases children voluntarily enlist in armed groups and forces, but do so in an environment of limited choices. They are often enticed by offers of money and food, the chance for gaining more power or exacting revenge against those who have harmed them or their community, or to escape abuse at home.[25] Mark Drumbl proposes viewing the voluntary involvement of children in armed forces and groups through the lens of circumscribed action, where children exercise their agency and decision making powers as best they can in an environment of limited choices, misinformation and considerable violence.[26]

Children and child soldiers are only mentioned briefly in the ICISS report, and not at all in the relevant paragraphs of the WSO document. The ICISS report briefly notes the use of child soldiers in modern intrastate wars and their deadly impact on civilians,[27] the basic need to protect children from starvation,[28] and the jurisdiction of the International Criminal Court (ICC) over the war crime of child soldier recruitment.[29]

From the legal perspective, war crimes are a potential trigger for the Responsibility to Protect under the terms of the WSO document. Under the Rome Statute of the ICC, the enlistment of children under the age of 15 into the national armed forces during an international armed conflict,[30] or the conscription or

24 Ibid., p. 22.

25 Ibid.

26 Mark Drumbl, *Reimagining Child Soldiers in International Law and Policy* (Oxford: Oxford University Press, 2012), pp. 61–101.

27 ICISS, *The Responsibility to Protect*, 1.18.

28 Ibid., 2.29.

29 Ibid., 3.30.

30 'Rome Statute of the International Criminal Court', A/CONF.183/9, 1 July 2002, https://www.icc-cpi.int/nr/rdonlyres/ea9aeff7-5752-4f84-be94-0a655eb30e16/0/rome_statute_english.pdf, accessed 11 January 2017, Article 8, 2(b)(xxvi).

enlistment of children under 15 into armed forces and groups, or their participation in hostilities,[31] constitute war crimes, and hence are subject to the Responsibility.

While it is unlikely that the Responsibility would ever be invoked solely in the case of child soldier recruitment, the use of child soldiers seldom if ever occurs in the absence of other crimes of the gravity required to invoke the Responsibility. For instance, the Global Centre for the Responsibility to Protect currently lists 14 countries as either in crisis, at imminent risk, or of serious concern for populations at risk of mass atrocity crimes.[32] Of those 14 countries, 10 of them are currently listed by the United Nations for the use and recruitment of child soldiers, while 4 of the countries listed by the UN are not listed by the Global Centre.[33] Countries such as Syria, Iraq, South Sudan, and the DRC that are listed by both organisations all have widespread use of child soldiers and have been the scene of crimes against humanity that clearly fall under the scope of the Responsibility to Protect.

Child Soldiers as an Early Warning Indicator

From an instrumental point of view, placing children at the top of the peace and security agenda has significant benefits, not only in protecting children from the horrors of war, but also in preventing conflict and building peace. The use of child soldiers is an important feature of most modern wars, enabling armed groups to build their numbers faster, last longer due to the increased length of service that young soldiers can provide, perpetuate severe human rights abuses, and survive with less support from the civilian community. The proliferation of small arms and the large youth populations of many countries provides a large pool of both weapons and people to wield them. The long-term physical, psychological, and social damage resulting from children fighting instead of going to school makes conflicts more difficult to end, and more difficult to recover from.[34] Consequently, a focus on children and youth in the

31 Ibid., Article 8, 2(e)(vii).

32 Global Centre for the Responsibility to Protect, 'Populations at Risk', http://www.globalr2p.org/regions/, accessed 7 July 2017.

33 'Children and Armed Conflict: Report of the Secretary-General', 20 April 2016, http://www.un.org/ga/search/view_doc.asp?symbol=A/70/836&Lang=E&Area=UNDOC, accessed 11 January 2017, pp. 37–40.

34 Shelly Whitman, 'The Responsibility to Protect and Child Soldiers', in Andy Knight and Fraser Egerton (eds.), *The Routledge Handbook on the Responsibility to Protect* (London: Routledge, 2012).

prevention of conflict which may lead to mass atrocities is particularly important from the perspective of the Responsibility to Protect.

Prevention has a number of facets, and one of the most proximate to conflict is early warning. A variety of different definitions and systems of early warning have been put forward, but all aim to examine a variety of factors that lead to armed conflict and mass atrocities and monitor countries for them to warn of violence before it breaks out, allowing for prevention.[35] Various early warning systems exist at both the regional and global levels, operated by governments and organisations.

The Early Warning Project, based at the United States Holocaust Memorial Museum, 'produces risk assessments of the potential for mass atrocities around the world by combining state-of-the-art quantitative and qualitative analysis'.[36] This system uses two elements to assess the risk of mass atrocities: a statistical model, drawing on patterns found in analysis of previous mass atrocities, and consultation with expert opinions.[37] As of July 2017, they list Sudan, Yemen, Myanmar, Nigeria, and Afghanistan, respectively, at highest risk of mass atrocity.[38] All of these countries are currently listed for the use and recruitment of child soldiers by the United Nations.

Another prominent early warning system is the Fragile States Index, published by the Fund for Peace. Using an analytical process developed from extensive social science research, the FSI assesses the rankings in the index based on 12 primary indicators, comprised of over 100 sub-indicators, drawn from literature and reports on the countries ranked.[39] As of July 2017, they rank South Sudan, Somalia, the Central African Republic, Yemen, and Syria, respectively, as most at risk.[40] All of these countries are listed by the United Nations for the use and recruitment of child soldiers.

---

35 Shelly Whitman and Sam Holland, 'Understanding the Recruitment and Use of Child Soldiers as an Early Warning Indicator', the Roméo Dallaire Child Soldiers Initiative: Working Paper, June 2015, http://www.childsoldiers.org/wp-content/uploads/2016/07/Understanding_the_Use_of_Child_Solders_Early_Warning-min.pdf, accessed 11 January 2017, p. 5.

36 Early Warning Project, 'About the Project', https://www.earlywarningproject.org/about, accessed 11 January 2017.

37 Early Warning Project, 'FAQ: Statistical Risk Assessments', https://www.earlywarningproject.org/faq#risk_assessments, accessed 11 January 2017.

38 Early Warning Project, 'Statistical Risk Assessments', https://www.earlywarningproject.org/risk_assessments, accessed 7 July 2017.

39 Fund For Peace, 'Methodology Behind the Index', http://fsi.fundforpeace.org/methodology, accessed 11 January 2017.

40 Fund For Peace, 'Fragile States Index 2017—Annual Report', May 2017, http://fundforpeace.org/fsi/2017/05/14/fragile-states-index-2017-annual-report/, accessed 7 July 2017.

The aforementioned Global Centre for the Responsibility to Protect's 'Populations at Risk' tracks countries at risk of mass atrocities falling under the Responsibility to Protect. It currently lists Syria, Sudan, South Sudan, Myanmar, North Korea, Iraq, Yemen, and Eritrea as countries which have ongoing mass atrocities,[41] of which all but North Korea and Eritrea are listed by the United Nations for the use and recruitment of child soldiers.

Various other mechanisms exist, such as the Early Warning System under the ECOWAS Conflict Prevention Framework in West Africa. These various systems however often provide different results, with some overlap in particularly high-risk countries. The disagreement between different models only adds to the inability of the international community to act preventatively. As one of the authors has previously argued, adding a specific focus on children, particularly their use and recruitment as soldiers, could provide a valuable additional early warning indicator common to most situations of mass atrocity.[42]

These connections between the inclusion of children on the peace and security agenda, and the implementation of the Responsibility to Protect, indicate the need for greater attention to their interaction and the potential for mutual reinforcement. Similar to the argument by Davies and Teitt in 2012 about the need for the Women, Peace, and Security and the Responsibility to Protect agendas to reinforce each other,[43] the inclusion of children and armed conflict in the Responsibility to Protect could be greatly beneficial. Better cooperation and alignment between these agendas would be mutually reinforcing: attention to children in R2P would make sufficient preventative action more likely, which in turn would better protect children during armed conflict and reduce the likelihood of their recruitment and their involvement in future mass atrocities.

Syrian Children as Targets of Violence and Recruitment

From the very beginning of the crisis in Syria, children have been at the forefront of events, whether as protestors, victims, or perpetrators of violence. The trigger for the uprising was the detention and torture of a group of teenage

41 Global Centre for the Responsibility to Protect, 'Populations at Risk'.

42 Whitman and Holland, 'Understanding the Recruitment and Use'.

43 Sara E Davies and Sarah Teitt, 'Engendering the Responsibility to Protect: Women and the Prevention of Mass Atrocities', *Global Responsibility to Protect*, 4/2: 198–222 (2012).

boys by the government for spray-painting anti-government graffiti.[44] In the aftermath of the Arab Spring, the Syrian government was prepared to crush any dissent, and responded to peaceful protests against the teenagers' arrest with violence. A quickly accelerating spiral of protests and crackdowns ensued, as repression was simply met with more protests.[45] Children were often intentionally targeted by government forces during protests and military operations,[46] and were beaten, killed, or arrested and tortured.[47] In one particularly disturbing and indicative incident reported by the UN Human Rights Commissioner's Commission of Inquiry, a military defector reported that he witnessed a Syrian military officer kill a 2-year-old girl expressly to prevent her from becoming a member of the opposition when she grew up.[48] As the conflict has escalated, children have become an ever larger portion of the dead as well: a study in *Lancet Global Health* found that children made up 8.9% of civilian deaths in 2011, rising to 23.3% in 2016.[49]

As the crisis in Syria began to transform from violent government suppression of peaceful protests to armed resistance against the state, evidence began to emerge of the use of children as soldiers. The 2012 report of the UN Secretary-General's Special Representative (SRSG) on Children and Armed Conflict, published on April 26th, reports on credible allegations of the Free Syrian Army and other opposition armed groups recruiting children as young as 14, and of government and government-aligned forces using children as young as 8 as human shields.[50]

Over the course of 2012, various media outlets and advocacy organisations began to report on the use of child soldiers by various armed opposition groups. However, their use did not receive widespread attention outside of the

---

44 Kareem Fahim and Hwaida Saad, 'A Faceless Teenage Refugee Who Helped Ignite Syria's War', *The New York Times*, 8 February 2013, http://www.nytimes.com/2013/02/09/world/middleeast/a-faceless-teenage-refugee-who-helped-ignite-syrias-war.html?_r=1, accessed 10 January 2017.

45 Ibid.

46 'Children and Armed Conflict: Report of the Secretary-General', A/66/782-S/2012/261, 26 April 2012, p. 120.

47 '1st report of the Commission of Inquiry on the Syrian Arab Republic', A/HRC/S-17/Add.1, 23 November 2011, pp. 70–72.

48 Ibid., p. 71.

49 Debarati Gua-Sapir, Benjamin Schlüter, Jose Manuel Rodriguez-Llanes, louis Lillywhite, and Madelyn Hsiao-Rei Hicks, 'Patterns of civilian and child deaths due to war-related violence in Syria: a comparative analysis from the Violation Documentation Center dataset, 2011–16', *Lancet Global Health*, 6: 103–10. doi: 10.1016/ S2214-109X(17)30469-2.

50 A/66/782-S/2012/261, 26 April 2012, pp. 122–24.

child rights community until the emergence of the so-called Islamic State and their high-profile use and promotion of child soldiers in 2014.[51] By this point, however, child soldiers had already been heavily used in the war for the previous two years.

Since the beginning of the conflict, children have increasingly been used as soldiers, and are making up an ever-larger proportion of front line combatants. Humanitarian officials familiar with the situation in Syria as of August 2016 informed the authors of the worrying increases in use of child soldiers in Syria over the past few years. This includes the recruitment of children by all sides in the conflict, at rates that are substantially higher in 2015 compared to 2014, an increasing proportion of children who serve in front line combat roles versus support roles, and the use of children as young as 6 years old.

The most recent UN verified numbers, from 2016 (published in October 2017 in the annual report of the Secretary-General), found 851 incidents of child recruitment and use in Syria. The real number of course is much higher than this, due to the strict requirements the UN has for verification through its Monitoring and Reporting Mechanism (MRM), and the difficulties of acquiring such information on the ground in a situation with as limited access as Syria's. Therefore, the scope of child recruitment and use in Syria is certainly much greater than this. However, the proportions recorded do offer some idea of the scale of the problem.[52]

Of the verified cases of child recruitment and use, 60% were committed by the Free Syrian Army, a substantial change from the 75% committed by the so-called Islamic State in the 2016 report. Most of the remaining incidents were perpetrated by the so-called Islamic State, pro-government militias, and the YPG. 20% of recruited children were under the age of 15. Recruitment was driven by ideological motivations, the payment of salaries, and pressure from children's communities to join armed groups.[53]

This increase in the use of child soldiers in Syria, and the movement of children from support roles to front line combat roles, demonstrates the increasingly grim and intractable nature of the Syrian conflict. When taken alongside the use of chemical weapons, bombing of civilians, widespread torture, and other atrocities of the war, the crimes against children which have been committed by all sides provide an indicator of the nature of the conflict. The use

51 Josh Boyter (Director of Communications, the Roméo Dallaire Child Soldiers Initiative), personal communication, 10 January 2017.

52 'Children and Armed Conflict: Report of the Secretary-General (2017)', A/72/361-S/2017/821, 24 August 2017, p. 25.

53 Ibid., p. 25.

of child soldiers is one of a series of escalations in the actions of armed groups and forces in the Syrian conflict.[54]

Several issues stand out with the use and recruitment of children by the so-called Islamic State. Most prominent is the use of very specific propaganda and targeted language to describe the recruitment and use of children as soldiers in Syria and in Iraq. The so-called Islamic State has deliberately used the phrase 'a generational war' to describe how it aims to inculcate and indoctrinate the very youngest fighters to join their movement. It is therefore a natural progression to understand that the recruitment of very young children is an attempt to create a generation that believes in the 'jihad' as a commitment from a young age, and that it is their duty in life to carry it on. Having been introduced to the ideology at a young age with no external reference point, children are more likely to consider it normal and therefore defend its practices and thus secure its long-term survival.[55]

This deliberate tactical and strategic use of children combined with social media propaganda, not only impacts its efforts inside Syria but also increases the global fear of the 'caliphate'. Such a fear is meant to paralyse any political will to intervene by framing the war as one that is unwinnable and therefore not worthy of foreign troop intervention.

The so-called Islamic State also seeks to normalise the use of extreme violence and desensitise children to it from a very early age. This includes the children: practicing beheading prisoners by cutting off the head of a teddy bear; attending public executions which are carried out particularly brutally by crucifixion, beheading, immolation, or stoning, and displaying them on public TV screens; making them torture prisoners and execute them by shooting, beheading, or blowing them up; making children hold up severed heads and play football with them; and distributing high-production-quality 'action movies' made from actual combat footage. All of this is designed to make children think that use of such extreme violence is normal for dealing with enemies of the 'caliphate', and combined with the ideological indoctrination discussed above, increases the longevity of the conflict and the difficulty of rehabilitating these children.[56]

---

54 Simon Adams, 'Failure to Protect: Syria and the UN Security Council', Global Centre for the Responsibility to Protect Occasional Paper Series No. 5, March 2015, http://www.globalr2p.org/media/files/syriapaper_final.pdf, accessed 11 January 2017.

55 Noman Benotman and Nikita Malik, *Children of Islamic State* (London: Quilliam Foundation, 2016), p. 27. Note: one of the authors of this paper (Shelly Whitman) contributed to this report.

56 Ibid., pp. 49–50.

While the use of child soldiers by the so-called Islamic State has been the most prolific and well-documented, other groups have also relied extensively upon them, particularly the Free Syrian Army, Jabhat Fateh al-Sham (formerly the al-Nusra Front), and the Kurdish People's Protection Units (YPG).

The Free Syrian Army, the primary opposition group that formed after the beginning of the war in Syria, was first listed by the UN Secretary-General's report for recruitment and use of children in 2013, using 2012 data.[57] Human Rights Watch first documented the use of child soldiers by the Free Syrian Army in November 2012, with boys as young as 14 acting in support roles and as young as 16 in front line combat roles. Those used in support roles carried supplies and spied on enemy positions. Many of the boys interview by Human Rights Watch had joined due to the presence of family and community members within Free Syrian Army units, and in some cases were specifically prevented from taking part in front line duties by their commanders.[58]

At various points, the leadership of the Free Syrian Army has claimed that they have a policy of not recruiting children, but Human Rights Watch found that many adolescents simply lied about their age, and no proof of age was asked for by recruiters, or the policy is actively ignored.[59] As of 2017, the UN continues to list the Free Syrian Army as a recruiter of children.

Jabhat Fateh al-Sham, formerly al-Nusra Front, is an extremist opposition group in Syria, affiliated with al-Qaeda. They were first listed by the UN for recruitment and use of children in 2014.[60] They continue to be listed in 2017. Human Rights Watch found that children were recruited through educational opportunities that Jabhat Fateh al-Sham provided, financial incentives for them and their families, and protection from government forces.[61] However, the UN was only able to verify two cases of child recruitment by them in its 2016 report.

The Kurdish People's Protection Units (Yekîneyên Parastina Gel, YPG) are the armed wing of the PYD, a Kurdish political party that took advantage of the war in Syria to gain control over a large portion of northern Syria. They have been the principal ally on the ground for the coalition fighting the so-called Islamic State, and have received extensive training and air support from the

57 'Children and Armed Conflict: Report of the Secretary-General (2013)', A/67/845*-S/2013/245*, 15 May 2013, Annex I.

58 Human Rights Watch, *"Maybe We Live and Maybe We Die": Recruitment and Use of Children by Armed Groups in Syria* (New York: Human Rights Watch, 2014), pp. 16–20.

59 Ibid.

60 'Children and Armed Conflict: Report of the Secretary-General (2014)', A/68/878-S/2014/339, 15 May 2014, Annex I.

61 Human Rights Watch, *"Maybe We Live"*, pp. 25–26.

United States and other foreign powers. The YPG was first listed by the UN for recruitment and use of children in 2014,[62] and remain listed in 2017. Research by Human Rights Watch found that both the YPG and the Asayish, the PYD's police force, had recruited and used children, both boys and girls, primarily to guard checkpoints. Similar to the FSA, recruitment of children as young as 13 continued despite statements from senior YPG and Asayish officers that they had instituted and enforced policies to prevent the recruitment of children under 18, and had removed children from their ranks.[63]

Pro-government militias have been listed by the UN for recruitment and use of child soldiers, and there is evidence that children have been recruited by government armed forces as well, which was verified by the UN in their 2017 report.[64]

Despite the widespread acknowledgement of the use of child soldiers in the Syrian conflict by all sides, and routine media coverage of this fact since 2012, there has been comparatively little attention paid to it in research by non-government and international organisations besides the Office of the SRSG for Children and Armed Conflict, and some reports focusing on the so-called Islamic State.

Finding solutions to address the Syrian conflict is becoming harder by the day. Various challenges have arisen as the war has become protracted and prolonged including unprecedented refugee flows, increased radicalisation worldwide, and a generation that is growing up in complete devastation. The exposure of these children to extreme violence and the teachings of groups like the so-caled Islamic State increases the potential that they will continue to carry on the war. Our lack of collective action over the past years will likely haunt us for years to come.

Implications for Early Warning and Prevention

The current conflict in Syria serves as an example of the difficulties facing the Responsibility to Protect, despite the clear presence of mass atrocities falling under its umbrella. Many scholars have examined the case of Syria, and the barriers that have prevented a resolution of the crisis, through an R2P lens: the skepticism of Russia and China after Libya of R2P due to its use as a cover by

62 'Children and Armed Conflict: Report of the Secretary-General (2014)', Annex I.

63 Human Rights Watch, *"Maybe We Live"*, pp. 27–28.

64 'Children and Armed Conflict: Report of the Secretary-General (2017)', A/72/361-S/2017/821, 24 August 2017, Annex I.

western countries for regime change;[65] the practical and strategic considerations that did not allow any credible options for intervention;[66] and the Russian government's view of its place in the world;[67] among others.

As discussed above, children were directly targeted from the very beginning of the Syrian crisis, which should have demonstrated to the international community the seriousness of the situation and the potential for escalation. The conflict's effect on children has evolved from targeting them for repression and death to actively enlisting them in the fighting in ever greater numbers, with more and more children on the front lines. Throughout the conflict its impact on children has been widely known and documented, from the iconic photo of Aylan Kurdi's body on a Turkish beach to the propaganda videos of the so-called Islamic State. However, it is only recently that concerned organisations and governments have begun to take seriously the use of children as soldiers in the conflict and their impact.

Attention to the targeting and use of children in the conflict as a more central issue could have had a number of beneficial impacts. As an early warning indicator, these attacks and recruitment demonstrated the seriousness of the conflict at an early stage and the willingness of parties to the conflict to flout international law in pursuit of their objectives. Recognition of this could have increased the urgency of attempts to find a political settlement. Consideration of the centrality of children and youth in conflicts such as Syria's has the potential to open up new areas of agreement between opposing groups.[68] Where seemingly intractable conflicts exist, it may be possible to leverage the near-universal belief in the need to protect children to begin a dialogue between opposing sides.

What does this mean for early warning and conflict prevention at large? Children can be a rallying point for peace and security discussions. We can highlight the violations against children, improve the protection of children through concerted and deliberate actions, as well as to ensure that those negotiating understand the importance of recognising the plight of children to the overall conflict.

A critical element of addressing the role of children in armed conflict in this way is the availability of timely and accurate information on violations

65 Andrew Garwood-Gowers, 'The Responsibility to Protect and the Arab Spring: Libya as the Exception, Syria as the Norm?', *UNSW Law Journal*, 36 (2013): pp. 594–618.

66 Cronogue, 'Responsibility to Protect'.

67 Derek Averre and Lance Davies, 'Russia, Humanitarian Intervention and the Responsibility to Protect: The Case of Syria', *International Affairs*, 91/4: 813–834 (2015).

68 Whitman and Holland, 'Understanding the Recruitment and Use'.

against children, particularly the recruitment and use of child soldiers. As discussed previously, such information from the war in Syria has often been sporadic and not always easy to verify. While the UN through its MRM takes pains to thoroughly verify each case of child recruitment and use, the security situation on the ground means it is only able to document a tiny fraction of the existing cases. Organisations concerned with human rights such as Amnesty International and Human Rights Watch are faced with a situation where the recruitment and use of children is only one of a plethora of violations being committed as a concerted strategy by all sides of the conflict, making it difficult to dedicate resources to monitoring the use of child soldiers. Finally, the reports of news organisations and local monitoring organisations such as the Syrian Observatory for Human Rights can provide valuable information, but are not always given sufficient weight.

The UN's Monitoring and Reporting Mechanism (MRM) was established by Security Council Resolution 1612 (2005) in order to:

> Collect and provide timely, objective, accurate and reliable information on the recruitment and use of child soldiers in violation of applicable international law and on other violations and abuses committed against children affected by armed conflict.[69]

The MRM is activated in situations of armed conflict on the agenda of the Security Council, or in others as required by the Secretary-General, as presented in the annual Secretary-General's report on Children and Armed Conflict. Consequently, the formal MRM is not triggered until sufficiently grave violations have already occurred, as reported by UN staff and others on the ground.[70]

The MRM focuses on the Six Grave Violations, selected for their particular gravity and harm done to children: killing and maiming, recruitment and use, attacks on schools and hospitals, sexual violence against children, abduction, and denial of humanitarian access. The MRM monitors all parties to a conflict, even when only one has triggered the interest of the UN, and focuses on non-state armed groups that have some degree of structure and intent, rather than more random violence committed by civilians.[71]

---

69 S/RES/1612 (2005), 25 July 2005, 2(a).

70 UNICEF, 'Guidelines: Monitoring and Reporting Mechanism on Grave Violations against Children in Situations of Armed Conflict', June 2014, http://www.mrmtools.org/mrm/files/MRM_Guidelines_-_5_June_2014(1).pdf, accessed 31 January 2017, pp. 7–8.

71 Ibid.

Information is gathered at the country level by UN representatives including from UNICEF, other UN human rights bodies, military and police peacekeeping forces, and members of special political missions. Local and international NGOs operating in country are also part of the process and provide information to the MRM, with sufficient consideration for the quality of information provided, the neutrality of the organisations, and the safety and security of their staff and of children. This information is collated by the Country Task Force for Monitoring and Reporting, and transmitted by the UN SRSG or Resident Coordinator (RC).[72]

Reports are considered by the Secretary-General, the SRSG for Children and Armed Conflict, and the Security Council, and are released publicly. They provide the basis for advocacy work by many organisations, and are considered the most reliable information on the use of children in armed conflict. As previously discussed however, they are not able to provide a comprehensive number of violations due to the difficulty of verification in situations of armed conflict.

In order for this information from the MRM and from other sufficiently credible sources to be useful as an early warning indicator, several improvements as to how it is used are needed. First, ongoing advocacy is required at the level of the international community and with individual governments and organisations to move the recruitment and use of child soldiers, and violations against children during armed conflict, to the top of the peace and security agenda. Only when relevant actors fully appreciate that the involvement of children in war is a central peace and security concern and not only a specialist humanitarian issue will we be able to fully and constructively address it.

Even when relevant actors properly consider information on the recruitment and use of children, it is critical that this information is received in a timely manner. All too often data is only collected once violations and violence have begun, when it is too late to take many of the more efficient and productive preventative actions. Better mechanisms are needed to collect and consider information on recruitment and use of children in fragile situations that have not already erupted into war. This could include better reporting by UN and regional peacekeeping forces on the ground, support to local and international NGOs operating in fragile states, and earlier formal triggering of the MRM.

The various early warning projects discussed earlier provide a guide as to which countries are most likely to face increased violence, and monitoring

72 Ibid., pp. 9–13.

resources and attention should be directed to such fragile countries before violence and atrocities occur.

Finally, for early warning indicators of any kind to be effective, they must be acted upon. As discussed earlier, preventative action is much more efficient and likely to succeed than reactive measures, particularly if we wait until military intervention is the only option. The mobilisation of greater resources and political will for preventative measures in fragile states and situations will require efforts by the UN, national governments, and advocacy by NGOs and other concerned organisations.

The international community as a whole ought to focus more attention on situations where there are credible reports of the recruitment of children by state or non-state armed groups and forces. When such reports are received, people on the ground should be mobilised to verify and gather more information, which should be widely shared among relevant state, non-state, and international organisations. Relevant governments, UN bodies and other groups should then seek to take appropriate steps to prevent the situation from escalating further, whether that is dialogue with the groups conducting recruitment, training for security forces facing those groups, changes to humanitarian and development programs, increased attention from peacekeepers, or the thoughtful application of sanctions and similar measures.

In one glimmer of hope in this area, the new UN Secretary-General António Guterres called for greater emphasis on preventative measures and called out the international community for too often only reacting to crises after they erupt.[73] The emphasis on the use of child soldiers, and other violations of children's rights, presented in this paper serves as one mechanism that the international community can use to implement this call to action.

Conclusion

The current conflict in Syria has shocked the conscience of the world who have watched as Syrian children have been caught up in the violence as victims of war and as soldiers and perpetrators of crimes. While the Responsibility to Protect has been largely discussed in terms of the use of intervention and the difficulties of applying it to Syria, preventative action is more important, more

73 António Guterres, 'Remarks to the Security Council Open Debate on "Maintenance of International Peace and Security: Conflict Prevention and Sustaining Peace"', 10 January 2017, https://www.un.org/sg/en/content/sg/speeches/2017-01-10/secretary-generals-remarks-maintenance-international-peace-and, accessed 31 January 2017.

efficient, and more likely to succeed if conducted well. An important component of prevention is early warning indicators of mass atrocities, which can provide time for the international community to act before a situation devolves into crimes against humanity. Attention to the role that children play in a conflict, particularly as soldiers, provides a valuable indication of the potential for escalation and willingness of parties to flout international law. The Syrian crisis presents clear usage of child soldiers, but this knowledge was not acted upon in a coordinated fashion by the international community. Learning from the example of Syria, we may be able to respond preventatively to head off future crises and save the lives of children and other civilians.

Conclusion

Of Responsibilities, Protection, and Rights: Children's Lives in Conflict Zones

Bina D'Costa
UNICEF Office of Research–Innocenti, Italy
bdcosta@unicef.org

Abstract

The endorsement of R2P by the UNGA and the UNSC does not give the doctrine legal status, however, such broad acceptance in the international community gives the concept some normative force. Although the UNGA formulation of R2P can be considered to be the most authoritative, as demonstrated by the articles in this special issue, the doctrine could be further advanced in relation to children in conflict zones. This article provides some reflections about recent UNICEF emergency response experiences in dealing with the Rohingya displacement in Cox's Bazar, Bangladesh.

Keywords

forced displacement – trafficking – armed conflict – the Rohingya – child labour

Introduction

While my co-editor, Luke Glanville, and I were in the midst of organising this special issue publication, I was called to provide research support to the Rohingya emergency response in Cox's Bazar, Bangladesh. The humanitarian emergency with which the global community was dealing involved a

* The author gratefully acknowledges the editorial support provided by Mary-Louise Hickey, the Department of International Relations, ANU.

 | DOI:10.1163/9789004379534_013

mass-scale displacement of the Rohingya from Myanmar across the border to Bangladesh. Now recognised as one of the most persecuted minorities of the world, the Rohingya are also stateless people, long invisible in international discourses of the Responsibility to Protect (R2P).

The children of this world have inherited the history of Somalia, Bosnia, Kosovo, Rwanda, and the countless 'never again' promises that came with the genocidal experiences of the 1990s. Despite much improved early warning systems, children encounter similar kinds of violence in many parts of the world including in Myanmar, Darfur, Syria, and elsewhere. Following on from Glanville's Introduction, the deep insights of our contributors and my most recent field experience in Rohingya refugee camps, I lay out three observations for the R2P agenda relating to children in conflict zones. None of these are new and in most instances they are also interlinked. However, as the contributors in this special issue argue, we need innovative and multi-dimensional approaches to global R2P that makes sense to local practices and opportunities of child protection and rights.

The Scope of R2P in Protecting Children

While R2P incorporates well-established theory, concepts, and principles, the doctrine developed the emerging concept of sovereignty as responsibility into an alternative and unifying theoretical and practical framework for human protection. In the context of an international human rights framework, increasing recognition of human security and emerging state practices, the international community by now has recognised a modern understanding of sovereignty as responsibility. R2P, as endorsed by the United Nations General Assembly (UNGA), was reaffirmed in United Nations Security Council (UNSC) Resolution 1674.[1] Endorsement of R2P by the UNGA and the UNSC does not give the doctrine legal status; however, such broad acceptance in the international community provides the concept some normative force. Although the UNGA formulation of R2P can be considered to be the most authoritative, as demonstrated by this special issue, the doctrine could be further advanced in relation to children in conflict zones. Reflecting on the plight of the Rohingya children, I would also like to emphasise that the protection of forcibly

1 Teresa Chataway, 'Towards Normative Consensus on Responsibility to Protect', *Griffith Law Review*, 16/1: 193–224, at 199 (2007).

displaced children must be one of the key issues discussed and debated in the context of R2P.

According to the UNGA, R2P is owed to the 'population' of a state. The UNGA did not further elaborate on this term. The International Commission on Intervention and State Sovereignty used the terms 'people', 'populations', 'civilians', and 'citizens' interchangeably to refer to the beneficiaries of R2P despite the different meanings of these terms. These different terms raise questions about the scope of R2P. If R2P is a corollary of sovereignty, then arguably, it is only owed to the nationals of a state. This would exclude both temporary and permanent residents. Alternately if 'population' is taken to mean the persons permanently inhabiting a state, does R2P then extend to temporary residents and refugees? Does Bangladesh have a responsibility to protect Rohingya refugees living in camps in Bangladesh from the Burmese Army/Tatmadaw?

The term 'civilians' is even more problematic given that many situations which give rise to R2P involve armed conflict. R2P is best viewed as being owed to a population. This is most consistent with the purpose of the doctrine. Despite the centrality of sovereignty in the doctrine, the purpose of the doctrine is first and foremost to protect vulnerable people. Narrower terms or an interpretation of the term 'population' which failed to extend protection to some of the most vulnerable groups such as refugees would not be consistent with the purpose of the doctrine. However, the use of the term population, which refers to a defined geographical area, relevantly the borders of a state, raises further questions about a state's nationals who reside outside its borders.

Armed conflicts dramatically increase children's vulnerability to human rights and humanitarian law violations – from impeded access to education, health and humanitarian assistance, family separation and displacement, to more acute risks of killing and maiming, recruitment and sexual violence. The nexus between armed conflict, displacement, and increased risk of human trafficking is also clear. Further, in displacement, increased push and pull factors for harmful coping mechanisms including early marriage and the worst forms of child labour are established, as well as impeded freedom of movement, lack of access to essential services and legal documentation, and heightened risk of detention and refoulement.

Different formulations of the R2P doctrine are also consistent in attributing responsibility to the international community to protect the people of a state if the state fails to discharge its own responsibility to protect. However, as several authors in this issue articulate (Timea Spitka, Myriam Denov and

Atim Angela Lakor, and Jeremy Shusterman and Michelle Godwin), the distribution of this collective responsibility within the international community, and the extent to which the exercise of this responsibility is incumbent upon individual states, is not always clear.

In her article, Katrina Lee-Koo, draws attention to the tension between protection systems as political agenda and the failures of the UNSC to protect children caught up in conflict zones. The R2P doctrine has been used to a varying extent to reinvigorate and reinforce the UN Charter model of collective security. The UNGA ascribed to the international community the responsibility *through the United Nations* to use appropriate diplomatic, humanitarian and other peaceful means, in accordance with Chapters VI and VIII of the Charter, to help to protect vulnerable populations. But interventions are also incredibly expensive, in particular when dealing with protracted conflicts. This has significant implications for how R2P is implemented. By giving the UN primary responsibility for exercising R2P, states have arguably limited their individual responsibility to the extent of their contribution to UN actions. The UNGA also ascribed to the international community responsibility to take collective action *through the Security Council* in accordance with the Charter, including Chapter VII, should peaceful means be inadequate and where national authorities are manifestly failing to protect their populations.

While the UN may be the most appropriate body to implement R2P, its capacity to do so is limited by resource constraints, although even those limited resources must be used strategically and meaningfully to have a more holistic approach of protecting children. For example, Jana Tabak and Leticia Carvalho provide a critique of the representation of displaced and fleeing children as vulnerable which could be counterproductive in the long run as those not only at risk but as risks to global community. How then could a global agenda of R2P meaningfully reflect children's perspectives and interests? Contributors in this issue, such as J. Marshall Beier and Erin Goheen Glanville, provide responses to this important question.

As Figure 1, drawn by a Rohingya child, reveals, children carry with them memories of violence. The R2P agenda already includes visions for rebuilding peaceful societies. Providing protection to children fleeing violence is critical for healing and rebuilding societies as well.

Children are vulnerable when they cross treacherous borders to seek refuge. On 25 August, the Arakan Rohingya Salvation Army, a Rohingya insurgent group, which, according to the International Crisis Group, was formed after the 2012 violence, attacked police posts and attempted to raid an army base in 25 locations. The disproportionate counter-offensive carried out by Tatmadaw

FIGURE 1 *Drawing by a Rohingya child*

forced the Rohingya population to flee across the border to Bangladesh.[2] From 25 August until 7 January 2018, 655, 500 new arrivals are reported in Bangladesh.[3] Approximately 60% are children under 18.

Referring to the humanitarian crisis and the resulting displacement, UN Secretary-General António Guterres called for 'swift action' to prevent further instability and find durable solutions. UN agencies are now seeking more funds to cope with the massive displacement. As UNICEF's former Executive Director, Anthony Lake advised, 'We shouldn't let the numbers of this crisis numb us to the fact that everyone of these numbers represents a human life, the majority of whom are children – children who need our urgent help'.[4]

The persecution of the Rohingya has been highlighted not only in the UN but also in global media, raising new questions about whose responsibility it is

2 Bina D'Costa, 'Life (and Death) of Rohingya Children: No Place to Hide', http://www.thedailystar.net/star-weekend/the-shadow-violence/no-place-hide-1475062 (accessed 11 January 2018).

3 Inter sector coordination group situation update, 6 January 2018. On file with author.

4 'Joint Statement by Emergency Relief Coordinator and United Nations Under-Secretary-General for Humanitarian Affairs, Mark Lowcock and UNICEF Executive Director, Anthony Lake', 4 October 2017, https://reliefweb.int/report/bangladesh/joint-statement-emergency-relief-coordinator-and-united-nations-under-secretary, accessed 11 January 2018.

to protect the most vulnerable? What are the roles and responsibilities of the civil society and business actors in protection?

Protecting Rights in Genocidal Violence

In modern history, the inadequacies of legislative measures, the lack of a sincere commitment of parties caught up in conflicts, and a failure to form a strong and unified regulatory regime capable of dealing with children's rights in armed conflicts are some of the major obstacles in protecting children. Simply sparing children in the context of armed conflict clearly falls far short of providing for their wellbeing and development. Under international humanitarian law (IHL) – a body of treaty law that regulates the conduct of hostilities[5] and the protection of victims during armed conflict[6] – specific measures can be taken to protect child civilians, and these are applicable to both international and non-international armed conflict. However, the deficiencies of international law in this area are compounded by the problem that under the laws of war, the definition of a 'child' has yet to be agreed.

The most significant IHL treaties are the Geneva Conventions drafted after the Second World War and the two Additional Protocols adopted in 1977. In the international context, prior to 1949 there was no specific mention of the vulnerability of children in conflict. The experiences of the Second World War demonstrated the inadequacies of existing laws to protect children in conflict

5 An armed hostility is broader than the customary definitions of armed conflicts and/or war. It includes any hostile act or attempted hostile act, if the severity rises to the level of an 'armed attack' or if it is intended to contribute to such acts. It is also relevant to note that the International Committee of the Red Cross proposes the following definitions, which reflects strong prevailing legal opinion: 1. International armed conflicts exist whenever there is *resort to armed force between two or more States*. 2. Non-international armed conflicts are *protracted armed confrontations* occurring between governmental armed forces and the forces of one or more armed groups, or between such groups arising in the territory of a State (party to the Geneva Conventions). The armed confrontation must reach *a minimum level of intensity* and the parties involved in the conflict must show *a minimum level of organisation*. International Committee of the Red Cross, 'How is the Term "Armed Conflict" Defined in International Humanitarian Law?', International Committee of the Red Cross Opinion Paper, March 2008, p. 5, emphasis in original, http://www.icrc.org/eng/assets/files/other/opinion-paper-armed-conflict.pdf, accessed 5 January 2018.

6 Françoise J. Hampson, 'Legal Protection Afforded to Children Under International Humanitarian Law', Report for the Study on the Impact of Armed Conflict on Children, May 1996, http://www.essex.ac.uk/armedcon/story_id/000578.html, accessed 5 February 2015.

zones. A major impediment with most of the Convention provisions was the lack of a legal definition before 1949 of children as persons under eighteen years of age. This was only accepted with the adoption of the Convention on the Rights of the Child (CRC) in 1989.

Although the majority of children affected by armed conflicts are child civilians caught up in the theatres of war, a disproportionate percentage of the international community's attention focuses on child soldiers and children who are in conflict with the law. Even during the drafting of the CRC, stakeholders' considerations centred on the protection of child soldiers, most of whom are male. While the CRC Optional Protocols offer safeguards, legal theorists believe that the 'blinkered vision of the drafters of the Convention may have contributed to the weakening of standards in respect of child civilians.'[7]

In this regard, domestic and international civil society play a central role in advancing the rights of the child – from filling critical gaps in service provision, leading public advocacy on behaviour change campaigns, and lobbying governments through private advocacy and treaty-based mechanisms. UN agencies and various other international humanitarian actors have made it abundantly clear that contemporary identity-based domestic armed conflicts abuse and consciously target children (see Johnson, Whitman and Soroka in this issue), leaving them physically scarred and psychologically traumatised. UNICEF, the International Committee of the Red Cross (ICRC), Save the Children, and Plan International have referred to the lack of accountability of those wielding military, economic, and political power as the root cause of violence against children. International advocacy to resolve children's vulnerability in conflicts, for example, has adopted four specific approaches: publicly naming those who target children; establishing children's peace zones; lobbying for a more rigorous normative framework; and establishing international alerts to ensure that states and non-state actors comply with existing humanitarian and human rights norms.[8] At the international level, non-governmental organisations (NGOs) have become significant actors and norm-shapers. The experience of NGOs – especially child rights organisations at local levels – became crucial to ensuring the compliance of state and non-state actors during times of conflict. The mainstreaming of children's concerns through the UN protection

7 Geraldine van Bueren, *The International Law on the Rights of the Child* (The Hague: Martinus Nijhoff Publishers, 1998), p. 341.

8 Bina D'Costa, 'Who Speaks for Children? Advocacy, Activism and Resistance', in Kim Huynh, Bina D'Costa and Katrina Lee-Koo, *Children and Global Conflict* (Cambridge: Cambridge University Press, 2015).

agenda for children affected by armed conflict (Children and Armed Conflict Agenda – CAAC) has focused on four specific elements defining the specificities and the scope of application of its campaign: systematic monitoring and reporting of grave violations against children as a basis for action to end the impunity of those committing abuses; mainstreaming of CAAC concerns into the policies, priorities, and programs of the entities and institutional processes of the UN and beyond; strategic advocacy, awareness raising, and dissemination of CAAC norms and standards; recognition, support, and enhancement of local civil society actors, organisations, and networks who represent the front line protection and rehabilitation of CAAC.[9] Children's visibility is also raised in both global and local advocacy by drawing attention to their vulnerabilities and marginalisation (see Jeremy Shusterman and Michelle Godwin's essay in this special issue). However, this strategy also includes initiatives to integrate children's voices into advocacy programs, and from early 2000 in encouraging children's representation in peace movements.

Over the last two decades in particular, countries that have focused largely on laws and strategies countering 'terrorism', 'extremism', and 'radicalisation' relied upon a range of assumptions and views about young people's motivation and participation in projects of political and/or genocidal violence.

In addition to CAAC, the CRC was expanded in 2000 with the adoption of an Optional Protocol on the involvement of Children in Armed Conflict. The optional protocol entered into force in 2002 with currently 167 State parties to the Protocol[10] – the only countries in the Asian and European region not full parties being Myanmar (signatory only), North Korea, and Papua New Guinea (non-signatories). The optional protocol establishes eighteen as the minimum age for compulsory recruitment and participation in hostilities.[11] More recent initiatives including the Countering Violent Extremism/Preventing Violent Extremism (CVE/PVE) agenda being pursued through the UNSC and UNGA by several member states can present challenges in practice for ensuring the continued protection of children affected by armed conflict.[12]

---

9 Ibid.

10 See United Nations Office of the High Commissioner on Human Rights, 'Ratification of 18 International Human Rights Treaties', http://indicators.ohchr.org/, accessed 11 October 2017.

11 Radhika Coomaraswamy, 'The Optional Protocol to the Convention on the Rights of the Child on the Involvement of Children in Armed Conflict – Towards Universal Ratification', *The International Journal of Children's Rights*, 18/4: 535–49 (2010).

12 It could, however, be argued that this agenda is rarely discussed within the rights framework and enables rights violations.

It is important in this regard to recognise that the CVE/PVE agenda has the potential to inadvertently yet significantly undermine over twenty years[13] of hard fought advocacy to better protect children exploited during armed conflict, also rolling back or placing constraints around women's engagement in peace and peacebuilding.[14] CVE/PVE-related measures have tended to be intimately linked with legislation that overrides rule of law and due process principles in practice, giving state actors far-reaching powers at the detriment of human rights obligations, especially for children detained, charged, and tried under such legislation.[15] As provided in Human Rights Council resolution 30/15 in 2015 on human rights and preventing violent extremism, the resolution makes clear the need for any CVE/PVE measures to comply with state obligations under international human rights, refugee and humanitarian law, including human rights education and training capacity-building for state and local entities involved in implementing such measures.[16] Further work is needed to re-orient the CVE/PVE agenda to addressing the root causes and drivers of social exclusion and youth marginalisation in development, as well as establish the necessary firewalls with humanitarian action.

Better Protecting the Forcibly Displaced

The now-iconic image of three-year-old Aylan Kurdi's body washed up on a beach in Turkey in September 2015 sparked a public outcry and turned the world's attention to Europe's forced migration dilemmas involving children. However, it is critical *not* to frame the pressing concerns of a displaced child's migration in Europe or elsewhere as a 'crisis'. Just a simple internet search on Italian media provides an interesting insight. In 2014, in Italian media 'migration crisis' appeared 6,990 times and in 2016, 26,990 times. Similarly, 'refugee

13 Office of the Special Representative of the Secretary-General for Children and Armed Conflict, '20 Years to Better Protect Children Affected by Conflict' (New York: Office of the Special Representative of the Secretary-General for Children and Armed Conflict, 2017).

14 UN Women, *Preventing Conflict, Transforming Justice, Securing the Peace: A Global Study on the Implementation of United Nations Security Council Resolution 1325* (New York: UN Women, 2015).

15 This had already been noted to a large extent in the ten-year review of the Graça Machel study. See UNICEF, OSRSG-CAAC, *Machel Study 10-Year Strategic Review: Children and Conflict in a Changing World* (New York: UNICEF-OSRSG-CAAC, 2009), p. 13.

16 United Nations Office of the High Commissioner on Human Rights, 'Human Rights and Preventing and Countering Violent Extremism', http://www.ohchr.org/EN/Issues/RuleOfLaw/Pages/PCVE.aspx, accessed 11 October 2017.

crisis in Europe' appeared 4,800 times in 2014 and in 2016 it rose to 44,900 times.[17]

Throughout global history, children have been on the move, with and at times without their families and communities. Also, there are more refugees and migrants in Africa and the Asia-Pacific region, which host approximately 60 per cent of displaced children. Although the intention might be worthy and the language of 'crisis' evokes certain urgency and emotion that stakeholders believe to be appropriate, it also accentuates anxiety and social unrest that have a political impact on the world's recent encounters with rapidly evolving migration dynamics. A fearful political climate, focusing only on border security, undermines the objective to develop a sustainable and thoughtful methodological approach essential for a child-friendly migration governance structure. There is also a risk that the 'crisis' label will result in exceptional or differential treatment of the children involved either to their disadvantage or the disadvantage of other migrant children.

The real crisis in forced displacement and irregular migration in today's world is that border regimes worldwide make desperate people turn to desperate measures and dangerous journeys. The large-scale movements of people and the rising number of children who are compelled to take risky and unsafe sea, land and air routes is a serious concern. Data from the International Organization for Migration (IOM) tells us that by 23 April 2017, 43,204 migrants and refugees entered Europe by sea, with over 80 per cent arriving in Italy and the rest in Spain and Greece, and there were 1,089 fatalities in the Mediterranean route.[18]

Globally, 50 million children have been uprooted[19] including 28 million children forced to move due to conflict and violence. One in every two refugees is a child.[20] In Europe, one in four asylum applications is from a minor. While this subject matter is recognised as one of the most pressing humanitarian challenges of our time, there is a significant lack of understanding of children's mobility. There is a heavy focus on drafting new regulations and frameworks

17 Michelle Godwin et al., 'Floods and Flows: How We Frame Children in Migration Debates', Innocenti Research Brief (Florence: UNICEF Office of Research–Innocenti, forthcoming).

18 International Organization for Migration, 'Mediterranean Migrant Arrivals Top 43,000 in 2017; Deaths: 1089', https://www.iom.int/news/mediterranean-migrant-arrivals-top-43000-2017-deaths-1089, accessed 11 January 2018.

19 UNICEF, 'Nearly a Quarter of the World's Children Live in Conflict or Disaster-Stricken Countries: UNICEF', Press Release, 9 December 2016, https://www.unicef.org/media/media_93863.html, accessed 11 January 2018.

20 UNHCR, '2016 in Review: Trends at a glance', http://www.unhcr.org/5943e8a34.pdf, accessed 11 January 2018.

instead of addressing some of the underlying and to some extent invisible challenges entrenched in region/state-specific policies and practices which contribute to implementation gaps in migration systems and the responsibility to protect children. There is a need to explicitly recognise the rights of children in the migration pathway, not as migrants or as refugees, but as children first.[21]

Supporting displaced children is a shared responsibility and governments hold legal obligations under the UN CRC to protect and safeguard children. The best interests principle set forth in Article 3.1 in the CRC stipulates 'the best interests of the child shall be a primary consideration'. In addition, Article 2 (non-discrimination), Article 6 (the right to life and survival and development), and Article 12 (the right to be heard) are extremely important in the context of children on the move. Finally, CRC General Comments, the authoritative guidance to states issued by the Committee on the Rights of the Child about the interpretation and implementation of the CRC, provide important legal frameworks to respond to the needs of children in the migration pathway. Migration is also broadly mentioned throughout the 2030 Sustainable Development Goals (SDG) Agenda that links closely to the R2P agenda. The SDG and targets[22] codify strategies of engagement on migration. Children's migration is relevant but not limited to SDGS 10.7, 1.2, 3.2, 4.1, 4.2, 4.5, 4.a, 5.2, 8.6, 8.7, 8.8, 16.1, and 16.2.

As the SDG agenda articulates, gendered violence is also incredibly important to consider in the context of R2P (see Myriam Denov and Atim Angela Lakor's essay in this issue). The International Day of the Girl 2017 highlighted the grossly inequitable status quo for girls across the world and significant challenges ahead for reaching the gender equality-related SDGs.[23] One girl dies every five minutes as a result of violence, one in four girls are married as a child, 71 per cent of known trafficking victims are female, 63 million girls

21 General Comments, Status of the Convention on the Rights of the Child, Seventy-first session. Resolution adopted by the General Assembly on 19 December 2016. Available at http://www.un.org/en/development/desa/population/migration/generalassembly/docs/globalcompact/A_RES_71_177.pdf, accessed 11 January 2018. Child migrants, child immigrants, refugee children, unaccompanied and separated children, and children seeking asylum are used interchangeably and generally to refer to immigrant children who are under the age of eighteen.

22 On 25 September 2015, the United Nations General Assembly adopted seventeen SDGs and 169 accompanying targets as part of a global agenda to promote sustainable development over the next fifteen years.

23 To end all forms of violence against girls, put all girls in school, end the aids epidemic, and end child marriage.

have undergone female genital mutilation/cutting, 130 million girls are out of school, and girls are twice as likely to be infected with HIV.[24]

Migration assistance systems including existing laws, policies, and practices in Europe are not always child-friendly.[25] Family reintegration is one of the most important challenges. In addition, the risk of statelessness experienced by children globally has increased dramatically. Recent UN meetings on forced displacement cover the plight of unaccompanied and separated children but overlook accompanied, undocumented, and/or missing children. Assumptions about accompanied children who are with their families not needing child protection are also problematic. There remains insufficient understanding of children who are returned to their country of origin or to a third country, either voluntarily or forcibly.[26] There is a global responsibility to develop a comprehensive, well-governed, child-sensitive, and child-responsive rights-based approach to migration. This approach must be informed by not only sending and receiving country data, but also with relevant evidence from transit countries, in Europe and beyond.

The UNGA adopted the New York Declaration for Refugees and Migrants in September 2016. The 193 member states also committed to two Global Compacts: A Global Compact on Refugees; and a Global Compact on Safe, Regular and Orderly Migration. UNICEF called for an Agenda for Action, outlined in the Global Compacts. While not legally binding these global commitments are positive steps towards protecting children. In December 2017, the United States withdrew from the Global Compact on Migration, stating that 'the global approach in the New York declaration is simply not compatible with US sovereignty.' While this is unfortunate, states must ensure humane and appropriate legislative, administrative, social and educational measures to protect children seeking sanctuary. We further need to recognise that one of the most inhumane ways of assessing a child's refugee status is housing children in detention facilities. Advocacy and evidence-based research reveals the harmful consequences of detention on children. The outputs of such research need to

24 Global Goals for Sustainable Development, http://www.globalgoals.org/dayofthegirl, accessed 11 January 2018.

25 UNICEF reviews for eight countries (Austria, Czech Republic, Germany, Greece, Hungary, Italy, Serbia, and Turkey). On file with author. See summary published in UNICEF, 'Building the Future: Children and the Sustainable Development Goals in Rich Countries', UNICEF Innocenti Report Card 14 (Florence: UNICEF Office of Research – Innocenti, 2017), p. 43.

26 The Directive on Return that was adopted by the European Union in 2008 includes prolonged pre-removal detention and a ban on re-entering the EU. The Returned Directive also breaches the principles of the CRC. See for details, http://eur-lex.europa.eu/LexUriServ/LexUriServ.do?uri=OJ:L:2008:348:0098:0107:EN:PDF, last accessed 11 January 2018.

be communicated effectively to state parties for strong policy advocacy at the global and national levels.[27]

The Global Responsibility to Protect Those Falling through the Cracks

Armed conflict, situations of fragility, and the subsequent breakdown in the protective environment and the rule of law facilitates transnational crime including the trafficking of children. Further, significant risks of trafficking arise during displacement and subsequent onward movement for refugee, asylum seeking, and migrant children. This is often due to restricted legal movement options, lack of trust in authorities (and resulting push and pull factors with smugglers/traffickers), lack of access to accurate information on their rights and asylum processes, unacceptably slow family reunification processes, and the opportunism of smugglers/traffickers. The *Global Report on Trafficking in Persons 2016* highlighted an increasing number of trafficking victims from Syria, Iraq, and Somalia in destination countries in Europe, Asia, and the Middle East.[28] Meanwhile, some 152 million children worldwide are believed to be engaged in child labour, with nearly half engaged in its worst forms.[29] Reliable data, however, is difficult to come by given the nature of the work children in which are engaged (e.g., slavery and situations similar to slavery, commercial sexual exploitation, and recruitment in armed forces and groups, among others). Nevertheless, member states need to ensure adequate prevention and response measures are in place to protect those vulnerable, disrupt and prosecute criminal and other exploitative networks, and provide appropriate responses to child survivors that are too often lacking.[30]

It has long since been established that childrens' and adolescents' participation in work that does not affect their health, personal development, and well-being is generally regarded as positive. On the other hand, child labour,

---

27 Rayyan Sabet-Parry, 'Why Research Should Be a Priority in the Global Response to the Child Migration Crisis', 5 October 2016, https://blogs.unicef.org/evidence-for-action/research-priority-global-response-child-migration-crisis/, accessed 11 January 2018.

28 United Nations Secretary-General, *Report of the Secretary-General on the Implementation of Measures to Counter Trafficking in Persons*, S/2016/949, 10 November 2016; United Nations Office on Drugs and Crime, *Global Report on Trafficking in Persons 2016* (Vienna: UNODC, 2016).

29 International Labour Organization, 'Global Estimates of Child Labour' (Geneva: ILO, 2017).

30 Bina D'Costa and Ton Liefaard, 'Background Paper of the Rapporteurs for 17th ASEM Seminar on Human Rights and Children', Sofia, Bulgaria, November 2017. On file with author.

in its most extreme forms, involves children being enslaved, separated from their families and communities, exposed to serious hazards and illnesses, and/or left to fend for themselves on the streets of large cities, all of these often at a very early stage.[31]

International policy commitments and action plans to reduce the risk of children's forced labour run into the problem of semantics that must also be appropriately understood/redefined. For example, 'modern slavery', 'trafficking in persons', and 'human trafficking' have been used as umbrella terms for the act of recruiting, harbouring, transporting, providing, or obtaining a person for compelled labour or commercial sex acts through the use of force, fraud, or coercion. The Protocol to Prevent, Suppress and Punish Trafficking in Persons, Especially Women and Children, supplementing the United Nations Convention against Transnational Organized Crime (the Palermo Protocol), describe this compelled service using a number of different terms, including involuntary servitude, slavery or practices similar to slavery, debt bondage, and forced labour.

From the literature, including research, and international and national advocacy reports, we can see the differences of opinions: in terms of legal usage and ramifications of using such terms for policy purposes; tensions about mobilizing resources (financial, intellectual, and other forms) to invest in research; criticism of modern-day abolitionists for creating a moral panic, particularly when it involves women and children by appropriating the framework of slavery and historical injustices for which, generations later, advocacy groups are still seeking some forms of reparation; concern that an umbrella term to capture diverse experiences of vulnerabilities and risk reduces the importance of distinct categories and responses; lack of data and evidence; and finally, political and socio-cultural approaches of understanding the differences, even in the context of in-country situations.[32]

Those who advocate the use of the term either as 'modern slavery' or 'modern-day slavery', argue that in contemporary slavery, 'legal ownership is bypassed, slavery itself may be short-term rather than over a lifetime, and slaves are plentiful and extraordinarily cheap.'[33] Critics suggest that the modern-day slavery framework has 'helped ignite outrage and galvanise political support for

31 *Eliminating the Worst Forms of Child Labour: A Practical Guide to ILO Convention No. 182*, Handbook for Parliamentarians No. 3 (Geneva: International Labour Organization, 2002), http://www.ilo.org/pardev/partnerships/civil-society/parliamentarians/WCMS_172685/lang--en/index.htm, accessed 11 January 2018.

32 Bina D'Costa, 'Trafficking and "Modern-Day Slavery": Thinking Beyond Conceptual Boundaries', UNICEF Office of Research–Innocenti Briefing Paper (Florence: UNICEF Office of Research–Innocenti, 20 February 2017).

33 Robin T. Byerly, 'Combating Modern Slavery: What Can Business Do?' *Journal of Leadership, Accountability and Ethics*, 9/5: 25–34, at 26 (2012).

modern anti-slavery campaigns.'[34] Sharapov, for example, observes that there is a need to interrogate representations of 'problems' implicit in dominant anti-trafficking discourses, and to highlight what they include and what they leave out. For her, this interrogation provides both conceptual and methodological tools to explore how what may seem to be a universally accepted 'problem' – 'the scandal of human trafficking'[35] – may not exist as an objective phenomenon that can be fully understood and eradicated, but is, in fact, constructed by national governments within specific socio-economic, political, and cultural contexts.[36] In this way, it becomes possible to understand why and how current anti-trafficking policies are developed, and to identify and confront power involved in producing and sustaining dominant discourses. There is an enormous popular appeal in framing the anti-trafficking agenda as modern day anti-slavery abolitionism. As such it depoliticises and absolves – behind a humanitarian agenda – the state for its role in creating the structures that permit, if not encourage, coercive exploitation of workers, especially migrants. The resulting prescriptions thus narrowly focus on punishing the enslavers and rescuing innocent victims. They suggest that governments, corporations, and individuals can eradicate slavery simply by engaging in more ethical consumption of goods and services.[37]

An added complication is families are prepared to send their children to journeys despite being aware of the extreme dangers children often encounter. UNICEF's recent report on Libya further highlights, 'Most migrants are prepared for the possibility of sexual violence and many take precautions depending on the routes they plan to travel.'[38] Some women and girls from Somalia, Ethiopia, and Eritrea who pass through Khartoum get contraception shots and

34 Janie Chuang, 'The Challenges and Perils of Reframing Trafficking as "Modern-Day Slavery"', *Anti-Trafficking Review*, 5: 146–9, at 146 (2015).

35 'Secretary-General's remarks at the General Assembly's high-level meeting on Improving the Coordination of Efforts against Trafficking in Persons' https://www.un.org/sg/en/content/sg/statement/2013-05-13/secretary-generals-remarks-general-assemblys-high-level-meeting, accessed 11 January 2018.

36 See for example, Kiril Sharapov, 'Traffickers and Their Victims': Anti-Trafficking Policy in the United Kingdom' *Critical Sociology*, 1: 91–111 (2017).

37 Ibid.

38 Key informant interview on women and children migrants in Libya. Interview conducted in Tunis, Tunisia by Tufts University; 27 September 2016. Key informant interview on women and children migrants in Libya. Interview conducted in Tunis, Tunisia by Tufts University. See 'Harrowing Journeys Children and youth on the move across the Mediterranean Sea, at risk of trafficking and: exploitation', available at https://www.unicef.org/publications/files/Harrowing_Journeys_Children_and_youth_on_the_move_across_the_Mediterranean.pdf.

often bring emergency contraception with them on the journey. Three fifteen-year-old girls reported that they were raped but did not become pregnant because they received the shots. They received information about the importance of taking these precautions through stories from other migrants as well as from smugglers who provided these precautions as part of the transport package.[39] Although this may seem as if the smugglers are making efforts to help protect the migrants, women and girls are often raped by them after the precautions have been taken. Nevertheless, the women and children migrants take the risk and embark on the journey.'

There are significant gaps in our understanding of these different *concepts* and how these manifest in refugee and migrant children's lives, particularly in conflict zones. Current normative and institutional frameworks mandated to cover migration fail to respond to the specific needs of children who are vulnerable to trafficking and modern-day slavery. Overwhelmingly, the literature on children and forced labour focuses on sexual exploitation, drug trade, and armed conflicts, but overlooks *trafficked children's forced labour* in agriculture, factories, construction, brick kilns, mines, bars, the tourist industry, and domestic work.[40] Many children are also severely exploited through marriage, especially when no consent is involved. Although there is increased global advocacy on child marriage, we have limited knowledge about the links between *child marriage* and children's displacement.

Business actors, both national and transnational, have a dual responsibility, the first to ensure children are not exploited through the conduct of their operations. Practically, this involves having a publicly available zero-tolerance policy on exploitative activities involving children, including those classified as the worst forms of child labour. The second is to take proactive voluntary measures to support the realisation of children's rights. In 2012, UNICEF, Save the Children, and the UN Global Compact released the Children's Rights and Business Principles (the Principles) designed to guide both responsibilities.[41]

---

39 Ibid.

40 International Organization for Migration, 'UN Migration Agency Warns of Trafficking, Labour Exploitation, Sexual Abuse of Rohingya Refugees', 14 November 2017, https://www.iom.int/news/un-migration-agency-warns-trafficking-labour-exploitation-sexual-abuse-rohingya-refugees, accessed 11 January 2018.

41 1. Meet their responsibility to respect children's rights and commit to supporting the human rights of children.

2. Contribute to the elimination of child labour, including in all business activities and business relationships.

3. Provide decent work for young workers, parents and caregivers.

4. Ensure the protection and safety of children in all business activities and facilities.

There is significant potential to expand and innovate on the proactive role of business actors in positively contributing to children's rights through corporate social responsibility initiatives. For example, this could entail offering work placements, training, scholarships, and other capacity-building support to vulnerable caseloads including children in alternative care and ethnic minorities.

This special issue begins the conversation about different formulations of R2P and its application to children's lives. Key questions still remain regarding relative responsibility of different actors in the international community, particularly between the UN and individual states (see in particular Jacob, and Prantl and Nakano in this issue). In an international community suspicious of self-interested and pre-emptive interventionism in the wake of Iraq and Afghanistan, the price of consensus on R2P in the UN was a narrowing of the threshold criteria, the omission of criteria for intervention, and limited recognition of the responsibility to prevent and the responsibility to rebuild. This was a price to high for people of Myanmar and Darfur, however, now that the responsibility concept is accepted by the international community, perhaps when it gains greater shape and recognition, it will prevent a future Rwanda.

---

5. Ensure that products and services are safe, and seek to support children's rights through them.

6. Use marketing and advertising that respect and support children's rights.

7. Respect and support children's rights in relation to the environment and to land acquisition and use.

8. Respect and support children's rights in security arrangements.

9. Help protect children affected by emergencies.

10. Reinforce community and government efforts to protect and fulfil children's rights. UNICEF, 'The Children's Rights and Business Principles', https://www.unicef.org/corporate_partners/index_25078.html, accessed 10 September 2017.

Bibliography

Acharya, Amitav, 'How Ideas Spread: Whose Norms Matter? Norm Localization and Institutional Change in Asian Regionalism', *International Organization*, 58/2: 239–75 (2004).

Acharya, Amitav, 'Norm Subsidiarity and Regional Orders: Sovereignty, Regionalism, and Rule-Making in the Third World', *International Studies Quarterly*, 55/1: 95–123 (2011).

Acharya, Amitav, 'The Responsibility to Protect and a Theory of Norm Circulation', in Ramesh Thakur and William Maley (eds.), *Theorising the Responsibility to Protect* (Cambridge: Cambridge University Press, 2015).

Adams, Simon, 'Failure to Protect: Syria and the UN Security Council', Global Centre for the Responsibility to Protect Occasional Paper Series No. 5, March 2015, http://www.globalr2p.org/media/files/syriapaper_final.pdf.

Akello, Grace, 'Experiences of Forced Mothers in Northern Uganda: The Legacy of War', *Intervention*, 11/2: 149–156 (2013).

Amir, Noam, and Maariv Hashavua, 'IDF Chief: No Need To Pump Bullets Into Palestinian Girl With Scissors', *Jerusalem Post*, 17 February 2016.

Amusan, Lere, 'Libya's Implosion and its Impacts on Children', *Journal of International Women's Studies*, 14/5:66–79 (2013).

Anderson, Zoe, 'Borders, Babies, and "Good Refugees": Australian Representations of "Illegal" Immigration, 1979', *Journal of Australian Studies*, 36/4: 499–514 (2012).

Annan, Kofi, 'Two Concepts of Sovereignty', *Economist*, 18 September 1999.

Apio, Eunice, 'Uganda's Forgotten Children of War' in Charli Carpenter (ed.), *Born of War: Protecting Children of Sexual Violence Survivors in Conflict Zones* (Bloomfield, CT: Kumarian Press, 2007).

Appadurai, Arjun, *Modernity at Large* (Minneapolis: University of Minnesota Press, 1996).

Archard, David, *Children: Rights and Childhood* (New York: Routledge, 2004).

Auschwitz Institute for Peace and Reconciliation, 'Pursuing Institutionalization of the Prevention Agenda: National Mechanisms for the Prevention of Genocide and other Atrocity Crimes' (New York: Auschwitz Institute for Peace and Reconciliation, 2017).

Autesserre, Séverine, 'International Peacebuilding and Local Success: Assumptions and Effectiveness', *International Studies Review*, 19/1: 114–132 (2017).

Averre, Derek, and Lance Davies, 'Russia, Humanitarian Intervention and the Responsibility to Protect: The Case of Syria', *International Affairs*, 91/4: 813–834 (2015).

Barcelona, Antonio (ed.), *Metaphor and Metonymy at the Crossroads: A Cognitive Perspective* (Berlin, DE: De Gruyter Mouton, 2003).

Barthes, Roland, *Image, Music, Text*, trans. by Stephen Heath (New York: Hill & Wang, 1977).

Baudrillard, Jean, *The Illusion of the End*, trans. by Chris Turner (Stanford: Stanford University Press, 1994).

Beier, J. Marshall, 'Grave Misgivings: Allegory, Catharsis, Composition', *Security Dialogue*, 38/2: 251–269 (2007).

Beier, J. Marshall, 'Dangerous Terrain: Re-Reading the Landmines Ban Through the Social Worlds of the RMA', *Contemporary Security Policy*, 32/1: 159–175 (2010).

Beier, J. Marshall (ed.), *The Militarization of Childhood: Thinking Beyond the Global South* (New York: Palgrave Macmillan, 2011).

Beier, J. Marshall, 'Shifting the Burden: Childhood, Resilience, Subjecthood', *Critical Studies on Security*, 3/3: 237–252 (2015).

Beier, J. Marshall (ed.), *Childhood and the Production of Security* (Abingdon: Routledge, 2016).

Bellamy, Alex J., 'Conflict Prevention and the Responsibility to Protect', *Global Governance*, 14/2: 135–156 (2008).

Bellamy, Alex. J., 'The Responsibility to Protect - Five Years On', *Ethics and International Affairs*, 24/2: 143–169 (2010).

Bellamy, Alex J., 'Libya and the Responsibility to Protect: the Exception and the Norm', *Ethics and International Affairs*, 25/3: 263–269 (2011).

Bellamy, Alex J., 'Mass Atrocities and Armed Conflict: Links, Distinctions, and Implications for the Responsibility to Prevent', Policy Analysis Brief (Muscatine, IA: The Stanley Foundation, February 2011).

Bellamy, Alex J., *Massacres and Morality: Mass Atrocities in an Age of Civilian Immunity* (Oxford: Oxford University Press, 2012).

Bellamy, Alex J., 'The Responsibility to Protect: Added Value or Hot Air?', *Cooperation and Conflict*, 48/3: 333–357 (2013).

Bellamy, Alex J., 'The Responsibility to Protect and the 2014 Conflict in Gaza', *E- International Relations*, 22 July 2014.

Bellamy, Alex J., 'The First Response: Peaceful Means in the Third Pillar of the Responsibility to Protect', The Stanley Foundation, December 2015, http://www.stanleyfoundation.org/publications/pab/Bellamy3rdPillarPAB116.pdf.

Bellamy, Alex J., and Tim Dunne (eds.), 'R2P in Theory and Practice', *The Oxford Handbook of Responsibility to Protect* (Oxford: Oxford University Press, 2016).

Benotman, Noman, and Nikita Malik, *Children of Islamic State* (London: Quilliam Foundation, 2016).

Berenschot, Ward, *Riot Politics: Hindu–Muslim Violence and the Indian State* (New York: Columbia University Press, 2011).

Berents, Helen, 'Children, Violence, and Social Exclusion: Negotiation of Everyday Insecurity in a Colombian Barrio,' *Critical Studies on Security*, 3/1: 90–104 (2015).

Berents, Helen, 'Hashtagging Girlhood: #IAmMalala, #BringBackOurGirls and Gendering Representations of Global Politics', *International Feminist Journal of Politics*, 18/4: 513–527 (2016).

Berger, Thomas, *Cultures of Antimilitarism: National Security in Germany and Japan* (Baltimore, MD: The Johns Hopkins University Press, 1998).

Betts, Alexander, and Phil Orchard (eds.), *Implementation and World Politics: How International Norms Change Practice* (Oxford: Oxford University Press, 2014).

Bhabha, Jacqueline, 'The Child: What Sort of Human?', *PMLA*, 121/5: 1526–1535 (2006).

Bhabha, Jacqueline, *Child Migration & Human Rights in a Global Age* (Princeton: Princeton University Press, 2014).

Bigo, Didier, 'Protection: Security, Territory and Population' in Jef Huysmans, Andrew Dobson, and Raia Prokhovnik (eds.), *The Politics of Protection: Sites of Insecurity and Political Agency* (New York: Routledge, 2006).

Blatter, Ariela, and Paul D. Williams, 'The Responsibility Not To Veto', *Global Responsibility to Protect*, 3/3: 301–322 (2011).

Bookmiller, Robert J., and Kirsten Nakjavani Bookmiller, 'Canada and the Human Security Network (1998–2010): RIP?', *British Journal of Canadian Studies*, 23/2: 246–71 (2010).

Brass, Paul R., *Theft of an Idol: Text and Context in the Representation of Collective Violence* (Princeton, NJ: Princeton University Press, 1997).

Brass, Paul R., *The Production of Hindu–Muslim Violence in Contemporary India* (New Delhi: Oxford University Press, 2003).

Brocklehurst, Helen, *Who's Afraid of Children? Children, Conflict and International Relations* (Aldershot: Ashgate, 2006).

Brocklehurst, Helen, 'The State of Play: Securities of Childhood – Insecurities of Children', *Critical Studies on Security*, 3/1: 29–46 (2015).

Brownmiller, Susan, 'Making Female Bodies the Battlefield', in Alexandra Stiglmayer (ed.), *Mass Rape: The War against Women in Bosnia-Herzegovina* (Lincoln, NE: University of Nebraska Press, 1994).

Bulley, Dan, 'Shame on EU? Europe, R2P, and the Politics of Refugee Protection', *Ethics & International Affairs*, 31/1: 51–70 (2017).

Burke, Kenneth, *A Grammar of Motives* (Berkeley: University of California Press, 1945).

Burman, Erica, 'Innocents Abroad: Western Fantasies of Childhood and the Iconography of Emergencies', *Disasters*, 18/3: 238–253 (1994).

Burman, Erica, *Deconstructing Developmental Psychology* (New York: Routledge, 2008).

Burman, Erica, *Developments: Child, Image, Nation* (New York: Routledge, 2008).

Butler, Judith, 'Photography, War, Outrage', *PMLA*, 120/3: 822–827 (2005).

Byerly, Robin T., 'Combating Modern Slavery: What Can Business Do?' *Journal of Leadership, Accountability and Ethics*, 9/5: 25–34 (2012).

Cabezas, Mar, and Gottfried Schweiger, 'Girlhood and Ethics: The Role of Bodily Integrity', *Girlhood Studies*, 9/3: 37–53 (2016).

Canavera, Mark, Kiryn Lanning, Katherine Polin and Lindsay Stark, '"And Then They Left": Challenges to Child Protection Systems Strengthening in South Sudan', *Children & Society*, 30/5: 356–368 (2016).

Carlson, Khristopher, and Dyan Mazurana, *Forced Marriage Within the Lord's Resistance Army*, (Medford MA: Feinstein International Center, Tufts University, 2008).

Carpenter, R. Charli, '"Women, Children and Other Vulnerable Groups": Gender, Strategic Frames and the Protection of Civilians as Transnational Issue', *International Studies Quarterly*, 49/2: 295–334 (2005).

Carpenter, R. Charli, *'Innocent Women and Children': Gender, Norms and the Protection of Civilians* (Aldershot: Ashgate, 2006).

Carpenter, R. Charli, 'Recognizing Gender-Based Violence against Civilian Men and Boys in Conflict Situations', *Security Dialogue*, 37/1: 83–103 (2006).

Carpenter, R. Charli, *Forgetting Children Born of War: Setting the Human Rights Agenda in Bosnia and Beyond* (New York: Columbia University Press, 2010).

Castaneda, Claudia, *Figurations: Child, Bodies, Worlds* (Durham, NC: Duke University Press, 2002).

CBC, 'Refugee Crisis, Drowned Syrian Boy Shift Focus of Election Campaign', *CBC News*, 3 September 2015.

CBC, 'Katelynn Sampson Inquest: Institutions Too Slow to Assess Case, Says Children's Aid Lawyer', *CBC News*, 29 February 2016.

Chataway, Teresa, 'Towards Normative Consensus on Responsibility to Protect', *Griffith Law Review*, 16/1: 193–224 (2007).

Child Protection Working Group (CPWG), 'Minimum Standards for Child Protection in Humanitarian Action', September 2012, https://reliefweb.int/sites/reliefweb.int/files/resources/Minimum-standards-for-child-protection-in-humanitarian-action.pdf.

Chouliaraki, Lilie, 'The Humanity of War: Iconic Photojournalism of the Battlefield, 1914–1912', *Visual Communication*, 12/3: 315–340 (2013).

Chuang, Janie, 'The Challenges and Perils of Reframing Trafficking as "Modern-Day Slavery"', *Anti-Trafficking Review*, 5: 146–9 (2015).

Cochrane, Liam, 'Myanmar Could be on the Brink of Genocide, UN Expert Says', ABC News, 6 September 2017.

Coen, Alise, 'Capable and Culpable? The United States, R2P, and Refugee Responsibility-Sharing' *Ethics & International Affairs*, 31/1: 71–92 (2017).

Cohen, Dara Kay, 'Explaining Rape During Civil War: Cross National Evidence (1980–2009)', *American Political Science Review*, 107: 461–477 (2013).

Cohen, Dara Kay, *Rape during Civil War* (Ithaca, NY: Cornell University Press, 2016).

Cohn, Carol, '"Maternal Thinking" and the Concept of "Vulnerability" in Security Paradigms, Policies, and Practices', *Journal of International Political Theory*, 10/1: 46–69 (2013).

Cole, Teju, 'The White Savior Industrial Complex', *The Atlantic*, 21 March 2012.

Coleman, Daniel, Erin Goheen Glanville, Agnes Kramer-Hamstra, and Wafaa Hasan 'Introduction', in *Countering Displacements: The Creativity and Resilience of Indigenous and Refugee-ed Peoples* (Edmonton: University of Alberta Press, 2012).

Cook, Daniel, 'When a Child is Not a Child, and other Conceptual Hazards of Childhood Studies', *Childhood*, 16/1: 5–10 (2009).

Cook, Daniel, 'A Politics of Becoming: When "Child" is Not Enough', *Childhood*, 22/1: 3–5 (2015).

Cook, Daniel, 'Childhood as a Moral Project', *Childhood*, 24/1: 3–6 (2017).

Coomaraswamy, Radhika, 'The Optional Protocol to the Convention on the Rights of the Child on the Involvement of Children in Armed Conflict – Towards Universal Ratification', *The International Journal of Children's Rights*, 18/4: 535–49 (2010).

Cottrell, M. Patrick, *The Evolution and Legitimacy of International Security Institutions* (New York: Cambridge University Press, 2016).

Cronogue, Graham, 'Responsibility to Protect: Syria: The Law, Politics, and Future of Humanitarian Intervention Post-Libya', *International Humanitarian Legal Studies*, 3/1: 124–159 (2012).

Csanady, Ashley, 'Children Who Die in Care in Ontario Will Get a New Voice Under Bill to Expand Advocate's Powers', *National Post*, 3 December 2015.

Cumming-Bruce, Nick, 2016. '"Worst Annual Death Toll Ever": Mediterranean Claims 5,000 Migrants', *New York Times*, 23 December 2016.

Cunningham, Hugh, *Children and Childhood in Western Society Since 1500* (United Kingdom: Pearson Education Limited, 2005).

D'Costa, Bina, 'Marginalized identity: new frontiers of research for IR?' in Brooke A. Ackerly, Maria Stern and Jacqui True (eds.), *Feminist methodologies for International Relations* (Cambridge; New York: Cambridge University Press, 2006).

D'Costa, Bina, *Nationbuilding, Gender and War Crimes in South Asia* (New York: Routledge, 2011).

D'Costa, Bina, 'The Rights of the Child: Political History, Practices and Protection', in Kim Huynh, Bina D'Costa and Katrina Lee-Koo, *Children and Global Conflict* (Cambridge: Cambridge University Press, 2015).

D'Costa, Bina, 'Children and Justice: Past Crimes, Healing and the Future' in Kim Huynh, Bina D'Costa, and Katrina Lee-Koo, *Children and Global Conflict* (Cambridge: Cambridge University Press, 2015).

D'Costa, Bina, 'Who Speaks for Children? Advocacy, Activism and Resistance', in Kim Huynh, Bina D'Costa and Katrina Lee-Koo, *Children and Global Conflict* (Cambridge: Cambridge University Press, 2015).

D'Costa, Bina (ed.), *Children and Violence: Politics of Conflict in South Asia* (Cambridge: Cambridge University Press, 2016).

D'Costa, Bina, 'Life (and Death) of Rohingya Children: No Place to Hide', *The Daily Star*, 13 October 2017.

D'Costa, Bina, 'Trafficking and "Modern-Day Slavery": Thinking Beyond Conceptual Boundaries', UNICEF Office of Research–Innocenti Briefing Paper (Florence: UNICEF Office of Research–Innocenti, 20 February 2017).

D'Costa, Bina, Kim Huynh and Katrina Lee-Koo, 'Introduction: Why Children Matter to Global Conflict', in Kim Huynh, Bina D'Costa and Katrina Lee-Koo (eds.), *Children and Global Conflict* (Cambridge: Cambridge University Press, 2015).

D'Costa, Bina, and Ton Liefaard, 'Background Paper of the Rapporteurs for 17th ASEM Seminar on Human Rights and Children', Sofia, Bulgaria, November 2017.

Dahl, Gudrun, 'Sociology and Beyond: Agency, Victimisation and the Ethics of Writing', *Asian Journal of Social Sciences*, 37/3: 391–407 (2009).

Dallaire, Roméo, 'Preventing the Use of Child Soldiers, Preventing Genocide', *UN Chronicle*, 52/1 & 2 (2015).

Davis, J. Francis, 'The Power of Images: Creating the Myths of Our Time', *Impact of Images: Life and Culture in the Media Age*, 57 (1992), http://www.medialit.org/reading-room/power-images-creating-myths-our-time.

Davies, Graeme A.M., and Robert Johns, 'R2P from Below: Does the British public view humanitarian interventions as ethical and effective?', *International Politics*, 53/1: 118–137 (2016).

Davies, Sara E., 'Addressing the Gender Gap in R2P', in Alex J. Bellamy and Tim Dunne (eds.), *The Oxford Handbook of the Responsibility to Protect* (Oxford: Oxford University Press, 2016).

Davies, Sara E., and Sarah Teitt, 'Engendering the Responsibility to Protect: Women and the Prevention of Mass Atrocities', *Global Responsibility to Protect*, 4/2: 198–222 (2012).

de Certeau, Michel, *The Practice of Everyday Life* (California: University of California Press, 1988).

De Vries, Maya, Asmahan Simry, Ifat Maoz, 'Like a Bridge Over Troubled Water: Using Facebook to Mobilize Solidarity Among East Jerusalem Palestinians During the 2014 War in Gaza', *International Journal of Communication*, 9: 2622–2649 (2015).

Dearden, Lizzie, 'Israel Approves New Law to Jail Child "Terrorists" as Young as 12', *Independent*, 3 August 2016.

Defense for Children International, Palestine, 'Child Fatalities', http://www.dci-palestine.org/child_fatalities_statistics.

Defense for Children International, 'Palestinian Children Being Used as Human Shields', 1 February 2015, http://www.dci-palestine.org/palestinian_children_being_used_as_human_shields.

Defense of Children International, 'Year in Review, Worst Abuses against Palestinian Children in 2016', 1 January 2017, http://www.dci-palestine.org/year_in_review_2016.

Denov, Myriam, 'Children Born of Wartime Rape: The Intergenerational Complexities of Sexual Violence and Abuse', *Ethics, Medicine and Public Health*, 11: 61–68 (2015).

Denov, Myriam, and Atim Angela Lakor, 'When War is Better Than Peace: The Post-Conflict Realities of Children Born of Wartime Rape in Northern Uganda', *Child Abuse and Neglect*, 65: 255–265 (2017).

Denov, Myriam, Leah Woolner, Jules Pacifique Bahati, Paulin Nkusi, and Obed Shyaka, 'The Intergenerational Legacy of Genocidal Rape: The Realities & Perspectives of Children Born of the Rwandan Genocide', *Journal of Interpersonal Violence*, 1–22 (2017).

Department of Peacekeeping Operations, 'Child Protection in the United Nations Peacekeeping' (United Nations: Spring 2011).

di Tomasso, Laura, 'More Equal than Others: The Discursive Construction of Migrant Children and Families in Canada', *International Journal of Child, Youth and Family Studies* 3/2–3: 331–348 (2012).

Dieng, Adama, Special Advisor for the Secretary-General on the Prevention of Genocide, United Nations, INoGS Conference, Keynote Speech, 'Preventing Genocide Today: Applying the Lessons of the Past to Protect Future Generations', Jerusalem, 26 June 2016.

Drumbl, Mark, *Reimagining Child Soldiers in International Law and Policy* (Oxford: Oxford University Press, 2012).

Dunne, Tim, 'The Responsibility to Protect and World Order', in Ramesh Thakur and William Maley (eds.), *Theorising the Responsibility to Protect* (Cambridge: Cambridge University Press, 2015).

Duschinsky, Robbie, 'Slaughtered Innocents: Child Victims in Political Discourse During the Second Intifada and Gaza Conflict', *Social Semiotics*, 21/1: 33–51 (2011).

Eliasson, Jan, 'The United Nations' Human Rights up Front Initiative', Academic Council on the United Nations Systems Quarterly Newsletter, 2015.

Eliminating the Worst Forms of Child Labour: A Practical Guide to ILO Convention No. 182, Handbook for Parliamentarians No. 3 (Geneva: International Labour Organization, 2002).

Eliot, T.S., *Four Quartets* (New York: Houghton Mifflin Harcourt, 1943).

Elliott, Heather (ed.), 'Children and Peacebuilding: Experiences and Perspectives', World Vision Discussion Paper (Melbourne: World Vision, 2002).

Ercan, Pinar Gözen, 'Responsibility to Protect and Inter-state Crises: Why and How R2P Applies to the Case of Gaza', *The International Journal of Human Rights*, 19/8: 1018–1111 (2015).

Erjavec, Karmen, and Zala Volčič, '"Target", "Cancer", and "Warrior": Exploring Painful Metaphors of Self-Presentation Used by Girls Born of War Rape', *Discourse & Society*, 21/5: 524–543 (2010).

European Union, 'EU Guidelines on Children and Armed Conflict', 9 December 2003, 15634/03.

Evans, Gareth, 'The Responsibility to Protect: An Idea Whose Time Has Come … and Gone?', *International Relations*, 22/3: 283/298 (2008).

Evans, Gareth, *The Responsibility to Protect: Ending Mass Atrocity Crimes Once and For All* (Washington, DC: Brookings Institution Press, 2008).

Faek, Rasha, 'Educational Toll of Gaza War: At Least 2 Universities, 148 Schools', *Al Fanar Media*, 3 August 2014.

Fahim, Kareem, and Hwaida Saad, 'A Faceless Teenage Refugee Who Helped Ignite Syria's War', *The New York Times*, 8 February 2013.

Faulkner, Joanne, 'Vulnerability of "Virtual" Subjects: Childhood, Memory, and Crisis in the Cultural Value of Innocence', *SubStance* #132, 42/3: 127–147 (2013).

Ferrales, Gabrielle, Hollie Nyseth Brehm, and Suzy McElrath, 'Gender-Based Violence against Men and Boys in Darfur: The Gender–Genocide Nexus', *Gender & Society*, 30/4: 565–89 (2016).

'Final Report of the Commission of Experts Established Pursuant to Security Council Resolution 780 (1992)', S/1994/674, 27 May 1994.

Finnemore, Martha, and Kathryn Sikkink, 'International Norm Dynamics and Political Change', *International Organization*, 52/4: 887–917 (1998).

Finnström, Sverker, 'Wars of the Past and War in the Present: The Lord's Resistance Movement/Army in Uganda', *Africa: Journal of the International African Institute*, 76/2: 200–220 (2006).

Finnström, Sverker, *Living with Bad Surroundings* (Durham, North Carolina: Duke University Press, 2008).

Foucault, Michel, *Discipline and Punish: The Birth of the Prison* (New York: Vintage Books, 1995).

Foucault, Michel, *Security, Territory, Population: Lectures at the Collège de France 1977–1978* (New York: Picador, 2009).

Fund For Peace, 'Fragile States Index 2017 – Annual Report', May 2017, http://fundforpeace.org/fsi/2017/05/14/fragile-states-index-2017-annual-report/

Fund For Peace, 'Methodology Behind the Index', http://fsi.fundforpeace.org/methodology.

Gagiano, Annie, '*Ice-Candy-Man* and *In the Country of Men*: The Politics of Cruelty and the Witnessing Child', *Stellenbosch Papers in Linguistics*, 39/1: 25–39 (2010).

Gallant, Jacques, 'Coroner Announces Inquest Into Death of Katelynn Sampson', *Toronto Star*, 13 August 2015.

Garcia, Denise, *Small Arms and Security: New Emerging International Security Norms* (Abingdon: Routledge: 2006).

Garwood-Gowers, Andrew, 'The Responsibility to Protect and the Arab Spring: Libya as the Exception, Syria as the Norm?', *UNSW Law Journal*, 36/2: 594–618 (2013).

'Gaza Could Become Uninhabitable in Less than Five Years Due to Ongoing "De-development"', UN Conference on Trade and Development, *UN News Centre*, 1 September 2015.

Gelb, Leslie H., 'Shoot to Feed Somalia', *New York Times*, 19 November 1992.

Gen, Watye Ki, *Documentation of Children Born in Captivity* (Unpublished Report: Gulu, Uganda).

Glanville, Luke, *Sovereignty and the Responsibility to Protect: A New History* (Chicago: University of Chicago Press, 2014).

Godwin et al., Michelle, 'Floods and Flows: How We Frame Children in Migration Debates', Innocenti Research Brief (Florence: UNICEF Office of Research–Innocenti, forthcoming).

Goldenberg, Susan, 'Making of a Martyr', *The Guardian*, 3 October 2000.

Guha-Sapir, Debarati, Benjamin Schlüter, Jose Manuel Rodriguez-Llanes, Louis Lillywhite, and Madelyn Hsiao-Rei Hicks, 'Patterns of Civilian and Child Deaths Due to War-Related Violence in Syria: A Comparative Analysis from the Violation Documentation Center Dataset, 2011–16', *Lancet Global Health*, 6: 103–10 (2018).

Hampson, Françoise J., 'Legal Protection Afforded to Children Under International Humanitarian Law', Report for the Study on the Impact of Armed Conflict on Children, May 1996, http://www.essex.ac.uk/armedcon/story_id/000578.html.

Hansen, Lene, 'Theorizing the Image for Security Studies: Visual Securitization and the Muhammad Cartoon Crisis', *European Journal of International Relations*, 17/1: 51–74 (2011).

Hanson, Karl, 'Embracing the Past: "Been", "Being" and "Becoming" Children', *Childhood*, 24/3: 281–285 (2017).

Harff, Barbara, 'No Lessons Learned from the Holocaust? Assessing Risks of Genocide and Political Mass Murder since 1955', *American Political Science Review*, 97/1: 57–73 (2003).

Harff, Barbara, 'Genocide and Political Mass Murder: Definitions, Theories, Analyses' in Michael Stohl, Mark I. Lichbach and Peter Nils Grabosky (eds.), *States and Peoples in Conflict: Transformations of Conflict Studies* (Abingdon: Routledge, 2017).

Harris Rimmer, Susan, *Gender and Transitional Justice: The Women of East Timor* (Abingdon: Routledge, 2010).

Harris Rimmer, Susan, 'Refugees, Internally Displaced Persons and the "Responsibility to Protect"', (*New Issues in Refugee Research*, 185 UN High Commissioner for Refugees, 2010).

Härting, Heike, 'Global Humanitarianism, Race, and the Spectacle of the African Corpse in Current Western Representations of the Rwandan Genocide', *Comparative Studies of South Asia, Africa, and the Middle East*, 28/1: 61–77 (2008).

Harvey, Stella Leventoyannis, *The Brink of Freedom* (Winnipeg: Signature Editions, 2015).

Harvey, Stella Leventoyannis, 'Halt, who goes there?', *BC Booklook*, 5 November 2015.

Hass, Amira, 'Is the IDF Conducting a Kneecapping Campaign in the West Bank?', *Haaretz*, 27 August 2016.

Heathcote, Gina, 'Women and Children and Elephants as Justifications for the Use of Force', *Journal of the Use of Force and International Law*, 4/1: 66–85 (2017).

High Level Independent Panel on Peace Operations, *Uniting Our Strengths for Peace: Politics, Partnership and People* (New York: United Nations, 2015).

High Level Panel on Threats Challenges and Change, *A More Secure World: Our Shared Responsibility*, (New York: United Nations, 2004).

Hockey, Jenny, and Allison James, *Growing Up and Growing Old: Ageing and Dependency in the Life Course* (London: Sage Publications, 1993).

Hogwood, Jemma, Christine Mushashi, Stuart Jones and Carl Auerbach, '"I learned who I am": Young People Born from Genocide Rape in Rwanda and their Experiences of Disclosure', *Journal of Adolescent Research*, 33/5: 1–22 (2017).

Holt, Victoria, Glyn Taylor, and Max Kelly, *Protecting Civilians in the Context of UN Peacekeeping Operations: Successes, Setbacks and Remaining Challenges* (New York: United Nations, 2009).

Holzscheiter, Anna, *Children's Rights in International Politics: The Transformative Power of Transnational Discourse* (New York: Palgrave Macmillan, 2010).

Hook, Glenn D., *Militarization and Demilitarization in Contemporary Japan* (London and New York: Routledge, 1996).

Hubert, Don, and Ariela Blätter, 'The Responsibility to Protect as International Crimes Prevention', *Global Responsibility to Protect*, 4/1: 33–66 (2012).

Human Rights Watch, *"Maybe We Live and Maybe We Die": Recruitment and Use of Children by Armed Groups in Syria* (New York: Human Rights Watch, 2014).

Human Rights Watch, 'Ensure Consistency in Children and Armed Conflict Report', 27 April 2015.

'Human Rights Organizations in Israel: Politicians' Calls to Police and Soldiers to Shoot Rather than Arrest Endorse the Killing of Palestinians', *Adalah*, 14 October 2015.

Huynh, Kim, 'Children and Agency: Caretakers, Free-rangers and Everyday Life', in Kim Huynh, Bina D'Costa and Katrina Lee-Koo, *Children and Global Conflict* (Cambridge: Cambridge University Press, 2015).

Huynh, Kim, Bina D'Costa, and Katrina Lee-Koo, *Children and Global Conflict* (Cambridge: Cambridge University Press, 2015).

ICISS, *The Responsibility to Protect: Report of the International Commission on Intervention and State Sovereignty* (Ottawa: IDRC, 2001).

ICRC, 'Professional Standards for Protection Work Carried out by Humanitarian and Human Rights Actors in Armed Conflict and Other Situations of Violence', (Geneva: International Committee of the Red Cross, 2013).

Ignatieff, Michael, 'How Syria Divided the World', *The New York Review of Books*, 11 July 2012.

Ignatieff, Michael, 'Human Rights, Global Ethics, and the Ordinary Virtues', *Ethics & International Affairs*, 31/1: 3–16 (2017).

Imoh, Afua Twum-Danso, 'Children's Perceptions of Physical Punishment in Ghana and the Implications for Children's Rights', *Childhood*, 20/4: 472–486 (2013).

International Committee of the Red Cross, 'How is the Term "Armed Conflict" Defined in International Humanitarian Law?", International Committee of the Red Cross Opinion Paper, March 2008.

International Committee of the Red Cross, 'Children Affected by Armed Conflict and Other Situations of Violence', Workshop Report (Geneva: ICRC, 14–16 March 2011).

International Labour Organization, 'Global Estimates of Child Labour' (Geneva: ILO, 2017).

International Organization for Migration, 'Mediterranean Migrant Arrivals Top 43,000 in 2017; Deaths: 1089', https://www.iom.int/news/mediterranean-migrant-arrivals-top-43000-2017-deaths-1089.

International Organization for Migration, 'UN Migration Agency Warns of Trafficking, Labour Exploitation, Sexual Abuse of Rohingya Refugees', 14 November 2017, https://www.iom.int/news/un-migration-agency-warns-trafficking-labour-exploitation-sexual-abuse-rohingya-refugees.

'Israeli soldiers who Used Palestinian boy, 9, as a Human Shield Avoid Jail', *The Guardian*, 21 November 2010.

Jacob, Cecilia, *Child Security in Asia: The Impact of Armed Conflict in Cambodia and Myanmar*(Abingdon: Routledge, 2014).

Jacob, Cecilia, '"Children and Armed Conflict" and the Field of Security Studies', *Critical Studies on Security*, 3/1: 14–28 (2015).

Jacob, Cecilia, 'State Responsibility and Prevention in the Responsibility to Protect: Communal Violence in India', *Global Responsibility to Protect*, 7/1: 56–80 (2015).

James, Allison, and Adrian L. James, *Constructing Childhood: Theory, Policy and Social Practice* (Basingstoke: Palgrave Macmillan, 2004).

James, Allison, Chris Jenks, and Alan Prout, *Theorizing Childhood* (Cambridge: Polity Press, 1998).

Jenks, Chris, *Childhood* (London: Routledge, 2005).

Jervis, Robert, *System Effects: Complexity in Political and Social Life* (Princeton: Princeton University Press, 1997).

Johnston, Alastair Iain, *Social States: China in International Institutions, 1980–2000* (Princeton, NJ: Princeton University Press, 2008).

Jones, Adam, 'Gendercide and Genocide', *Journal of Genocide Research*, 2/2: 185–211 (2000).

Kalyvas, Stathis N., *The Logic of Violence in Civil War* (Cambridge: Cambridge University Press, 2006).

Kaplan, Robert D., *Balkan Ghosts: A Journey through History* (New York: St. Martins, 1993).

Karstedt, Susanne, 'Contextualizing Mass Atrocity Crimes: Moving Toward a Relational Approach', *Annual Review of Law and Social Science*, 9: 383–404 (2013).

Katsuma, Yasushi, 'Buryoku Funso ka no Eikyo wo Uketa Kodomo no Anzen Hosho wo meguru Kokusaiteki na Torikumi' [A Search for the Security of Children Affected by Armed Conflicts], *Ajia Taiheiyo Tokyu*, 17: 125–126 (October 2011).

Keating, Tom, 'Mobilising the troops: generating the political will to act', in W. Andy Knight and Frazer Egerton (eds.), *Routledge Handbook of the Responsibility to Protect* (Abingdon: Routledge, 2012).

Kelly, Lyndsey, 'The Downfall of the Responsibility to Protect: How the Libyan and Syrian Crises Secured the Fate of the Once-Emerging Norm', *Syracuse Journal of International Law and Commerce*, 43/2: 381–409 (2016).

Kestler-D-Amours, Jillian, Peter Edwards, Tonda MacCharles, and Jacques Gallant, 'Tima Kurdi's Pleading Letter to Allow Brother to Enter Canada Revealed', *Toronto Star*, 3 September 2015.

Ki-Moon, Ban, 'Foreword' in *20 Years to Better Protect Children Affected by Conflict*, Office to the Special Representative of the Secretary-General for Children and Armed Conflict, https://childrenandarmedconflict.un.org/wp-content/uploads/2017/01/Twenty-Years-of-Work-Booklet_web.pdf.

Kingsbury, Damien, *Sri Lanka and the Responsibility to Protect: Politics, Ethnicity and Genocide* (New York: Routledge, 2012).

Knudsen, Anita, and Michelle Godwin, 'Pinning Down a Paper Tiger: Some Practice Observations on the Monitoring and Reporting Mechanism in Nepal and Asian Contexts' in Bina D'Costa (ed.), *Children and Violence: Politics of Conflict in South Asia* (Cambridge: Cambridge University Press, 2016).

Krook, Mona Lena, and Jacqui True, 'Rethinking the Life Cycles of International Norms: The United Nations and the Global Promotion of Gender Equality', *European Journal of International Relations*, 18/1: 103–127 (2012).

Ladisch, Virginie, *From Rejection to Redress: Overcoming Legacies of Conflict-Related Sexual Violence in Northern Uganda,* International Centre for Transnational Justice, October 2015, www.ictj.org/sites/default/files/ICTJ-Report-Uganda-Children-2015.pdf.

Lang, Hazel, and Anita Knudsen, '"Your Subject of Protection is a Dangerous One": Protracted Internal Conflict and the Challenges for Humanitarian Agencies', *Norsk Geografisk Tidsskrift – Norwegian Journal of Geography*, 63/1: 35–45(2009).

Lantis, Jeffrey S., *Arms and Influence: U.S. Technology Innovations and the Evolution of International Security Norms* (Stanford: Stanford University Press, 2016).

Lee, Nick, *Childhood and Society: Growing Up in an Age of Uncertainty* (Maidenhead: Open University Press, 2001).

Lee-Koo, Katrina, 'Horror and Hope: (Re)presenting Militarised Children in Global North–South Relations', *Third World Quarterly*, 32/4: 725–742 (2011).

Lee-Koo, Katrina, 'Not Suitable for Children: The Politicisation of Conflict-Affected Children in Post-2001 Afghanistan', *Australian Journal of International Affairs*, 67/4: 475–490 (2013).

Lee-Koo, Katrina, 'Children and Armed Conflict: Mapping the Terrain', in Kim Huynh, Bina D'Costa and Katrina Lee-Koo, *Children and Global Conflict* (Cambridge: Cambridge University Press, 2015).

Levitt, Matthew, 'Hamas from Cradle to the Grave', *Middle East Quarterly*, Winter: 3–15 (2004).

Levy, Gideon, and Alex Levac, 'Israeli Police Help Palestinian Girls Commit Suicide', *Haaretz*, 3 June 2016.

Loriggio, Paola, 'Toronto Girl Murdered by Guardians Was Once Struck So Hard Her Liver Ruptured, Pathologist Tells Inquest', *National Post*, 10 November 2015.

Lynch, Colum, 'Confidential UN Report Accuses Saudi Coalition of Killing Hundreds of Yemeni Kids', *Foreign Policy*, 16 August 2017.

MacFarlane, S. Neil, and Yuen Foong Khong, *Human Security and the UN: A Critical History* (Bloomington: Indiana University Press, 2006).

Macfarlane, S. Neil, Carolin J. Thielking and Thomas G. Weiss, 'The Responsibility to Protect: Is Anyone Interested in Humanitarian Intervention?', *Third World Quarterly*, 25/5: 977–992 (2004).

Machel, Graça, *Impact of Armed Conflict on Children*, A/51/306, 26 August 1996.

Mackenzie, Megan, 'Securitizing Sex? Towards a Theory of the Utility of Wartime Sexual Violence', *International Journal of Feminist Politics*, 12/2: 202–221 (2010).

MacKinnon, Catherine A., 'Rape, Genocide and Women's Human Rights', in Alexandra Stiglmayer (ed.), *Mass Rape: The War against Women in Bosnia-Herzegovina* (Lincoln, NE: University of Nebraska Press, 1994).

MacMillan, Lorraine, 'The Child Soldier in North-South Relations', *International Political Sociology*, 3/1: 36–52 (2009).

MacMillan, Lorraine, 'Children, Civilianhood, and Humanitarian Securitization', *Critical Studies on Security*, 3/1: 62–76 (2015).

Mahmood, Saba, *Politics of Piety: The Islamic Revival and the Feminist Subject* (Princeton, NJ; Woodstock: Princeton University Press, 2012).

Makman, Lisa Hermine, 'Child Crusaders: The Literature of Global Childhood', *The Lion and the Unicorn*, 26: 287–304 (2002).

Mamdani, Mahmood, 'Responsibility to Protect or Right to Punish?', *Journal of Intervention and State Building*, 4/1: 53–67 (2010).

Mani, Rama, and G Thomas. Weiss (eds.) *Responsibility to Protect: Cultural Perspectives in the Global South*: (Abingdon Routledge, 2011).

Mani, Rama, and Thomas G. Weiss, 'R2P's Missing Link, Culture', *Global Responsibility to Protect*, 3/4: 451–472 (2011).

Martin, Susan, 'Forced Migration, the Refugee Regime and the Responsibility to Protect', *Global Responsibility to Protect*, 2: 38–59 (2010).

Maslow, Abraham H., 'A Theory of Human Motivation', *Psychological Review*, 50/4: 370–396 (1943).

Mazower, Mark, *Governing the World: The History of an Idea* (New York: The Penguin Press, 2012).

McElroy, Theresa, Herbert Muyinda, Stella Atim, Patricia Spittal, and Catherine Backman, 'War, Displacement and Productive Occupations in Northern Uganda', *Journal of Occupational Science*, 19/3: 198–212 (2012).

McEvoy, Kieran, and Kirsten McConnachie, 'Victims and Transitional Justice: Voice, Agency and Blame', *Social & Legal Studies*, 22/4: 489–513 (2013).

Meade, Amanda, 'Charlie Hebdo Cartoon Depicting Drowned Child Alan Kurdi Sparks Racism Debate', *The Guardian*, 14 January 2016.

Midford, Paul, *Rethinking Japanese Public Opinion and Security* (Stanford: Stanford University Press, 2011).

Miller-Graff, Laura E., and E. Mark Cummings, 'The Israeli-Palestinian Conflict: Effects on Youth Adjustment, Available Interventions, and Future Research Directions', *Development Review*, 43: 1–47 (2017).

Morris, Justin, 'Libya and Syria: R2P and the Spectre of the Swinging Pendulum', *International Affairs*, 89/5: 1265–1283 (2013).

Murdie, Amanda, and Dursun Peksen, 'The Impact of Human Rights INGO Shaming on Humanitarian Interventions', *Journal of Politics*, 76/1: 215–228 (2014).

Niland, Norah, Riccardo Polastro, Antonio Donini and Amra Lee, 'Independent Whole of System Review of Protection in the Context of Humanitarian Action' (Norwegian Refugee Council, on behalf of the Inter-Agency Standing Committee and the Global Protection Cluster, 2015).

Nordstrom, Carolyn, 'The Jagged Edge of Peace,' in Siobhan McEvoy-Levy (ed.), *Troublemakers or Peacemakers? Youth and Post-Accord Peace Building* (Notre Dame, IN: Notre Dame University Press, 2006).

Nussbaum, Martha C., 'Capabilities as Fundamental Entitlements: Sen and Social Justice', *Feminist Economics*, 9/2–3: 33–59 (2003).

Nyers, Peter, *Rethinking Refugees: Beyond States of Emergency* (New York: Routledge, 2006).

O'Toole, Megan, 'Guardians Get Life for Killing 7-Year-Old Girl', *National Post*, 1 May 2012.

OCHA, 'Aide Memoire for the Consideration of Issues Pertaining to the Protection of Civilians in Armed Conflict' (New York: United Nations, 2014).

OCHA, 'Protection of Civilians Report', 7–20 March 2017.

Ono, Kent A., and John M. Sloop, *Shifting Borders: Rhetoric, Immigration and California's Proposition 187* (Philadelphia, PA: Temple University Press, 2002).

Ontario, Office of the Chief Coroner, 'Inquest Touching the Death of Katelynn Sampson: Jury Verdict and Recommendations', 29 April 2016, Toronto.

Ontario, Office of the Provincial Advocate for Children and Youth, 'Suggested Recommendations for Jury Consideration: Inquest into the Death of Katelynn Sampson', 26 February 2016.

Orford, Anne, *International Authority and the Responsibility to Protect* (Cambridge: Cambridge University Press, 2011).

'Palestinian teens armed with scissors shot in Jerusalem', *Al Jazeera*, 23 November 2015.

Park, Tina Kiwon, 'From Promise to Practice, UN Marks 10 Years of R2P', *Open Canada*, 16 September 2015.

Peterson, V. Spike, 'Security and Sovereign States: What is at Stake in Taking Feminism Seriously?' in V. Spike Peterson (ed.), *Gendered States: Feminist (Re)Visions of International Relations Theory* (Boulder: Lynne Rienner Publishers, 1992).

Petrie, Charles, 'Report of the Secretary-General's Internal Review Panel on United Nations Action in Sri Lanka' (New York: United Nations, 2012).

'Playing with Fire: Israel's Sweeping Disregard for the Wellbeing and Security of East Jerusalem Residents has Led to Four Fatalities and Dozens of Injuries, and Disrupted the Lives of Tens of Thousands of Residents', *B'TSELEM*, 24 July 2017.

Ponthieu, Aurelie, Christoph Vogel, and Katharine Derderian, 'Without Precedent or Prejudice? UNSC Resolution 2098 and Its Potential Implications for Humanitarian Space in Eastern Congo and Beyond', *Journal of Humanitarian Assistance*, 21 January 2014.

Porter, Catherine, 'Katelynn Sampson Tragedy Shows We Forget Children Are People: Porter', *Toronto Star*, 30 April 2016.

Powell, Betsy, 'Katelynn Sampson: Guardians Sentenced to Life in Prison For Murdering 7-Year-Old Toronto Girl', *Toronto Star*, 1 May 2012.

Powers, Maggie, 'Responsibility to Protect: Dead, Dying, or Thriving?', *The International Journal of Human Rights*, 19/8: 1257–1278 (2015).

Prantl, Jochen, and Ryoko Nakano, 'Global Norm Diffusion in East Asia: How China and Japan Implement the Responsibility to Protect', *International Relations*, 25/2: 204–223 (2011).

Prevent Genocide International, 'Rome Statue of the International Criminal Court', 17 July 1998, https://www.icc-cpi.int/NR/rdonlyres/ADD16852-AEE9-4757-ABE7-9CDC7CF02886/283503/RomeStatutEng1.pdf.

Pruitt, Lesley, *Youth Peacebuilding: Music, Gender, Change* (New York: SUNY Press, 2013).

Pulse, Lindsay, 'Women Dress in Tribute to *The Handmaid's Tale* to Protest New Texas Abortion Bills', *Newsy*, 21 March 2017.

Pupavac, Vanessa, 'Misanthropy Without Borders: The International Children's Rights Regime', *Disasters*, 25/2: 95–112 (2001).

Pupavac, Vanessa, 'The International Children's Rights Regime' in David Chandler (ed.), *Rethinking Human Rights: Critical Approaches to International Politics* (New York: Palgrave Macmillan, 2002).

Quota, Samir, and Eyad El Sarraj, 'Prevalence of PTSD Among Palestinian Children in the Gaza Strip', *Arabypsynet Journal*, 2: 8–13 (2004).

Qvortrup, Jens, 'Editorial: The Waiting Child', *Childhood*, 11/3: 267–273 (2004).

Qvortrup, Jens, 'Varieties of Childhood' in Jens Qvortrup (ed.), *Studies in Modern Childhood: Society, Agency, Culture* (New York: Palgrave Macmillan, 2005).

Ramzy, Austin, 'At Risk in Rohingya Exodus: 230,000 Children, Hundreds All Alone', *New York Times*, 15 September 2017.

Rasmussen, Kim, 'Places for Children – Children's Places', *Childhood*, 11/2: 155–173 (2004).

Razack, Shereen, *Dark Threats and White Knights: The Somalia Affair, Peacekeeping and the New Imperialism* (Toronto: University of Toronto Press, 2004).

Razack, Shereen, 'Stealing the Pain of Others: Reflections on Canadian Humanitarian Responses', *Review of Education,Pedagogy, and Cultural Studies*, 29/4: 375–394 (2007).

Regan, Paulette, *Unsettling the Settler Within* (Vancouver: UBC Press, 2010).

Reichhold, Urban, and Andrea Binder, 'The Metrics and Ethics of Protecting Civilians', *Global Responsibility to Protect*, 6/2: 204–226 (2014).

Reike, Reuben, Serena Sharma, and Jennifer Welsh, 'A Strategic Framework for Mass Atrocity Prevention', Policy Paper 03/2013 (Queanbeyan, NSW and Oxford: Australian Civil–Military Centre and Oxford Institute for Ethics, Law and Armed Conflict, 2013).

Ricoeur, Paul, 'Interview with Richard Kearney', in Lucy Burke, Tony Crowley, Alvin Girvin (eds.), *The Routledge Language and Cultural Theory Reader* (London: Routledge, 2000).

Rose, Nikolas, *Governing the Soul: The Shaping of the Private Self* (London: Free Association Books, 1999).

Roy, Ananya, 'Praxis in the Time of Empire', *Planning Theory*, 5/1: 7–29 (2006).

Ryan, Patrick, 'How New Is the "New" Social Study of Childhood? The Myth of a Paradigm Shift', *Journal of Interdisciplinary History*, 38/4: 553–576 (2008).

Sabet-Parry, 'Rayyan, Why Research Should Be a Priority in the Global Response to the Child Migration Crisis', 5 October 2016, https://blogs.unicef.org/evidence-for-action/research-priority-global-response-child-migration-crisis/.

Sami, Samira, Holly A Williams, Sandra Krause, Monica A Onyango, Ann Burton, Barbara Tomczyk, 'Responding to the Syrian Crisis: the Needs of Women and Girls', *Viewpoint*, 8 November 2013.

Sammon, E., M.L. Godwin, A. Rumble, A.B. Matsika Nolan and N. Mayanga, 'Make the Promise True: A Monitoring and Evaluation Framework for Measuring Quality in Child Protection Service Delivery in Zimbabwe', *Child Indicators Research*, 8(3): 623–640 (2015).

Sandholtz, Wayne, 'Dynamics of International Norm Change', *European Journal of International Relations*, 14/1: 101–131 (2008).

Sato, Yukio, 'Nihon no Kokuren Gaiko to Ningen no Anzen Hosho', *Kokusai Mondai*, 530 (March 2004).

Save the Children, 'Untold Atrocities: The Stories of Syria's Children' (London: Save the Children, 2012).

Save the Children, 'Unspeakable Crimes against Children: Sexual Violence in Conflict' (London: Save the Children, 2013).

Save the Children International, 'Rising to the Challenge: Save the Children Annual Report' (London: Save the Children, 2016).

Schnabel, Albrecht, 'The Responsibility to Rebuild' in W. Andy Knight and Frazer Egerton (eds.), *The Routledge Handbook of the Responsibility to Protect* (London: Routledge, 2012).

Schott, Robin May, 'War Rape, Natality and Genocide', *Journal of Genocide Research*, 13/1–2: 5–21 (2011).

Sengupta, Somini, 'Saudi Arabia Resists Independent Inquiry on Yemen Atrocities', *New York Times*, 27 September 2017.

Serrano, Mónica, 'National Focal Points for R2P: Institutionalizing the Responsibility to Protect', in Serena K. Sharma and Jennifer M. Welsh (eds.), *The Responsibility to Prevent: Overcoming the Challenges of Atrocity Prevention* (Oxford: Oxford University Press, 2015).

'Settlers' Presence in Batan al-Hawa Results in Local Minors Being Arrested and Detained by Security Forces', *B'Tselem*, 28 December 2016.

Shanahan, Fiona, and Angela Veale, 'How Mothers Mediate the Social Integration of Their Children Conceived of Forced Marriage Within the Lord's Resistance Army', *Child Abuse & Neglect*, 51: 72–86 (2016).

Shapiro, Michael, *Reading the Postmodern Polity: Political Theory as Textual Practice* (Minneapolis: University of Minnesota Press, 1992).

Sharapov, Kiril, 'Traffickers and Their Victims': Anti-Trafficking Policy in the United Kingdom', *Critical Sociology*, 1: 91–111 (2017).

Sharlach, Lisa, 'Rape as genocide: Bangladesh, the former Yugoslavia, and Rwanda', *New Political Science*: 22(1), 89–102 (2000).

Sharma, Serena K., and Jennifer M. Welsh, 'Conclusion: An Integrated Framework for Atrocity Crime Prevention' in Serena K. Sharma and Jennifer M. Welsh (eds.),

The Responsibility to Prevent: Overcoming the Challenges of Atrocity Prevention (Oxford: Oxford University Press, 2015).

Shinyo, Takahiro, 'Nihon no Ningen Anzen Hosho Seisaku to Sono Gaikoteki Jissen' [Japan's Policy on Human Security and Its Implementation], *Kokusai Kokyo Seisaku Kenkyu*, 13/1: 39–52 (2008–2009).

Singer, Hanaa, 'Statement by Hanaa Singer, UNICEF Representative for Syria on Attack on the Al Hayat Primary School in Eastern Damascus', 7 November 2014, https://www.unicef.org/media/media_76951.html.

Singer, Peter, *One World Now* (New Haven & London: Yale University Press, 2016).

Slim, Hugo, *Killing Civilians: Method, Madness and Morality in War* (Oxford: Oxford University Press, 2010).

Slim, Hugo, and Andrew Bonwick, *Protection - An ALNAP Guide for Humanitarian Agencies* (London: ALNAP/ODI, 2005).

Smith, Joanna, 'Judge Cleared in Katelynn Complaint', *Toronto Star*, 19 December 2008.

Stahn, Carsten, 'Responsibility to Protect: Political Rhetoric or Emerging Legal Norm?', *The American Journal of International Law*, 101/1: 99–120 (2007).

Stamnes, Eli, 'Speaking R2P and the Prevention of Mass Atrocities', *Global Responsibility to Protect*, 1: 70–89 (2009).

Steffler, Margaret, 'The Production and Use of the Globalized Child: Canadian Literary and Political Contexts', *Jeunesse: Young People, Texts, Cultures*, 1/2: 109–124 (2009).

Stephens, Sharon, 'Introduction', in Sharon Stephens (ed.), *Children and the Politics of Culture* (Princeton: Princeton University Press, 1995).

Stiglitz, Joseph E., 'The Ideological Crisis of Western Capitalism', *Project Syndicate*, 6 July 2011.

Stiglmayer, Alexandra, 'The Rapes in Bosnia', in Alexandra Stiglmayer (ed.), *Mass Rape: The War against Women in Bosnia-Herzegovina*, (Lincoln, NE: University of Nebraska Press, 1994).

Stoltenberg, Jens, 'Our Children: the Key to Our Common Future', *The Lancet*, 368/9541: 1042–1044 (2006).

Strange, Susan, *The Retreat of the State: The Diffusion of Power in the World Economy* (Cambridge: Cambridge University Press, 1996).

Straus, Scott, *The Order of Genocide: Race, Power, and War in Rwanda* (Ithaca, NY: Cornell University Press, 2006).

Straus, Scott, 'Triggers of Mass Atrocities', *Politics and Governance*, 3/3: 5–15 (2015).

Straus, Scott, *Fundamentals of Genocide and Mass Atrocity Prevention* (Washington, DC: United States Holocaust Memorial Museum, 2016).

Stuenkel, Oliver, 'The Bricks and the Future of R2P: Was Syria or Libya the Exception?', *Global Responsibility to Protect*, 6/1: 3–28 (2014).

'Sudan Summons Unicef Representative to Protest Jem Pact', *Sudan Tribune*, 25 July 2010.

Tabak, Jana, *In the Best Interest of Whom? Rethinking the Limits of the International Order through the (Re)constructions of the World Child and Child-soldiers*, Ph.D, Pontifícia Universidade Católica do Rio de Janeiro, 2014.

Task Force on the EU Prevention of Mass Atrocities, 'The EU and the Prevention of Mass Atrocities: An Assessment of Strengths and Weaknesses' (Budapest: Budapest Centre for the International Prevention of Genocide and Mass Atrocities, 2013).

Taylor, Charles, *Modern Social Imaginaries* (London: Duke University Press, 2004).

Tazreiter, Claudia, *Asylum Seekers and the State: The Politics of Protection in a Security-Conscious World* (Aldershot, England: Ashgate, 2004).

Thakur, Ramesh, 'R2P after Libya and Syria: Engaging Emerging Powers', *The Washington Quarterly*, 36/2: 61–76 (Spring 2013).

Thakur, Ramesh, and Thomas G Weiss, 'R2P: From Idea to Norm—and Action?', *Global Responsibility to Protect*, 1/1: 22–53 (2009).

The Sphere Project, *Humanitarian Charter and Minimum Standards in Humanitarian Response* (Rugby: The Sphere Project - Practical Action Publishing, 2011).

'This is How We Fought in Gaza: Soldiers' Testimonies and Photographs from Operation "Protective Edge"', *Breaking the Silence*, 2014.

Thompson, Shamala Kandiah, 'Children and Armed Conflict', in Jared Genser and Bruno Stagno Ugarte (eds), *The United Nations Security Council in the Age of Human Rights* (Cambridge: Cambridge University Press, 2014).

Tocci, Nathalie, 'On Power and Norms Libya, Syria, and the Responsibility to Protect', *Global Responsibility to Protect*, 8/1: 51–75 (2016).

Toole, Dan, 'Statement on the protection of the rights of children who may be transferred from Nauru to Cambodia', 17 April 2015, https://www.unicef.org/eapro/media_23969.html.

Tourinho, Marcos, Oliver Stuenkel, and Sarah Brockmeier, '"Responsibility while Protecting": Reforming R2P Implementation', *Global Society*, 30/1: 134–150 (2016).

Truth and Reconciliation Commission of Canada, *Honouring the Truth, Reconciling for the Future: Summary of the Final Report of the Truth and Reconciliation Commission of Canada* (Winnipeg: National Centre for Truth and Reconciliation, 2015).

Tulloch, Sara (ed.), *Oxford Dictionary of New Words* (Oxford: Oxford University Press, 1991).

Tuttle, Brad, 'Sales of Dystopian Novels Have Been Spiking on Amazon Since the Election', *Money*, 25 Jan 2017.

Udagawa, Mitsuhiro, 'Nihon no Enjo Rinen to shite no Jijodoryoku Shien no Kokusai Seijiron teki Kosatu' [The Study of Self-help as Japan's ODA Philosophy in International Politics], *Kokusai Seiji*, 186: 113–128 (January 2017).

'UN: Ensure Integrity of Children's "List of Shame"', *Human Rights Watch*, 4 June 2015, https://www.hrw.org/news/2015/06/04/un-ensure-integrity-childrens-list-shame.

UN Women, *Preventing Conflict, Transforming Justice, Securing the Peace: A Global Study on the Implementation of United Nations Security Council Resolution 1325* (New York: UN Women, 2015).

UNICEF, *World Declaration on the Survival, Protection and Development of Children*, 30 September 1990.

UNICEF, 'State of the World's Children 1996' (New York: UNICEF, 1996).

UNICEF, *The Paris Principles: Principles and Guidelines on Children Associated with Armed Forces or Armed Groups*, February 2007.

UNICEF, *Machel Study 10-Year Strategic Review: Children and Conflict in a Changing World* (New York: Office of the Special Representative of the Secretary-General for Children and Armed Conflict, 2009).

UNICEF, 'Children in Israeli Military Detentions: Observations and Recommendations', February 2013.

UNICEF, 'Guidelines: Monitoring and Reporting Mechanism on Grave Violations against Children in Situations of Armed Conflict', June 2014.

UNICEF, 'HA2 Position Paper: UNICEF's Roles and Responsibilities in the Children and Armed Conflict Agenda of the Security Council', August 2014.

UNICEF, 'Guidance Note: UNICEF Roles and Responsibilities in the Children and Armed Conflict Agenda of the Security Council', November 2015.

UNICEF, 'Malak and the Boat: a Journey from Syria', UNICEF video, March 2016.

UNICEF, 'Mustafa goes for a Walk: a Journey from Syria', UNICEF video, March 2016.

UNICEF, 'The Story of Ivine and Pillow', UNICEF video, March 2016.

UNICEF, 'UNICEF Launches "Unfairy Tales" of Refugee and Migrant Children', 29 March 2016.

UNICEF, 'Protecting Children from Violations and Abuse in Gaza', 25 October 2016.

UNICEF, *Uprooted: The Growing Crisis for Refugee and Migrant Children*, 30 October 2016.

UNICEF, 'Nearly a Quarter of the World's Children Live in Conflict or Disaster-Stricken Countries: UNICEF', Press Release, 9 December 2016.

UNICEF, 'Building the Future: Children and the Sustainable Development Goals in Rich Countries', UNICEF Innocenti Report Card 14 (Florence: UNICEF Office of Research – Innocenti, 2017).

UNICEF, *Hitting Rock Bottom: How 2016 Became The Worst Year for Syria's Children*, March 2017.

UNICEF, *A Child is a Child: Protecting Children on the Move from Violence, Abuse and Exploitation*, 3 May 2017.

UNICEF, *In Search for Opportunities: Voices of Children on the Move in West and Central Africa*, July 2017.

UNICEF, 'Children Under Attack at Shocking Scale in Conflicts Around the World, Says UNICEF', Press Release, 28 December 2017.

UNICEF, OSRSG-CAAC, *Machel Study 10-Year Strategic Review: Children and Conflict in a Changing World* (New York: UNICEF-OSRSG-CAAC, 2009).

'United Nations Chief Exposes Limits to His Authority by Citing Saudi Threat', *The New York Times*, 9 June 2016.

United Nations Office for the Coordination of Humanitarian Affairs (OCHA), 'Fragmented Lives: Humanitarian Overview 2014', 26 March 2015.

United Nations Office on Drugs and Crime, *Global Report on Trafficking in Persons 2016* (Vienna: UNODC, 2016).

US Congress, 'Opposing Any Endorsement or Further Consideration of the Report of the United Nations Fact Finding Mission on the Gaza Conflict', *Congressional Record*, 3 November 2009.

Valentino, Benjamin A., *Final Solutions: Mass Killing and Genocide in the Twentieth Century* (Ithaca, NY: Cornell University Press, 2004).

Valentino, Benjamin, 'Why We Kill: The Political Science of Political Violence against Civilians', *Annual Review of Political Science*, 17: 89–103 (2014).

van Bueren, Geraldine, *The International Law on the Rights of the Child* (The Hague: Martinus Nijhoff Publishers, 1998).

Van Ee, Elisa, and Rolf J. Kleber, 'Growing Up Under a Shadow: Key Issues in Research on and Treatment of Children Born of Rape', *Child Abuse Review*, 22/6: 386–397 (2013).

Van Reenen, Piet, 'Children as Victims in the Israeli/Palestinian conflict, Policing Realities and Police Training', in Charles W. Greenbaum, Philip E. Veerman and Naomi Bacon-Shnoor (eds.), *Protection of Children During Armed Political Conflict, A Multidisciplinary Perspective* (Oxford: Intersentia, 2006).

Vigh, Henrik, 'Crisis and Chronicity: Anthropological Perspectives on Continuous Conflict and Decline', *Ethnos*, 72/1: 5–24 (2008).

Wadley, Jonathan D., 'Gendering the State: Performativity and Protection in International Security', in Laura Sjoberg (ed), *Gender and International Security: Feminist Perspectives* (New York: Routledge, 2010).

Wall, John, 'Human Rights in Light of Childhood', *International Journal of Children's Rights*, 16/4: 523–554 (2008).

'War in the Cities', *International Review of the Red Cross*, 98/1 special issue (2016).

Watson, Alison M.S., 'Saving More than the Children: The Role of Child-Focused NGOs in the Creation of Southern Security Norms', *Third World Quarterly*, 27/2: 227–237 (2006).

Watson, Alison M.S., 'Children and International Relations: A New Site of Knowledge?' *Review of International Studies*, 32/2: 237–50 (2006).

Watson, Alison M.S., *The Child in International Political Economy: A Place at the Table* (London: Routledge, 2009).

Watson, Alison M.S., 'Resilience is its Own Resistance: The Place of Children in Post-Conflict Settlement', *Critical Studies on Security*, 3/1: 47–61 (2015).

Watters, Charles, *Refugee Children: Toward the Next Horizon* (London: Routledge, 2008).

Weinstein, Jeremy M., *Inside Rebellion: The Politics of Insurgent Violence* (Cambridge: Cambridge University Press, 2007).

Weitsman, Patricia A., 'The Politics of Identity and Sexual Violence: A Review of Bosnia and Rwanda,' *Human Rights Quarterly*, 30: 561–578 (2008).

Welle, Deutsche, 'Child Migrants Face Risks from Cold Weather, Boat Crossings, Says UNICEF', 13 January 2017.

Welsh, Jennifer M., 'Implementing the "Responsibility to Protect": Where Expectations Meet Reality', *Ethics and International Affairs*, 24/4 (2010).

Welsh, Jennifer M., 'Remarks of the Special Advisor to the Secretary General on Responsibility to Protect', 11 September 2013, http://www.un.org/en/preventgenocide/adviser/pdf/Special%20Adviser%20Jennifer%20Welsh%20remarks.GA%20Dialogue%202013.pdf.

Welsh, Jennifer M., 'The Individualization of War: Protection, Liability, and Accountability', Lecture, Trudeau Foundation, Ontario, 25 March 2014.

Welsh, Jennifer M., 'The Responsibility to Prevent: Assessing the Gap between Rhetoric and Reality', *Cooperation and Conflict*, 51/2: 216–32 (2016).

Wessells, Michael G., *Child Soldiers: From Violence to Protection* (Cambridge: Harvard University Press, 2006).

Wessells, Michael G., 'Bottom-up Approaches to Strengthening Child Protection Systems: Placing Children, Families, and Communities at the Center', *Child Abuse & Neglect*, 43: 8–21 (2015).

Wessells, Michael G., 'Children and Armed Conflict: Introduction and Overview', *Peace and Conflict: Journal of Peace Psychology*, 22/3: 198–207 (2016).

Wessells, Michael G., 'Children and Armed Conflict: Interventions for Supporting War-Affected Children', *Peace and Conflict: Journal of Peace Psychology*, 23/1: 4–13 (2017).

Western, Jon, and Joshua S. Goldstein, 'R2P after Syria, To Save the Doctrine Forget Regime Change', *Foreign Affairs*, 13 March 2013.

Wheeler, Nicholas J., 'Pluralist or Solidarist Conceptions of International Society: Bull and Vincent on Humanitarian Intervention', *Millennium: Journal of International Studies*, 21/3: 463–487 (1992).

Wherry, Aaron, 'Life, Death and Politics: The Death of Alan Kurdi and the Federal Election Campaign of 2015', *Maclean's*, 3 September 2015.

Whitman, Shelly, 'The Responsibility to Protect and Child Soldiers' in W. Andy Knight and Frazer Egerton (eds.), *The Routledge Handbook of the Responsibility to Protect* (London: Routledge, 2012).

Whitman, Shelly, and Sam Holland, 'Understanding the Recruitment and Use of Child Soldiers as an Early Warning Indicator', the Roméo Dallaire Child Soldiers Initiative: Working Paper, June 2015.

Whitman, Shelly, Tanya Zayed, and Carl Conradi, *Child Soldiers: A Handbook for Security Sector Actors* (Halifax, NS: The Roméo Dallaire Child Soldiers Initiative, 2014).

Will to Intervene (W2I), 'Mobilizing the Will to Intervene: Leadership and Action to Prevent Mass Atrocities', 2009, https://www.concordia.ca/research/migs/projects/will-to-intervene/about-w2i/report.html.

Williams, Michael C., 'Words, Images, Enemies: Securitization and International Politics', *International Studies Quarterly*, 47/4: 511–531 (2003).

'With Only Three Hours of Electricity a Day, Gaza Is "On Verge of Explosion"', *Haaretz*, 4 January 2017.

Wood, Elisabeth Jean, 'Armed Groups and Sexual Violence: When is Wartime Rape Rare?' *Politics and Society*, 37/1: 131–62 (2009).

Worley, Will, 'Queen Rania of Jordan commissions Aylan Kurdi cartoon in response to Charlie Hebdo', *The Independent*, 17 January 2016.

Wyness, Michael, Lisa Harrison, and Ian Buchanan, 'Childhood, Politics and Ambiguity: Towards an Agenda for Children's Political Inclusion', *Sociology*, 38/1: 81–99 (2004).

Young, Iris Marion, 'The Logic of Masculinist Protection: Reflections on the Current Security State', *Signs: Journal of Women in Culture and Society*, 29/1: 1–25 (2003).

Zerrougui, Leila, 'Harnessing the Potential of Boys and Girls to Fulfil the Promise of the Sustainable Development Goals', April 2016, https://unchronicle.un.org/article/harnessing-potential-boys-and-girls-fulfil-promise-sustainable-development-goals/.

Zifcak, Spencer, 'The Responsibility to Protect After Libya and Syria', *Melbourne Journal of International Law* 13/1: 1–35 (2012).

Index

www.ingramcontent.com/pod-product-compliance
Lightning Source LLC
Chambersburg PA
CBHW072243240926
51846CB00012B/151
9789004284197